Consulting

*Facilitating
Human Potential and
Change Processes*

Don Dinkmeyer
DePaul University

Jon Carlson
Governors State University

Charles E. Merrill Publishing Company
A Bell & Howell Company
Columbus, Ohio

038443|

Published by
Charles E. Merrill Publishing Co.
A Bell & Howell Company
Columbus, Ohio 43216

International Standard Book Number: 0-675-08958-1

Library of Congress Catalog Card Number: 72-97006

1 2 3 4 5 6 7 8 9 10 — 77 76 75 74 73

Quoted material on pp. 277–78 reprinted by
permission from TIME, the Weekly News-
magazine; © Time Inc.

Printed in the United States of America

*To Jane and Laura, our consultants,
the real facilitators of human potential*

Preface

The schools are currently in the midst of a crisis with a growing wave of discontent on the part of students, parents, and teachers. Students are crying for relevance, parents are concerned about the lack of discipline and the rebellion of youth, and teachers are finding administration inefficacious in improving teacher-student relationships. In an era of accountability, the services of pupil personnel specialists, whether they be psychologists, counselors, or social workers, are being reevaluated. Society and educators are insisting on innovative approaches which will help teachers and parents to fulfill their human development responsibilities.

It is our conviction that the schools presently place an overemphasis on achievement and the acquisition of facts through memorization. Mere lip service is being given to meeting human needs, educating and facilitating the whole child, and creating a climate which builds self-esteem and humaneness. The purpose of this book is to rectify the current situation through the development of strategies for understanding and promoting education in a humane context. We do not view our approach as a new "ism" but, perhaps, as an integration of existing procedures which are designed to systematically develop a humane environment. By bringing together the resources in an integrated fashion and establishing a hierarchy or priority of function, we believe our aforementioned goal can be reached. This is an approach which we believe to be practical and effective for the pupil personnel specialist as well as staff, parents, and children.

The text is intended for basic courses in pupil personnel work offered to administrators, school counselors, psychologists, and social workers. It is also designed for a basic text in consultation, and it is hoped that it will be of use to administrators searching for more viable processes.

The impetus to write this text was derived from our personal experiences in consulting with school districts locally and throughout the nation. Our experience in full-time personnel positions illustrated dramatically the limitation of individual diagnosis and counseling. The presentation of workshops using these procedures in over forty states convinced us of the necessity of developing a text to systematically present the constructs basic to consultation. We bring to the text many years of experience as elementary and secondary school teachers and counselors, school psychologists, consultants, private-practice psychologists, and counselor educators.

In writing the text, we began by looking at the current situation and first established the imperative nature of humaneness, then detailed specific suggestions for developing humane institutions through consulting with the system. Learning is considered from a humane viewpoint, and specific processes which make the learning situation humane are discussed.

We present a theory of human behavior which permits one to understand behavior in light of its consequences. Specific illustrations and implications of the theory are included. We discuss the school as an organization which inhibits humaneness and include procedures for utilizing group dynamics to promote development. Consultation processes with individuals and groups are explained in detail.

The consultant role is proposed as a constructive alternative for new approaches to pupil personnel problems. The role is developed in terms of a hierarchy of functions, with the consultant being truly a facilitator of human potential. Attention throughout the text is given to procedures for both individual and group consultation with administration, staff, and parents. The classroom which promotes humaneness and human potential is described, and the relationship of the consultant to this development is set forth.

We would like to thank Jane Dinkmeyer and Gloria Brown for preparation of the manuscript. We are especially grateful to Jim Muro of the University of Maine and Dan Fullmer of the University of Hawaii for their detailed and constructive critique of the first draft of the manuscript. We would also like to thank our graduate students who worked with a mimeographed version of the text and helped us refine the concepts. It also seems important at this time to indicate the stimulation generated by the important others in our lives—Don, Jim, Kirstin and Matthew. It is their actions that constantly reaffirmed our belief in the human potential of man and that "Everything is gonna be all right!"

Contents

0384431

1

An Educational Imperative: Humaneness*

The headlines of the *New York Times* on September 20, 1970 reported the findings of a three-and-one-half-year study conducted by Charles E. Silberman (1970) and endorsed by the Carnegie Corporation. Silberman concluded that most schools not only fail to educate children adequately, but also are "oppressive," "grim," and "joyless." The report recommended a radical reordering of the classroom along more informal lines, so that a student would be free to use his own interests as a starting point for education and would no longer be dominated by his teacher. It contended, among other things, that most schools are preoccupied with order, control, and routine; that students are essentially subjugated by the schools; that by practicing systematic repression, the schools create many of their own discipline problems; and that they promote docility, passivity, and conformity in their students.

The schools are confronted with a crisis. There is a growing wave of discontent on the part of students, parents, and teachers. Students are dissatisfied with the irrelevance of material and what they consider a lack of challenge. They often feel a lack of belonging or identification with the educational enterprise. Education does not meet their intellectual, social, and emotional needs (Silberman 1970).

Parents are concerned about the inadequacy of the educational product. They feel inept at dealing with the rebellion and lack of respect

---

* See Appendix A for a detailed list of resources for promoting humaneness. List includes books, periodicals, films and tapes, and organizations.

for authority and standards. Teachers often feel unprepared for the challenge of educating youth in this era. They may know the subject matter, but they are not equipped to motivate the learner. They espouse the "whole child" doctrine, but are not truly equipped to deal with the child's feelings, attitudes, and values. However, if teachers are to educate, they must be capable of dealing with emotions, motives, and the total personality. The child comes as a whole child, and we need whole teachers to cope with the challenge. The whole teacher is able to relate personally, sense feelings, and use the student's emotions to energize the learning process.

Our purpose in this book is to develop procedures for facilitating education in a humane context. A balance must be developed between the emphasis on achievement and the need for developing fully functioning persons. The schools must create a climate which builds humaneness, self-esteem, and resultant achievement.

EQUALITY AND CHANGE NOW

Our society is undergoing a rapid shift from the passive acceptance of autocratic procedures and unequal treatment to a pressure to deal with *all* (nations, races, creeds, husband and wife, parent and child) as equals. There is social pressure to institute democratic procedures. We are becoming increasingly cognizant of the fact that we cannot talk about democracy theoretically while demonstrating authoritarian administrative procedures and conducting autocratic classrooms. Our relationships and actions speak louder and more forcefully than our lectures. Children cannot learn about democracy vicariously; they must live it. However, teachers cannot be free to practice democracy in the classroom if they fear autocratic supervisors or if they are untrained in group procedures which enable them to provide democratic leadership. Teacher education and school administration must reassess human values if they expect the broad objectives which deal with the whole child to be more than meaningless platitudes.

We have reacted to the knowledge explosion by placing more demands on staff and students. We have failed to recognize that the increase in knowledge was not accompanied by a commensurate increase in learning capacity on the part of students. The teacher can no longer be primarily a dispenser of knowledge; he must, instead, serve to motivate and facilitate the educative process. As Toffler (1970) stated, we are "citizens of the age of transcience" where things are increasingly temporary. Examples of engineers, advertising men, and men in industrial management living "half-lifes"—meaning that one-half of what they learn will be outdated within a decade—are numerous. The change process is so rapid that today's facts will be tomorrow's fictions.

The problem of youthful rebellion with which educators must cope, and the polarization and the communication gap between both generations and colleagues are symptoms of a need to restructure our institutions to service the community. Educators must be dedicated to renewal of self *and* society to promote personal and social growth so that we might live more effectively in a pluralistic society. We must increasingly develop educational experiences which are relevant for the children who must live in an urban and mechanized society that requires flexibility, adaptability, and spontaneity of its citizenry.

A close inspection of educational practices and methods indicates a great disparity between the objectives and claims and what is actually accomplished. Unlike business, which fires the unsuccessful salesman, we have suggested that when the teacher does not "sell" or motivate the child, the child is the failure. The system must be reevaluated and revised.

For example, William Schutz talks of his young son Ethan in his recent bestseller entitled *Joy: Expanding Human Awareness* (1967):

> When Ethan smiles, every cell of his body smiles, including his turned up toes. When he is unhappy, he is thoroughly unhappy, all over. When he is interested in a new object, only he and the object exist. He touches it, tastes it, smells it, puts it in things, puts things in it, gives it to people, takes it from people, looks at it from far and near. The total absorption is beautiful to watch (p. 9).

Ethan is a whole being, thinking, feeling, and acting at once. He has access to all his human resources and is totally involved. He is engaged in a self-educative process; he is exploring. Will this be Ethan's experience when he meets with formal education?

The single most important characteristic that our schools often share in common is a preoccupation with *order* and *control*. Teachers become disciplinarians with the terminal goal of "the absence of noise and movement."

We insist that children "sit silent and motionless," which is quite unnatural, and we assume and expect that all students will be interested in the same thing at the same moment and for the same length of time.

As Barry Stevens states:

> Essentially there are two views of man. One of them is that man has made to behave. This becomes internalized and I also push myself to be pushed around, filled with information, molded, manipulated,

around, etc. The other concept of man—a more religious one, in my view—is that we are born with the ability to find our own way, make our own discoveries, choose for ourselves. This is not a *new* view. It keeps being rediscovered (Dimick and Huff 1970, p. 240).

Silberman (1970) states that children are not disruptive—it is the formal classroom that is disruptive, i.e., disruptive of childhood itself. We must not forget that our prisons, mental hospitals, welfare lines, employment offices, street corners, and other societal sties are inhabited by ex-elementary school children—who once were asking for help. Others who were also searching for early help in life would include the millions of Americans that lead unproductive and unhappy "daily" lives (Van Hoose, Pietrofesa, and Carlson 1973). This situation is the result of a fragmented education, an education that has failed to deal with the whole person (teacher or child). It has failed to help children to understand themselves and their life tasks, resulting eventually in apathy, divorce, rebellion, alienation, etc.

Perhaps the teacher who wrote the following essay captures the dehumanistic nature of today's schools best:

> I have taught for ten years. During that time I have given assignments, among others to a murderer, an evangelist, a pugilist, a thief, and an imbecile.
>
> The murderer was a quiet little boy who sat on the front seat and regarded me with pale blue eyes; the evangelist, easily the most popular boy in the school, had the lead in the school play; the pugilist lounged by the window and let loose at intervals with a raucous laugh that startled even the geraniums; the thief was a gay-hearted lothario with a song on his lips; and the imbecile, a soft-eyed little animal seeking the shadows.
>
> The murderer awaits death in the state penitentiary; the evangelist has lain a year now in the village churchyard; the pugilist lost an eye in a brawl in Hong Kong; the thief, by standing on tip toe, can see the windows of my room from the county jail; and the once gentle-eyed moron beats his head against a padded cell in the state asylum. All of these pupils once sat in my room, sat and looked at me grimly across worn brown desks. I have been a great help to these pupils—I taught them the dates of battles, the boundaries of states and how to find square roots by the algebraic method (Dimick and Huff 1970, p. xvi).

At least one-half of our country's hospital beds are filled with people who have mental illness (Coleman 1964). Drugs, suicide, and other forms of dropping out have become a way of life for tomorrow's leaders—today's youth.

JUST THINK, ONCE WE WERE ALL LIKE ETHAN!

Some educators say this is the price that we have to pay for knowledge or a "good" academic education. But we are not getting that either! Educators have concentrated on subject matter and paid little attention to how children learn. As an example:

> A cluster of children are examining a turtle with enormous fascination and intensity. The teacher tells the children to put the turtle away because, "we're going to have our science lesson!"

The two components of learning are *information* and *meaning*. What we have is more information than we need. When we fail it is because we have not discovered the meaning of the information we have. Nothing is learned until it has become personally meaningful and it actually influences our perceptions and behavior. We know we should listen to the feelings and beliefs of our students, but we have so many "pages to cover." We clearly have not learned the importance of listening.

Teachers don't fail because they don't know their subject matter—they fail because they are unable in one way or another to make this information meaningful. The information component of the learning process lies outside the learner, and because of this, other people can do something about it. However, the meaning aspect lies within the learner and is not so open for us to change. But American educators want to change—so, we are altering the *information* component. This is the only part of the learning process with which we are attempting to cope.

Our rationale follows along these lines: if a little information is a good thing, then a lot must be a whole lot better! Subsequently we are *drowning* kids in information—and more is coming.

longer days at school
fewer vacations
more courses
less physical education or anything considered a frill (music, drama, art)
more *solid* subject matter
less frills, more facts
foreign language in the elementary school
more math and *so on*

Most of us need more information like we need the plague. More important than the giving of information is helping people to understand the personal meaning of the information. Take the dropout for example. He didn't drop out because of a lack of information—*everybody* offered him that! He was not, however, helped to see the relationship between the information and his personal needs. Involvement and meaning were not developed. There is a big difference between knowing and behaving. Knowing results from acquiring new information. A change in behavior comes with the discovery of meaning.

Children need to feel safe and secure before they can feel challenged. If they are not safe, they feel threatened. Threat deters learning! Challenge fosters learning! Yet we continue to threaten children all the time (grades, no recess, "I'll send a note home . . .").

Society is currently characterized by turmoil, rebellion, strife, insecurity, and fear. There is much rebellion and concern about one's rights, whether this be child versus adult, adolescent versus parent, woman versus man, labor versus management. All have the same concern—to get what they believe is their just due. This general feeling of futility is accompanied by a basic striving to become more than one is socially, intellectually, and monetarily.

Throughout the nation there is also a general feeling of alienation, polarization, inadequacy, and social remoteness. We must recognize that the most fundamental motivation of all is the desire to belong. This is not being met in the typical educational organization. Hence, we note the growth of sensitivity groups and the attractiveness of social groups which value persons more than things. Few of us feel that we really belong and that we make a major contribution to our community. As Burt Bacharach wrote in a recent song, "What the World Needs Now is Love Sweet Love!" Only people can humanize—not things.

Our economic and political system appears to reward material gains over human values. Social responsibility, spiritual values, and character are discussed and verbally lauded, but they are not prized and rewarded. Material values push us to compete in an unending, unrewarding battle to have more than others. We are engaged in talking about equality while we demonstrate inequality at all levels. The administrator feels superior to the teacher, the teacher feels superior to the child, and the child struggles to get his rights. From all of this emerges the "getting" person, one concerned about what he can accomplish for self and unconcerned about others.

The schools present a major dilemma insofar as they attempt to teach democracy but attempt to do it in an authoritarian manner. We are more concerned with whether children know the correct answers to the eighth-grade constitution test than whether they have an experience in democratic living with each other. In practice, it appears that our goals and objectives are limited to acquiring facts. We tell children that democracy, cooperation, peace, and brotherhood are the goals of a happy and successful life. Yet, we introduce, train for, and demonstrate these concepts in an authoritarian and competitive manner (getting ahead at the expense of others)—the direct opposite of the stated objectives or eventual goals. Students learn from what we do rather than from what we say. The model of the benevolent autocrat who fosters competition is internalized.

We must meet the challenge of our times—to live *truly* as equals! This recognizes that we are equal in value even though we might not be equal in social position. The basic social conflict involves the struggle for control, the overambition to be more than others, and the resultant nagging feeling of inadequacy and alienation. Our dilemma is clear—how do we live as equals?

> Today husband and wife cannot live separately with each other if they do not treat each other as equals. Nor can parents get along with their children if they assume the children can be subdued. There can be no harmony and stability in the community unless each member of it has his safe place as an equal to all others. There can be no cooperation between management and labor unless each group feels respected and trusted by the other. There can be no place on earth unless one nation respects the rights and dignity of another (Dreikurs 1971, p. xiii).

The revolution against authority and autocratic methods is already here—the signs are everywhere in our culture. We must become familiar with democratic procedures if the society is to survive. The democratic system is not faulty, but we have people attempting to operate the system who have not learned how to function democratically. Their experiences have trained them to deal with superior-inferior relationships, but not to live as equals. Democratic procedures require that man must choose, become responsible for his behavior, and as a result, be in control of himself. This requires that he recognizes his status as a social equal in a democratic society.

> In his fear of being inferior, he tries to establish his superiority over others. He cannot recognize others as his equals at a time when they really are. He is a free agent but does not feel free. He must discover himself in order to find personal peace and to live at peace with others (Dreikurs 1971, p. xiv).

We must decide on the type of society we value and the kinds of adults we should be as products of the educational experience. Each of us can and should take responsibility for our own corner of the world.

Our classroom, school, and consulting relationships do not have to be autocratic and inhumane. Our actions are evidence of our decisions. We are suggesting that we can strive for nothing less than an enlightened and compassionate electorate. This clearly recognizes that we do not produce compassionate, humane people by focusing only on enlightenment and intellectual gain. If we are to exist together as equals, humaneness must become a stated rather than implied goal of the educational process.

The manpower needs and the uniqueness of democratic life are contributing to much of today's human displeasure with life. It is this technocracy and the subsequent depersonalization of American life, which counselors helped to create, that our youth are rebelling against. The guidance movement not only needs to grow, but to change. We need to stand strong against the imposing societal dictates and create new worlds for children that focus on such overworked yet underpracticed terms as love, trust, freedom, and so on—education for humaneness has become imperative in our increasingly technologically influenced society (Van Hoose, Pietrofesa and Carlson 1973). "The wonderful progress of science has brought no improvement to the hearts of man" (Golden 1970, p. 11). The education of children does not need "better" ways of neglecting the *needs* of children.

We must dispel the depersonalization that is impinging on us with an environment that is flavored with the satisfaction of human needs. We can *no* longer rationalize these dilemmas away with such frequently deployed statements as, "Maybe things are not so bad after all!" This is the kind of defense mechanism that typifies the majority of our people and has helped us to reach our present state. (What rationalizations have you already built for why you and your school are not functioning this way?)

Man is physically and emotionally distant from his neighbor, anonymous in a mass society, often alienated from his work and his fellow man (Scobey and Graham 1970)—it is possible and imperative to help man to grow and develop his human capabilities. But what is possible is not necessarily easy.

The evolution of the humane person will require changes in education, changes as radical as the technological shifts of the 1970s. These changes will require boldness, imagination, and hard work. Wishing will not bring them about. Change requires optimism, belief in the intrinsic worth of man. Change requires changing the people who set the policy, make the decisions, and facilitate the growth of the students. This change can only occur by dealing with a person's beliefs and values. Traditional change processes and in-service programs have exposed the populace to ideas and concepts but have not permitted the person to internalize these concepts in terms of his own attitudes and beliefs.

Education should prepare people not just to make or earn a living, but to live a life—a creative, humane and sensitive life—a life of joy where man can reach out with a sensitive hand to his total environment. This calls for a liberal humanizing education. The purpose of a liberal education is to educate educators—to turn out men and women who are capable of educating their friends, their communities, and most importantly, themselves. Education is not a spectator sport; it is *life* and each individual needs to get involved.

FEELINGS OF ADEQUACY AND FAILURE

There are an increasing number of children and adolescents who do not succeed in the educational process as it is presently organized. These data are apparent when one looks at the problems related to under-achievement, dropouts, and the apathy of some students who remain within the system. Our society is regularly producing a large number of children and adults who perceive themselves as inadequate and as failures.

Glasser, a psychiatrist interested in education, drew some generalizations related to failure and discovered the following principle: "Regardless of how many failures a person has had in his past, regardless of his background, his culture, his color, or his economic level, he will not succeed in general until he can in some way first experience success in one important part of his life" (Glasser 1969, p. 5). It is Glasser's contention that if the child is able to succeed in school, he will have an excellent chance for success in life. In contrast, failure in the school diminishes his chance to be a success in life.

One of the major problems of the schools is that they are a product of a failure-oriented evaluation system and a mistake-centered approach to instruction. We are more concerned with children's weaknesses and liabilities than we are with their strengths and assets. However, if we are to truly meet with the problems of the "rebel," the "unmotivated," the "apathetic," the "alienated," and the general social disorganization that surrounds us, we must start to examine the deficiencies which appear in parts of the educational system.

Glasser (1965) has projected in his *Reality Therapy* that man has two basic needs: the need for love and the need for self-worth. They are the pathways which lead to a successful identity. Glasser (1972) feels that this identity or *role* is the basic motivation of Western society. Social rather than economic stress *now* governs man's life. It is only as we help man to provide for these needs that he can think of self in a positive manner. Love, in terms of the educational task, is found in the opportunity to be socially responsible, to give as well as receive love.

Our current emphasis on standards, threats, and punishment prevents the development of a feeling of genuine self-worth. Schools have failed to teach children how to maintain a successful identity and to become socially responsible, contributing persons. It is apparent that children come to school feeling capable and comparatively adequate. But the school quickly creates feelings of inadequacy. Combs and Soper (1963) found that between kindergarten and first grade children's perceptions tended to become less favorable with respect to (a) general adequacy, (b) strength and athletic prowess, (c) relationships to teachers and other adults, and (d) adequacy to do school work.

The significance of the early school years for the formulation of selfhood has been recently demonstrated in a number of research studies. Bloom (1964) indicated the significance of the first three grades for predicting the total pattern of achievement. Kagan and Moss (1962) released a study which indicated that many of the behaviors exhibited by the child during the period from six to ten years of age were moderately good predictors of theoretically related behavior during early adulthood. There were clear indications from this study that the child who was achieving well early in school would continue to achieve well.

It is apparent that there are a number of factors in school which have a negative influence upon self-concept and feelings of self-esteem. Mosher and Sprinthall (1971) feel that this can be attributed to a curriculum that is psychologically crippling. It is obvious that as one passes through school, an increasing emphasis is placed upon memorizing if one is to achieve the typical rewards of the school— grades. This is accompanied by the fact that education unfortunately becomes increasingly less relevant for the child's personal and social needs.

Schools also discourage students from developing the capacity to learn *by* and *for themselves,* because the schools are structured in such a way as to make students totally dependent upon the teachers. Students' curiosity, spontaneity, and courage, along with their ability—and perhaps most serious, their desire—to think and act for themselves are destroyed. Schools deny children sufficient experience to understand modern complexity and to translate that understanding into action. But a stated educational goal is to help children to develop responsibility for the direction of their lives. This is only one example of the conflict between our stated objectives and practices.

In our society we do not let children assume responsibility for their future until they reach the age of sixteen. At that time they are expected to make responsible decisions and choices. Upon completion of high school for example, children are required to choose their vocation, mate, and possible college. Yet, prior to this time they have had little training and no experience in decision-making. Thus, a high college drop-out rate, a high divorce rate, and much vocational transfer (Carlson and Mayer 1971, p. 193).

A child cannot become human by learning only from the experience of others. In order to become human, one must establish his own anchors and his own contact with reality. He must begin to get involved and to evaluate his performance. Teachers don't have to evaluate everything a child does.

The knowledge explosion had a tremendous impact upon American education. The launching of the Russian Sputnik in 1957 is recognized as the date when the United States first felt challenged by the scientific achievement of other cultures. It was increasingly apparent that there was a greater amount of knowledge than one could readily master through traditional methods. Thus, we were at a turning point where we had to decide whether we should emphasize facts and information, or instead, attitudes. Obviously the decision was made to place an emphasis upon acquiring knowledge. This resulted in the placement of college subjects into the high school curriculum and the moving of high school subjects to the elementary level. One might only speculate on the results if, instead, we had abandoned any attempt to master all the current knowledge (which is being outdated by scientific research) and had focused on developing positive attitudes towards learning and a desire to become involved in the educational process as a lifetime task.

It might be interesting to note what the Russians have been doing since Sputnik.

It took the shock of Sputnik to cause Americans to reject the permissiveness of the 'thirties and 'forties in favor of pressure for academic excellence. It may, therefore, come as something of a surprise to learn that the primary education emphasis on Soviet society during the past ten years has been not on academic excellence, but on character education—the development of such qualities as altruism, industry and service to one's community and nation. Moreover, following Makarenko,

Soviet leaders have emphasized that effective character training requires imposing on the child challenging responsibilities for service and self-discipline not only within the family but, equally importantly, in his collective or peer group both within and outside the school (Urie Bronfanbrenner's introduction to A. S. Makarenko's book *The Collective Family*, 1967).

While the Americans have been going all out for cognitive scholarship (math, science, chemistry), the Russians have been focusing on character or psychological education! Perhaps our emphasis should have been on persons who are truly committed to the learning process instead of memorization. In contrast, we have found schools focusing far too often on memorization and failure and far too little on problem solving, spontaneity, creativity, involvement, interest, and the capacity to think. In our overemphasis upon a mistake-centered type of education which places emphasis upon the one right answer, we have failed to develop citizens who care, are concerned, and who are committed to action. Our citizenry read *Time* and *Newsweek* and understand social problems, but generally they do not act. It is important that we look at the total scene and recognize that an educated citizen in a democracy only learns how to become an effective human being by participating in the decision-making processes related to his own education. He learns how to decide by being given choices. He becomes responsible by accepting responsibility for the consequences of his decisions, attitudes, and behavior.

A HUMANIZED AND PLURALIZED SOCIETY

To teach students in humane living the teacher must experience humaneness first. The results will not come quickly and will require courage. To meet our current problems, schools need creative leadership which can meet all of the challenges of an urban, pluralized society. The present revolt in society has been characterized by Jourard (1970) as "Them Against Us." "THEY are everyone who does not share our perspective of life and time and how these should be spent . . . OUR Utopia is not for THEM" (p. 52). Adults represent the Establishment, those in power who resist change in society and keep THEM unheard and unresponded to. The system works so that those who are not in power are treated in such a manner as to discourage their participation in the democratic process. It almost appears as if "THEM" are treated as if they were non-existent or certainly as if they do not count.

Out of all this we have produced a vast array of social disorders: riots, adolescent rebellion, refusals to fit into the system, bored housewives, large numbers of mentally ill and extremely poor—barely existing in a society which is basically affluent.

Jourard (1970) has really posed a challenging question when he asks, "Do we get sick because of germs? Or because we live sickening ways of life to preserve the status quo, ways we could change if we could find viable alternatives, if someone would help us invent them? Is sickness the price we pay for our one-dimensional way of life?" (p. 54). For many, drugs are a method of escape, protest, and rebellion against the status quo. Drugs create excitement and escape in a world that provides little satisfaction of the basic psychological needs.

The educational system, then, must be restructured to educate for what is real. It must become concerned with the real problems of society and practical ways of dealing with them. We must focus on developing means of educating for a pluralistic society in which we welcome varied ways of living, believing, feeling, and acting, because they produce a rich and varied society. In the past our educational systems have focused on limited goals; they have trained more than educated, and they have valued material in contrast to spiritual, humanistic values.

Our programs in the social sciences must become rich, dynamic, and varied. We must encourage and support research in the social sciences that provides experiments in more effective ways of understanding self and of relating to others. Education must focus on ways to renew both self and society. We must encourage teachers to become persons who get out from behind masks which cause them to focus on achievement and limited goals. We must encourage them to become real persons who develop dialogue and communication with students which enable the pupils to become more aware of the varied alternatives available for decision-making beings.

We need new approaches to the organization and administration of schools. There is a need for a new look at the problems of curriculum, administration, and pupil personnel. We can no longer view these as separate functions, but must see them as totally intertwined and interlocked. Jourard (1970) suggests the necessity of new approaches:

> And perhaps there should be not only psychological clinics in every school, but also a resident guru or teacher of teachers. Not an expert in curricular subjects, not a behavioral repairman, but an exemplar of dedication to becoming fully grown. And perhaps the students should have the opportunity to involve themselves in dialogue and group encounter so that their perspectives will broaden (p. 62).

This person would work as an agent of change, a catalyst, a facilitator with specialization in human behavior and human relationships. He could well be the missing ingredient in providing an education for humaneness.

Knowledge and Human Capabilities

One of our concerns should relate to what type of knowledge is the most valuable in developing the individual capabilities to be distinctly human. Chase (1970) attempts to answer this in terms of the following criterion:

1. Knowledge of self, insofar as it enables one to make an intelligent assessment of his needs, desires, and powers. This assessment becomes the basis for maximum development of capabilities. However, the advancing self-knowledge requires the development of teachers capable of developing dialogue which promotes the full range of self-inquiry. There is, at present, considerable information with simulation games, psychodrama, and role playing as routes for self-knowledge.

2. To develop humane capabilities, individuals must have knowledge of other persons. There is a great need for developing more effective interaction and communication in order to obtain what is valued. If our basic need is to belong, we need to become more effective in our social relationships. In many instances this suggests that we improve methods of communication and interaction and utilize group procedures which develop mutual understanding between peers, members of varied generations, and ethnic groups.

3. To become humane, individuals need knowledge of the evolution and functioning of institutions. Such knowledge is essential because it is through institutions that human capabilities are developed, human rights and freedom secured, and justice and welfare promoted.

If education is to stress humaneness, there must be a systematic emphasis in the following areas:

1. Vigorous measures are needed to strengthen the knowledge base from which education operates. The emphasis needs to be on making current information meaningful rather than on giving more information.

2. Greatly increased effort must be directed to establishing the essential preconditions for effective learning.

3. Continuous curriculum adaptation is necessary in order to receive new inputs which reflect (a) the current state of knowl-

edge in each subject of instruction, and (b) the behavioral knowledge applicable to teaching and learning.

4. New life patterns emerging in response to changing knowledge and technology will require schools and colleges to function decreasingly as primary sources of knowledge and increasingly as developers of capacities to process information and reorganize experiences obtained in family, community, work situations, and a variety of complementary institutions.

5. Education needs better processes for helping individuals to order their values so as to help them make better choices as to how their energies, and eventually their lives, are spent.

The Humane Person

The purpose of the educational experience is directed towards developing a fully functioning person who is secure, sensitive, and particularly aware of self and open to others. He is capable of developing relationships with others and becoming sensitive to their problems. Because he is responsible to self, he is capable of being responsible to others. The humane person is involved in his environment and not concerned with superiority and competition. He has a high level of social interest and concern for participating in the give-and-take of life. He feels that he belongs to the human race, and as such is free to be altruistic, concerned about ways of providing as well as receiving love. His openness and personal freedom enables him to encourage his own creativity.

The focus, then, is on self-evaluation in contrast to external evaluation. He values uniqueness and idiosyncracy. He is capable, purposeful, and curious. He pursues knowledge for personal satisfaction, not to be more than others. He is most often involved in purposive inquiry, which is different than activities which involve the acquisition of information or the development of skills in order to pass some external evaluation or judgment. He is enlightened and compassionate, the product of an educational system which has developed his cognitive and affective domains. It is apparent that if we are to train citizens capable of dealing with the present problems of society, we can no longer stress cognitive gain while raising people essentially immature and retarded in terms of their social and emotional development.

Programs to Implement Humane Schools

We are making the assumption that the prime purpose of education becomes a development of humane individuals. These are persons who operate in a school situation which is open in contrast to closed. This system provides for option, choice, and decision making. Procedures and policies are able to be challenged when new and more appropriate solutions are proposed. The atmosphere of the school encourages the individual to grow, develop, and change. This kind of atmosphere obviously is in contrast to a rigid, stifling, tradition-bound schooling which characterizes many school organizations. It is in opposition to lock-step promotions, fixed curriculum patterns, and competitive training systems. A close look at the schools forces us to recognize that very often we are setting up rigidities and traditions which tend to dehumanize everyone affiliated with the system, from the superintendent and the parents to the youngest child.

A philosophy which espouses educating the whole child with full recognition of his individuality in ability, interests, and motivation has in practice not provided procedures for achieving these lofty goals.

Thus, we must look to the social sciences to provide us with methods designed to facilitate personal and social development to become mature humane persons. This will become a reality as we recognize democratic procedures and knowledge about facilitating humaneness is already available. Our task is to establish educational priorities which insure achieving these goals. It has not been the purpose of this chapter to destructively attack the school and emphasize the gloom and pessimism of the times. But rather, we have intended to paint a picture of how things exist and where we can go. We feel like Bertrand Russell in that we would rather be mad with the truth, than sane with lies.

The remainder of the material will focus on ways to enhance growth and humane potential. We believe as does George Brown (1971):

> The greatest potential for change and significant improvement in our individual predicaments and in our dilemma as a society is in the school. It is the one institution in Western civilization outside the family that most profoundly affects the human conditions. It is also the institution that, though resistant, is the most practical in which to innovate (p. 8).

If theory is to influence practice and if humanism is to be implemented, there must be a systematic provision for consultation. The consultant utilizes his skill in interpersonal relations, learning processes, and group procedures to facilitate the development of the helping relationship between staff and with students.

This book will present a humane viewpoint of the learning process and provide a theory of human behavior which is designed to facilitate more effective human relationships. It includes a theoretical rationale for the consultant as a specialist in human relationships; the theory and practice of consulting with teachers, administrators and parents; and practical examples of work with individuals and groups. The classroom, as well as the system as a whole, are discussed and methods for releasing their inherent humane potential are presented.

REFERENCES

Bloom, B. *Stability and Change in Human Characteristics.* New York: Wiley, 1964.

Brown, G. I. *Human Teaching for Human Learning.* New York: Viking, 1971.

Carlson, J. and Mayer, G. R. "Fading: A Behavioral Procedure to Increase Independent Behavior." *The School Counselor* 17 (1971): 193–197.

Chase, F. S. "Educational Implications of Changing Knowledge." In *To Nurture Humaneness: Commitment for the '70's,* edited by Mary-Margaret Scobey and Grace Graham. Washington, D.C.: Association for Supervision and Curriculum Development, 1970.

Coleman, J. C. *Abnormal Psychology and Modern Life.* Glenview, Illinois: Scott, Foresman and Company, 1964.

Combs, A. W. "An Educational Imperative: The Humane Dimension." In *To Nurture Humaneness: Commitment for the '70's, edited by Mary-Margaret Scobey and Grace Graham. Washington, D.C.: Association for Supervision and Curriculum Development, 1970.*

Combs, A. W. and Soper, D. *The Relationship of Child Perceptions to Achievement and Behavior in the Early School Years.* Cooperative Research Project #815, Gainesville, Florida: University of Florida, 1963.

Dimick, K. and Huff, V. *Child Counseling.* Dubuque, Iowa: William C. Brown, 1970.

Dreikurs, R. *Social Equality: The Challenge of Today.* Chicago: Henry Regnery, 1971.

Farber, J. *The Student as Nigger.* New York: Pocket Books, 1969.

Glasser, W. *Reality Therapy: A New Approach to Psychiatry.* New York: Harper & Row, 1965.

Glasser, W. *Schools Without Failure.* New York: Harper & Row, 1969.

Glasser, W. *Identity Society.* New York: Harper & Row, 1972.

Golden, H. "What It Means to be Humane." In *To Nurture Humaneness: Commitment for the '70's,* edited by Mary-Margaret Scobey and Grace Graham. Washington, D.C.: Association for Supervision and Curriculum Development, 1970.

Jourard, S. "Human Revolution: Confronting the Realities of 'Them' and 'Us.'" In *To Nurture Humaneness: Commitment for the '70's,* edited by

Mary-Margaret Scobey and Grace Graham. Washington, D.C.: Association for Supervision and Curriculum Development, 1970.

Kagen, J. and Moss, H. *Birth to Maturity*. New York: Wiley, 1962.

Makarenko, A. S. *The Collective Family: A Handbook for Russian Parents.* New York: Doubleday & Company, 1967.

Mosher, R. L. and Sprinthall, N. A. "Psychological Education: A Means to Promote Personal Development During Adolescence." *The Counseling Psychologist* 2 (1971): 3–85.

Schutz, W. C. *Joy: Expanding Human Awareness*. New York: Grove Press, 1967.

Scobey, M. and Graham, G., eds. *To Nurture Humaneness: Commitment for the '70's*. Washington, D.C.: Association for Supervision and Curriculum Development, 1970.

Silberman, C. E. *Crisis in the Classroom: The Remaking of American Education*. New York: Random House, 1970.

Toffler, A. *Future Shock*. New York: Random House, 1970.

Van Hoose, W. H., Pietrofesa, J. J. and Carlson, J. *Elementary School Guidance and Counseling: A Composite View*. Boston: Houghton Mifflin, 1973.

2

The Consultant:
Facilitator of Human Potential

School pupil personnel workers are involved in a reanalysis of their role and identity. Although in some instances school administrators are willing to accept a limited role for the counselor as a specialist in educational, vocational, and personal counseling, in many schools administrators question the priority and value of these functions for the general educational enterprise. They believe the function must involve more than system maintenance and that there is need for a consultant who helps the organization to be adaptable (Holeman 1970).

The ACES-ASCA Committee (1966), in a study of the role of the elementary school counselor, identified three basic functional processes: counseling, consultation, and coordination. But another significant area exists—that which involves collaboration among *all* of the significant adults. School psychologists and social workers are also developing new role definitions which do not limit them to the traditional diagnostic and therapeutic functions. The major focus of the educational process—helping children to achieve their human potential—necessitates a reevaluation of role and function.

A number of well-known psychologists have suggested that man uses a small fraction of his potential. Herbert Otto (1969) has estimated that we use but 5 percent of our creative capacity. It is becoming more apparent that all people have creative capacities which can be developed. However, our educational system, with its emphasis upon conformity, memory, and rote learning, serves as a force which limits and often represses the development of creativity which releases human potential. If the school is to meet the challenge of developing creative, purposeful beings who actualize their human potential, then all aspects of the educational process must become humanized.

The consultant should recognize that pupil problems which now necessitate diagnosis, therapy, individual and group counseling, and special classes are often the products of the school's sociological environment. Current practice too often focuses on educating and assigning counselors to assist the child in adjusting to the structure of the school. However, in many instances the counselor will be more successful in resolving the problems of the schools and the pupils if he helps to restructure the social setting of the school. The consultant must be concerned with the total milieu or life space.

Leacock (1968), an anthropologist, indicates that teachers, administrators, and counselors should consider the sociological sources of pupil problems. All too frequently the schools are prone to see an individual problem as something arising from the pupil, rather than from the societal context of the school. We need to examine the organization and methods of the school as possible precursors of academic difficulty. Perhaps a close look at the instructional, curricular, and administrative policies within the school would be of greater service to pupils than effort focused primarily on getting the child to adjust to school.

As John Gardner (1964) has indicated:

> If we indoctrinate the young person in an elaborate set of fixed beliefs, we are ensuring his early obsolescence. The alternative is to develop skills, attitudes, habits of mind and the kind of knowledge and understanding that will be the instrument of continuous change and growth on the part of the young person. Then we will have fashioned a system that provides for its own continuous renewal (p. 25).

We should focus on using the mind to create and innovate, instead of using it for storing and repeating.

CONSULTANT ROLE

The type of professional identity we are suggesting, then, is one that is concerned and involved with the total school process. The consultant is not an ancillary or auxiliary service. He is in the mainstream of the educational endeavor, involved with the total environment and school milieu. He exists to be of service to all the persons in the educational environment—the administrator, teacher, specialist, parent, and child. He participates in decision making about the most effective way to enhance the learning process for the children—his main focus. However, he recognizes that he often achieves his goals and helps children most through indirect service to administrators, teachers, and parents.

The consultant is a resource and a catalyst for administration, teachers, parents, and children. His expertise is in the area of understanding affect and its impact upon the educational process.

His role, as McNassor (1967) has suggested, is

> . . . to aid the school in keeping itself open, flexible and humane, a hygienic place for human development through learning. He is there to help make it possible for some children to become what never was intended for them. He is there to help assure that all children develop the spirit along with the brain (p. 86).

Alvin Toffler has indicated that the creation of curiosity and awareness is the basic task of education (Toffler 1970). If we are to educate youth to meet the impact of change, based upon the assumption of a continuing rise in transciences, novelty, and diversity, students will need new skills in three areas: learning, relating, and choosing.

If this is the consultant's focus, then his effectiveness might be judged on an entirely new criterion. We would not be concerned with the number of cases he works with or the number of teacher contacts or pupil counseling sessions he has. Instead, he might be evaluated on whether his absence would cause administration and staff to feel they no longer had a vital resource, and as a result, the learning of children was no longer facilitated as it had been with his presence.

PROFESSIONAL PREPARATION OF THE CONSULTANT

The professional preparation of the consultant will place an emphasis upon creating an awareness of the significance of the school climate, the total milieu, and the way in which consultants may work through group procedures to influence the milieu. The consultant would be trained in counseling and learning theory and group process because they are basic to many of the skills of consultation. He would have special expertise in group dynamics and group procedures. The program for the consultant would provide intensive training in counseling so that he might utilize the process in working with pupils, parents, and teachers. The suggested course of studies would cover two years of preparation.

The educational experience from its inception would include role playing, micro-exercises in basic skills, demonstration, beginning experiences with clients in the appropriate area, and a continuous experience in developing awareness of self and others. Class time would be planned so as to allow opportunities for the students to participate in all facets of these experiences. Before completion of the training each candidate would be examined in terms of his competency in the required skills.

PROGRAM IN CONSULTATION

First Year

1. Philosophy, Principles, Organization and Administration of Pupil Personnel Services
2. Modification of Motivation and Behavior Change
3. Learning Processes and Educational Development
4. The Teacher: Human Potential and Guidance Procedures in the Classroom
5. Counseling Theory and Practice
   Understanding Human Behavior and Counseling Procedures
6. Techniques and Processes of Counseling: Counseling Laboratory
7. Guidance Consulting
   Techniques and Processes of Consulting Parents and Teachers: Application of Modification Processes
8. Human Appraisal Procedures (Tests and Measurement)
9. Research and Accountability Procedures
10. Practicum and Lab Internship
11. Group Counseling
12. Interpersonal Relations
    A personal experience in developing understanding of self and human relationships

Second Year

1. Research Procedures in Behavioral Sciences
2. Community Psychology and Social Organization
3. Advanced Group Dynamics—Theory and Practice
4. Advanced Group Counseling Theory and Practice: Group Counseling Practicum
5. Consultation and The System

6. Supervised Laboratory Experiences:
   Consultation with Parent, Teacher, Administrator
7. Internship in Practicum and Supervision
8. Seminar in Professional Development
9. Electives: Reading
               Curriculum
               Philosophy
               The Exceptional Child
               Human Services
10. Sociology, Psychology or Intergroup Relations
11. Psychology elective
12. Anthropology elective

It should be apparent that this type of training program places some new priorities in the education of pupil personnel specialists. In order to underline some of the differences, we would like to note some of the following emphases:

1. Concentration in understanding psychological processes and their relationship to the educational process would be emphasized. The counselor must be a specialist in understanding the child, the teaching process, the curriculum *and* the procedures for improving conditions for learning in the classroom.

2. Concentration would be focused on the development of an expertise in actual classroom procedures. If he is to be available to the teachers as a resource, the consultant must have some experiences which enable him to go into the classroom and demonstrate group guidance, classroom discussions, role playing, puppetry, sociometrics, scattergrams, classroom procedures for identifying guidance needs, procedures for developing understanding of self and others, and methods for individualizing and personalizing the educational process.

3. There would be an emphasis upon understanding counseling theory, techniques, and practical experiences in counseling with individuals.

4. There would be a special emphasis upon the significance of group dynamics and group process as a basic competency. The consultant would not only know about group consulting procedures but would be competent in their leadership. Group procedures would be studied in terms of their application to work with teachers and parents as well as children.

5. Effecting the whole learning climate is a basic emphasis of the program. The course work would give supervised training experiences in leading administrative, teacher, parent, and child groups.

6. Focus would be on developing a specialist who understood his role as a human relations specialist. His identity and the strategy for the development of such a program would be discussed, role played, and experienced in practicum and internship settings.

7. This specialist would also have training which would make him knowledgeable in behavioral sciences such as sociology, psychology, and anthropology. He would also be acquainted with special procedures related to curriculum and reading.

THE CONSULTANT AS A PERSON

One must not be confused that the type of consultant we are seeking is necessarily the product of a set of courses. It is essential that he possess a number of important personal qualities and capacities if he is to have any effectiveness as a facilitator of human potential. Thus, the course work which we have suggested must be taught in a democratic and open-system fashion which permits not only the freedom for the individual to become totally involved, but also provides a number of required group experiences which enable him to become more aware of himself, his impact upon others, and his own personal values and purposes.

The consultant will be expected to demonstrate competency in the following areas:

1. He must be empathic and be able to understand how others feel and experience their world.

2. He must be able to relate to children and adults in a purposeful manner. While he should be effective in developing rapport and working relationships, he must be judicious in the use of this time. This necessitates the capacity to establish relationships with his clientele which are in line with the purposes of this program.

3. He must be sensitive to human needs. He would understand Maslow's hierarchy of needs, but more than that, it is vital that he be able to perceive a need and be available as a facilitator to help the person meet that need.

4. He must be aware of psychological dynamics, motivations, and purpose of human behavior. His training qualifies him not only to talk about psychological dynamics, but actually to deal with them in the here and now.

5. He must be perceptive of group dynamics and its significance for the educational establishment. This suggests that he is aware of the impact of group forces upon the teacher, that he sees the teacher in the context of forces from *without* (such as administration and parents) and forces from *within* (such as his own goals and purposes).

6. He must be capable of establishing relationships which are characterized by mutual trust and mutual respect. His appearance as a consultant to either a group or an individual should inspire confidence. His personal approach to people should make it apparent that they are collaborators with him.

7. He must be personally free from anxiety to the extent that he is capable of taking a risk on an important issue. He must be able to take a stand on significant issues that affect human development. The consultant's role requires a courageous approach to life. He has the courage to be imperfect, recognizing that he will make mistakes, but realizing mistakes are learning experiences and he must not be immobilized by the fear of making one. This courage is developed through group experiences and in the supervised practical experience.

8. Perhaps the most important of all, assuming he is able to establish the necessary and sufficient conditions for a helping relationship, the consultant should be creative, spontaneous, and imaginative. The consultant position, by its very nature, demands flexibility and the ability to deal with a variety of expectations—on one hand, the principal's need for order and structure; on the other, the child's need for participation, care, and concern. Thus, the consultant will find his creativity continuously challenged.

9. He should be capable of inspiring leadership at a number of levels from educational administrators who look to him as a specialist in understanding human relations and human behavior to parents who see him as a specialist in child psychology. Teachers would see him as a resource in connection with pupil personnel problems. He would be available to children who see him as a resource in helping them to understand self and others.

It is our belief that this type of person emerges most readily from a program which places an emphasis from the very start upon not only the cognitive skills of the graduate student, but upon developing an awareness of self and one's impact upon others. We believe that this type of personal development is best arranged through regularly scheduled group experiences which enable the individual to become more aware of himself and his human qualities and their effect upon his colleagues. The helping profession cannot tolerate the ineffectual

person, the one who is able, perhaps, to relate to children but not to adults, or vice versa. The consultant must be capable of establishing human relationships with his entire clientele.

It is recognized that the goals established for the consultant set high standards for the professional person engaged in this position. Not all consultants will attain this level upon completion of training, and personal growth is always a continual process. However, it is important to recognize that these traits are not mere platitudes. No single factor is more destructive to consultant progress than lack of ability to develop effective helping relationships. The data from the Combs' studies (1969) indicate that a premium must be placed on the concept of self as instrumental for consulting. A comprehensive set of courses cannot compensate for failure to develop the type of person we are suggesting.

THE CONTEXTUAL APPROACH TO CONSULTATION

The concept of a consultant has already been advocated by Patouillet (1957), Lee (1963), Dinkmeyer (1962), and Faust (1967). They have suggested that if we are truly to develop services for all children, we must become involved in the consultant approach.

It is apparent that the need for comprehensive services for all students cannot be met through an approach which focuses only on individual counseling. Direct services must be combined with an awareness of the significance of the consultant's role as a milieu facilitator. In this role he is concerned with the total life space that surrounds the child and all of the forces that motivate development and retard growth. This is done with an awareness that the child is not an independent agent entirely free to decide his destiny. Significant elements in his life space, e.g., parents and teachers, must be contacted if the child is to be assisted.

This approach works on an extension of some of the original constructs of Lewin (1951) in his field theory. Lewin believed that behavior is a product of the totality of coexisting factors in a dynamic field, wherein one section of the field depends on every other sequence of that field. Behavior, thus, is always dependent upon the present field. If one is to understand the behavior of a given individual, it is necessary to comprehend how he experiences and interprets his present psychological environment.

Life-space consulting involves helping people to cope with life's problems in the actual context and setting. It necessitates that the consultant leave the office and enter into the life spaces of administrators,

teachers, parents, and children. We must enter their world and understand their feelings, thoughts, and actions in a manner that is empathic and conveys an understanding concern.

The contextual approach is in contrast to much that has been happening in pupil personnel. It does not suggest that we study the child and see if we can adjust the child to school. Instead, it suggests that we look at the school and the curricular experience and see in what ways they can be adjusted to the uniqueness of the child. This approach requires going beyond ancillary roles to involvement in the mainstream of educational programs.

The contextual approach requires all persons to become involved deeply in the very context that surrounds the behavior. It suggests providing a service which deals with problems when they occur. It implies that the consultant cannot always be available when a child has a fear of tests, hesitates to approach a school task, exhibits apathy, or acts out aggressively. The teacher usually is the closest and, therefore, primary resource during most of these situations. While the teacher could refer the child to a specialist, we are suggesting that he can learn to cope with the *real* situation. The consultant's knowledge and skills in human behavior and interpersonal relations must be integrated into the teacher's approach to children.

Learning must become an active process which embraces not only the cognitive or intellectual, but also the affective domain. It is not merely concerned with what can be poured in and abstracted regularly in the form of a test, but in contrast, it is concerned with the total learning situation and human development.

The contextual approach recognizes that an individual's reaction is determined not only by the actual event itself, but by his perception of it. Learning is always dependent upon the personalized meanings and purposes which are derived from it. The contextual approach has access to the whole teacher—thoughts, feelings, and perceptions—and through these the teacher is enabled to work with children in context.

Contextual procedures make use of the total situation—the child's thoughts, feelings, and actions. In some instances, the child is discouraged and needs specific encouragement. The teacher must be aware of the significance of pointing out the child's assets or things he can do well. In another instance, the child may lack an understanding of what it is that is really expected of him and will need to role play the situation in order to become aware of the expectations. In many instances, dealing with the problem in context provides an opportunity for the child to recognize choice as a significant factor in his own life. He is taught to recognize the consequences of his behavior and to be responsible for his actions.

Consultant Behavior and the School Climate

There is a growing body of research which indicates that schools have quite different climates, which are supportive of varied types of student and staff behavior. The climates, as discussed in detail in Chapter 3, may be opened or closed, and they have a significant influence on the total system. There are actually identifiable institutional norms and goals which have an effect upon the overall atmosphere of the school. There are also student subcultures and deviant subgroups which have special problems adjusting to school. It appears that these climates have a considerable impact upon values, behavior, and student interaction.

The consultant must be aware of the impact of the school climate if he is to obtain faculty support and participation in the guidance program. It is important to know: (1) who has social power, (2) who must be involved in decisions, (3) when to meet and (4) the purpose and rationale for involvement of individuals and group.

In many instances it appears that faculty and staff are in a sense alienated from each other. They have little hope that they can participate in determining the school's progress through the development of educational goals. In some instances the staff exists in a closed climate, where communication and support are extremely difficult and accomplishing daily tasks takes on greater significance than planning for the future. It would appear obvious that the consultant's effectiveness will no longer be thought of in terms of developing bigger programs and providing more effective counseling service.

In contrast, it may be vital that he understand the values of the student subgroups and be flexible enough to adopt consultant strategies and interventions which are relevant to the needs of the varied subgroups. The consultant, in this sense, becomes aware of the total climate and student needs and works to respond imaginatively to all the needs which exist in the total milieu (Walz and Miller 1969). He would recognize that human behavior is always influenced by significant groups in which the persons feel belonging and hold membership, and would work to create necessary groups and facilitate present groups.

Whenever student behavior relates to values and attitudes, it appears to be in a large part group-determined. Belonging is a basic need; thus, it is inefficient to respond to students as if they were individuals without significant referent groups. The consultant of the future may find that one of his more significant tasks necessitates being involved with groups of students to determine what might be an appropriate service to that student group.

The research on school climates indicates that schools do have quite different climates which are supportive of diverse types of students and staff behavior. It appears that the adjustment and success of an individual student may well be a function of (a) the type of climate of the school he attends, and (b) the extent to which the school climate is supportive of his individual needs and values (Walz and Miller 1969, p. 860).

There has been a number of interesting studies on school climates. Walberg and Anderson (1967) developed a model of school climates which considered two factors comprising the school climate.

1. The *structural* factor, the role expectations held by students for their own behavior. These include the student behavior expectations which the entire student group holds as acceptable behavior for a group member. These role expectations are determined by the way in which the classroom is structured and organized. Walberg and Anderson defined three dimensions: co-action (the amount of compulsive restraint or coercion used by the teacher); organization (the efficient direction of activity); and isomorphism (the tendency for class members to be treated equally).

2. The *affective* factor, determined by individual student's predisposition to act. This was divided into two dimensions: synergism (the personal relations among class members) and synality (the extent of the individual student's identification with group goals). It was found that isomorphism and organization predicted learning better than co-action and synergism predicted better than synality.

Halpin and Croft (1962) developed the concept of open and closed school climates. This concept suggests that the open school climate is one where the staff group is characterized by a mutual caring among members and openness of communication. In contrast, a closed school climate is one in which the staff group feels little commitment to the group and is unwilling to be open with other staff members. Halpin and Croft suggest that the major variable determining the school climate is the leadership style of the school administrator.

It would appear that this study suggests the significance of the consultant analyzing the school climate and working closely with school administration. In this instance, the consultant can be a resource person who helps to process feedback to administration about ways to develop a climate which increases communication and develops caring among the staff.

Walz and Miller (1969) summarize the extensive research on school climate:

> Overall, it is intriguing to consider what a greater attention to studying the school climate will do for counselor role. It is interesting to envisage the counselor as a researcher on school climate who consults with both students and staff regarding their behavior in a particular climate, who is resourceful in assisting people to adopt more adaptive and constructive behaviors and who serves as a linking agent between the school faculty and students with regard to the development of viable change strategies (p. 866).

GROUP DYNAMICS

Group dynamics is concerned with the nature of groups, their development, and the relationship among individuals, groups, and institutions. This approach understands man as a social being who needs other individuals to increase his self-awareness and regulate his behavior through group norms (Zimbardo and Ebbesen 1969). Group dynamics is concerned with all of the forces affecting social change.

If we recognize that the consultant is seeking to operate within a frame of reference which is based upon understanding the life space and the psychological field, then awareness of group dynamics cannot be incidental; it must be central to his understanding of role and function in the school. This implies that the consultant not only has didactic instruction in group procedures, but practical supervised experiences which enable him to observe and study the influences of social factors and forces in the educational scene.

The consultant is aware that the individual and the group are inextricably intertwined and the mixture of group and individual personalities should result in the development of a group of persons who are aware of these relationships and move towards a goal that is mutually acceptable. Cartwright (1951) suggested that there are eight factors significant in the strategy of achieving change. These factors include:

1. Cohesiveness: those who are to be changed and those who attempt to influence change must have a strong feeling of belonging to the same group. There must be developed, through equal participation, a feeling of psychological interdependence. It is important to use

organizational training procedures which treat all as equals and which enhance the feeling of belonging. (Schmuck and Miles 1971)

2. Attractiveness: the more attractive the group is to the members, the greater is the potential influence of the group. This suggests that it is critical to give attention to the selection of any group in the educational setting, and to do things which enhance the attractiveness of the group. This is most often facilitated by assuring that people who are socially powerful or attractive become members of the group. Attractiveness is also influenced by time and location of meetings and the strong support of administration.

3. In order to achieve change, one must identify which values and attitudes are the basis for attraction to the group. Those which are held in common can be used as forces for change. The group will have less influence on attitudes which are not related to the basis for group membership.

4. The greater the prestige of a group member in the eyes of others, the more significant the influence he will exert.

5. Efforts to change individuals or groups so as to make them deviate from group norms will encounter resistance. The pressure to conform to group norms must be considered in any strategy to achieve change. Attempts to change individuals through special programs, while failing to deal with the group norms, are not only unproductive but may increase tension within the group.

6. Everyone in the group should share perception of the need for change if the source of pressure for change is to lie within the group. It is important that members have a clear conception of purpose and personal commitment to individual and group goals.

7. Changing the group requires the opening of communication channels. It is important that all affected by the change are informed about the need for change, plans for change, and the consequences of change.

8. Changes in one part of a group produce strain in other related parts. This strain can be removed only by eliminating the change or readjusting the parts. Frequently a change in the substructure, such as a pairing of friends or opponents, will create increased tension in the total group.

Some of the most significant forces in the group include: goals, aspirations, leadership, anticipations, attitudes, and cohesiveness. In order for a group to become meaningful, a group goal must emerge. Unless the group is working towards some announced goal, it will tend to be unproductive until the goal is clarified. Clarification of group goals generally leads to an increase in members' interdependence, coopera-ation, and movement (Hollander 1967). Thus the goal is essential to the development of the group.

It has been demonstrated that moderate but realistic increases in the level of aspiration tend to generate a comparable increase in perform-ance. Aspirations are essential to a group that desires to succeed, and they tend to result in both individual satisfaction and increased group performance. Therefore, moderately increasing the level of a group goal will usually result in a corresponding increase in the level of group performance (Cartwright and Zander 1968).

The style of leadership appears to have an important effect on group results. The original experiment by Lewin, Lippitt, and White (1939) with varied styles of leadership found that children worked more effec-tively with the democratic form of leadership, and that democracy also fostered participation and involvement.

When the group goal becomes more important than the individual's goal, the group usually seeks an authoritarian form of leadership to attain the goal. This force sees to it that individual aspirations do not interfere with the group goal. However, as stress on group-oriented achievement decreases, the group will increasingly tend to seek a demo-cratic form of leadership (Cartwright and Zander 1968, p. 361).

Attitudes are the organization of beliefs which point the individual towards a preferred response. Groups are formed to facilitate the ex-pression of attitudes. However, we must distinguish between attitudes and values. Although they are interrelated, an individual generally holds many more attitudes than he possesses values, and the attitudes are more subject to change, while the values are closely related to a specific culture and, hence, tend to be sustained. In order to change attitudes, one must become open to the processing of new information and must find this information of value in developing social identifica-tions. Too often in education we have attempted to change attitudes by telling and advising. Change efforts which only involve the cognitive process, and omit the affective domain, usually do not change values or bring action.

Cohesiveness plays the most significant role in group dynamics. It has been established that the properties of the cohesive group include: attractiveness of members, similarity between members, and established group goals. The attractiveness of the group and the amount of com-munication between the members have a significant influence upon group cohesiveness. Cohesiveness often meets needs which can never be met in isolation. Thus, the more that norms and standards among members are shared, the greater the cohesiveness of the group. The more cohesive the group, the more it can influence the members.

It is apparent that the group forces play a significant part in the school climate and the psychological environment in which the consultant must work. It is only as he understands these group forces and applies group procedures that he can be effective as a facilitator and catalyst in the educational milieu.

Implications for consulting based on a knowledge of group dynamics include:

1. An understanding of the consultee's concern or challenge in its social context. Problems should be seen in terms of a total psychological field.
2. Usage of group strategies and procedures which recognize the importance of social power, attractiveness, prestige, belonging, cohesiveness, and commitment to change both in the formation and maintenance of the group.
3. A clear understanding among group members about the structure and purpose of the group. Group goals should be established which serve as guidelines and norms.
4. An involvement of both the affective and cognitive processes, in order to change attitudes.

HUMAN EFFECTIVENESS

The development of human potential necessitates a change in priorities. The human potential approach does not place its primary concern upon vocational guidance, clinical assessment, or abnormalities. It recognizes that, due to the overconcern with abnormalities, psychology may be lacking in constructs which help to conceptualize the development of human effectiveness.

Blocher (1966a) has made some attempts to describe a framework for the analysis of human effectiveness, when he states:

In this framework, the effective person is seen as being able to commit himself to projects, investing time and energy and being willing to take appropriate economic, psychological, and physical risks. He is seen as reasonably consistent across and within typical role situations. He is seen as being able to think in divergent and original, i.e. creative ways. Finally, he is able to control impulses and produce appropriate response to frustrations, hostility, and ambiguity (p. 731).

The consultant, then, takes this model for human effectiveness and seeks to facilitate it in the total milieu. He finds ways in which he can assist the significant adults–administration, teachers, and parents—to become more adequate and effective persons. He is concerned with helping them to maximize themselves so that they might become more fully functioning individuals. A byproduct of this effectiveness will be seen in their service to children.

However, the consultant does not merely provide indirect service for the child; he not only looks at the milieu, but works at times with the child directly in order to help facilitate the child's effectiveness. Thus, his target is human effectiveness. His service necessitates that he look at the total contextual approach, give recognition to the influence of the life space, and utilize procedures which take full cognizance of group dynamics. Only such a comprehensive approach will enable him to maximize human effectiveness.

His theoretical orientation is social-psychological, which recognizes the significance of growth theory. This is in line with the positive direction toward self-actualization as purported by Maslow (1954). Maslow takes a holistic approach to the organism and goes beyond the basic drives when he considers the source of motivation. Recognition is given to the basic goals and purposes of the individual. The way in which needs are expressed reveals the person's motives and purposes.

Maslow has formulated a hierarchy of human needs which are certainly applicable to the consultant approach. He suggests that we cannot work with the needs which are critical for the educational process until we have fulfilled the basic needs. His schematic approach begins with the physiological needs—food, air, water, and sex. If these basic and urgent needs are gratified, then a new set of needs emerge which are involved with safety. Safety needs are usually met in an orderly world in which the child feels safe and secure. This security involves freedom from bodily illness, danger, and the disruption of routine. The consultant recognizes that the environmental forces have much to do with the development of a satisfaction of safety needs. When the needs are not met, we typically see the neurotic or psychotic child. After the physiological and safety needs are met, the child becomes free to experience the needs for love, affection, and belonging. These needs—for the opportunity to both give and receive love—help the child to overcome the threats toward maladjustment and psychopathology. When these basic needs are met, it enables the child to advance to the esteem needs, or the needs for competence, mastery, adequacy, achievement, and recognition. It is interesting to note that frequently the school attempts to help the child to meet his esteem needs and fails to recognize the priority and prerequisite of the physiological, safety, and love areas. Some governmental programs are attempting to recognize that until we meet the prior needs, we cannot get involvement from the students (e.g., lunch programs).

When esteem needs are not met by the school and the child does not feel he is adequate and/or is not getting recognition for achievement, he tends to become discouraged. Thus, esteem needs are best met when the curriculum is tailored to individuality. If esteem needs are met, a new force emerges—the need to self-actualize and be whatever one is capable of becoming. The self-actualizing person, the goal and target of the consultant, emerges only after we attend to prior needs.

It is a primary professional responsibility of the consultant to facilitate human development. The consultant's job is not to adjust or manipulate the individual to bring him into conformity with the institutions and the culture. The consultant is concerned with the importance of what the psychiatrists refer to as "milieu therapy," the creation of a milieu which maximizes human development for all the clients. Creation of a milieu which enhances development and facilitates learning is a primary task for the consultant. It is important to recognize the immensity of the task. Blocher has dealt with some of the problems involved (Blocher 1966b) when he questions whether the counselor is qualified by training, background, and experience to be such an agent of change. We are suggesting that the consultant must be a behavioral scientist, able to understand not only the individual, but the society and its institutions. His role in the institution is that of developing relationships which facilitate growth. However, he must recognize that if he is committed to serve as an agent of change, he may be perceived as a disturber of peace and a personal threat to many people who are within the institution. This is why it is essential that the consultant operate openly with the full support of administration and staff. He exists to help the administration facilitate an atmosphere which produces maximum growth for all concerned.

THE SCHOOL ADMINISTRATOR AND THE CONSULTANT

The type of program that we are proposing must be developed systematically if it is to achieve its objectives. The philosophy and psychological principles which undergird the program must first of all be established with the top administrator in the educational system. This type of role and function cannot be discussed without the full approval and support of administration. A consultant program will only occur with the endorsement and active support of school administration. So, in the end, it is the administrator who provides not only the verbal but nonverbal support for the functions of the type of consultant that we propose. The relationship of administrator and consultant should not be one of superior and inferior. In contrast, the relationship should be concerned with maximizing the potential of each to the benefit of students, staff, consultant, and administrator.

In the final analysis, it is the administrator who has the authority to experiment and develop new programs. It is from him that we must expect educational leadership and innovation. He must be the type of person who encourages creative thinking, spontaneity, and new approaches to educational involvement. When the consultant works with an administrator who is equally concerned with becoming a catalyst and who seeks to attack resistance and indifference, then the two can work in a collaborative relationship.

The consultant never accepts an assignment in a school district unless he has had complete communication with central administration on a number of basic issues. The most important contact is that with the administration for the purpose of aligning goals. The consultant can only make a major contribution to improving the system if he and the administrator experience clear communication and if he shows the administrator how he can help him to achieve his goals for the staff and the total system. There should be clarification and agreement reached regarding the following points:

1. Purpose of the consultant program. Is there agreement that services to pupils can be both direct and indirect, and that a premium must be placed on recognition of the role of staff and total milieu on educational development?

2. The types of experiences which will facilitate the accomplishment of these purposes. Will greater involvement be developed through large group meetings, a guidance committee, small buzz sessions of the staff, or teacher groups? What is the most effective strategy for maximizing human potential in the educational organization?

3. Procedures for organizing these experiences which provide continuous developmental guidance experiences. This involves looking at the way in which guidance is treated as part of the curriculum. Is each teacher concerned with seeing himself involved in the guidance process with students? Is there a planned, sequential set of experiences in the guidance area that exists throughout the student's stay in the school?

4. Responsibility for directing the program. Who is providing the leadership for the developmental program? What is the relationship between administration and the pupil personnel staff? Because this relationship is critical, it is vital that responsibilities for direction be spelled out clearly.

5. Involvement in stimulation of the total staff. Has a schedule been developed which encourages staff to participate on a regular basis in direct contact with the consultant? The consultant should not attempt to proceed in his work with students, teachers, or parents until this contact has been successfully accomplished. The administrator has human needs, feelings, and values which must be dialogued. Failure to develop clear communication with administration can serve as a permanent deterrent to progress in the consultant program.

It is suggested that administrative decisions which are oriented toward maximizing human development be based on some of the following guidelines:

1. A premium is placed on recognizing that the educational process is effective only when it recognizes individual differences and is involved in reconciling programs to the uniqueness of the individual. This contrasts with services which attempt to fit the student into the predetermined curriculum.

2. A real priority is given to developing teachers who possess not only a guidance philosophy and a child-centered point of view, but also competencies which enable them to carry on instructional processes which are always integrated with a guidance approach. Staff members are hired with the expectation that they will work as part of a team, combining with the consultant to facilitate the maximum development of each pupil.

The total guidance program involves a continuous sequence of experiences which assist the child in meeting his personal developmental tasks and environmental demands. This type of program is more than incidental and haphazard. Instead, it presents a sequence of experiences which help the individual to cope with the discontinuity between his own development and environmental demands.

3. The total staff is involved with the development of a program which sees pupil personnel services as an integral part of the total educational process. It must be recognized that it is the administrator who provides the consultant with leadership and personal support. It is he who decides the delegation of responsibilities, who answers the question, "Is the consultant free to observe in classrooms, arrange for staff meetings, schedule small 'C' groups with teachers?" This is in contrast to setting up priorities which make it impossible for the consultant to facilitate this kind of development. It will soon be apparent to the staff whether the consultant is really valued as someone who can make a difference in their professional growth or whether he is another administrative assistant or clerical aide in the central office.

The administrator provides the physical facilities, amount of supplies, type of clerical assistance, and qualified staff. As the school schedule is developed, it is the administrator alone who can establish teaching teams and flexible schedules which facilitate regular individual and group contacts with staff and students. The consultant cannot be available primarily to react to crisis. He functions in such a way as to have a developmental impact which reduces the necessity of continual crises or "brush fire" fightings in the schools. Thus, he is more than a reactor; he is a force for change. If he is to be conceptualized as a catalyst in the school environment, then he must focus on stimulating new ideas and humanizing the curriculum.

The consultant's focus still is on serving all the children of all the people. However, he must learn to avoid the trap which has often encapsulated other specialists in pupil personnel—that of failing to establish a role or purpose and to communicate functions. He must establish some priorities for administrator, teacher, and parent contacts.

The set of priorities and a hierarchy of services will always be dependent upon the skills of the consultant and the distinct work setting. However, it is suggested as a model that the consultant might establish the following priorities:

1. *Collaboration and consultation with administration.* The consultant meets with central school administration and the local principals to consider school policy insofar as it affects human potential within the system. He looks at this in terms of the impact upon both teachers and children. He is concerned about the learning environment and the learning climate. In some instances, this will necessitate his meeting with specialists in curriculum to process feedback about the effect of certain curricular programs upon the staff and students. The consultant brings to administration his expertise in human relations, group dynamics, and the affective domain. He functions to help the administration to implement effective educational procedures. He can serve as a consultant to the principal by dialoguing and consulting on concerns which originate as an outgrowth of his role with the principal, staff, parents, and children.

2. *Collaboration and consultation with groups of teachers.* We are suggesting that collaboration implies working together, in contrast to establishing a superior-inferior relationship. This consulting may focus on a specific child or group of children. The model used is the "C" group, which will be discussed in Chapter 8. This approach helps the teachers to clarify their thinking about specific children and the relationship between teacher beliefs and attitudes and the ensuing student beliefs and attitudes. It is an approach that is concerned with develop-

ing better relationships between staff members and facilitating commitment to change.

If the consultant is to work with groups of teachers, schedules must be developed which allow time for group meetings. While the members of the group must come out of their own willingness to participate, administration, as a minimum, should develop schedules which permit regular contacts.

3. *Counseling with groups of children.* This type of counseling will work with either developmental groups concerned with typical kinds of problems, or crisis-oriented groups in which students have particular difficulties which require more intensive assistance. The consultant becomes accessible to groups of children and in this way he maintains a close contact with pupil needs so that he may process them into the general feedback which he relays to administration, curriculum, and the instructional staff.

4. *Consultation with parents in groups.* This type of consultation, which is developed more extensively in Chapter 11, focuses on parent education, child study, and parent groups. The concern is with reaching a large number of parents to help them to understand more effective ways to relate with and motivate their children.

The consultant's role is that of humanizing the educational process. He is a facilitator concerned with maximizing the human potential of administrators, teachers, parents and students. To accomplish this task as an agent of change, he utilizes a strategy and establishes priorities.

REFERENCES

ACES-ASCA Joint Committee Report on the Elementary School Counselor. In *Guidance and Counseling in the Elementary School,* edited by Don Dinkmeyer. New York: Holt, Rinehart & Winston, 1968.

Blocher, D. "Wanted: A Science of Human Effectiveness." *Personnel and Guidance Journal* 44, no. 7 (March 1966a): 729–733.

Blocher, D. "Can the Counselor Function as an Effective Agent of Change?" *The School Counselor* 13, no. 4 (May 1966b): 202–205.

Cartwright, D. "Achieving Change in People: Some Applications of Group Dynamics Theory." *Human Relations* 4 (1951): 381-393.

Cartwright, D. and Zander, A. *Group Dynamics.* New York: Harper & Row, 1968.

Combs, A. et al. *Florida Studies in the Helping Professions.* Gainesville, Florida: University of Florida Press, 1969.

Dinkmeyer, D. "The Consultant in Elementary School Guidance." *Guidance Journal* 1, no. 4 (Spring 1962): 95–101.

Faust, V. "The Counselor as a Consultant to Teachers." *Elementary School Guidance and Counseling* 1, no. 2 (March 1967): 112–117.

Gardner, J. *Self-Renewal.* New York: Harper & Row, 1964.

Halpin, A. W. and Croft, D. "The Organizational Climate of Schools." Salt Lake City: Utah University, U.S. Office of Education Research Report, July 1962.

Holemon, R. "Toward Viewing Guidance and Counseling as Adaptive Organizational Functions." Indiana State University, *Contemporary Education* 41, no. 5 (April 1970): 240–243.

Hollander, E. *Principles and Methods of Social Psychology.* New York: Oxford University Press, 1967.

Leacock, E. "The Concept of Culture and Its Significance for School Counselors." *Personnel and Guidance Journal* 46 (May 1968): 844–851.

Lee, J. M. "Is a Guidance Consultant Needed in the Elementary Schools?" *Illinois Guidance and Personnel Association Newsletter* (Fall 1963): 56–59.

Lewin, K. *Field Theory in Social Science.* New York: Harper, 1951.

Lewin, K., Lippitt R. and White, R. "Patterns of Aggressive Behavior in Experimentally Created 'Social Climates.'" *Journal of Social Psychology* 10 (1939): 271–299.

McNassor, D. "High Priority Roles for Elementary School Counselors." *Elementary School Guidance and Counseling* 2, no. 2 (December 1967): 83–92.

Maslow, A. H. *Motivation and Personality.* New York: Harper, 1954.

Otto, H. "New Light on Human Potential." *Saturday Review*, December 20, 1969, pp. 14–17.

Patouillet, R. "Organizing for Guidance in the Elementary School." In *Guidance and Counseling in the Elementary School*, edited by Don Dinkmeyer, pp. 54–63. New York: Holt, Rinehart & Winston, 1968.

Schmuck, R. A. and Miles, M. B. *Organization Development in Schools.* Palo Alto, California: National Press Books, 1971.

Toffler, A. *Future Shock.* New York: Random House, 1970.

Walberg, H. J. and Anderson, G. "Classroom Climate in Individual Learning." Cambridge: Harvard University, 1967. Research Report of Harvard Project Physics in cooperation with Carnegie Corporation of New York, National Science Foundation, Sloan Foundation, and the U.S. Office of Education.

Walz, G. and Miller, J. "School Climates and Student Behavior: Implications for Counselor Role." *Personnel and Guidance Journal* 47, no. 9 (May 1969): 859–867.

Zimbardo, P. and Ebbesen, E. *Influencing Attitude and Changing Behavior.* Reading, Massachusetts: Addison-Wesley, 1969.

3

The Consultant and the System

Traditionally, consultants have been viewed as professionals who work in a clinical sense, helping staff members to understand individuals who present special problems. Less traditional and more dynamic approaches have suggested that the consultant might use group dynamics and group counseling procedures to work with staff members in groups. The case staff approach usually has focused upon the child, in contrast to creating awareness of the relationship between the child and needs and values as perceived by the teacher. In certain instances, such as the "C" group, groups have focused on understanding both children and themselves. It is our contention that the self must be safe and free from threat in order to be open to consultation. The consultant must be enabled to enter the consultee's perceptual field. His diagnostic skills must be tuned to assessing and reinforcing the positive behaviors of the consultee.

We are now suggesting that the consultant needs to move beyond a limited clinical role to utilize his skills and behavioral science knowledge to help members of the organization to help themselves. The type of organization development that we are suggesting has been described clearly by Blocher, Dustin, and Dugan (1971):

> . . . organization development is a function for the social system that is almost completely analogous to the counseling function with individuals. Just as counseling is primarily concerned with helping clients

41

"learn how to learn," so the broader guidance function is aimed at helping the total system learn how to adapt, innovate, and plan on a continuous and orderly basis or in other words develop the capacity for self renewal (p. 86).

The primary function of the consultant role is to develop the capacity for self-renewal within individuals, groups, and the total system. As John Gardner has succinctly stated, "Most of us have potentialities that have never been developed simply because the circumstances of our lives never called them forth" (Gardner 1964, p. 13). The capacity for self-renewal requires that one possess the courage to be imperfect. If we fear failure it prevents exploration, experimentation, and growth. It is important to get people involved in doing things they care about enough that they represent convictions which are energized by feelings of real commitment to a position, point of view, or role. They are impatient with formalities, trivia, and bureaucracy.

We are suggesting in this particular function that the consultant go beyond his role of working only with the consultee, who may be an administrator, specialist, teacher, or parent and take a broader view of his role. In this sense, he is a systems analyst in that he helps the members of the system to conceptualize their problems in ways that allow them to ask significant questions and develop problem-solving capacities. This approach suggests that guidance must go beyond any traditional format which limits its concern to vocational planning, career or college selection, diagnostic appraisal, or counseling and psychotherapy.

GOALS FOR GUIDANCE IN THE SYSTEM

The goals for guidance in this sense are most in line with those developed by Cook (1971, pp. 542-543):

1. Guidance should assist persons to develop the capacity to be as concerned about others as about the self.
2. Guidance should enable students to expand their awareness of life to the extent that a global comprehensiveness can develop.
3. Guidance should enable students to develop a sense of self-worth that liberates them to an acceptance of the full reality of both self and situation.
4. Guidance should facilitate the development of instructional approaches that enhance the full participation and the full development of potential in the learner.

5. Guidance should facilitate the development of open systems of structure and communication in education to the end that meaningful participation in the school structure becomes possible for those outside the structures—primarily students and parents.

6. Guidance should facilitate change in the educational structures to enable the continual renewal of both persons and institutions.

7. Guidance should enable every youngster of school age to pursue an educational experience relevant to his needs and to the full limit of his interests and capacities.

These goals are broad-based and obviously eventually must be described in terms of specific performance objectives. Cook sets forth a number of examples of how to transcribe these objectives into specific performances.

One of the major functions of guidance, as currently conceived in the educational system, is to help the system to design learning experiences which enhance self-awareness, empathy, and social interest—in other words, the capacity to give and take. The crucial problem in human development and all living is developing a better understanding of self and more effective procedures for relating with others. Clients who come for counseling almost always bring a problem which does not reflect a lack of technical skill, but in contrast, a deficit in terms of understanding oneself in his social context. Consultation procedures also frequently require the consultant to help the consultee to get in touch with his own resources. The false dichotomy between counseling which deals with affect and consultation which is concerned with information and not feelings is *not* the type of consultation we are proposing.

If we are to really help the client and the consultee, we must effectively modify the environment. The history of pupil personnel services has been one of attempted remediation of deficits originally created by the system. We can no longer afford to employ large numbers of specialized personnel who only attack fragments of the problem and fail to look at the total situation. The consultant looks at the total system and its potential and seeks to develop mutual goal alignment among administration, staff specialists, teachers, students, parents, and the community. It is his task to inspire and free their creativity and improve their relationships so that progress towards common goals may be obtained. The consultant is concerned with developing a climate which fosters creative, purposeful, and meaningful behavior.

The consultant must have training which helps him to comprehend the school climate and the interpersonal relationships which affect learning, personal development, and the acquisition of skills (Walz and Miller 1969). The consultant has procedures which enable him to work as an agent of change within the school climate. He must be able to see patterns in the interrelationships among the significant persons in the system. As one begins to comprehend the system holistically, he is able to perceive the social organization of the school. This capacity enables him to see causes, consequences, interactions, their pattern, and at the same time to develop procedures for processing feedback. His task involves getting the staff together to focus on common concerns. This can only be accomplished by eliminating anxiety and fear and building trust, open communication, and a feeling of belonging to a group which espouses and works for common purposes.

TYPES OF SYSTEMS

One examines the structure of the organization of the school in order to develop a meaningful theoretical framework for describing the relationships that occur in the school situation. The consultant who wants to make an impact on the total system must be aware that most organizations have an inertia which enables them to resist any effort to examine themselves or change. It is almost as if the staff were banded together to act as if change could never occur. The security they feel from continuing in the way in which they have always operated is something of which the consultant must be aware; he must work instead to develop the security which comes from involvement in decision making. It is important that staff members become aware that change and decay are all about us and that the one thing that no man can resist is constant change. Change is a given in any system. However, groups with well-established norms are resistant to any change or innovation.

Systems can be categorized into one of two general types: closed or open. The *closed system* occurs when an organism has no procedures for recognizing or responding to input, nor does it have any channel for routing information it receives so that it can be dealt with as feedback and thus be used to guide modification of internal processes. In simple terms, the closed system is completely isolated from its environment. It refuses to admit any matter from outside of itself. It is primarily concerned with maintaining position and status, and change is resisted strongly because it breaks the current fantasy that in the self-perpetuating system we can grasp security. Thus, the closed system is static, and its greatest danger is it can only be nourished by itself; hence, it becomes self-destructive.

The *open system* emphasizes full and open communication of beliefs, attitudes, perceptions, and feelings. It believes that feedback is vital for orderly and organized growth. There is a continuous exchange of energy or information within the environment. Administration communicates openly to staff and vice versa. There is an intake and output of both matter and energy that is dynamic and self-renewing.

"Understanding the behavior of the individual requires, in fact demands, conceptualization of man-system relationships" (Sarason 1967, p. 232). The consultant is a contact point among the different points in the social system. To bring about change that improves both the learning climate and relationships for children, administrators, teachers, and parents involves dealing with the transactions between people and the interacting systems. This awareness of systems is particularly crucial if one is to avoid change merely on the surface while basic conditions are not altered. Some urban school systems have been characterized as the "fastest changing status quos," indicating there is a lot of paper shuffling and little real action in terms of the change process.

We must recognize that behavior takes place in the context of organizations or social systems. Sarason states, "I am not maintaining that social systems cause behavior. I am only maintaining that any theory which purports to explain behavior and which does not come to grips with man-system relationships is a naive, incomplete, and mischief producing theory" (Sarason 1967, p. 230). We need a psychology of change and innovation which sustains the change processes, and this is best accomplished through a psychological approach which is holistic in contrast to reductionistic.

The school, its clientele and professionals, as well as the consultant, are members of a system which sets conditions. Consultants often have failed in attempting to initiate even routine changes because they have not accounted for the system. Failure to recognize the complexity of the social system results in attempting to operate in the school without cognizance of a most significant variable. We must deal with the transactional processes which include the individuals and subsystems which are part of a larger field of relationships. The transactional process is reciprocal and cyclical in that an action evokes a response, feedback, and then an action. The new action involves a new level of awareness and a perception which is different from the original action as a result of the feedback.

Thus, the relationship is truly collaborative insofar as the consultant recognizes and utilizes the expertise of staff members. Any attempt to exert authority and impose his judgments may produce resistance and slow the change process. Even if the authority role were accepted, it would make the staff dependent and less able to manage their educational and personal change efforts. Collaboration is an essential requisite because it enhances the abilities of the consultant through utilizing additional resources, while at the same time it values and therefore increases the self-esteem of the staff. The consultant helps the staff to become aware of the children's needs, their own need systems, and the potential for meeting these needs through more creative utilization of their resources. To develop this type of approach necessitates beginning with a small group of people who have been carefully selected and who represent social power and critical needs within the system. An over-ambitious program to change everything and everybody is predestined to failure. The model of selecting a group of teachers for the "C" group with the intention of demonstrating effectiveness (Chapter 8) is obviously applicable to consultant-system relationships.

DIMENSIONS OF THE CONSULTANT'S JOB

The consultant that we are describing really serves or functions best as a catalyst. In this sense we mean that he is there to "make things happen," to promote growth and change in human potential. He has been described by Doress (1971) as "a responsible, humane, decent, courteous, loving, non-violent, respectable and respecting revolutionary." In other words, his task is making the school environment suitable for the development of human potential, and seeing to it that the institution fulfills its real purposes. He is concerned with making certain that all participate in decisions which influence and affect them. In this sense, then, he does not become overinvolved in paper work and nonfunctional communication or in indirect conversations which do not involve the principles, but instead focuses upon the major concerns, the total system, and its organization.

Lippitt (1959) describes the consultant position dramatically when he states: "The consultant asks such questions as: What seems to be the difficulty? Where does it come from? What's maintaining it?" (p. 6). Typical diagnoses include: (1) inappropriate distribution of power, (2) blockage of productive energy, (3) lack of communication between subparts of the system, (4) lack of correspondence between external reality and the situation perceived by the client (the system), (5) lack of clarity or commitment to goals for action, and (6) lack of decision-making and action-taking skills.

Lippitt (1959, p. 10) also suggests that we take a close look at the different phases of the process of changing. He identifies seven phases of the change process:

1. The development of a need for change.
2. The establishment of a consulting relationship

3. The clarification of the client problem
4. The examination of alternative solutions and goals
5. The transformation of intentions into actual change efforts
6. The generalization and stabilization of a new level of functioning or group structure
7. Achieving a terminal relationship with the consultant and a continuity of change-ability.

Therefore, this type of intervention is based upon the belief that, as a result of consulting contacts with the total system, the organization will learn to more adequately attack current and future problems by acquiring new procedures and formats for adapting to change.

We must become increasingly cognizant that we cannot change human behavior very much by interventions that are aimed solely at individuals. Our psychological theories must be social as well as psychological if they are to have a real impact. As we will explain in Chapter 5, man by nature is a social creature, and his behavior is best understood in a social context (Dreikurs 1950). Sarason has added a dimension to this by recognizing the importance of understanding behavior in terms of man-system interrelationships.

The counselor becomes involved in helping the administrator to initiate change. He has a number of possible change agent roles. Cook (1971, p. 477) has characterized some of these roles. He suggests that the counselor who takes on the change agent role does not have the leadership designation, the authority, and other responsibilities for the total institution. He can only account for his goals in collaboration with the administration. It is increasingly apparent that leaders in the field of school administration are recognizing that the guidance function must go beyond mere system maintenance (Holeman 1970). The counselor must do more than merely interpret the school structure or serve to attempt to "adjust students" so square pegs can squeeze into round holes. Instead, it is suggested that they help the organization to become more flexible and able to solve problems.

The six-stage adaptive-coping cycle which guidance personnel might execute include the following stages (Schein 1965):

1. Sensing changes in the environment
2. Imparting this information into the system
3. Changing internal processes
4. Stabilizing internal change
5. Exporting new and presumably improved goods or services
6. Getting feedback on the new export.

Many administrators are eagerly seeking pupil personnel specialists who are able to go beyond the limited clinical roles which they have designed for themselves and deal with the major problems of educational institutions.

Popper (1970) talks about the counselor's latent role capacity as a communications hub and institutional balance wheel. This, he suggests, can be accomplished by having a teacher-centered ratio in contrast to a pupil-centered ratio and having the consultant focus on ways to make classroom guidance by teachers the central focus of the guidance process.

Cook (1971, pp. 478–482) sees some possibilities in the following types of roles:

1. The *creative critic* who is committed to change and who questions the traditions of the institution.

2. The *feedback agent* who processes feedback from students— their general attitudes and experiences—to the staff. He becomes alert to aspects of the current structure which are opposed to educational and therapeutic development.

3. The *sociotherapist* who focuses on activities which will improve the climate of the institution; a resident sociologist who looks at how the system is functioning.

4. The *ombudsman* who acts as a trouble shooter not concerned with adjusting the student to a system which may be faulty or sick in itself, but rather with attempting to bring about an improvement in the situation. He is concerned with much more than adjusting individuals to the system.

5. *Manager of conflict* who brings out conflict in such a way as to facilitate development and better human relationships.

6. A *model of an open system* insofar as the counselor exemplifies an open-system person who offers himself as a fully functioning being—the liberal and the conservative. He respects persons.

7. *Developer/preventer* who, through his awareness of the developmental needs of students, functions to prevent the development of problems which might emerge.

8. *Researcher* who examines the school climate insofar as he serves as a linking agent between faculty and students in the development of change strategy.

Cook summarizes all of this material by introducing his own tripartite role model: "In this model the counselor is a combination of three roles: 1) an enabler/facilitator; 2) a disturber of the peace; and 3) a Don Quixote" (p. 482). He recognizes the necessity for confrontation and disturbance of the status quo and at the same time he "dreams the impossible dream." As stated by Robert Kennedy, "Some men dream and ask why; I dream and ask, why not?" He creates expectancies of fulfillment and wholeness for the individual. He emphasizes an optimistic and encouraging outlook.

ADMINISTRATIVE PATTERNS AND ORGANIZATIONAL CHANGE

Griffiths (1964) suggested that systems theory can serve as a model for administrative change and developed the following propositions:

Proposition 1. The major impetus for change in organizations is from the outside.

Proposition 2. The degree and duration of change is directly proportional to the intensity of the stimulus from the supra-system.

Proposition 3. Change in an organization is more probable if the successor to the chief administrator is from outside the organization, than if he is from inside the organization.

Proposition 4. Living systems respond to continuously increasing stress first by a lag in response, then by an over-compensatory response, and, finally, by catastrophic collapse of the system.

Proposition 5. The number of innovations is inversely proportional to the tenure of the chief administrator.

Proposition 6. The more hierarchical the structure of an organization, the less the possibility of change.

Proposition 7. When change in an organization does occur, it will tend to occur from the top down and not from the bottom up.

Proposition 8. The more functional the dynamic interplay of subsystems, the less the change in an organization.

(Miles 1964, pp. 431–435)

It is important to recognize that the school was conceived as a social system to achieve educational goals. However, over a period of time it is apparent that there has been and still is a discrepancy between the stated goals of the organization and the procedures and means which are used to achieve the end. Bureaucratic procedures, mass education, and a number of other ills have limited the productivity of the system and the organization. Thus, as a social system, the school has tended to become hierarchal and impersonal.

It is imperative, then, that consultants deal with the real roots of the problems and gain an understanding of why the school, as a social system, has created such problems as limited educational opportunities, alienation, and lack of personal-social or intellectual growth. The schools can only become more effective in reaching their stated objectives by introducing new concepts of organization which enable them to be sensitive to all the people they intend to affect.

The hierarchial structure of the school involves both the authority and leadership hierarchy in the system. It is this structure which gives coherence and meaning to the system. One must recognize and be aware of both formal and informal structures. The consultant must not be on the periphery as an ancillary or auxiliary service, but be part of the vital interaction that occurs within the school. He recognizes the difference between authority, which is the designated capacity to invoke compliance and cooperation from people, and leadership, which induces cooperation in others without possessing designated authority. The system, of course, functions at its optimal level when those who have designated authority also have that quality of leadership that enables them to motivate and stimulate cooperation. Systems have their greatest conflict when the designated authority and the actual leadership is divided. The guidance worker as a consultant must be able to cooperate and communicate closely with the designated authority structure in order to promote the greatest growth of the system.

We conceive of the administrator and consultant as collaborators who work together with the system in order to apply democratic problem-solving procedures. It is essential that the organization develop in such a way that the goals sought are collaborative and mutually align those in authority and the total staff. Etzioni (1961) has indicated that research evidence clearly suggests that the more an organization relies upon force or coercion, the less it is capable of producing changes in either attitudes or feelings. It is important that the planning develops a structure whereby there is interaction and continuous communication for the purposes of collaboration and total clarification throughout the system. There must be articulation between significant groups within the system. The consultant serves as one of the articulators, but he must be aware of the importance of identifying other articulators in the system, those who have social power. It is possible to identify these people by watching social transactions that go on within the faculty lounge and faculty meetings. The consultant should note who tends to speak frequently on points and issues that are important within the system and who is listened to by the rest of the staff.

ORGANIZATIONAL TRAINING

Planned organizational change often has grown out of many of the assumptions originally developed in T-group training. However, a number of specialists, especially Schmuck, Runkel, and Langmeyer (1971), have suggested that the goals of organizational development require a different kind of training than that designed to develop increased self-understanding. They indicate that organizational training is concerned primarily with the organizational roles and norms and their interrelationship, and is based more on general systems theory and group dynamics than on interpersonal relations. Organizational training recognizes that knowledge about self will not in many instances bring individual changes and certainly will not effect structural change in the schools. Thus, the sensitivity training may still leave people in the organization resistant. The targets for this type of training are all members and subgroups of the system, and the concern is with increasing the effectiveness of the system as a task-oriented entity so that members may function more effectively as part of the total body.

The consultant should become aware that the total staff has a number of characteristics which are different from those of individual members. These are called the school's systemic characteristics. The orientation of Schmuck and his colleagues to organizational training is as follows:

1. Interventions will be more efficient if they deal with subsystems and not just random selected components. The training is concerned with the relationships within and among the subsystems.

2. Intervention should make the school aware of the discrepancy between the stated goals and the actual achievements.

3. Intervention should be concerned with making every subsystem in the school more open to the influences of all the other subsystems.

4. Intervention should help the school to identify system-wide resources and build communication systems between all of the basic units and subsystems.

Organizational training, then, is concerned with helping schools achieve more capability for efficiently bringing about structured changes (Buckley 1967). The emphasis is upon training subsystems—intact working groups—so they deal with their communications, norms, transactions, and relationships. Giving and receiving feedback is carried out most effectively by using the four communication skills, which are as follows:

1. *Paraphrasing*—making sure you understand the other person's message. Check your perception of the meaning—be sure you understand the idea as he *intended* it to be understood. Allow

the speaker to assess the listener's understanding. The goal is to increase the degree of mutual understanding and to convey interest.

2. *Description of behavior*—describing what you see behaviorally, avoiding inference. Report specific observable behaviors without evaluating them.

3. *Description of your own feelings*—describing feelings, not inferences or thoughts. This goes against old cultural norms of expressing and acknowledging feelings in self and others.

4. *Perception checking*—focusing on affective message, describing what you believe to be his feeling. Check your perceptions of another's feelings by describing to another how you think he is feeling so that he can verify or deny your supposition.

"Organizational training proposes to make substantial improvements in the school's responsiveness to its environment by helping it modify its internal features, including its roles and norms, and to become more self renewing" (Schmuck, Runkel and Langmeyer 1971, p. 186). It does not merely work with problems as defined by administration but attempts to explore problems from the perspective of all parts of the organization. The goal, then, is to attain an adaptable, self-renewing organization.

Organizational training focuses on helping members of the organization who are not performing their roles effectively to take on new behaviors in their actual work group setting, while other members of the group observe their new behavior. It is suggested that norms within the school organization are altered most effectively when members see their colleagues actually taking on new patterns of behavior within the school setting. This contrasts with the concept of going away to T-group or sensitivity training to develop a better understanding of self and coming back unable to actualize it within the work setting.

The type of training Schmuck is suggesting is holistic.

Because we believe that man's rational and emotional sides are inextricably mingled, we believe also that an organizational intervention can be successful only if it adequately takes account of man's emotional experience. Substantial research evidence shows that men invest emotion in at least three domains: 1) striving toward achievement, also labeled curiosity, exploration, or activity 2) affiliation, also delineated by some as the interpersonal dimension of the love, indifference, and hostility, and 3) influence or power, also described as the dimension of dominance-submission. We assume that all interpersonal relations and the motivations concomitant with them can be construed as having achievement, affiliation, and influence components (p. 187).

Thus, it is suggested that this emotional component, which some have formerly considered a threat to progress, now can be utilized to generate the energy for growth and change. Feelings about achievement, for example, can be utilized best when staff members of the school clearly recognize each other's goals. Open awareness of goals is usually more growth producing than the frustration generated by ambiguity about goals and directions. Schmuck and his colleagues point out the following goals for organizational training in terms of their theory:

These serve as objectives as we intervene in a school district to improve its organizational functioning. 1) Increase understanding of how people in different parts of the school affect one another. 2) Develop clear communication networks up and down and laterally. 3) Increase understanding of the various educational goals in different parts of the school. 4) Develop new ways of solving problems through creative use of new roles in groups. 5) Develop new ways of assessing progress toward educational goals in the school. 6) Involve more people at all levels in decision-making. 7) Develop procedures for searching out innovative practises both within and outside the school (p. 188).

These objectives are achieved through several steps. First, communication skills must be improved. Staff members must increase their capacity to deal with interpersonal or interrole problems more effectively by practising new procedures for communication. The function of the trainer or consultant is to help them to build increased openness and ease of interpersonal communication by training them in the skills of paraphrasing, describing behavior, describing their feelings, and checking their perceptions of other's feelings.

The next step involves changing to new norms that support interpersonal openness and helpfulness on the staff. These changes in the organizational norms are facilitated because staff members are now aware that they can behave in new ways which will be supported by their colleagues. The final phase involves the building of new functions, roles, procedures, and policies which become part of the basic school organization. They should be formal and institutionalized, actually supported as part of the total budget.

Once there is readiness and acceptance of the problem with verbal commitment from all who will participate, one may begin with a demonstration. Generally Schmuck and his associates follow this succession: 1) interpersonal communication, 2) choosing goals, 3) conflicts in the group and norms, 4) learning more effective group procedures, 5) solving problems, and 6) making decisions.

The core ingredients of organizational training are 1) improving communication skills, 2) changing norms, and 3) structural change. Schmuck and his colleagues (p. 188) suggest that in this aspect of consultation which they call "communication consultants" the relevant skills involve:

1. Increased understanding of how people in different parts of the total school system affect one another by setting up feedback sessions.

2. Development of a clear communication network through the use of the communication skills of paraphrasing and behavior description and by providing for communication skill workshops.

3. Increased understanding of various educational goals in the school organization by writing specific behavioral objectives and specifying the outcome.

4. Development of new ways of solving problems through creative use of new roles in groups by using problem-solving sequences and training exercises with people in leadership positions.

5. Development of new ways of assessing progress toward goals in the schools.

6. Involvement of more people at all levels of decision making through smaller groups and organized confrontations to reduce the distance between the various levels in the system's hierarchy.

7. Development of procedures to search out innovative practises within and outside of the school by identifying creative practises wherever they may be occurring.

Organizational training aims at increasing the effectiveness in problem-solving of groups as task oriented entities. It attempts to help participants to function more effectively as components of working bodies carrying out specific tasks in that particular job setting. Unlike sensitivity training, it does not aim at helping individuals to understand themselves better or to help them be more skillful in personal relationships generally (Schmuck et al. 1971, p. 190).

The consultant functions as a change agent acquainted with the democratic procedures for facilitating social change. He must be capable of developing relationships which emphasize mutual respect, equality, and trust. He must be capable of avoiding legalistic authority or authoritarian-type decisions forced from on top. In contrast, he develops common goals and cooperation. This involves dealing sometimes with hostility which may come from his peers, other members of the professional staff. He works eventually to develop commitments from staff members.

PRINCIPLES OF SOCIAL CHANGE PHENOMENA

Blocher, Dustin, and Dugan (1971) have done an excellent job of summarizing the nature of the social change process.

1. Change processes operate largely from within the system affected. Those who expect to facilitate change must belong to or find ways of belonging to the system which is to be changed. . . .

2. The more cohesive the system—that is, the greater the degree to which it meets the needs of members—the more intense will be the resistance to change and the more fruitful the change will be in producing changed behavior of members. Cohesion then is both the source of resistance and the energizer of change.

3. The basis on which proposed changes will be accepted in a system is the degree to which they are perceived as relevant to the core values that constitute the nucleus of the system. . . .

4. The degree to which an individual member of a system is able to facilitate or resist change in the system is a function of the status and respect that he is accorded within the system. . . .

5. The rate at which planned change can occur within a system is largely a function of the communication processes that operate within the system. Planned change cannot occur faster than the channels of communication operating within the system allow information, feelings, and attitudes about the change to be shared by all relevant members of the system.

6. A system that is pathologically resistant to change is probably one in which strong barriers to effective communication, particularly expressive or emotional communication, exists. . . .

7. When barriers to expressive communication are suddenly removed, the resultant outpouring of emotional communication may be frightening to members of the system, particularly to those in authority positions for whom the barriers have served as insulators against negative feedback or hostility. . . .

8. Change in one system results in changes in all systems with which linkages occur. . . .

(p. 84–86)

The consultant should be aware of some of the basic strategies which have proven to be effective in facilitating change. Obviously one must be aware of the setting and situation which he is attempting to change. He must get the feel of the situation—assessing staff and learning who are his potential allies and who are those who may provide major resistance. He must develop a guidance committee which helps to get feedback about his procedures as well as access to the system.

The guidance advisory committee can be either voluntary or appointed by the administration. Steps should be taken to insure that it represents a variety of positions relative to the guidance function and includes experienced staff members as well as those who can contribute primarily in terms of the pertinent educational courses and training they have experienced. This committee makes suggestions, serves as a sounding board, is a procedure for getting reactions from teachers concerning existing practices, and promotes and interprets the aims and purposes of the program. The committee provides a unique form of feedback for the consultant. It meets monthly and "on call."

If, by chance, the consultant is in a system that is already open, he may need only to find out how to facilitate his function within it. However, in most situations the consultant will find the system more closed than open. This suggests that one should first select some issues that are central to the problems which beset the organization but also present an opportunity for a chance of successfully changing the situation. First attempts at innovation should be those which have a high possibility of positive change. Plans for change and steps to be taken should be those which involve taking on small components of what may be an eventual long-term change process. All attempts to bring about change involve developing procedures for collaboration, negotiation, and communication. Long-range goals will be in line with those which Lippitt (1959) has suggested.

Lippitt indicates successful interventions end with at least three kinds of learning. The organization should have learned to cope more adequately with the problems which initiated the consulting process. The organization should have learned how to function more adequately in clarifying future problems as they emerge and to make appropriate decisions about seeking outside help. The organization should have learned new procedures and types of organization to help it adapt to change.

ORGANIZING THE CURRICULUM FOR GUIDANCE

It is the responsibility of the school to provide each child with a teacher who will be concerned about his personal social development and interested in him as an individual. This is promoted best when there is an open system which has a genuine concern for the personal growth needs of staff members. It frees the teacher to see the need for doing the same for children. As he develops his personal identity, values, and goals, and is enabled to have contact with other staff, he is able to do the same for his students.

The whole student comes to the school with his intellect, feelings, and behavior and can no longer be fragmented into parts. Personalized interaction must be based on an awareness of the basic dignity of all persons. Our current approach to children is basically depersonalizing for the typical youngster. Sachs (1966) states we are actually saying, "Because you are only normally human, there does not seem to be point in interacting with you on a personal and intimate basis" (p. 269). So, despite the fact that these students constitute the vast majority, they may receive the least attention.

Sachs has proposed that the school make two basic commitments: 1) provide personalized learning experiences, and 2) see that each student has at least one continuing small group experience that forms for him a link between the egocentricity of the individual and the commonality of mankind. Sachs then presents in a comprehensive fashion a core curriculum which involves both personalized contact with a teacher and an ongoing group experience. Each student is able to find himself through these various roles which perform a service to him and society. We must not overlook the fact that the curriculum always occurs in a social context which, in turn, influences the learning experience.

THE HUMAN RELATIONS SYSTEM

Human psychological needs are met in the human relationships that go on within the school system. Effective organizational relationships are characterized (just as therapeutic relationships) by warmth, empathy, and positive regard. Blocher and his colleagues have set forth five psychological constructs that are involved in relationship development (Blocher, Dustin and Dugan 1971). They are conceived of as patterns of interpersonal behavior that can be learned by all members of the organization, and the relationship system of the school should be designed to implement learning experiences that facilitate the acquisition of these constructs.

1. *Role adaptability*—the capacity of the individual to respond to his immediate feelings and impulses to the extent that within the relationship one is free to respond to his own immediate

feelings and impulses so he can contribute maximally to not only his own growth but that of others.

2. *Cognitive flexibility*—the openness and tentativeness with which people approach new ideas and new adaptations. There is no tendency to early closure but a willingness to tolerate ambiguity and to look for solutions from experience rather than from tradition or authority.

3. *Perceptual sensitivity*—or the ability to receive accurately the communications of others and to respond to their needs empathically.

4. *Consistency of communication*—or the quality of being able to communicate unambiguously by saying what one really means. One should check to see whether disagreements are expressed openly and voice tone is compatible with verbal content.

5. *Interpersonal involvement*—the ability to relate ways to communicate warmth, caring, and personal consideration, or the ability to show a mutual concern rather than a giving of approval or disapproval.

It will be important for each consultant to develop a hierarchy and set of priorities in his strategies for change. It is interesting to note that Cook (1971), Dinkmeyer and Muro (1971), and Faust (1968) have all indicated that one of the top priorities in the strategy for change is group counseling with teachers. This should be accompanied by group procedures and self-awareness training for both administration and staff. This can facilitate the development of classroom groups such as have been suggested by Dreikurs (1968) and Glasser (1969).

COMMUNICATION SYSTEMS

The agent of change must be aware of all the communication patterns that are involved in the structures and all the messages that are being sent within the system—these are pertinent in determining the methods that he uses to implement change. It is important that he be aware of all the messages that are being sent within the system; this will only be facilitated as he becomes an active listener who is able to catch feelings. This is why, as we have already indicated, his counseling skills enable him to develop a healthy, cooperative, growth-inducing social system. It is important to see the communication pattern that operates within the system, because there is a pattern existing there just as there is between the client and the consultee, the consultee and the consultant. There will be both formal and informal communication channels. The goal in dealing with the communication system is to promote a consistency of expectations to the extent that the staff is able to predict expectations. Then one can develop a climate for change in the expectations of members.

The consultant serves as a linkage-type person in that he can function as the communicator between teacher and principal, school and family, pupil and staff, etc. He needs to analyze the official communications which go out from the administrative hierarchy and those which proceed from his office. He must try to avoid sending one-way communications which inhibit or limit feedback, e.g., the memo, directive, or announcement over the P.A. system.

He must clarify the type of messages being sent. Some are instrumental, only intended to produce a specific action in the receiver, while others are expressive and intended primarily to convey the feelings of the sender. It will be important to facilitate the sending of congruent messages which include both instrumental and expressive intentions. Often, the administration of the school system is operating on the basis of the fantasy or mythology which tends to believe the expression of feelings in a system is unhealthy. The consultant helps the administration to understand how failure to develop open expression of feelings in a system is usually a sign of pathology. He will need to analyze the communication flow within the system and discover how accessible people at the top level of administration are to negative messages. Many systems provide little opportunity for flow upward in the vertical hierarchy.

Blocher and his colleagues (1971) point out the importance of two-way communication when they suggest:

> One of the factors that increases difficulty in facilitating direct two-way communication within a system is the mistaken belief that it is safer to communicate difficult or tension arousing messages in one-way, indirect channels, rather than in direct face to face exchanges (p. 161).

The successful implementation of social change should produce an organization which eventually develops in the members new processes, norms, and skills so that there can be a continuous flow of information and fulfillment of its goals. The consultant always must be aware that, as has been indicated, "the medium is the message" and he must be concerned not only with the content but the form that the message takes.

The consultant who is interested in reorganization of the system will analyze well the power structure and find ways in which to help implement growth. In many instances, he will need to be extremely flexible, having his long-range goals, but also being willing to adapt to anything which he sees as a step forward. He carefully selects issues which will be important to staff people and to those with social power who are also concerned with the development of a more humane environment. He lays the groundwork of good human relations through the model of his behavior, and he seeks as many "allies" as possible.

REFERENCES

Blocher, D. H., Dustin, E. R. and Dugan, W. E. *Guidance Systems*. New York: Ronald Press, 1971.

Buckley, W. *Sociology and Modern Systems Theory*. Englewood Cliffs, New Jersey: Prentice-Hall, 1967.

Cook, D. R. *Guidance for Education in Revolution*. Boston: Allyn & Bacon, 1971.

Dinkmeyer, D. and Muro, J. *Group Counseling: Theory and Practice*. Itasca, Illinois: Peacock, 1971.

Doress, I. "Counselors as Catalysts" Unpublished paper. Northeastern University, March 29, 1971.

Dreikurs, R. *Psychology in the Classroom*. New York: Harper & Row, 1968.

Dreikurs, R. *Fundamentals of Adlerian Psychology*. Chicago: Alfred Adler Institute, 1950.

Etzioni, A. *Complex Organizations*. New York: Free Press, 1961.

Faust, V. *The Counselor-Consultant in the Elementary School*. Boston: Houghton Mifflin, 1968.

Gardner, J. W. *Self-Renewal*. New York: Harper & Row, 1964.

Glasser, W. *Schools Without Failure*. New York: Harper & Row, 1969.

Griffiths, D. E. "Administrative Theory and Change in Organizations." In *Innovation in Education,* edited by M. B. Miles. New York: Teachers College Press, Columbia University, Bureau of Publications, 1964. (Can also be found in Blocher, Dustin, Dugan, p. 42–43).

Holeman, R. "Toward Viewing Guidance and Counseling As Adaptive Organizational Functions." Indiana State University, *Contemporary Education* 41, no. 5 (April 1970): 240–243.

Lippitt, R. "Dimensions of the Consultant's Job." *Journal of Social Issues* 15, no. 2 (1959): 5–12.

Popper, S. "The Guidance Counselor as an Institutionary Balance Wheel In Early Adolescent Education: A Probe Into Latent Role Capacity." Indiana State University, *Contemporary Education* 41, no. 5, (April 1970): 232–239.

Sachs, B. *The Student, the Interview, and the Curriculum.* Boston: Houghton Mifflin, 1966.

Sarason, S. "Toward a Psychology of Change and Innovation." *American Psychologist* 22, no. 3 (March 1967): 227–233.

Schein, E. *Organizational Psychology.* Englewood Cliffs, New Jersey: Prentice-Hall, 1965.

Schmuck, R., Runkel, P. and Langmeyer, D. "Theory to Guide Organizatonal Training in Schools." *Sociological Inquiry* 41, no. 2 (Spring 1971): 183–191.

Waltz, G. and Miller, J. "School Climates and Student Behavior: Implications for Counselor Role." *Personnel and Guidance Journal* 47, no. 9 (May 1969): 859–867.

4

Application of Learning
Principles in Consulting

There is no teaching until the pupil is brought into the same state or principle in which you are: A transfusion takes place; he is you, and you are he; there is a teaching; and by no unfriendly chance or bad company can he ever quite lose the benefit. Emerson (1803–1882)

There are two ways of coming at any sort of learning and a moral conduct of life: the one is by instruction in, the other by practical exercises. Josephus (37–96 A.D.)

The first thing, I believe, for mankind is education. Whenever anyone does the beginning of anything correctly, it is likely also that the end will be right. As one sows, so one can expect to reap. If in a young body one sows a noble education, this lives and flourishes through the whole of its life, and neither rain nor draught destroy it. Antiphon (5th Century B.C.)

... It is in fact nothing short of a miracle that the modern methods of instruction have not yet entirely strangled the holy curiosity of inquiry; for this delicate little plant, aside from stimulation, stands mainly in need of freedom; without that it goes to wrack and ruin without fail. Albert Einstein (1879–1955)

The analysis of the process of learning is not a recent interest, as we can observe above. The question of how one acquires knowledge and the finding of the best way to do it have perplexed modern man since his inception. The points of view expressed above demonstrate a poetic flare toward the desire to enhance the humaneness of man through learning. Yet man's attempts at transcribing this goal through modern learning processes is presently described as "sick," "failure-oriented," "corrupt," and "mistake-centered" (Glasser 1969, Postman and Weingartner 1969, Toffler 1970). Perhaps the current educational learning process is best captured in a poem "The Memoirs of Jesse James" by Richard Brautigan (1970). Brautigan depicts school as a place where one waits—for lunch, to go home, or to return again to life. Teachers are portrayed as forcing children to stay in school and are, therefore, responsible for stealing part of "life." The present situation may be depicted as a contest—how much can one get by competition, power struggles, etc. School becomes a game in which the authoritarian teacher tries to control, but the child in actuality dictates all the rules.

The learning system appears dichotomized. We have the espoused goal and the practical model. How can they be merged? Or to use current terminology, "How can we get it (this age-old problem) together?" What must the consultant know to facilitate this development? What can the consultant do? How does the consultant use the learning process?

RATIONALE: THE LAKE WILDERNESS CONFERENCE

The need for change in today's schools and the necessity for developing humane learning already has been established in a previous chapter. The call for a refocusing and reordering of the basic principles regarding the learning process, environment, participants, and facilities is now clear.

In June of 1971 a National Conference of Pupil Personnel Services, sponsored by the U.S. Office of Education, was held at Lake Wilderness, Washington. Thirty-two persons, representing a variety of roles in education and related fields, met for the purpose of examining and seeking new directions for Pupil Personnel Services.

The conference produced a new model or role for the Pupil Personnel Worker—that of *Learning Development Consultant* (LDC). The LDC is primarily concerned with matching the learning process to each individual's needs. The many subsystems (e.g., family, neighborhood, school, and future systems such as university, world of work, military services, and the new family) in which the individual functions are understood and shared with other learning facilitators.

The LDC is perceived as a generalist who serves as an advocate for the learner as a developing human being. He seeks to reach this goal through the dual roles of *facilitator* of communication and *coordinator* among those involved in contributing to learning and development. He is totally involved in the learning process and school environment. The consultant recognizes the diversity of needs and the subsequent concerns and the necessity of involving all those concerned (e.g., learners, parents, learning developers, administrators) in order to establish the dimensions of the problem.

In order to function in the proposed role, the LDC is seen as needing skills of the following kinds:

1. Sensitivity to and recognition of *needs* as expressed in words and behavior, and ability to conceptualize those needs in relation to appropriate theories and systems.

2. Ability to help learners and others to identify their own needs and goals and to plan and carry out appropriate action to satisfy those needs and attain those goals.

3. Ability to work with groups (of learners, learning developers, parents, and others) in such ways as to assist the groups and the individual members to become increasingly aware of their own resources, of effective communication, and of the dynamics of change.

4. Ability to transmit to others in the learning community his/her own knowledge and skills in sensing and analyzing needs, improving communication and in facilitating change.

5. Ability to help create an atmosphere of collaboration, of flexibility, of change, and to stimulate others, in and out of school, to participate actively in the total educative enterprise.

(U.S.O.E. 1971, p. 7)

The goal of the new model is to facilitate the satisfaction of the major needs of learners at a high level. The significance of this new model lies in its focus on learning. The emphasis is not just timely, but perhaps the mystery ingredient in the search for a humane environment. The consultant is primarily concerned with learning.

THE CONSULTANT'S ROLE IN LEARNING

The consultant should strive toward a theory of human behavior that contains a theory of *action* (that which describes the process by which behavior is elicited and carried out) and a theory of *acquisition* (that which describes how behavior is learned) (Baldwin 1968). In Chapter 5, we will deal with a theory of action and the remainder of this section will deal with *acquisition* of human learning.

In general, educators have been concerned with developing different and novel approaches in order to more effectively communicate material to their students. They have been concerned about how to interest students in the teacher's concerns, plans, and curriculum. It is interesting to contemplate what might happen if they began with the concerns and interests of the learner. Interests and needs do not need to be created—they are already present (Weinstein and Fantini 1970, Borton 1970).

Specifically, the consultant needs to become competent in the learning process in order to facilitate an *understanding* of himself and to help others to understand themselves. The knowledge of learning does not stop here; it becomes most important in the second stage of the helping process—*change*. The consultant is constantly helping to facilitate change in himself, his consultees, classrooms, teachers, the organizational system of the school, administration, and the community. The consultant realizes that learning does not take place until a behavioral change occurs, and therefore, comprehension or understanding is just not enough. To put it another way, one's perception of the learning process closely parallels one's view of behavior.

Comprehension of the learning process allows the consultant to realize how he can assist others in bringing about the changes they seek. He can help the consultee not only to become aware of his goals and purposes but also how to achieve them in an efficacious manner. Through his knowledge of the learning process, he can foster the production of institutional as well as individual change. It is through such changes that we can reach *our* goal of humaneness—or the full development of human potential. The importance of this change has been captured by Loughary (1970):

> The technological revolution will have two major impacts on education. The obvious one, at least that receiving the most attention, concerns the actual use of technology in education; for example, the impact of computers and other audio-visual hardware and software. The second, and in my opinion the more forceful, will be the new requirements which a technological society places on formal education. These two developments create situations both conducive and inimical to the growth of humaneness, at the same time that they make educating for humaneness imperative (p. 75).

He goes on to describe the imperative conditions for education. Among them are the need to deal with the whole person throughout his total life span; the necessity (rather than luxury) of individualized instruction; the need to involve the learner in the process; and the need to help each individual to get more information *and* satisfaction out of life (rather than just more information about it).

Daig (1969) states that competition is the main source of motivation in the school classroom where *ideas* are shared, not *feelings*. He sees this as an unhealthy environment for learning because it is not a real environment. Combs et al. (1971) support this contention: "When understood in terms of the effects of challenge and threat, competition turns out to be a motivating force of limited value for some and downright destructive for others" (p. 109). Three things become apparent about competition. (1) It appears to be a motivating force for only those who believe they have a chance of winning. (2) Persons who are forced to compete and who do not believe they have a chance of success are not motivated by the experience; they are threatened by it. (3) When competition becomes too important, any means becomes justified to meet the ends. Daig (1969) therefore feels that we should concentrate on *people* in our schools rather than things and treat the school experience as "life itself" where "risks and rewards are here and now and very real."

Rogers (1969) feels that learning is *not* "lifeless, sterile, futile, quickly forgotten stuff which is crammed into the mind of the poor helpless individual tied into his seat by ironclad bonds of conformity" (p. 3)! He feels that significant or experiential learning consists of the following elements:

1. The *whole* person is involved *in* the learning situation.
2. Learning must begin from within the individual; it is self-initiated.
3. Behavior, attitudes, and sometimes the personality of the individual change.
4. Evaluation by the learner determines the result of whether or not the experience is meaningful.

It is such learning, that which has relevance for the whole person, that consultants attempt to model, encourage, and reinforce. An experiential type of learning is based on involvement of the total being, i.e., intellect, affect, and behavior, and provides the opportunity to experience the concept being emphasized in the process. The content of the experience is the behavior of children reacting openly, honestly, authentically, and the personal experience of working with beliefs and feelings the children produce. The children's beliefs, feelings, attitudes, perceptions, and values become the content of the course. The direction the class will take follows intrinsic motives and response patterns of the children. There are not preconceived right answers; tentative hypotheses and alternative courses of action are considered. Through the lack of correct answers, involvement, excitement, and challenge are added and interaction becomes valued.

It is important that we comprehend that the terms "teaching" or "instruction" are not synonomous with "learning." These terms only become equated when the teaching or instruction has *meaning* for the learner. The dropout heard the lesson on "don't drop out!" Yet he left. The pregnant teenager heard and saw the movie on "birth control," yet she's expecting a child. This instruction was not personally meaningful. Meaning occurs when lessons or knowledge become personalized and enter into the learner's world and experiences.

It was perhaps Piaget's greatest contribution to education when he demonstrated that the *child* or learner is the *principal agent* in his own education. It is up to the learner to decide if he will assimilate or accommodate the instruction. How then does teaching become learning? It will help if we utilize the following conditions and qualities which were identified by Carl Rogers (1969) for use in the facilitation of learning. The consultant can use these guidelines in order to facilitate learning in the consulting session as well as to help his consultee to understand how to apply these conditions.

1. The consultant sets the beginning climate of the consulting experience.

2. The consultant helps to elicit and clarify the consultee's purposes.

3. He relies upon the desire of each individual to implement those goals which have meaning for him as the motivational force behind significant learning.

4. He strives to organize and make readily available the widest possible range of resources for learning.

5. The consultant regards himself as a flexible resource to be utilized by individuals and groups.

6. In responding to expressions, he accepts both the intellectual content and the emotionalized attitudes, attempting to understand each aspect in regard to the degree of emphasis it has for the individual.

7. As the acceptant climate becomes established, the consultant is able to become a participant learner, expressing his views as those of an individual only.

8. He takes the initiative in sharing himself—his feelings as well as his thoughts—in ways which do not demand nor impose, but simply represent a personal sharing which one may take or leave.

9. Throughout the consulting experience, he remains alert to the expressions indicative of deep or strong feelings.

10. In functioning as a facilitator of learning, the consultant endeavors to recognize and accept his own limitations.

Perhaps most important of all, the consultant needs to be authentic. He must live the theory he purports.

It is therefore necessary to understand how one learns to become humane. It is from the way we live that we learn. The experiential component of the learning process is of paramount importance. This is popularly depicted in Dorothey Law Nolte's children's creed entitled "Children Learn What they Live."

It is important for the individual not only to learn through doing, but also to be humanly involved in the process. The learning activity should complement the individual's unique life purposes. This necessitates becoming truly involved with the person of the learner in order to comprehend his purpose. Real learning, that which influences perceptions, skills, and behavior, comes when teacher and pupil goals are aligned. When this happens the teacher will no longer say, "Class, open your book to page fifty-two, and we will do the first ten problems." Some class members will need more or less problems; others will need to be on different pages or in different books. According to Grams (1966), effective learners are also emotionally healthy people. Thus, the consultant can help school to become a place where emotionally healthy people don't just *do*, but rather *do* and *be!*

KINDS OF LEARNING

The consultant directly controls the *message* to be delivered and the mode or method of delivery. Postman and Weingartner (1969) stress the fact that the medium (or method of delivery) is the message. This implies that the critical content of any learning experience is the method or process through which the learning occurs. Krumboltz (1966) separates learning into four types:

1. *Operant learning,* in which the reinforcement given depends upon the ability of the pupil to "operate" in a situation or to proceed to master a difficulty.

2. *Imitative learning* based upon modeling, role playing, films, video tape, demonstrations, books—especially autobiographies, which make a certain behavior visible.

3. *Cognitive learning* which may involve a "transaction" or "contact" in regard to future behavior, also a type of learning in which, again, modeling and role playing may assist a pupil in trying out or understanding a particular behavior, thus allowing the cues of reinforcement to be well timed.

4. *Emotional learning* whereby tension release is achieved and the stress in a situation reduced, again using reinforcement and encouragement, models, role playing, or other means to achieve a different feeling by trying and strengthening a new, less stressful behavior pattern.

Education and most educators are concerned with methods—not meanings.

> Education has been highly successful in gathering information and making information available to people, but has been far less successful in helping people to make information so much a part of themselves that they would behave differently as a result (Combs and Snygg 1959, p. 149).

We plan the learning of subject matter in a careful fashion and leave the learning about self and others to chance. Thus, the lack of learning in this critical area takes its toll in the individual's failure to cope with the tasks of work and social relationships. The students "know about" a number of things which can have no personal meaning.

The importance of integrating affective and cognitive learnings is essential.

> Oh, yes, it would greatly simplify matters if we could somehow isolate intellectual experience from emotional experience, but at the moment this is possible only in textbooks and experimental designs. The cold, hard, stubborn reality is that whenever one learns intellectually, there is an inseparable accompanying dimension. The relationship between intellect and affect is indestructibly symbiotic (Brown 1971, p. 11).

Affective components are learned just as cognitive. We need to facilitate an individual's personal development by becoming involved with him as a total being: intellect, feelings, attitudes, values, purposes, and behavior. Rather than trying to deny the "holism" of the individual, it is time we began to make good use of these interrelationships.

We need to change our emphasis from training computers or memory banks *to* fully functioning persons. We need to move education back into reality. Education is not preparation for life, but life itself! A humanized approach which centers upon learning about one's self and assists each individual to become responsible for his choices and behavior is needed, an approach that allows the learner to become intrinsically involved with the curriculum (Dinkmeyer 1971). This type of involvement in the learning experience comes when the motivation to learn is intrinsic, from within, and the experience possesses or provides meaning for the learner.

Schools Without Failure demonstrates a total program founded on increased involvement, relevance, and thinking. Glasser (1969) states:

> . . . schools usually do not teach a relevant curriculum; when they do, they fail to teach the child how he can relate this learning to his life ouside of school (p. 50).

Relevant learning or the "blending of one's own world with the new world of school" (p. 53) does *not* prevail in schools today. The relevance problem is seen as two-fold.

1. Too much taught in school is not relevant to the world of the children. When it is relevant, the relevance is too often not taught, thus its value is missed when it does exist.
2. The children do not consider that what they learn in their world is relevant to the school (Glasser 1969, pp. 52–53).

Holt (1969) feels that "true learning—learning that is permanent and useful, that leads to intelligent action and further learning—can arise only out of the experience, interests, and concerns of the learner" (p. 3).

> Every child, without exception, has an innate and unquenchable drive to understand the world in which he lives and to gain freedom and competence in it. Whatever truly adds to his understanding, his capacity for growth and pleasure, his powers, his sense of his own freedom, dignity, and worth may be said to be true education. . . . Education therefore is something a person gets for himself, not that which someone else gives or does to him (pp. 3–4).

The quality of humaneness cannot be learned via a non-humane approach. As Holt (1969) states:

> What we do in the school (never mind what nice things we preach) says in effect to young children, "Your experience, your concern, your hopes, your fears, your desires, your interests, they count for nothing. What counts is what *we* are interested in, what *we* care about, and what *we* have decided you are to learn" (p. 200).

The consultant, in his relations with others, must not fall victim to this authoritarian/traditional mode of imparting knowledge. The consultant relationship cannot be one of superior and inferior, or the pronouncement of authoritarian diagnostic statements. The history of pupil personnel services is replete with case studies and recommendations which, due to their autocratic presentation and failure to consider the personality components of the consultee, have become only paper work and material for the file folder.

When we better understand the ways, conditions, and spirit in which individuals do their best learning, and are able to make school a place where thinking and learning may become natural, school may then become a place in which all involved may grow in all areas (Holt 1967, viii).

THEORIES OF LEARNING

It seems apparent from the myriad of learning theories that *the* theory of learning has not completly unfolded.

All theoretical systems are imperfect and fail to describe all types of learning with equal validity. Theories are useful not because they answer all questions or indicate the correct way to manage all learning situations, but because they do a reasonable job of organizing the vast amount of experimental and empirical information about the learning process. They do provide a relatively consistent and functional frame of reference for an educational practitioner to use in the assessment of the consistency and the effectiveness of teaching (Pittenger and Gooding 1971, pp. 78–79).

It would be helpful, therefore, to acquire an understanding of some of the popular or "accepted" theories. The following descriptions are the results of the basic thinking of many men. The use of one name is used in order to demonstrate a specific approach and to give the reader an introduction or starting point for discovering where additional data may be found.

Field Theory

Kurt Lewin and J. S. Bruner are among the leading proponents of cognitive field theory. The primary emphasis of this approach is that learning is goal-directed. The goals are seen as being self-set and dynamic (will change with new experiences). They describe motivation as a product of disequilibrium in a life space. The life space consists of those parts of the individual's world which stand out as psychologically meaningful. Lewin pictured the life space in a potato-shaped paradigm marked with routes and barriers to represent the types of activity allowed and available or restricted and blocked. The routes lead to goals with positive and negative valences which indicate whether the goals are attractive or repulsive. The individual in this field is then moved or stopped by the force of these valences on the routes or courses of action available. The field or the surroundings in which learning occurs (e.g., the self, the family, the classroom atmosphere) is emphasized.

Lewin presented the life space as an empty circle, so that the individual would not be described in terms of capacities but rather in terms of his environment. Lewin (like Skinner) is therefore not speaking of stupid and intelligent people, but is talking about more or less intelligent environments. Intelligence is not seen as a property of the nervous system but of how the individual perceives the world, its qualities, flavors, meanings, and possibilities for action. The goal of education is to help the individual to learn to become more intelligent by teaching him what the environment consists of, how it operates, and how he can interact with it.

Whereas other theories have tried to analyze learning and the corresponding psychological functions in terms of their elements, field theory is concerned with the qualities of organized things as a whole (or gestalt). For example, the field theorist would point out that a square constructed of lines or dots is seen in terms of its squareness (or the *whole quality*) rather than in terms of the particular elements that make it up. This comprehension of the whole is thought to be fundamental to the understanding of the parts. When describing the learning process, constructs such as goals and barriers to goals, as well as tension toward goals, are utilized.

The field theorists define perception in terms of each unique individual and how things exist for *him* at a particular time. Meaning and order are prescribed individually in terms of one's own needs, abilities, and purposes. The child's perceptions and the context of the learning experience determine the value of a learning experience and the resultant motivation of a pupil. Learning and involvement are dependent upon the pupil's perceptions of the meaning, worth, and purpose of the activity.

Bruner (1960) indicates that the process is more important than the content. Any topic in which the child is totally engaged is totally educating. The goal of education then is to create a more humane person, not a memory book. The content is important but it must be related or have bearing to the world outside the classroom or future events. The separation of cognitive and affective learning is seen as a false dichotomy that has a crippling effect upon the development of thought and feeling. *Man is whole.* An example of Bruner's theory in practice can be seen in "Man: a Course of Study" (Bruner 1966). In this course, Bruner focuses on man—what is human about him, how he got that way, and how he can be made more human. In pursuit of these objectives, the five great humanizing forces (tool making, language, social organization, management of man's prolonged childhood, and man's urge to explain his world) are stressed.

Selections for Further Exploration

Bigge, J. L. *Learning Theories for Teachers.* New York: Harper & Row, 1964.

Bruner, J. S. *The Process of Education.* Cambridge: Harvard University Press, 1961.

Bruner, J. S. *Toward a Theory of Instruction.* Cambridge: Harvard University Press, 1966.

Cartwright, D., ed. *Field Theory in Social Science: Selected Theoretical Papers by Kurt Lewin.* New York: Harper & Row, 1951.

Jones, R. M. *Fantasy and Feeling in Education.* New York: Harper & Row, 1968.

Kounin, J. S. *Discipline and Group Management in Classrooms.* New York: Holt, Rinehart & Winston, 1970.

Lewin, K. "Field Theory and Learning." In *The Psychology of Learning,* 41st Yearbook, Part 2, pp. 215–242. National Society for the Study of Education, 1942.

Tolman, E. *Purposive Behavior in Animals and Men.* New York: Appleton-Century-Crofts, 1932.

Phenomenological Approach

This theory also stresses the wholeness of the learning process rather than an analysis of its elements. Learning is seen as a process by which the individual changes his behavior. Learning according to Combs and Snygg (1959) is an active process resulting from an individual's efforts to satisfy his needs.

Cronbach (1963, pp. 125–126) felt that the following needs are probably the most important in school:

1. Need for affection
2. Need for approval by peers
3. Need for approval by authority
4. Need for independence
5. Need for competency and self-respect

Carl Rogers (1969) pictures a learning process which produces an individual who is more self-confident, flexible, self-directed, and less rigid in his perception. Learning will be more meaningful and rapid when the learner perceives the problem he wishes to resolve, Learning then would be enhanced by making resources available to the child and allowing him to choose—rather than being forced.

Kelley (1947) states:

> I can get my stimuli from the same objects as you do, but I cannot bring the same purpose and experience to them that you do. Therefore, they are never the same to you as they are to me (p. 58).
>
> It is the only kind of knowing (mine not yours) which will serve my purpose. . . .
>
> The knowing that will serve me best is that which I seek out of a welter of infinite possibilities. Rather than take what has served another, which he offers for my services, I will do better if I seek my own (p. 60).
>
> Subject matter is set out to be learned to a degree. It can be briefly studied against examination day, but unless it attains more meaning than the requirements of that day—unless its meaning takes on importance to the learning person—it will not abide long. In fact, it might be said not to have been learned at all, but perhaps only memorized, since when we learn, a modification of the organism is said to occur. That is, the organism behaves differently after true learning has taken place (Kelley 1947, p. 63).

The goal in learning from the consultant's stance is to help facilitate meaningful and real learning. This necessitates dynamic rather than static purposes. The purposes in learning should not be to do well on an examination, but rather to do well in life! The learning acquisition required on the examination should complement and fit the schema of the learner's life and become a catalyst for future growth. Too much learning is viewed now as a "stop sign" or the *end* rather than the means. The knowledge does not fit the learner's purpose but rather the instructor's purpose.

Kelley (1962) states that the acquisition of subject matter is not educational in itself; we all know people who have acquired much subject matter yet have remained uneducated.

We extract meaning from our surroundings as a whole. Meaning is as broad as life itself. It cannot be felt or understood in segments or separated into pieces. We may do it briefly, but schools and laboratories do it entirely. If we want to produce whole men, we will have to abandon our efforts to train or educate them in parts.

Selections for Further Exploration

Combs, A. W., ed. *Perceiving, Behaving and Becoming.* Washington, D.C.: Association for Supervision and Curriculum Development, 1962.

Combs, A. W., Avila, D. L. and Purkey, W. W. *Helping Relationships.* Boston: Allyn & Bacon, 1971.

Combs, A. W. and Syngg, D. *Individual Behavior.* Rev. ed. New York: Harper & Row, 1959.

Kelley, E. C. *Education for What is Real.* New York: Harper & Row, 1947.

Maslow, A. H. *Motivation and Personality.* 2nd ed. New York: Harper & Row, 1970.

Pittenger, O. E. and Gooding, C. T. *Learning Theories in Educational Practice.* New York: John Wiley & Sons, 1971.

Rogers, C. R. *Freedom to Learn.* Columbus, Ohio: Charles E. Merrill, 1969.

Scobey, M. and Graham, G., eds. *To Nurture Humaneness: Commitment for the 70's.* Washington, D.C.: Association for Supervision and Curriculum Development, 1970.

Gagne's Theory

Robert Gagne is particularly interested in the practical aspects of learning in the school or home. He sees learning as a change in human disposition or capability which can be retained and which is not simply ascribable to the process of growth. He is concerned with human performance. He proposes that four basic conditions of learning need to be met if learning is to take place. They are (1) stimulation, (2) response, (3) assessment and feedback, and (4) transfer.

Stimulation includes the motivational value of instructional methods and materials. In considering stimulation, internal and external components need to be examined. The internal components refer to the learner, his attitudes, beliefs, background, etc. The external components refer to anything that may be observed during the learning interaction, directions, information, materials used, etc.

Response refers to what the learner does. Gagne (1970) feels we should strive for responses that are meaningful as well as overt.

Assessment and feedback refers closely to B. F. Skinner's concept of reward; the more immediate, informative, positive, motivating, and unthreatening it is, the better.

Transfer refers to the generalizability and breadth of application of the new learning. Whether or not it provides new insights or is applicable to other situations is not important.

Gagne (1970) feels that "the external events that are called instruction need to have different characteristics, depending on the particular class of performance change that is the focus of interest (p. v)." He found the following eight different classes of learning and corresponding sets of conditions associated with each: (1) signal learning, (2) stimulus-response learning, (3) chaining, (4) verbal association, (5) discrimination learning, (6) concept learning, (7) rule learning, and (8) problem solving.

The identification of kinds of learning in terms of the conditions that produce them clearly has some definite implications for education. The necessity of careful planning for learning, the management of learning, the function of instructing (arranging the conditions of learning that are external to the learner), and the choice of media are obvious examples of activities that could be enhanced by a specification of the conditions of learning.

Selections for Further Exploration

Gagne, R. M. "The Acquisition of Knowledge." *Psychological Review* 69 (1962): 355–365.

Gagne, R. M. *Conditions of Learning.* 2nd ed. New York: Holt, Rinehart & Winston, 1970.

Gagne, R. M. "Contributions of Learning to Human Development." *Psychological Review* 75 (1968): 177–191.

Montessori Method*

Maria Montessori developed a training schema which focuses upon the specific elements as opposed to the organism as a whole. She felt that training in each of the specific sense modalities (i.e., touch, taste, sight, hearing, smelling) would allow the learner to become more aware of his external world. The specific procedure is one of providing learning materials which predominately require the use of one sense (auditory, visual, tactile, baric (weight), gustatory, olfactory, and stereognostic). The classroom structure is open and the learner is free to choose his own materials and work at his own rate.

The Montessori method, in a nutshell, involves (1) the CHILD AS AN INDEPENDENT LEARNER interacting with (2) the PREPARED ENVIRONMENT featuring (3) the NEW TEACHER as observer. The goal of (4) the LEARNING PROCESS AS AUTOEDU-

---

* This section prepared with the help of Leni Cowling, a graduate student at Wayne State University and a former Montessori teacher.

CATION is the emergence of (5) a NEW MAN able to cope with today's complex world. These five key facets of the Montessori approach are briefly reviewed below:

1. CHILD AS INDEPENDENT LEARNER

   Motivated to develop himself, utilizing his formative period, absorbent mind, and sensitive periods.

   Child as explorer displaying remarkable powers of concentration in making discoveries in his world leading to mastery of himself and environment.

2. PREPARED ENVIRONMENT

   Organized to provide the child with interesting materials and a milieu of liberty and autoeducation.

   Designed to promote expansion of child's physical, emotional, intellectual, and social life.

3. NEW TEACHER

   Teacher as trained observer who teaches indirectly, intervening only when necessary.

   Teacher as scientist prepared in spirit as well as in mechanical skill to conduct learning experiments in the classroom laboratory.

4. LEARNING PROCESS AS AUTOEDUCATION

   Sensory, motor, and language education with programmed materials encouraging individual self-choice and self-pacing.

   Multisensory, intrinsically motivated sequential activity with flexible scheduling and grouping, and a cosmic curriculum.

5. NEW MAN

   Independent yet socially aware individual who is self-disciplined, confident, competent, spontaneous, creative, and psychologically fully functioning.

   Inner harmony growing from release of, respect for, and response to human potential for perceptual proficiency, motor coordination and intellectual development leading to internal order of "prepared mind."

The Montessori method is actually a point of view which allows the child to work on self-selected tasks of interest to him in an environment that has been set up and programmed by the teacher (whose main function is to preserve and "protect" the learning process).

Selections for Further Exploration

Hainstock, E. G. *Teaching Montessori in the Home: The Pre-school Years.* New York: Random House, 1968.

Montessori, M. *The Montessori Method.* Cambridge, Massachusetts: Robert Bentley, 1965.

Standing, E. M. *The Montessori Revolution in Education.* New York: Schocken Books, 1966.

Piaget

Jean Piaget has devoted a lifetime to studying the cognitive processes of learning. As a result of his research he has postulated each individual moves through set stages of cognitive growth. The four major levels or stages are as follows.

1. Sensory-Motor Period (birth to eighteen months or two years)
2. Pre-Operational Thought Period (two years to six or seven years)
3. Concrete Operations Period (eight years to eleven years or later)
4. Formal Logic Period

Although each individual will move through these states in an invariant sequence, *the rates will vary* with the individual.

Piaget visions that the learning process occurs when the learner adapts knowledge via the processes of accommodation or assimilation. *Accommodate* essentially means to *modify self to fit the new material,* while *assimilate* means to *modify the material to fit the self.* The self in Piagetian terms would be referred to as schema or methods to deal with the external world. This theory, then, places the child as the principal agent in his education.

Learning is seen as resulting from the complex and continuous process of interaction between the individual and the external world. This interaction process is life-long, from birth to death. It is the individual's task to assimilate these experiences and accommodate to them. In essence, the individual learns through *his* doing—and no one else's.

Piaget feels that learning is always related to one's developmental period. The individual does not develop alone. The social environment affects him as much as the physical world.

The learning facilitator's job is to provide the individual with situations that encourage experimentation, manipulation of objects and symbols, and the subsequent results. The learner must be allowed to "do" and to progress at his own rate. The individual only has *real* comprehension if he invents himself. Whenever we teach or present material *too* quickly, we prevent the individual from reinvesting it for himself. Perhaps, Piaget's goal of education best summarizes his theory.

The principal goal of education is to create men who are capable of doing new things, not simply of repeating what other generations have done—men who are creative, inventive, and discoverers, who have minds which can be critical, can verify, and not accept everything they are offered (Silberman 1970, p. 219).

Selections for Further Exploration

Beard, R. M. *An Outline of Piaget's Developmental Psychology for Students and Teachers.* New York: Basic Books, 1969.

Elkind, D. and Flavell, J. H., eds. *Studies in Cognitive Development: Essays in Honor of Jean Piaget.* New York: Oxford University Press, 1969.

Furth, H. G. *Piaget and Knowledge: Theoretical Foundations.* Englewood Cliffs, New Jersey: Prentice-Hall, 1969.

Furth, H. G. *Piaget for Teachers.* Englewood Cliffs, New Jersey: Prentice-Hall, 1970.

Piaget, J. *Six Psychological Studies.* New York: Random House, 1968.

Piaget, J. and Inhelder, B. *The Psychology of the Child.* New York: Basic Books, 1969.

Skinner

B. F. Skinner sees all people as arriving at any behavior through a series of progressive approximations that eventually obtain what the person is seeking. When the behavior works, it is kept and when it does not work it is eliminated.

To bring about the learning or type of behavior that is desired, it first must be carefully described. The second phase involves observing the learner carefully until he behaves in a way that resembles the desired behavior or goal. When the learner "emits" this behavior, he is given a reward or reinforcer. Unrelated or undesirable behavior is not reinforced. If the learner is rewarded *immediately* for any behavior that resembles what is desired and if the reinforcer is sufficient (important or valuable), the new learning or behavior will be as planned. Thus, through the selective use of reinforcers, Skinner accounts for how new learnings are acquired. This procedure is described in detail later in this chapter.

The "operant conditioning" approach of Skinner works not only in the laboratory (with his famous studies on pigeons and rats) but the home (Patterson and Gullion 1968), school (Blackham and Silberman 1971, Homme 1969, Sulzer and Mayer 1972) and is the basis for the self-instructional methods of programmed instruction and learning machines.

Selections for Further Exploration

Blackham, G. J. and Silberman, A. *Modification of Child Behavior.* Belmont, California: Wadsworth, 1971.

Reese, E. P. *The Analysis of Human Operant Behavior.* Dubuque, Iowa: William C. Brown, 1966.

Skinner, B. F. *The Behavior of Organisms.* New York: Appleton-Century-Crofts, 1938.

Skinner, B. F. "Are Learning Theories Necessary?" *Psychological Review* 57 (1950): 193–216.

Skinner, B. F. *Science and Human Behavior.* New York: Macmillan, 1953.

Skinner, B. F. *Beyond Freedom and Dignity.* New York: Alfred A. Knopf, 1971.

Sulzer, B. and Mayer, G. R. *Behavioral Modification Procedures for School Personnel.* Hinsdale, Illinois: Dryden Press, 1972.

Social Learning Theory

Bandura and Walters (1963) are perhaps the major proponents of social learning theory. This theory describes a set of learning principles that emphasizes the role of social variables to a greater extent than previous theories. The principle of social learning centers around the acquisition of new behavior through imitation of others. Bandura (1965) feels that appropriate models who exhibit the desired behavior may greatly reduce trial and error and provide real dividends in learning.

The effects of modeling are not limited to the physical domain, but also directly affect cognitive and affective components. Imitative learning involves a number of variables related to conditions operating in the learner as well as the manner in which modeled activities are presented. Characteristics of the model (i.e., sex, age, dress), the type of reinforcement that the model and learner receive, and the learner's prior learning experiences are also important variables.

Selections for Further Exploration

Bandura, A. "Social Learning through Imitation." In *Nebraska Symposium on Motivation*, edited by M. R. Jones, pp. 211–269. Lincoln: University of Nebraska Press, 1962.

Bandura, A. *Principles of Behavior Modification*. New York: Holt, Rinehart & Winston, 1969.

Bandura, A. and Walters, R. H. *Social Learning and Personality Development*. New York: Holt, Rinehart & Winston, 1963.

Bourdon, R. D. "Imitation: Implications for Counseling and Therapy." *Review of Educational Research* 40, no. 3 (1970): 429–457.

COMMON ELEMENTS

The task specifically required of education is to promote the best learning situation possible. Thus it should not confine its efforts to the implementation of any one theory of learning. Means should be found in the classroom for an interchange of learning theories and teaching procedures which combine the best features of each (Thorpe and Schmuller 1954, p. 446).

In each of the approaches to learning that were presented, the following concepts were shared:

1. The uniqueness of each *individual* is basic.

2. The *consequences* of learning are important (whether in terms of purposes or reinforcement).

3. *Motivation* is identified as a state of disequilibrium (whether internal, external or internal-external).

4. Comprehension of the *total situation* is important.

5. *Empathy* or perceiving the world as the individual learner sees it is important.

6. One must account for each individual's rate of learning, practise the concept of readiness, and begin where the child is at.

7. The effect of the environment on the individual takes precedence over hereditary components.

8. Behavior change is recognized as the index of learning.

From these common theoretical elements the following basic principles of learning were developed.

BASIC PRINCIPLES OF LEARNING

Interestingly enough, while the experiential approaches were, in effect, becoming more behavioristic, the behavioristic approaches were becoming more experiential. There was a growing recognition on the part of many behaviorists that the behavior schedule or program was not enough. Indeed, there was a recognition that the effects of the behavior program were to some great degree dependent upon the relationship established between the counselor and client. Wolpe, himself, has conceded that as much as 60 percent of the effectiveness of the counter-conditioning process may be due to "non-specific relationship factors." Thus, while the relationship researchers moved toward specifying and operationalizing these "non-specific" variables, the behaviorists moved toward acknowledging the necessity for incorporating the experiential frame of reference into the total treatment process. . . . It is a singular tribute to the methodology of science that investigators beginning from diverse and seemingly antithetical viewpoints do converge in their explorations and their findings, if they are shaped by the results of their efforts and their inability to account for the major part of the variability in change indexes (Carkhuff 1971, p. 265).

1. One begins by identifying the child's needs and his position in the need hierarchy.
2. The learning task must be relevant to these needs and identified interests.
3. The learning situation requires that one be involved with the total field environment and aware of the holistic nature of learning—affective, cognitive, and actional.
4. One must identify the learner's basic purposes and goals and discover what is important to him. From this a mutual goal alignment should be developed.
5. Learning always occurs in a social context.
6. It is necessary to identify the perceptual field of the learner and its personal meaning—"where he is coming from."
7. One must diagnose strengths and offer encouragement.
8. The learning task is integrated and internalized when it reduces dissonance and builds feelings of adequacy.
9. Feelings and emotions energize the learning process. They are to be understood and used as catalysts rather than stifled.

10. The learner should be involved in continuous *self*-evaluation, utilization, and practise.
11. Behavior that helps one to meet needs is established.

BEHAVIOR CHANGE

In modifying or changing an individual's behavior it is necessary to alter his perceptual field or personal field of meanings. The fact that people behave in terms of their own field of meanings and that changes in meaning bring about corresponding behavior changes is not enough. The consultant needs to go beyond understanding to build an army of effective techniques for helping people to grow and solve problems in a healthy fashion.

The focus of this chapter is on learning, with the criterion for recognizing whether or not learning has taken place being that of behavior change. In developing techniques, the consultant needs to constantly consider the following basic questions.

1. Does the strategy have adequate and theoretical undergirding so that behavior change can be expected and predicted?
2. Is the application so consistent with desirable human goals?
3. Is the strategy efficient as well as effective?
4. Does its application lead to any negative or unsought consequences?

(Blackham 1969)

The consultant assumes the responsibility for socializing, training, and educating and therefore is involved in the process of enhancing or changing behavior. His goals in this area are essentially twofold: (1) to facilitate the acquisition and development of behavior not already present in the learner, and (2) to help change or eliminate behavior that is already present. In order to attain these goals, the consultant utilizes the following procedures.

Respondent Conditioning

An individual is in certain respects like *all* other men, like some other men, and like no other man. Respondent behavior refers to behavior that is unlearned or elicited automatically to a certain stimulus. The behavior is involuntary or not under the control of the individual, e.g., when light intensity is changed, the pupil contracts; when an onion is peeled, the eye sheds tears. These are common responses to stmiuli that *all* other people share.

Respondent conditioning utilizes these basic stimuli and develops response conditions by increasing the range of stimuli that produce a specific response. This process uses two kinds of stimuli and an involuntary response. One of these stimuli, the conditioned stimulus, is not sufficient to elicit a response (until learning has taken place), and the other, the unconditioned stimulus, does so automatically upon its occurrence. The involuntary response is labeled in two ways: *unconditioned response*, prior to conditioning, and *continual response*, once conditioning has occurred. The conditioning process basically consists of replacing one stimulus for another (sometimes refered to as *stimulus substitution*). This is accomplished by pairing or presenting together the conditional and unconditional stimulus several times until the response is elicited by the conditional stimulus alone.

The classical example of respondent conditioning is sometimes referred to as "Little Albert and the White Rat" (Watson and Raynor, 1920). Albert was an eleven-month-old boy who displayed approach reactions to a white rat and was taught to fear it. Before the conditioning began, he was tested for fear reactions to a number of stimuli (e.g., burning papers, a rabbit, a white rat). None of these elicited a fear reaction, and no one had ever seen Albert in a state of fear or rage until a loud noise was produced. The fear response was quickly conditioned by presenting a rat (conditioned stimulus) together with a loud noise (unconditioned stimulus). After seven pairings, the rat alone elicited the fear response (Reese 1966).

Blackham and Silberman (1971) discuss the following example of respondent conditioning in schools.

> . . . a first grade teacher (originally neutral stimulus) may present noxious stimuli (adequate to elicit fear) and come to be feared by first graders. And in accordance with the principle noted above, the fear of the first grade teacher may generalize to other teachers or to any stimulus or object in the school situation. Indeed some first graders' aversion to reading might well be explained on the same basis. Obviously a first grade teacher should erect those conditions (by the way she behaves) to ensure that she is regarded with positive feelings. Then first graders are more likely to generalize this positive feeling to learning stimulus objects in the environment of the school (p. 23).

Operant Conditioning

Operant behavior is influenced and controlled by consequences or events that follow the act; therefore, it is under voluntary control. According to Keller (1954), operant behavior includes all behavior that "operates on," changes, or affects the outside environment. Thus, it must be observable. Operant behavior as B. F. Skinner sees it "is simply a study of what used to be dealt with by the concept of purpose. The purpose of an act is the consequences it is going to have" (Evans 1968, p. 19). Thus, in an educational setting, when an appropriate behavior is observed (showing social interest or self-satisfaction), the *task* then should be reinforced. This is repeated until the behavior is learned and occurs when reinforcement is given less frequently and eventually eliminated.

Operant behavior is, therefore, strengthened or weakened by the events which follow the response. So, the consultant, when discovering a learning problem, needs to discover what was done about it or how it was strengthened or weakened.

When the desired behavior does not occur (or occurs very seldom), a procedure called *shaping* can be used. This procedure eventually involves identifying and reinforcing in a graduated fashion the responses that will eventually lead to the desired behavior. In the beginning steps some approximation of the desired behavior is reinforced. As advancement toward the goal occurs, reinforcement becomes more discriminating, reinforcing more and more *only* the desired behavior. For example, a child who is unwilling to read might initially receive a warm teacher response for touching the book. The next positive response would be for putting the book on the desk, then one for opening it, etc. Finally, the teacher's approval would come only for a minimum quantity and quality, i.e., reading.

Behavior, however, is not a simple matter of learning separate units. Most behavior is characterized by a series of units connected or *chained* in a sequence.

Essentially all school related behaviors actually consist of sequences or chains of behaviors. The links in the chains are each composed of simpler behavioral components. For example, the behavior "going to lunch"* can be broken down into a set of component behaviors: lining up outside the lunchroom, handing a ticket to the lunchroom monitor, picking up a tray, silverware and napkin, placing food on the tray, going to a table, sitting down and eating. Each of the component behaviors could also be broken down into smaller components. Eating for instance, may be composed of these behaviors: Placing food on a spoon, bending arm, opening mouth, chewing food, swallowing. Procedures which effectively produce such complex behavior sequences can help school personnel to do a better teaching job (Sulzer and Mayer 1972, p. 83).

---

* This illustration is a modification of one presented by Reynolds (1968, p. 53).

The chaining process then involves the placing of simple behaviors into more complex combinations. According to Sulzer and Mayer (1972), chains may be facilitated by(1) forming chains from established links, (2) starting with the final link, (3) utilizing discriminative stimuli, and (4) combining imitative prompting with the chaining procedure. The following example gives a simple school-related illustration of how chains are established.

> . . . take the complex behavior of coming in from recess, sitting quietly and attending to the teacher. If sitting quietly and attending to the teacher has in the past been consistently paired with a reinforcing stimulus (s+) in the form of approval from the teacher, the assumption of such a posture will become a signal that reinforcement is imminent; it will become a discriminative stimulus (S^D). Through further pairings with reinforcement (s+), the discriminative stimulus (S^D) itself, sitting quietly and attending to the teacher, will begin to reinforce (s+) the *prior* link in the chain, sitting down in one's seat. Through a similar process, sitting down in one's seat will become a discriminative stimulus (S^D) which sets the occasion for sitting quietly and attending to the teacher and a conditioned reinforcer (s+) for its prior link in the chain, say walking to one's seat, and so on. (Sulzer and Mayer 1972, p. 84)

Gagne (1965) describes the five *essential* conditions for learning response chains. (1) The separate units or links must be learned before they can be chained. (2) The learner must execute each link in proper sequence. (3) The units must be performed in "close time succession" to assure that they are connected together (long delays between links make this impossible). (4) The sequence needs to be repeated until the goal or desired learning has been reached. (5) Reinforcement needs to be present in the acquisition of chains (must be *immediately* after the final link).

The Use of Reinforcement

Reinforcement increases or maintains the frequency or strength of a behavior. If a behavior decreases in frequency (extinction), it is *not* receiving reinforcement.

The fastest way to increase the strength of a behavior is to reinforce it each time it occurs (regularly or continuously). In order to maintain a response after it has been established, an alternative *reinforcement schedule* is needed. The purpose is to gradually give less and less reinforcement (primary) for increasing amounts of behavior. The behavior, having initially been paired with the reinforcer, takes on reinforcing properties (secondary) and is able to sustain itself and resist extinction.

The major problem in the use of reinforcement techniques seems to be the identification of an appropriate reinforcer. Since each individual is unique, the identification of what is reinforcing is often difficult.

Does Sam respond rudely in class because his peers approve, because the teacher becomes angry, or because it gives him an opportunity to discharge aggression? Is it because his parents say "you show him he can't push you around," or because his parents give him negative attention for the behavior or what? What is reinforcing to one individual may not be to another (Sulzer, 1966). Candy may strengthen the behavior of one individual but not that of another. Cigarettes make some people sick, while others will work for a long period of time to receive them (Lindsley, 1956) . . . . . determination of an appropriate reinforcer must be based upon an objective observation of each individual's behavior (Sulzer, Mayer and Cody 1968, p. 42).

Once the reinforcer has been determined, different procedures may be used to teach behaviors in a classroom or similar learning environment.

Social reinforcers. These are presented by other individuals within a social setting. The following list presents a variety of possible social reinforcers:

Some Typical Social Reinforcers That Can Be Delivered
Immediately to Children and Adults

Children	*Young Adults and Adults*
Nod	Nod
Smile	Smile
Pat on shoulder, head, knee	Laugh (with, not at)
Wink	Wink
Signal or gesture to signify approval	Signal or gesture approval
Touch cheek	Orient glance directly towards his
Fulfill requests	face
Tickle	Give assistance when requested
Give assistance	Comment positively on
Say	appearance
yes	Pat on the back
good	Ask individual to discuss
fine	something before group

Children	Young Adults and Adults
Say	Ask individual about items of
very good	interest to him
very fine	Ask him to demonstrate something
excellent	Say
marvelous	very good
at-a-boy	o.k.
good boy (girl)	beautiful
right	good for you
that's right	_____ is excellent
correct	yeah
wonderful	right
I like the way you do that	I agree
I'm pleased with (proud of)	good idea
you	fine
that's good	what a clever idea
wow	you really are creative,
oh boy	innovative, and so on
very nice	see how you're improving
good work	that looks better than last time
great going	keep up the good work
good for you	you've apparently got the idea
that's the way	little by little we're getting
much better	there
o.k.	see how _____ has
you're doing better	improved
that's perfect	mmmm
that's another one you got right	you're really becoming an
you're doing very well	expert at this
look how well he (she) did	do you see what an effective
watch what he (she) did. Do it	job _____ has
again	done?
	you are very patient
	I admire your persistence,
	courage, idealism,
	enthusiasm, dedication,
	and so on

(Sulzer and Mayer 1972, pp. 31–32)

Token reinforcement. A token is an object that can be used by an individual at a later time for something reinforcing *(back-up reinforcer).* For example, the teacher can give stars, check marks, points, or plastic chips that may be used to gain special privileges. The back-up reinforcer can be any object or event that has been previously reinforcing to the individual. Campbell and Sulzer (1971) identified forty-two back-up reinforcers for use with a mentally handicapped class of children.

1. Extra swim period
2. Ten minutes for a game at milk break
3. Fifteen minutes in library
4. Film on Friday
5. Field trip (available once every two weeks)
6. Feed fish for a week
7. Choose story
8. Ride elevator
9. Turn filmstrip projector
10. Turn off lights
11. Five minutes writing on chalkboard
12. Crafts activity
13. Put blinds up or down
14. Leader in line
15. Get milk at break
16. Pass out milk at break
17. Pass out straws at break
18. Distribute milk at noon
19. Carry library books upstairs
20. Carry library books downstairs
21. Run errands by the day
22. Pull down screen
23. Erase and wash chalkboard
24. Clean erasers
25. Captain of team at recess
26. First up to bat at recess
27. Lead the pledge
28. Take care of calendar by the week
29. Sit at teacher's desk for reading
30. Sit at teacher's desk for spelling
31. File Peabody cards
32. Pass out paper
33. Pass out scissors
34. Buy extra straws
35. First in line for drink at recess
36. Help collect displays, and so on, for units
37. Time in science laboratory
38. Help custodian
39. Answer telephone by day
40. Make phone call
41. An extra cookie at break
42. Help secretary get milk for other classrooms

Sulzer and Mayer (1972, pp. 34–35) developed the following list of brief reinforcing activities for use with young children.

Blow up a balloon; let it go
Jump down from high place into arms of adult
Play with typewriter
Watch train go around track
Run other equipment, such as string pull toys, light switch
Listen to own voice on tape recorder
Build up, knock down blocks

Cut with scissors
Model with clay, putty
Throw ball, bean bag
Climb ladder
Turn on flash light
Sit on adult's lap
Look at projected slide
Listen to short recording
Watch short film, view master, filmstrip

Push adult around in swivel chair
Pull other person in wagon
Look out window
Play short game: tick tack toe,
    easy puzzles, connect the dots
Blow bubbles: soap, gum
Read one comic book
Write on blackboard: white or
    colored chalk
Paint with water on blackboard
Pour water through funnel, from
    one container to another, and
    so on
Blow out match
Comb and brush own or adult's hair
Look in mirror
Play instrument: drum, whistle,
    triangle, piano, and so on
Use playground equipment:
    slide, swings, jungle gym,
    merry-go-round, see-saw
Draw and color pictures

Walk around in high heels
Wear funny hats
Carry purse, briefcase
Roll wheeled toy down incline
Pop balloon, paper bag, milk carton
String beads
Play with magnet
Operate jack-in-the-box
Play with squirt gun
Solve codes and other puzzles
Sing a song
Listen to a song
Perform before a group; sing a
    song; tell a poem or riddle;
    do a dance, stunt, or trick
Be
    hugged
    tickled
    kissed
    patted
    swung around
    turned around in swivel chair
    pushed on swing, merry-go-
        round
    pulled in a wagon

Ordinary conditioned reinforcers such as attention and encouragement should be paired with the delivery of tokens. These typical or
ordinary reinforcers can eventually replace or substitute for the tokens.

Premack Principle.   This principle is based on the premise that activities an individual enjoys may be used as effective reinforcers for less
pleasurable behaviors. This is the equivalent of what Homme (1969)
calls contingency contracting or "arranging the conditions so that the
learner gets to do something he wants to do following something the
teacher wants him to do." Others have referred to this concept as
"Grandma's Law."

For educators, the most appealing aspect of a reinforcement procedure
in which the Premack Principle is employed is probably the fact that
potential reinforcers are already present in every classroom setting.
There are always some behaviors in which students engage (even if
they are sitting and "doing nothing") with greater frequency than
others. All that remains is to reorganize the classroom program in such
a way that access to those high frequency behaviors is made available
to the student directly following his performance of the low frequency

behavior that the teacher wishes to strengthen. Many students, for example, will work for extra minutes of recess (Sulzer and Mayer 1972, p. 36)

The reinforcing activity may be discovered through observation and the subsequent recording of how often and how long various behaviors occur. More information on this topic is presented in Chapter 5.

Modeling

Modeling or imitation can be used to promote behavior change, or more specifically, to increase the chances that a response will occur. The use of a model can be an extremely effective way of bringing about behavior change. It is a procedure that the individual began using early in life and has continued to use on a daily basis.

The chances of learning occurring through the exposure of an individual to a model's behavior is enhanced when (1) the imitated behavior is reinforced, (2) the model's behavior is reinforced, (3) simple behaviors are modeled, (4) the model is similar to the individual, and (5) the model is prestigious.

Applications of this basic procedure are plentiful. For example,

A child client may be asked to identify and describe the social situations and/or interpersonal relationships that create difficulty for him. When these situations have been defined, they may be arranged in a hierarchy from least to most difficult. A mini-situation is constructed for the rehearsal and enactment of each situation, starting with the least difficult. Reinforcement may be selectively administered at each stage. As the situations are being simulated, the enactments are video-taped. The video-tape is replayed and observed by child, client and therapist to provide appropriate feedback for the client and to enhance his role enactments. If necessary, the situation may be reenacted until the appropriate social behaviors are skillfully performed (Blackham and Silberman 1971, p. 41).

The use of movies and filmstrips, as well as certain guidance techniques such as role playing, simulation, audio- and video-taped examples, and group techniques (e.g., spectator therapy), involve specific applications of modeling which can be easily implemented by the consultant.

Other specific procedures are used in the weakening or de-learning or undesirable behavior. These methods, which include extinction, satiation, punishment, withdrawal or reinforcement, time-out, reinforcing incompatible behaviors, desensitization, and stimulus-change, are discussed in Chapter 5.

Relationship to Logical Consequences

The consequences are the main determinant of behavior and its change; thus, procedures that control contrived or logical consequences are of value. In the learning process, the consultant needs to help the learner to focus on the determinants of a situation by considering its natural and logical consequences (i.e., "What will be the outcome?" "Is it what I want?") The learner is searching to discover what behaviors will be attended to or will pay off. Once the learner accepts the responsibility for his actions, the logical and natural consequences of his behavior are consistent and appropriate (Dreikurs and Soltz 1964, p. 76).

It is important to consider the logical and/or natural consequences of an action in order to know either how to respond or to which behaviors to attend. Once the resulting realities of natural and logical consequences are identified, the use of behavior change techniques can become more appropriate or tailored. Gronert (1970) explains:

In combining a method of using natural and/or logical consequences with behavioral positive and negative reinforcement, we may think of the teacher or parent as analogous to a hot stove. A hot stove cooks meals (positive reinforcement). The logical consequence of using a hot stove properly is to eat hot meals; but, if one misuses the stove by bumping into it, he will be burned (negative reinforcement/natural consequence). Touching a hot stove repetitively would be similar to frequent disruption of a teacher's class by inappropriate behavior. The decision regarding how to use the hot stove is up to the individual, and he experiences in his behavior the natural consequences (good and bad). From such coping—experiences with life's consequences—the client should developmentally learn to side-step problems (p. 105).

Bullard (1970) pragmatically discusses this relationship:

"Very good. Your room looks neat and clean." The encouragement process was used. Then the author revealed the shallowness of understanding of the dynamics with this explanation. "If he doesn't (continue picking up) the mother reduces the allowance or permits no television that evening." If the behaviorists had understood the principles of "logical consequences" the contingency would have been more closely related to the failure in picking up the room. An Adlerian mother would have gently but firmly said, "You may join your playmates as soon as your room is picked up" (p. 3).

The emphasis is upon learning, and the contrived consequences are related to the desired or expected behavior. Dreikurs and Soltz's (1964) short-range goals of misbehavior add depth to this approach. For example, when punishment is applied to the goal or consequence of behavior in the violent stages of either power or revenge, rather than stopping the action, it would intensify the resistance.

Another use of the logical consequences would be with time-out, the behavioral procedure used to eliminate reinforcement for inappropriate behavior (Briskin and Gardner 1968).

> "Time-out" is a procedure by which the opportunity or likelihood that an individual will receive reinforcement for his actions is removed for a brief period of time (usually about 10 minutes). While extinction removes the reinforcement for a specific behavior, time-out removes the opportunity for the students to receive essentially any reinforcement. A school example should serve to illustrate this technique. Mary has been disrupting the class by speaking out loud about matters unrelated to the class discussion. The counselor and teacher might decide that each time Mary speaks out she should be removed from the classroom and placed in a location where no one will respond to her. Eventually Mary's "speaking out" behavior should be reduced. Of additional value is the fact that the class is not disrupted as a result of Mary during her absence (Sulzer, Mayer and Cody 1968, p. 43).

Thus, time-out is the logical consequence for inappropriate behavior. To strengthen the above example, Mary initially should be informed that *her* behavior put her in this situation and when she decides to behave in an appropriate fashion (according to class standards), she is welcome to come back to class.

BEHAVIOR CHANGE PROCESSES: FORMULATING LEARNING STRATEGIES

How one decides to reach his purpose or goals depends on such things as the environment, previous history, past reinforcements, recent ways of dealing with situations, and so on. Before the consultant can assist or facilitate this growth, he must understand what is to be treated. Learning strategies must be formulated that are connected to the enhancement or change of behavior.

The consultant is essentially confronted with the problem of ownership. Who is it that needs help? Teacher? Child? Parent? The relationship? The consultant must clearly delineate who is to be the *agent* of change and who is to be the *object* of change. Blackham and Silberman (1971) state:

> One must determine who the "real" or significant clients are and formulate a plan accordingly. It is neither efficient nor desirable to focus

treatment exclusively on a child when the significant people in his life continue to reinforce problem behavior. And since a child's behavior is largely influenced by the significant adults, they must be actively involved in the treatment process . . . it is necessary to identify the *variables* that appear to *maintain* it (p. 72).

Problem Behavior Defined and Analyzed

Once the agent(s) and object(s) of change have been identified, specific descriptions are needed. Anecdotes describing the behavioral difficulty in detail would be most helpful. This should include the ABCs of the action, i.e., (A) what the child did, (B) the teacher's reaction and his feelings, and (C) the child's response. It is important to know the context or situation (when, where, and with whom) and specifically what occurred (including the consequences or reinforcers). From the descriptions, an analysis can then be made to discover *what* and *who* maintain the behavior.

Developmental and Social History

A useful and necessary step in helping to discover where a person is "at" is a developmental and social history of the individual. This data should not be limited just to a collection of data indicating what the person *could* do, but must also provide data on what he *does* now. The focus needs to be on the individual's strengths, assets, and abilities as well as liabilities and weaknesses. This step calls for an overall evaluation of an individual's status.

Information on the person's life style or his characteristic way of looking at the world is essential, e.g., early recollections, family constellation, likes and dislikes, favorite fairy tale, three wishes, three animals, and what he would you like to be. The Life Style Guide in Figure 1 (pp. 96–97) is one form for gathering the data. This particular guide is adapted from the life style format used at the Alfred Adler Institute of Chicago.

Careful attention needs to be given to what is important or reinforcing to the individual. Blackham and Silberman (1971, pp. 173–174) use the following questions to help to identify potential reinforcers.

1. If you were going to the store to buy three games that you would like, what would they be?
2. What three special things do you like to work with or play with in the classroom?

LIFE STYLE GUIDE—CHILDREN

I. *Family Constellation:*   List all siblings in descending order, including the child in his position.

Name	Birthdate	Education
_____	_____	_____
_____	_____	_____
_____	_____	_____
_____	_____	_____
_____	_____	_____

   1. Who is most different from you?   How?

   2. Who is most like you?   How?

   3. Tell about your life before you went to school.

II. *Functioning at Life Tasks:*

   1. Socially: How do you get along with adults?

                How do you get along with children?

   2. Work: How do things go for you in school?

                What subject do you like best?   Why?

                What subject do you like least?   Why?

   3. What would you like to be when you grow up?   Why?

   4. What do you fear the most?

III. *Family Atmosphere:*

   1. What kind of a person is father?

   2. What kind of a person is mother?

   3. Which of the children is most like father?

   4. Which of the children is most like mother?

IV. *Rating:*

List highest and lowest sibling for each attribute:

Intelligent	Sensitive, feelings easily hurt
Hardest worker	Temper
Best grades in school	Materialistic, likes to get things
Conforming	Friends (most)
Rebellious	Most spoiled
Helps around the house	High standards of achievement, behavior morals
Critical	Athletic
Considerate	Strongest
Selfish	Prettiest
Tries to please	Most punished

V. *Early recollections:*

VI. *Three Wishes:*

If you were going to pretend to be an animal, which would you choose? Why?

3. What are three jobs in this classroom you like to do the most?
4. If you went to a store and had 25¢ to spend on whatever you wanted, what would you buy?
5. What things that you did not mention above do you like to do in your classroom or while you are at school (in the building or playground)?

A complete picture should emerge from the data. The individual's assets and liabilities, capabilities and inabilities, relationships and adjustments, as well as current problems, need to be discovered.

Behavior Change Goals Clearly Specified

In this step the consultant needs to determine who wants to learn and what specific behaviors need to be facilitated. Whether or not the behavior is harming the concerned individual or others, and whether the individual is ready to change or motivated, are important criteria in establishing priorities. The behaviors may be classified as *immediate*, short-range, long-range, or the focus of concern later. The goals in the behavior change plan *must* be clearly specified. The goals must be stated in operational (observable) and objective terms to be helpful in the promotion of learning. A goal such as "to improve one's self-concept" is just not acceptable. The goal needs be observable, e.g., "to smile for twenty minutes each day" or "to talk to three people I have never met before next Wednesday."

Formulation and Implementation of Change Strategies

Once the behavior-change goals have been identified, the specific learning strategies need to be devised. The change procedures must be stated clearly, including *specifically* how and with whom they will be accomplished. (Methods for helping others to become involved in the process are included in Chapter 7). For example, a statement such as "to reinforce his good behavior and ignore his inappropriate" needs further elaboration. "When Jimmy is sitting in his chair, Miss Brown is to reinforce him with a nod, touch on his arm, or a special privilege of his choice" is a more appropriate strategy.

Strategies for Promoting Behavior Change

Because the formulation and implementation of learning strategies is the final and most critical phase, the following strategies are presented as models for possible implementation.

Extinction and Positive Reinforcement. In eliminating or de-learning a behavior, the process can be made more effective when either an acceptable alternative behavior which will yield positive results or a reinforcement is available. The pairing or combining of these two procedures can be seen in the following example.

> . . . in an effort to obtain the teacher's attention or affection a student may withdraw and sulk in a corner. Such behavior could be ignored (the withdrawal of reinforcement, i.e., extinction), and whenever the student attempted to interact with other classmates the teacher could reinforce this behavior by giving him attention and praise (Sulzer, Mayer and Cody 1968, p. 43).

The change agent determines to which acceptable behavior the teacher will attend (reinforce) and which inappropriate behaviors will be ignored or reduced (extinction). Thus, in eliminating undesirable behavior, it is important to pair this with encouragement or reinforcement at pleasant times.

Modeling and Positive Reinforcement. Praising or reinforcing a model for certain behaviors, or reinforcing a learner once he has imitated or matched another individual, can bring about more efficacious learning. For example, the praising of the proper behavior of a classmate who is seated near a child who is misbehaving allows the misbehaver to see what he can do to be praised. This technique also has the advantage of surprise or "doing the unexpected" (assuming a different role or posture). The advantage of this procedure is to *demonstrate* an *appropriate behavior* that *pays off* or is of use or value to the individual. The procedure may be enhanced further if the learner is reinforced when he observes and imitates the preferred behavior.

"Pairing" Role Shift and Positive Reinforcement. A role shift, or behaving in a manner that is uncharacteristic or different than usual, necessitates a corresponding adjustment in the behavior of others. The old ways of behaving (roles) no longer pay off. For example, once the mother begins to adopt reciprocally to the teenager's new role behavior, additional shifts are promoted in the teenager, and conflict tends to decrease markedly (Keirsey 1965).

When the reciprocal behavior is emitted, it then can be reinforced and thus strengthened. The following example by Blackham and Silberman (1971) further clarifies this issue.

> Suppose a mother has the habit of constantly nagging her son each morning to get ready for school. The more mother nags, the more

Johnny resists. To help deal with this situation, she is instructed to perform a different role. She is told to make the request only once that he get ready for school. She is instructed not to nag, criticize or punish. If Johnny does not carry out the demand within ten minutes, she quietly goes to his room and indicates that she will help him get dressed. Johnny is allowed to assume as much of the responsibility as he wishes, and mother begins to reinforce these efforts. On each successive morning, the same procedure is followed, with reinforcement being given for each preparatory gesture. When Johnny has gotten dressed by himself, a bonus reinforcement (or reinforcing event) is given. When independent getting-dressed behavior has increased to reasonable frequency, tokens or points may be given, and the reinforcement schedule changed. It is apparent from the example that several things may be operative when role shift and positive reinforcement are used. The mother's behavior becomes more predictable, the child's old resistance and delay tactics are inappropriate and he gets reinforced for behaving differently. Since the mother's verbal behavior is no longer likely to evoke negative counter-reactions, Johnny's mini-rebellion is brought to a halt (p. 86).

Behavior Contract, Positive Reinforcement and Withdrawal of Reinforcement. This is a procedure in which an agreement is contracted between two or more parties (mother, father, child, teacher, principal . . .) to behave in certain ways in certain specific situations. The role of each person and the corresponding payoff (reinforcement) is clearly specified.

Summary

The following outline is a general summation of the steps involved in the learning or behavior change process.

1. *State the problem.* Define and analyze the problem behavior. State your reason for involvement.

2. *Gather behavior examples.* Give specific anecdotes or vignettes showing the ABCs of behavior and how the teacher or affected adult feels. Record carefully (A) what the child does, (B) the teacher's or parent's reaction and feelings, and (C) the child's response.

3. *Collect supplemental information.* Construct a developmental and social history.

4. *Make a tentative hypothesis* of the goal or life style of the individual. Clearly state what is reinforcing to the individual.

5. *Clearly specify the goals of behavior change.* Distinguish between the *agent* and the *object* of change.
6. *Formulate and implement the learning strategy.* Be very specific and thorough.

GOAL OF LEARNING

The goal of learning is to help the individual to become a fully functioning person and to reach new levels of humaneness. It is our belief that all individuals have the potential for change and improvement. The human organism is not doomed to its present state, but may continue to develop its capabilities through enhancing experiences. The following are characteristics of the fully functioning person (Kelley 1962, Rogers 1962):

1. He thinks well of himself and others.
2. He sees that man is a social animal, and therefore, self and others are interdependent.
3. He lives in the present. He is in an existential confrontation with each moment of life.
4. He sees himself as forward-looking or future- rather than past-oriented. He is anxious to face life's next challenge and has the confidence and courage to meet it.
5. He sees mistakes as steps rather than barriers.
6. He treasures people rather than material goods.
7. He lives in keeping with his values or authentically.
8. He lives an ever-moving and ever-becoming life.

These are important and essential goals, but they are general and serve the consultant as only general guidelines. Specific operational goals that quickly can be translated into action are required. The developmental tasks of Havighurst (1953) and the stages of man of Erikson (1963) are of this type.

1. Learning to give to others and accept from others affectional responses without expressing feelings of anxiety, guilt, embarrassment, or unworthiness.
2. Learning to express, assess, and consider one's feelings in relating appropriately to others as judged by peers and self-perception.
3. Learning to accept responsibility for one's behavior as determined by the acceptance of consequences following an act, making necessary psychological or material reparation.

4. Developing satisfying self-reinforcement patterns so that one feels comfortable with one's physical appearance, accomplishments, and ability to perform.
5. Learning appropriate social roles required as a participating member in a variety of groups.
   a. Developing the capacity to perform roles related to being son or daughter, boy or girl, pupil, leader, or follower as evidenced by being able to carry out responsibilities required in each role.

(Blackham and Silberman 1971, pp. 5–6)

The above desirable objectives of learning are stated in terms that more closely approxmiate the observable behavior wanted. An appropriately stated goal or objective, according to Mager (1962), must have two components: (1) the terminal behavior needs to be stated in terms that are overtly observable and hence measurable, and (2) the outcomes must identify behaviors to be performed and the exact conditions in which they should occur.

The consultant continually strives toward becoming a fully functioning person. In this process he encourages others to utilize their human potential. The learning process utilized is viewed as a problem of a total personality. Unless behavior has changed, one has not really learned. The key, then, to effective behavior change is an individual's personal discovery of meaning.

The purpose of consulting is to help to bring about more effective and satisfying means of behaving for the client. This calls for changes in personal meanings. Meanings, however, are inside people and cannot be changed directly by outsiders. *But they can be influenced by events in the outside world* (Combs, Avila and Purkey 1971). However, this necessitates that the consultant gain the understanding and skills involved in changing meaning. He must be constantly aware that a fact is not what is, but what a person believes is so! It is this meaning that is the goal of consulting contacts.

The Consultant's Function in the Learning Process

The consultant, his consultee, and the third party are all directly involved in the learning experience. All behavior, whether objective or subjective, is learned.

Learning, then, involves adaption of behavior. The emphasis is on behavioral change in the individual, based on his personal and purposeful perception of events, combined with his individual needs and goals.

The learner responds to the environment, but behavior is also determined by prior experiences and the way he perceives the situation. To be efficacious, learning must fulfill needs, meet goals, and make the individual more capable of dealing with his environment. Goal setting by the learner motivates learning. To improve learning, we need to improve the adequacy of guidelines as related to the learning process (Dinkmeyer 1965, p. 109).

Problems must precede answers. This is why advice is seldom so really helpful to other people and is usually avoided in the modern practice of counseling, consulting, psychiatry and social work. It is the active searching for answers to problems that helpers seek to encourage. We know that the process of searching for meaning even may be far more important for the growth of the individual than the answers he discovers. The following is an example of the consultant dealing with a learning problem.

Ms. Castillo, the second-grade teacher, came to the consultant with the following concern:

Ms. C:	"Matthew is a bright boy, but he just won't do his arithmetic. He does all of his other work and does a good job too. I've tried everything—he must have a learning disability."
Consultant:	"I can see you are very concerned. Can you give me a specific example of what is going on?"
Ms. C:	"Well today, I gave the arithmetic assignment and he just sat there. The other children took out their books and began working. He just didn't know where to begin."
Consultant:	"What did you do?"
Ms. C:	"I walked up to his seat, as I have to do every day, and gave him extra help. He seems to do OK as long as I stay and work with him, but as soon as I leave he just sits there and looks puzzled."

The consultant was already beginning to understand what was occurring and asked Ms. Castillo if she could think of another situation in which Matthew had trouble with arithmetic. She reported another situation in which he worked only when attention was given to him. The consultant realized that Ms. Castillo appeared to be reinforcing the "arithmetic" problem.

Consultant:	"Could it be that Matthew is not doing his arithmetic in order to get your attention?"
Ms. C:	"I was just thinking the same thing. He does so well in his other subjects."

Now that the learner's goal (i.e., attention) and the reinforcing behavior (i.e., teacher's physical presence and verbal messages) are established, a specific behavior change plan needs to be developed.

Consultant: "What could be done to eliminate Matthew's inappro-
               priate behavior during arithmetic class?"
Ms. C: "I suppose I could ignore it."
Consultant: "That sounds like a good way to eliminate the attention-
               getting behavior. Now I'm wondering what you would
               like Matthew to do. What is it that you hope he will do?"
Ms. C: "I would like him to do his arithmetic when I give the as-
               signment and without me helping him."
Consultant: "Perhaps whenever Matthew behaves in a manner that
               approximates this behavior, . . .

The consultant and Ms. Castillo now plan a procedure to collect specific data in order to establish a hierarchy of *very* specific behaviors
to reinforce in order to help Matthew to become a productive learner.
This involved specifying the *details* of just how Ms. Castillo was to
operate. The procedure involved eliminating or extinguishing one behavior and developing another.

Thus, through the thoughtful implementation of certain roles, the
consultant strives to enhance the total learning environment of the
school and community and to assist all children to fulfill their potential.

REFERENCES

Baldwin, A. L. *Theories of Child Development.* New York: John Wiley and
    Sons, 1968.
Bandura, A. "Behavior Modification through Modeling Procedures." In *Re-
    search in Behavior Modification,* edited by L. P. Ullman and L. Krasner,
    pp. 310–340. New York: Holt, Rinehart & Winston, 1965.
Bandura, A. and Walters, R. H. *Social Learning and Personality Develop-
    ment.* New York: Holt, Rinehart & Winston, 1963.
Berelson, B. and Steiner, G. A. *Human Behavior: Shorter Edition.* New York:
    Harcourt, Brace & World, 1967.
Blackham, G. J. "Strategies for Change in the Child Client." *Elementary
    School Guidance and Counseling* 3 (1969): 174–183.

Blackham, G. J. and Silberman, A. *Modification of Child Behavior.* Belmont, California: Wadsworth, 1971.

Borton, T. *Reach, Touch and Teach.* New York: McGraw-Hill, 1970.

Brautigan, R. *Rommel Drives on Deep into Egypt.* New York: Dell, 1970.

Briskin, A. and Gardner, W. "Social Reinforcement in Reducing Inappropriate Behavior." *Young Children* 2 (1968): 84–89.

Brown, G. I. *Human Teaching for Human Learning.* New York, Viking, 1971.

Bruner, J. *The Process of Education.* Cambridge: Harvard University Press, 1960.

Bruner, J. *Toward a Theory of Instruction.* Cambridge: Harvard University Press, 1966.

Bullard, M. "Human Operant Behavior and Individual Psychology in the Classroom." Paper presented at 9th Congress of International Association of Individual Psychology, New York, 1970.

Campbell, A. and Sulzer, B. "Motivating Educable Mentally Handicapped Students Toward Reading and Spelling Achievement Using Naturally Available Reinforcers in the Classroom Setting." Unpublished manuscript, Southern Illinois University, 1971.

Carkhuff, R. R. *The Development of Human Resources: Education, Psychology and Social Change.* New York: Holt, Rinehart & Winston, 1971.

Combs, A. W., Avila, D. L. and Purkey, W. W. *Helping Relationships: Basic Concepts for the Helping Professions.* Boston: Allyn & Bacon, 1971.

Combs, A. W. and Snygg, D. *Individual Behavior.* Rev. ed. New York: Harper & Row, 1959.

Cronbach, L. *Educational Psychology.* New York: Harcourt, Brace & World, 1963.

Daig, S. "Schools that Turn People Off." *The Education Digest* 35, no. 1 (September 1969): 41–43.

Dimick, K. and Huff, V. *Child Counseling.* Dubuque, Iowa: William C. Brown, 1970.

Dinkmeyer, D. *Child Development: The Emerging Self.* Englewood Cliffs, New Jersey; Prentice-Hall, 1965.

Dinkmeyer, D. "Understanding Self and Others: A Relevant, Purposeful Experience." *Canadian Counsellor* 5 (1971): 209–214.

Dreikurs, R. and Soltz, V. *Children: The Challenge.* New York: Meredith, 1964.

Erikson, E. *Childhood and Society.* 2nd ed. New York: W. W. Norton, 1963.

Evans, R. I. *B. F. Skinner: The Man and His Ideas.* New York: E. P. Dutton, 1968.

Gagne, R. *The Conditions of Learning.* New York: Holt, Rinehart & Winston, 1965.

Gagne, R. *The Conditions of Learning.* 2nd ed. New York: Holt, Rinehart & Winston, 1970.

Glasser, W. *Schools Without Failure,* New York: Harper & Row, 1969.

Grams, A. *Facilitating Learning and Individual Development.* St. Paul: Minnesota Department of Education, 1966.

Gronert, R. R. "Combining a Behavioral Approach with Reality Therapy." *Elementary School Guidance and Counseling* 5 (1970): 106–112.

Havighurst, R. J. *Human Development and Education.* New York: Longmans, 1953.

Holt, J. *How Children Learn.* New York: Pitman, 1967.

Holt, J. *The Underachieving School.* Belmont, Massachusetts: Dan Pinck and His Friends, 1969.

Homme, L. *How to Use Contingency Contracting in the Classroom.* Champaign, Illinois: Research Press, 1969.

Keller, F. C. *Learning: Reinforcement Theory.* New York: Random House, 1954.

Kelley, E. C. *Education for What is Real.* New York: Harper & Row, 1947.

Kelley, E. C. "The Fully Functioning Self." In *Perceiving, Behaving, Becoming,* edited by A. W. Combs. Washington, D.C.: Association for Supervision and Curriculum Development, NEA, 1962.

Keirsey, D. W. "Transactional Casework: A Technology for Inducing Behavioral Change." Paper presented at the Convention of California Association of School Psychologists and Psychometrists, 1965.

Krumboltz, J., ed. *Revolution in Counseling.* Boston: Houghton Mifflin, 1966.

Leonard, G. B. *Education and Ecstacy.* New York: Dell, 1968.

Lindsley, O. R. Operant Conditioning Methods Applied to Research with Chronic Schizophrenia." *Psychiatric Research Report* 5 (1956): 140–153.

Loughary, J. W. "Educating for Humaneness in the Technology Society." In *To Nurture Humaneness: Commitment for the 70's,* edited by Mary-Margaret Scobey and Grace Graham, pp. 75–85. Washington, D.C.: Association for Supervision and Curriculum Development, NEA, 1970.

Mager, R. F. *Preparing Instructional Objectives.* Palo Alto, California: Fearon Publishers, 1962.

McCandless, B. R. *Children: Behavior and Development.* New York: Holt, Rinehart & Winston, 1967.

Patterson, G. R. and Gullion, M. E. *Living with Children.* Champaign, Illinois: Research Press, 1968.

Pittenger, O. E. and Gooding, C. T. *Learning Theories in Educational Practice: An Integration of Psychological Theory and Educational Philosophy.* New York: John Wiley & Sons, 1971.

Postman, N. and Weingartner, C. *Teaching as a Subversive Activity.* New York: Delacorte Press, 1969.

Reese, E. P. *The Analysis of Human Operant Behavior.* Dubuque, Iowa: William C. Brown, 1966.

Reynolds, G. S. *A Primer of Operant Conditioning.* Glenview, Illinois: Scott, Foresman and Co., 1968.

Rogers, C. R. *Freedom to Learn.* Columbus, Ohio: Charles E. Merrill, 1969.

Rogers, C. R. "Toward Becoming a Fully Functioning Person." In *Perceiving, Behaving and Becoming,* edited by A. W. Combs. Washington, D.C.: Association for Supervision and Curriculum Development, NEA, 1962.

Silberman, C. E. *Crisis in the Classroom: The Remaking of American Education.* New York: Random House, 1970.

Skinner, B. F. *The Behavior of Organisms: An Experimental Analysis.* New York: Appleton-Century-Crofts, 1938.

Sulzer, B. "Match to Sample Performance by Normals and Institutionalized Retardates Under Different Reinforcing Conditions." Unpublished doctoral dissertation, University of Minnesota, 1966.

Sulzer, B. and Mayer, G. R. *Behavioral Modification Procedures for School Personnel.* Hinsdale, Illinois: Dryden Press, 1972.

Sulzer, B., Mayer, G. R. and Cody, J. J. "Assisting Teachers with Managing Classroom Behavioral Problems." *Elementary School Guidance and Counseling* 3 (1968): 40–48.

Thorpe, L. and Schmuller, A. *Contemporary Theories of Learning.* New York: Ronald Press, 1954.

Toffler, A. *Future Shock.* New York: Random House, 1970.

Watson, J. B. and Raynor, R. "Conditioned Emotional Reactions." *Journal of Experimental Psychology* 3 (1920) 1–14.

U.S.O.E. Report of the National Conference of Pupil Personnel Services. Washington. D.C.: U.S. Office of Education, August 28, 1971. (mimeo.)

Weinstein, G. and Fantini, M. D. *Toward Humanistic Education: A Curriculum of Affect.* New York: Praeger, 1970.

5

A Socio-Behavioral Approach
To Understanding
Human Behavior

In "Garments" Kahlil Gibran tells of a day when "beauty" and "ugli-ness" exchanged their exterior apparel. Some people mistook the one for the other because they failed to look beyond their exteriors, but others saw through their facades and recognized their true selves.

A similar analogy can be drawn between approaches to understand-ing human behavior. Many of the schools today employ the *"external frame of reference"* method. It may involve understanding by acquir-ing many facts and points of view. It is best demonstrated in attempts to be more "objective" in the case study or staffing which brings to-gether many points of view. In this approach the emphasis is on getting a collection of opinions, preferably representing a nonbiased scientific approach. For example, when a case study or an individual analysis is conducted, specialists from various disciplines (e.g., music, social work, administration, physical education, nursing, psychology) bring in facts and details as to how the child performs. The emphasis is on understanding *about* the child as he is seen from the outside observer.

In contrast, we are suggesting that behavior is better understood through the *"internal frame of reference,"* which acquaints one with the client's private logic. This approach helps us to understand the individual through his eyes and from his point of view. Combs, Avila, and Purkey (1971) refer to this as "reading behavior backwards," and feel that because behavior is a function of an individual's perceptions, it follows that if we observe his behavior carefully, it should be possible to reconstruct the feelings, attitudes, and purposes in the perceptual field of the behaver (p. 190). This does not mean that an elaborate and complicated theory based upon abstract constructs will be presented, but rather a simple practical approach that may be quickly understood and easily implemented.

RATIONALE

The major concern of the consulting process is to *maximize the human potential* of the teacher, administrator, parent, child—in other words, all people! It makes an assumption that everyone has considerable creative capacity which he seldom uses. The consultant helps the consultee to come in touch with his feelings and purposes. This can help the consultant to diagnose the purpose of behavior and can serve as the foundation for an improved relationship and corrective procedures. The consultant helps the concerned parties to work together in helping the child grow instead of competing, arguing, and bickering among themselves about theoretical positions or best procedures.

In order to help people, it is essential that we develop an understanding of them and how they deal with their environment. It is the purpose of this section to develop some practical guidelines that will enable the professional in the field to understand and modify human behavior. Too often psychological theorists have functioned as though the various approaches are completely different rather than possessing common elements. We believe and will attempt to demonstrate that much can be gained through observing the *common elements* in many of the *existing psychological theories.*

How a person behaves depends upon what he *believes* and how *authentically* he *acts* in terms of his beliefs. Combs et al. (1969) demonstrated that effective members of the helping professions have beliefs about people which are characteristically different from those held by ineffective members. Combs used the variable of congruency of behavior and correlated it with effectiveness in the helping professions. What Combs learned was it is not adequate just to have a theory of human behavior—we must act in accordance with our beliefs about people. Take, for instance, the consultant who, in theory, believes that all people are able, but refuses to allow others to function by taking on all responsibility himself, or the consultant who recommends to the teacher that he be a better listener when he exhibits poor listening in his own dialogue with the teacher. As an example:

Teacher: "They sure make me angry!"
Consultant: "I suggest you give them more love."
Teacher: "I'll try!"
Consultant: "It's also important to listen to hear their feelings."

In this case the consultant failed to listen to the message, to hear the teacher's feeling, or to realize that his proposed suggestion was not congruent with the teacher's problem.

A consistent or comprehensive approach to understanding human behavior allows one to deal effectively with others. It is this type of approach that allows for erroneous judgment and has a built-in evaluative mechanism that can modify a faulty hypothesis. From this point of view tentative hypotheses and guessing are valid procedures. They permit the consultant to process to the consultee his hunches based upon the probability in social transactions. By checking his ideas with the consultee through the feedback process, the consultant can determine if his hypotheses are correct, or he may get insight into a more valid hypothesis (Dreikurs 1950). In essence, this exchange allows one to accommodate for inaccurate understanding during the process of perceiving another individual's internal frame of reference.

The necessity of having a consistent operational understanding of our own as well as others' behavior can be fully understood in the example by McGehearty (1968) presented on page 112, in which the multiplicity (and potential for complexity) of the consultant's role is diagrammed.

Counseling as well as consulting has as its primary target the child, but because the consultant is forced to deal both directly and indirectly with other people, the behavioral analysis becomes more complex in consulting. In counseling, the counselor helps the child directly to understand himself and subsequently to modify his behavior. In consulting, the consultant helps the consultee to directly understand himself, the other person, and his relationship to others, and eventually to modify his behavior. The amount of human understanding necessary is multiplied as the consultant is forced to understand all parties involved, not just the client.

The consultant, therefore, needs a practical theory that will provide the following:

1. An *understanding* of human behavior.

2. A procedure that helps him to *accurately communicate* this understanding to others.

3. Operational knowledge of how to implement or put this new-found understanding into *practise*.

OVERT LEVEL OF COMMUNICATION

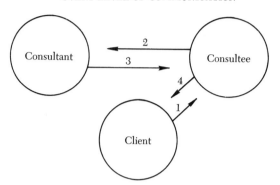

1. Client's input to consultee.
2. Consultee's perception of input from his phenomenological framework.
3. Consultant's feedback of professional expertise regarding client as reported by consultee, or feedback of support of consultee's interpretation.
4. Consultee's treatment based on gain in knowledge of reinforcement of previous tentative ideas.

COVERT LEVEL OF COMMUNICATION

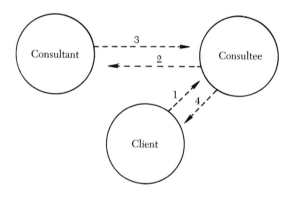

1. Client's impact upon internal dynamics of consultee.
2. Consultee's non-verbal cues, etc., communicating the nature of the blocking experienced.
3. Consultant's overt message incorporating input design to alleviate specific blocking or distortion.
4. Consultee's reception of message enabling more professional response to client.

FIGURE 1.   THE LEVELS OF COMMUNICATION INHERENT IN THE CONSULTING RELATIONSHIP.

UNDERSTANDING

Theory for theory's sake has value only to the intellectual. The practitioner requires a theory that can be comprehended as well as easily and quickly implemented. It has become apparent to the authors that such an approach to understanding human behavior is often lacking. Teachers, in their efforts to eliminate undesirable behavior in the classroom, many times reinforce it and cause it to occur more frequently, therefore making it harder to change.

> Miss Ropman, a fifth-grade teacher, wanted to keep Maryanne in her seat during class. Whenever Maryanne would get out of her chair, Miss Ropman would yell at her, "Get in that seat!" and she would quickly comply. After talking to the consultant she realized that Maryanne was trying to get her attention by getting out of her chair. Miss Ropman decided to ignore Maryanne's behavior in hopes that it would go away. After two days, she reported to the consultant, "It's no use. When I ignore her she gets worse! Pulls hair and drops books—I give up."

Many teachers are troubled by this and similar dilemmas. The knowledge that behavior, when going through the process of extinction, gets worse before it gets better, as well as the recognition that one must force onself to ignore misbehavior, may have helped Miss Ropman to ride out the transition. The end result, however, was that Maryanne's attention-getting behavior was strengthened rather than weakened and Maryanne's goal moved to power in an effort to control. Following is an attempt to reduce this void by proposing a practical approach to understanding human behavior that not only clarifies communication, but if adhered to, suggests direct steps for facilitating the development of active constructive behavior. Premises that are essential to understanding the behavior of man are included.

Human Personality is Best Understood In its Unity or Pattern

The holistic approach to understanding behavior comprehends man's actions in their total social and perceptual context. The total pattern is understood in its unity and in terms of its holism, in contrast to an analysis of its elements. The Ansbachers (1967, pp. 4–5) drew the distinction in terms of opposites:

Objective Psychology	Subjective Psychology
Emphasis on finding general laws: nomothetic laws	Emphasis on laws applying to the individual case: idiographic laws

Objective Psychology	Subjective Psychology
Atomism	Holism
Molecular units of analysis	Molar units of analysis
Analysis into elements	Phenomenological description
Classification into definite categories	Field theory
Behaviorism	Gestalt psychology
Stimulus-response psychology	Psychology emphasizing the variables intervening between stimulus and response
Mechanistic conceptions	Organismic conception
Motivation by pushes	Motivation by pulls
Genetic, historical approach	Ahistorical approach
Determinism	Immanent teleology

The significance of this may be seen in Figure 2 (p. 115). In Section A are many individual and unique components of the individual (e.g., IQ, health record, family constellation, nonverbal language). When these are viewed individually, their value has little meaning. But in Section B, the pieces are seen in their relationship to the total pattern. Just as each segment of a rainbow or a mosaic has limited meaning when taken individually, each aspect of an individual's character cannot be meaningfully understood until all are arranged into a special format and a pattern emerges.

In schools we continuously see the nurse approaching the individual from a physiological standpoint, the social worker from a social relationship approach, the psychologist from a mental competency position, and so on. Each professional analyzes a particular element. As Earl Kelley (1947) observed, *only in laboratories and schools are elements singled out—it is not that way in life.* If we want to develop whole men, we need to abandon our efforts at dichotomizing individuals into sections. "When a man meets a problem in his becoming world, he meets it with all he has—foot, ear, fist, purpose, value" (Kelley 1947, p. 65). The organism reacts as an organized whole to his phenomenal field (Rogers 1951). "These have to be marshalled together to meet not some, but all phases of the problem" (Kelley 1947, p. 65). A person responds to any stimuli as a total being with thoughts, actions, feelings, etc., and they are all part of a meaningful pattern. Thus, in order to understand the individual, we must perceive the pattern and help him in relation to it. Some of the patterns may involve desires to be special, to control, to get even, or to be served.

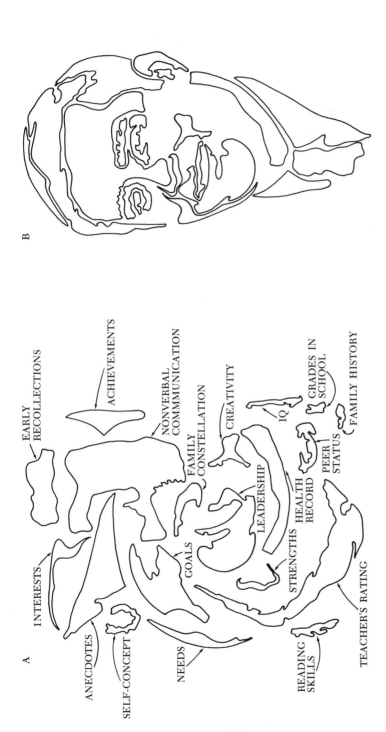

A

EARLY
RECOLLECTIONS

ACHIEVEMENTS

NONVERBAL
COMMUNICATION

FAMILY
CONSTELLATION

CREATIVITY

INTERESTS

ANECDOTES

SELF-CONCEPT

NEEDS

GOALS

LEADERSHIP

STRENGTHS HEALTH
RECORD

PEER
STATUS

IQ

GRADES IN
SCHOOL

FAMILY HISTORY

READING
SKILLS

TEACHER'S RATING

B

FIGURE 2. (A) SOME OF THE ELEMENTS WHICH HELP TO UNDERSTAND HUMAN BEHAVIOR. THESE ELE-
MENTS MEAN LITTLE WHEN TAKEN INDIVIDUALLY. (B) A PATTERN BEGINS TO EMERGE WHEN THE
PIECES OF INFORMATION ARE VIEWED COLLECTIVELY.

115

Advocates of the behavioral approach, such as Krumboltz and Thoresen (1969), have stated that the client initially must be understood *totally* before appropriate specific modifications may be implemented.

> Very seldom do clients begin by requesting help in accomplishing specific behavior changes. Very seldom does a client enter a counselor's office and state, "I want to learn to speak up in class," "I wish to reduce anxiety associated with viewing snakes," or "I wish to engage in information-seeking relevant to my career choice." When goals are so clearly and specifically expressed, it is relatively easy for a behavioral counselor to devise some kind of procedure that might help. But clients seldom behave that way. Most clients do not describe their difficulties in such simple straight-forward language. Most cannot specify what behavior they desire. They are usually confused and uncertain (pp. 7–8.)

The consultant must understand the whole individual if he is going to tailor his techniques to the unique individual he is working with.

> The counselor tries to understand and assess the client's *thoughts* and *feelings*. He first tries to see things from the *client's point of view*. He communicates his understandings to the client and attempts to determine if he is *accurately* perceiving the client's thoughts and feelings. . . . He also seeks answers to questions. *What precisely is going on in the client's everyday life?* In what ways do others respond to the client's words, thoughts and feelings? (Krumboltz and Thoresen 1969, p. 8).

A fragmentary analysis, however, is usually the precursor of misunderstanding.

> This is well illustrated in the case of Joanne. Here is a child with a high IQ, as measured by individual tests, and with considerable creativity and spontaneity. However, she is failing many of her school subjects. Upon first analysis, one might say that this behavior doesn't make sense. However, from this point of view we accept that the behavior always makes sense to the behaver. Thus, we focus on the pattern and psychological movement in contrast to the elements of high IQ, sponteneity, and low grades. We note that when she does not function, the teacher must make special efforts, and the parents are very disturbed. Joanne becomes special because she fails to function. She is known and must be dealt with in a unique manner by school and parents. Soon in this light, her behavior has a purpose. Thus, understanding behavior in terms of its total impact helps us to grasp a new insight into Joanne's actions (Dinkmeyer and Caldwell 1970, p. 34).

Often, although we protest our interest in the person, our traditional approaches lead us to consider him as a student, athlete, socially powerful person, etc. We have even studied "underachievement" by studying IQ and achievement scores and seeing them as discrepencies when they are highly related. All of the components of the individual are interrelated, and his behavior will only become comprehensible as we grasp his idiographic pattern. This seems to necessitate the understanding of each individual's unique life style.* Life style is the individual's characteristic approach and response to the tasks of life. Knowledge of these basic convictions permits an understanding of the individual as a whole. The life style reflects the child's goals, attitudes, and his "life plan." We can no longer pay homage to each distinct variable as though it were distinct, predictive, or helpful in understanding behavior.

Behavior is Goal Directed And Purposive

In contrast to other approaches, in the holistic approach behavior is understood in terms of its purpose (Dreikurs 1950). No time is wasted or effort expended in ascertaining the causes of behavior. We are involved in a discipline that focuses on the "here and now" and ascertains what the client *will* do (future), in contrast to one that completes a history (past). It is more important to predict the future and bring about change than to compile, contemplate, and recite the past. The historical approach to deciphering causes at best can only provide us with the frustration and anxiety of a situation beyond our control (e.g., broken home, death, physical disability). As was once said, "We can't move from where we aren't, only from where we are."

Behavior takes on new meaning in terms of its social purposes. The goal or purpose is subjective, created, and often not in awareness. The goal is influential in private logic (cognitive domains) and emotions (affective domains) which produce *action*. The purpose may be consciously or unconsciously sought; but because it becomes clear after the event, the purpose enables us to understand the consequences that the individual seeks. If we understand the consequences he desires, and henceforth the direction in which he is moving, we have access to understanding a basic area of motivation. We look beyond the present behavior which provides a static description and comprehend where the behavior is leading.

---

* The notion of life style is attributable to Alfred Adler but tends to overlap considerably with what Skinner (1969) has termed "rule-governed behavior," with what Galantier, Miller and Pribram (1960) call "plans," with Frank's (1961) "assumptive system," with Kelly's (1955) "supraordinate constructs," Rotter's (1966) "generalized expectancies of reinforcement (Allen 1971, p. 5)," and Berne's (1967) "life script."

Cal has been a "headache" to the teacher. Whenever she tries to help him with his work, an argument results. Upon checking the records, she discovered that Cal has "severe" problems at home. His father, for example, "does not allow him to go anywhere—not even to the library." The parents lock him in the basement for long periods of time as a means of discipline. Many other incidents of a poor home environment were noted. Thinking causally, the teacher would attribute his behavior to his poor home situation. But with the help of a consultant, the teacher begins to look at the way she responds to Cal and the pattern of their transactions. From this analysis, she poses the possible hypothesis that the only way Cal can feel special is to show that he is dominating. Through the process of extricating herself from Cal when the "power conflict" began and acting rather than talking, the teacher was able to help Cal redirect his energy into constructive channels.

Thus, behavior appears to be a function of the individual purpose or goal, which determines what is and is not reinforcing. In the case of Cal, his purpose was to show that he was "on top," and each confrontation with his teacher helped to reinforce the belief that this was a desirable way to be significant. The consequences of the action, therefore, tend to help us to comprehend behavior. Thus, as Sinnott (1961) indicated, "the end rather than the means seems to be the important thing" in understanding the individual. He contends that this goal directedness is not true just in psychological behavior, but in physiological behavior as well. Arieti (1955, 1956), for example, applied this rationale to the mental processes and discovered purposive short-circuiting of certain areas of the brain.

Dreikurs (1968) added insight to the goal-directed nature of behavior through his description of the four goals of misbehavior. These goals are attention getting, the struggle for power or superiority, the desire for revenge, and the display of inadequacy or assumed disability. (A chart indentifying these misbehaviors and their corrective measures, presented by Don Dinkmeyer and adapted from Edith Dewey's behavioral chart, can be found in Chapter 8, pages 220–221.)

The child who seeks attention prefers it in a pleasant way, but he will accept it negatively, as this is better than being ignored or not noticed. Children have the creative capacity to obtain attention in unique ways, some by being successful, other through charm, while others may obtain attention by annoying.

The child whose goal is power is attempting to assert his superiority and demonstrate he is boss and can do what he wants and not what anyone else wants him to do. As Dreikurs (1968) says, there is "no final 'victory' "; the more times we attempt to overpower the child, the more convinced he becomes of the value of power.

The child whose goal is revenge is characterized as one who has given up any hope of being liked or accepted by adults. As Dreikurs (1968) states, "The child no longer hopes merely for attention or even power; feeling ostracized and disliked he can see his place in the group only by his success in making himself hated" (p. 29).

The child whose goal is to display inadequacy is so dejected that he does not believe he can be significant. The child uses or develops his inability as a protective device in order to keep people from requiring or expecting things from him. By neither becoming involved nor contributing he hopes to avoid what he believes to be an even-more undesirable experience. This, in turn, becomes a self-fulfilling prophecy because since he believes he can't do anything, he doesn't do anything; therefore, his belief of his worthlessness is soon confirmed.

Whatever the goal, it is recognized as being subjective, created, and unconscious. It is frequently perceived only vaguely by the individual and is not a part of his awareness. The goal directs the individual's selective responses and can be seen in a cognitive and emotional form. In identifying the goals of a child, it is advantageous to check the reactions of both the teacher and child. This will be further explained in the section devoted to implementation.

Let it suffice to say that survival, whether biological, psychological, or social, is the basic goal of all humans. Thus, while many times behavior seems mysterious or incomprehensible because the purpose is not apparent, once the purpose is known, it becomes understandable (Dinkmeyer and Caldwell 1970).

The Individual is Constantly Striving for Significance

Each individual is striving for his own unique goal of success. (He is never the same.) Change is constant, necessary, and certain in the active and dynamic life of man. This striving for success arises when the individual experiences (either objectively or subjectively) a feeling of being different from his perceived self or is in dissonance (his behavior does not fit together psychologically) (Festinger 1957). The child very seldom realizes his goal because the striving for significance comes from his uniquely conceived goal or self-ideal.

The focus here is on recognizing the pull of the goal, a type of motivation which works with those forces that the individual anticipates, in contrast to the push of the drives or extrinsic rewards. Behaviorists (Hansen 1973, Krumboltz and Thoresen 1969, Sulzer and Mayer 1972) state that the specific response that an individual will make in a given situation seems to be a function of the reinforcement that follows the response. This is the same thing as saying that behavior is goal directed. The reinforcement or consequences become the goal. The significance of behavior lies in terms of its consequences or how the individual is seeking to be known. There is less concern with actual behavior and more with the direction in which the individual is moving. One of the most powerful parts of the person to deal with is his expectations and anticipations. When one works with "where the person is headed," "where he is going," or with his purposes, it is a deeper, more significant level of involvement. This is the next stage beyond empathy or working with feeling, as it can indicate not only "how you are now" but "what you *will* be doing." Thus, if a person becomes aware of and changes someone's anticipations, he really is reworking that person's perceptual field.

A seven-year-old boy was of considerable concern to his teacher. Not only was he a non-reader, but he attacked the smaller classmates with some fervor from time to time. The counselor's appraisal of the situation suggested that the goal of this behavior was becoming "special" in one way or another. It appeared that the boy saw himself as incapable of obtaining a secure place in the class by other means and therefore has hit upon the "problem behavior" as a vehicle to a unique position among his peers. Consequently rather than attacking this behavior directly, treatment consisted of providing him with opportunities to be "special" in a useful way, for example, helping classmates with tasks in which his greater strength and size gave him superior competence. Almost immediately other children began to comment on the favorable change in his demeanor and he began to read (Allen 1969, pp. 78–79).

The striving for significance becomes a motivating force behind human activity. While all humans do not seek to be significant in the same way, they do seek to establish a sense of importance. This is the same phenomenon that Maslow (1970) and Rogers (1951) refer to as self-actualization.

Therefore, the consultant needs to ask the question, "How is the child seeking to become significant?" The chart below can assist the consultant in answering this question.

Pattern	Purpose	Significance
Busy in all directions	To escape functioning	To be important
Always being right	To control	To be more than others
Always doing the "right" thing	To charm	To be accepted
Creating excitement	To make self noticed	To be dealt with

All Behavior Has Social Meaning

Man is primarily a social being and seeks human relationships. He learns very early in life that others are the suppliers of life's goodies. Thus, his behavior is best understood in terms of its social context and its distinct interpersonal relationships. The significance of behavior lies in terms of our interaction and transaction with others and the subsequent consequences. Socal striving, then, is of primary not secondary importance. Behavior is described in terms of social transactions in contrast to intrapersonal elements of classical psychoanalysis. Behaviorists, such as Hansen (1973), support the notion that the development of the child's pattern is a function of learning through relationships with other people, i.e., social learning. For further elaboration of the impact of the social environment on learning and behavior, see Bandura and Walters (1963) and Parke (1969).

Man, then, is understood as a social interacting individual whose problems arise because of the necessity of interaction with people. Behavior, then, is highly influenced by the consequences and the reactions of other people. For example, the consultant who recognizes the social significance of behavior is interested in how the child, as well as his peers, reacts to the behavior. In observing the teacher as he deals with the child, the consultant focuses not only on the child's responses to the teacher's attempts to direct him, but also the teacher's responses to the child's resistance, as it is of equal importance. The social meaning of behavior often can be discovered in the transactions between the teacher and the child, and the child and his peers.

The authors' approach utilizes experimental conditions and looks at observable social behavior. For example, Sulzer, Mayer and Cody (1968) discuss four methods of effecting the consequences (i.e., extinction, satiation, time-out, and reinforcement of incompatible behaviors) in helping to control behavior in a classroom setting. Their purpose was to help the ill-prepared elementary school worker to gain information concerning various management procedures. Kennedy (1968) discusses the use of reinforcing consequences in motivating learning. His methodology focuses on the relatively "normal" school learning problems frequently encountered by the classroom teacher. While Krumboltz (1966) uses this approach in counseling, he reinforces the appropriate behavioral consequences of the client in an attempt to help him reach his goal (i.e., the client's goal).

The following are specific procedures that the consultant can employ in helping to redirect goals toward a more positive function.

Premack Principle. This principle, which was previously mentioned, states that activities children enjoy can be used as effective consequences or reinforcers for other activities. "For any pair of activities, the more probable one will reinforce the less probable one" (Bandura 1969). In other words, if a child enjoys singing softly during class and it does not bother her classmates, but she does not like to read in her reading group, the singing can be used to reinforce the reading. When she reads in class for a specified period of time, she can sing for a period of time. This procedure then helps to redirect her goal in a more positive fashion. Homme (1963) illustrates this principle in a nursery school setting. Three-year-old children were engaging in a variety of undesired behaviors, including screaming, running around the room, and pushing chairs. Homme altered the situation so that for a specified time the children were asked to sit quietly and receive instruction from the teacher, then a bell would ring and the children were allowed to engage in any nondestructive activity they chose, including screaming, running around the room, and pushing chairs.

Logical Consequences. This is a procedure that allows the child to experience the logical consequences of an act. For example:

> A fourth-grade boy had been continuously in the habit of tipping his chair back while sitting in the classroom, despite the fact that he had indeed fallen back on the floor. He insisted on continuing this attention-getting device. Finally, the teacher asked him whether he would prefer to lean back in his chair or sit like the rest of the children. The boy indicated that he would prefer to lean back in his chair. The teacher then put two books under the front legs of the chair so that the boy was leaning back in an uncomfortable, but not dangerous, position. The boy was then asked to maintain this position until he decided to sit porperly. Before long he removed the books and no further episode of tipping his chair back occurred during the rest of the semester (Dreikurs and Grey 1968, pp. 78–79).

According to Kennedy and Seidman (1971), "because the consequences of behavior are its main causes, the teachers are, then, really in the best position to influence behavior, and its change, because they are in control of behavior's natural consequences, and may be trained to control contrived (or logical) consequences—for almost one-third of the child's waking hours during school age" (p. 4). However, this should not be confused with punishment, as Dreikurs and Grey (1968) point out:

1. Logical consequences express the reality of the social order, not of the person; punishment, the power of personal authority.
2. The logical consequence is related to the misbehavior; punishment rarely is.
3. Logical consequences involves no element of moral judgement; punishment inevitably does.
4. Logical consequences are concerned only with what will happen now; punishment, with the past.
5. The voice is friendly when consequences are invoked; there is anger in punishment, either open or concealed.

For additional examples of this procedure in operation, see Hillman (1967) and Grubbe (1968).

Time-Out. This procedure, which also was mentioned previously, is where the *opportunity that an individual will receive reinforcement for his actions is removed for a short period of time* (Sulzer, Mayer and Cody 1968). For example, David has been bothering the class by talking out in a loud voice at irregular intervals. The teacher might choose to remove David from the classroom and place him in a room where no one can hear or respond to his verbalizations. Eventually his behavior will be eliminated and not at the expense of a disrupted class.

Satiation. This is a process of *reducing behavior through the presentation of reinforcement.* For example, if a child who swears out loud is asked to repeat the word 1000 times out loud, he will probably not want to do it for a long time. The misbehavior that is enjoyable to the child must be repeated, not a similar form of the behavior. In this case, the swear word must be *verbally* repeated, not written 1000 times. (This would decrease the probability of his writing the word, but that's not the problem.)

Paradoxical Intention. In this procedure, the individual is invited to intend, even if only for a moment, precisely that which he fears. As Frankl (1963) stated, as soon as the client "stops fighting his obsessions and instead tries to ridicule them in an ironical way, by applying paradoxical intention, *the vicious circle is out* and the symptom diminishes and finally atrophies" (p. 203). For example:

When Mary was called on to read outloud in her fourth-grade class, she would stand up, get very embarrassed, begin to blush, and eventually have to sit down without reading. When asked about this Mary said, "Whenever I think of getting up in front of people, I get all flustered and clutch up! I can't help it." The consultant advised her that the next time this happened to try deliberately to show just how embarrassed and flustered she could get. Two weeks later, Mary informed the consultant that she was having no difficulty reading outloud in her classroom.

This procedure involves a reversal of the child's attitude, inasmuch as her fear is replaced by a paradoxical wish.

By using the consequences of behavior to explain the direction the individual is choosing, we would then seek to help him see the alternatives available and to make a commitment to a new choice. The social context of the behavior, however, is primary in both understanding and modification.

Each Individual Behaves According to His Beliefs

We are not concerned with how the events appear externally, but seek out the meaning the event possesses for the individual. This principle applies to understanding the child's private logic. The child who believes "It is safer to withdraw than try and fail," "I am not as able as others," or "I only try if I can be perfect" will function on the basis of these assumptions, regardless of their validity.

Adler (1957) stated, "A perception is never to be compared with a photographic image, because something of the peculiar and individual quality of the person who perceives it is inextricably bound up with it" (p. 49). Each individual has the ability to determine and explain his experiences to fit his own life style.

Behavior is not only reactive or a mere response to an external stimulus. That is, each individual has the capacity to creatively respond and produce a personally meaningful response. Behavior, therefore, is never understood solely within the framework of stimulus-response; it is always to be understood in terms of an S-O-R (Stimulus-Organism-Response) paradigm. Man, then, is always in search of his purposes and goals, evaluating and interpreting life as a truly decision-making organism.

Behavior always makes sense to the behaver but is often baffling to anyone else. For example, teachers are often confronted with behavioral problems which are difficult to cope with, and usually they feel they try to do everything to correct it (e.g., warnings, staying after school). A teacher may state to a child that he could have just as much of his time and attention if he performed properly—probably even more—yet, what the teacher does not understand is that because the behavior baffles him, he responds to the child in a confused fashion and sometimes excuses the child from having to complete certain tasks. These reprieves from functioning serve the direct purpose of the child.

Because teachers (parents, counselors, etc.) do not understand the child's goal or purpose, they tend to maintain or reinforce undesirable behavior (Krumboltz and Thoresen 1969). This increases the teacher's frustration by watching a behavioral response grow stronger rather than weaker.

> The crying baby cries louder before the crying subsides when ignored by its mother. The child who wants to get a drink may ask much more frequently for a few minutes before giving up. Though the increase in rate is a transitory one, in practice it can have some negative side effects. Mother and teacher may conclude too rapidly that their technique of ignoring the child is not effective, give up, and again reinforce the child. This situation sets the occasion for intermittent reinforcement. Its effect [is] increased resistance to extinction . . . In the long run the behavior then may actually become strengthened. When a mother or teacher complains, "I've tried everything and nothing works," they have probably been trapped into this bind (Sulzer, Mayer and Cody 1968, pp. 42–43).

The teacher whose previous training focused on the identification of factual and objective responses must learn to become aware of the unique meaning and significance that each individual derives from his behavior. This is the process of empathy—the ability to see how it looks from the other side. (Ask yourself, "How would I behave if I were he?") Or as Rogers (1951) states, "The best vantage point for understanding behavior is from the internal frame of reference of the individual himself" (p. 494). Behavior, therefore, is a function of the perceptual field of the behaver at the instant of action (Combs et al., 1969). Thus, it is our job as members of the helping professions to understand how the child views the world. (Objective data, such as anecdotal records, observation, etc. help the consultant accomplish this task.) Once we understand an individual's view of the world, his behavior makes sense. Each individual child perceives life as he has learned to perceive it. Through his experience, he develops beliefs: "People are kind," "Mother loves me most," "People are trustworthy," and so on. All of these beliefs affect his behavior. As Combs et al. (1969) states, we don't behave according to the facts, but we behave according to our beliefs.

In perceptual terms, behavior is always a function of perception. That is, how a person behaves at any moment will always be a function of the nature and condition of his perceptual field at the moment of his behavior. In everyday terms, "People behave according to how things seem to them" (p. 11).

Therefore, we behave according to how things appear and when we perceive things differently, we behave accordingly.

Belonging Is a Basic Need

Man can only be actualized as he finds his place and belongs to someone or something. Examples of this may be seen in schools where children attain identity from the place where they belong or are accepted (e.g., Miss Rotter's third grade, the Crow's reading group). Eventually, an individual's social significance can be attributed to his capability in identifying people to whom he belongs. When the individual doubts that he will be accepted or will not belong, anxieties and apprehension occur. When the child feels he will not be invited to the party, cannot gain admittance to the science club, or will not make the basketball team, a state of tension, as the result of the lack of a feeling of belonging, befalls him. Rudolf Dreikurs tells a story of the hermit who lived thirty miles from a small European city. The city burned completely to the ground, and the inhabitants decided to move elsewhere and not rebuild. The hermit then moved thirty miles from another city. In understanding the individual, it is oftentimes helpful to identify the source(s) of his acceptance and identity.

Understanding Behavior is Based on Idiographic Principles

In understanding human behavior, principles of an idiographic nature (principles that apply to the individual's unique life style) are of more concern than those of a nomothetic nature (laws that apply generally). Normative group descriptions cannot be universally applied to the individual. While it is interesting to know about the average ten year old, that type of data cannot be translated immediately into corrective procedures and practise.

Alfred Adler's original formulations pointed to the importance of iodiography. Behaviorists have also realized this principle for decades. The understanding of the singular nature of each individual is therefore practised in research that focuses on few subjects over long periods of time rather than groups of subjects for short periods of time. The popular story of the Skinnerian who answered a critic by saying, "Oh yes, I had a control group, but he died!" further elaborates the concentration on idiographic principles.

Nomothetic laws just do not lend much help in understanding the behavior of the individual from his point of view (e.g., "the terrible two's", "All nine year olds. . . .). Although accomplishing this "perceptual understanding" is difficult since perceptions lie inside people and are not susceptible to direct observation, Combs et al. (1969) found that ". . . techniques of inference can, indeed, provide reliable data if the researcher approaches the problem of measurement with the same discipline, care, and vigor demanded of science in any other field of exploration" (p. 70).

> It is necessary to understand the person's style of life and his particular laws of psychological movement. Each human organizes himself according to his personal view of things; he is not dependent solely upon objective circumstances. For example, the parents may really treat him fairly and his teacher may be giving equal assignments, but he does not believe this to be true and acts as though he were discriminated against. Then it is more important for us to understand his feelings, his attitudes, and convictions than to argue regarding the quality of treatment. We must learn to deal with the way in which the other sees things and not with some supposed objective evaluation (Dinkmeyer and Caldwell 1970, p. 44).

Total objectivity, then, would correlate with ineffectiveness. Thus, our concern is with both how the individual appears to himself as well as to others.

Psychology of Use vs. Psychology of Possession

The attributes an individual possesses are of less significance than what he decides to do with what he is endowed. We can only deal with what is—not what isn't! We need to concentrate on and understand where the individual is now and for what purpose.

How an individual selects to make use of his heredity or environment may further clarify this concept.

> In some instances we observe an individual who appears to have considerable physical or intellectual capacity but chooses not to utilize

it. The individual, for some reason, has decided that he is not wholly adequate, that it does not pay to function in terms of this specific capacity. The concern, then, becomes not one of trying to measure his capacity more accurately, but one of determining why he chooses not to use it (Dinkmeyer and Caldwell 1970, p. 45).

The important variable is what the child does with his possessions. The individual uses his capacities to suit his purposes.

Sources of Additional Understanding

The development of social interest is crucial for the individual's mental health. Thus, each individual should be assisted in finding his unique asset(s) in terms of making a contribution to the good of the entire group.

The effective person is capable of accepting himself and others. Combs and Snygg (1959) describe the adequate person as one who, (1) perceives himself in essentially positive ways, (2) is capable of accepting himself and others, and (3) perceives himself as closely identified with others.

Human needs arrange themselves in a hierarchy. As Maslow (1970) rates them, beginning with the most immediate: physiological, safety, belonging, love, self-esteem, and self-actualization. This allows us to understand that an individual must first deal with his lower hierarchy needs before he can become a fully functioning person.

COMMUNICATION

It is apparent that communication between the various disciplines has not been efficacious. A foundation for an interdisciplinary communication system for the helping professions is critical if current needs are to be met. Psychologists, social workers, teachers, principals, and counselors have jargon which is unique to their own profession. Each has its own system of classifying and dealing with the behavior of children and adults. The end result of this type of structure is to quote a song, "Communication Breakdown."

While in the past this pseudo-sophisticated approach was considered inevitable, it is apparent that educators and parents are increasingly less resigned to accepting the incapacity of professionals to practise their specialty—communication with their peers as well as their clients.

This becomes even more important for the consultant who needs to work closely with a myriad of different people. Until the message sent by the consultant is the same as that received by the teacher, and vice-versa, no communication or consultation can transpire. For example, when the teacher states, "Jack is a problem. I can't get him to do anything. I really have tried everything!" The consultant needs to get the full message and check out her feelings about the child (i.e., Is she annoyed? Angered? Hurt?). He then needs to send a message which shows (both in the cognitive and affective aspects): (1) recognition of the problem, (2) ownership of the problem, (3) awareness of the teacher's feelings, and (4) a check with the feedback process as to how the consultee understands his message.

We need to stop talking about the "underachiever," the child with "low motivation," "the overaggressive class agitator," and "the trouble-maker." These "descriptions" hinder the development of understanding. These terminologies mean different things to different people, and rather than clarifying the behavior, they tend to confuse. We need a system that will help cohese disciplines rather than add to the existing separation.

We need an approach to understanding behavior that *all* people who deal with children can understand, practise, and communicate. The approach presented below will not only clarify communication, but if adhered to, suggest direct steps for facilitating the development of active constructive behavior. This approach takes cognizance of the fact that a simple but direct and clear approach can be efficient and hence more productive for all concerned.

Implementation

The process is capsulized as follows:

1. *Observation.* See what happens in the child-teacher-child transaction. Record carefully what the child does, the teacher's reaction, his feelings, and the child's response.

2. *Consequences of Behavior.* Record the end result of the transaction. What happens to the participants and their resultant feelings and behavior?

3. *Identification.* Identify the goal of the behavior, for what purpose the individual behaves this particular way. What is the payoff?

4. *Modification.* Tentatively hypothesize possible solutions and begin to correct the misbehavior.

5. *Record.* Keep daily records as to what occurs to the child's behavior.

The following example will emphasize the teacher and the child, but the procedure is duly applicable to parent/child and counselor/child relationships.

Observation

In this phase, we observe and record what happens during the interaction between the child and the teacher. The most accurate way to do this is through the use of anecdotal records (Dinkmeyer 1965). In this process, the observer indicates simply what he sees and gives no subjective accounts of why the events are occurring. "An anecdote is a word picture of an incident in the life of a child, one significant piece in the jigsaw puzzle which when assembled, will contribute to a more complete picture of the child" (Dinkmeyer 1965, p. 54). Anecdotes provide the exact setting, detailed actions and reactions involving all the responses of those involved, while utilizing quotes and supplying nonverbal cues that are observed. The report should indicate the psychological movement of the situation or what the child does, how the teacher responds to it, and how the child reacts to the teacher. For example:

December 2, 1971, 10:10 A.M.

Bill was sitting at his desk during mathematics class while the teacher was talking to the other six-grade children from the front of the room. The teacher turned and began to write a problem on the blackboard, and Bill began talking to his neighbor. The teacher turned around, looked directly at Bill, and asked him to be quiet. She then turned around toward the blackboard, and Bill went back to talking.

L.C.

December 2, 1971, 11:50 A.M.

At the end of the physical education, period, the teacher blew her whistle and announced that it was time to put the basketballs away and to line up to return to the classroom. Bill continued to shoot baskets. After all of the children had lined up, the teacher asked Bill to please put the basketball away. He slowly dribbled the ball to the supply room and emerged with a grin on his face.

L.C.

December, 3, 1971, 3:00 P.M.

The children were told that they were to work on their homework, and they could read library books when they were finished. The teacher put the assignment on the board. All the children began to work on their assignments except Bill. He began reading his library book. The teacher noticed this and asked him if he had finished his assignment and he replied with a big grin on his face—"No." Bill then began to work on his assignment.

L.C.

December, 3, 1971, 3:00 P.M.

The children were told that they could get into line for dismissal. They all rushed for a position in line, except for Bill who slowly walked to the front of the line and stood.

L.C.

Anecdotes like these, coupled with similar reports regarding Bill's behavior, help to discover the social dynamics of the situation which will assist us in the next phase. For example, at this point, it seems as though Bill's goal of misbehavior is attention.

Another way of obtaining a picture of the present situation, as well as a description of how the teacher would like it to be, has been developed by Mayer and Benoit (1972) and can be seen in Figure 3, pp. 132–133.

Consequences of Behavior

We believe that the significance of behavior lies in its consequences. It is therefore essential that the end result of the transaction be recorded. It is necessary to discover what happens to each participant in regard to his feelings and behavior. This can be accomplished through observing as well as interviewing the participants. We need to understand how the teacher and child feel during the transaction.

Identification

Using the premise that all behavior is purposive, we then try to identify the goal of the child's misbehavior. The four goals of misbehavior as described by Dreikurs (1968) are as follows:

Goal 1: Attention-getting—he wants attention, to keep people busy with him.

Goal 2: Power—he wants to be boss, to control.

Present Antecedents to Behavior: A	Present Behavior: B	Present Consequences to Behavior: C
1. Subject matter being taught? ____	Describe the observable undesirable behavior and approximate frequency or duration of its occurrence.	1. How do you respond? ____
2. Seating location of child in classroom? ____		2. How do the students respond? ____
3. Activity of teacher? ____		3. What happens to the assigned task? ____
4. Activity of students? ____		4. Other? ____
5. What time does the behavior occur most frequently during the day (math, before recess, ten minutes into lesson, etc.) ____		
6. What is the previous experience of the child with subject matter? ____		
7. Other? ____		

132

Present Antecedents to Hoped For Behavior	Behavior "Hoped For"	Present Consequences to Hoped For Behavior
1. Subject matter being taught? ———	Describe the hoped for behavior in operational terms. Also give its approximate frequency or duration of occurrence.	1. How do you respond? ———
2. Seating location of child in classroom? ———		2. How do the students respond? ———
3. Activity of teacher? ———		3. What happens to the assigned task? ———
4. Activity of students? ———		4. Other? ———
5. What time does the behavior occur most frequently during the day (math, before recess, ten minutes into lesson, etc.)? ———		
6. What is the previous experience of the child with subject matter? ———		
7. Other? ———		

FIGURE 3. CONTINGENCY ANALYSIS CHART.

Goal 3: Revenge—he wants to hurt us, to get even.

Goal 4: Display of Inadequacy—he wants to impress us with his inadequacy, so he is excused with no demands made upon him.

The easiest and most efficient way to determine if the proper goal has been identified is to:

1. Understand the meaning of the child's behavior. What is the meaning of the psychological movement and the transaction that is occurring between the participants? Here you must be free to guess, use hunches, and make tentative analyses. These enable you to verify the purpose through feedback.
2. Check your spontaneous reaction. If you feel annoyed it is usually attention; if you feel personally challenged it is more likely to be power; if you feel hurt and mad it is usually revenge; or if you feel like giving up, it is probably inadequacy.
3. Watch the individual's response to correction. If he merely desired attention he will stop when it is obtained, but if he is power-seeking, controls will only bring more resistance.

Figure 4 (page 135) presents some of the typical feelings and reactions resultant from each goal. By using this classification, the problem of the school child is now in a more understandable and communicable form.

Modification

After identifying the child's purpose, we are ready to begin to correct the misbehavior. Some of the possible corrective measures are indicated in Figure 4. It must be remembered that this misbehavior did not develop instantly, and it will require consistent treatment to be modified. It is important to allow enough time for corrective measures to have an effect upon the child. Do not be alarmed if a sharp increase in the frequency of the behavior occurs initially, as this is typical in the extinction of behavior (Sulzer, Mayer and Cody 1968).

Record

This is the final step that determines what procedures are effective and what procedures are not. Keeping daily anecdotal records of the pupil's behavior helps to provide feedback as to whether or not the

GOAL OF MISBEHAVIOR	WHAT CHILD IS SAYING	HOW PARENT OR TEACHER FEELS	CHILD'S REACTION TO REPRIMAND	SOME CORRECTIVE MEASURES
ATTENTION	I only count when I am being noticed or served.	Annoyed Wants to remind, coax Delighted with "good" child	Temporarily stops disturbing action when given attention	Ignore Answer or do the unexpected Give attention at pleasant times
POWER	I only count when I am dominating, when you do what I want you to.	Provoked Generally wants power challenged, "I'll make him do it." "You can't get away with it."	Intensifies action when reprimanded Child wants to win, be boss	Extricate self Act, not talk Be friendly Establish equality Redirect child's stress into constructive channels
REVENGE	I can't be liked. I don't have power, but I'll count if I can hurt.	Hurt, mad, "How could he do this to me?"	Wants to get even Makes self disliked	Extricate self Win child Maintain order with minimum restraint Avoid retaliations Take time and effort to help child
INADEQUACY	I can't do anything right so I won't try to do anything at all; I am no good."	Despair "I give up."	No reprimand, therefore no reaction Feels there is no use to try Passive	Encouragement (may take long) Faith in child's ability

FIGURE 4. "CHILD'S MISTAKEN GOALS" BY MRS. PEARCY OF THE PARENT STUDY GROUPS, CORVALLIS, OREGON.

corrective measures are bringing about change. Another means of recording behavior is to mark down the frequency of the misbehavior on a daily basis and place the results on a graph. If no change has been evidenced after a reasonable period of time, a recycling process should begin. Perhaps the wrong goal of misbehavior is being treated.

In the case of Bill (previously mentioned), we can see the proposed methodology in simulation. In the first phase, data was gathered about Bill through observation (see anecdotes on pp. 130–131). Following the observation sequence, the consultant looks at the consequences of the interaction. He finds out how the teacher feels and what the child does in reaction to the teacher's behavior. In this case, the teacher was annoyed with his behavior, while Bill reacted to the teacher with a temporary cessation of his misbehavior after being reprimanded. From our superficial analysis of this hypothetical case, it appears as though Bill is striving for attention. Now that we have postulated the tentative goal of Bill's misbehavior, we must formulate some possible corrective procedures. In this case, we would suggest that the teacher ignore Bill when he misbehaves and give reinforcement in the form of attention during the more pleasant times when he is behaving in a desirable manner. We now need to try this new or unexpected approach and evaluate whether or not this technique is modifying Bill's behavior. If this technique does not prove to be successful after a reasonable period of time, there has been an incorrect appraisal of the goal and the process should be recycled and the phases of observation, consequences of behavior, identification, modification and record should be repeated.

IMPLICATIONS

The terminology and procedure presented here are both easy to understand and effective in improving the behavior of children. It is a method in which guidance workers, teachers, parents and others may be trained to deal with the problems they face in their relationships with children.

Through the utilization of this process, a more effective level of communication may be obtained among all who are concerned with helping children. Once it is understood, teachers and parents will be able to deal with many of the children that previously had to be sent to the counselor.

REFERENCES

Adler, A. *Understanding Human Nature.* New York: Fawcett Premier Books, 1957.

Allen, T. W. "Purpose is Alive and Well and Living in the Empty Organism." *The Counseling Psychologist* 1 (1969): 72–81.

Allen, T. W. "The Individual Psychology of Alfred Adler: An Item of History and a Promise of Revolution." *The Counseling Psychologist* 3 (1971): 3–24.

Ansbacher, H. L. and Ansbacher, R., eds. *The Individual Psychology of Alfred Adler.* New York: Harper & Row, 1967.

Arieti, S. *Interpretation of Schizophrenia.* New York: Robert Bruner, 1955.

Arieti, S. "The Possibility of Psychosomatic Involvement of the Central Nervous System in Schizophrenia." *Journal of Mental and Nervous Disorders* 123 (1956).

Bandura, A. *Principles of Behavioral Modification.* New York: Holt, Rinehart & Winston, 1969.

Bandura A. and Walters, R. H. *Social Learning and Personality Development.* New York: Holt, Rinehart & Winston, 1963.

Berne, E. *Games People Play.* New York: Grove Press, 1967.

Combs, A. W., Avila, A. L. and Purkey, W. W. *Helping Relationships: Basic Concepts for the Helping Professions.* Boston: Allyn & Bacon, 1971.

Combs, A. W., Soper, D. W., Gooding, C. T., Benton, J. A. Dickman, J. F. and Usher, R. H. *Florida Studies in the Helping Professions.* Gainesville: University of Florida Press, 1969.

Combs, A. and Snygg, D. *Individual Behavior.* New York: Harper & Row, 1959.

Dinkmeyer, D. C. *Child Development: The Emerging Self.* Englewood Cliffs, New Jersey: Prentice-Hall, 1965.

Dinkmeyer, D. C. "Contributions of Teleoanalytic Theory and Techniques to School Counseling." *Personnel and Guidance Journal* 9 (1968): 898–902.

Dinkmeyer, D. C. and Caldwell, E. *Developmental Counseling and Guidance: A Comprehensive School Approach.* New York: McGraw-Hill 1970.

Dreikurs, R. *Fundamentals of Adlerian Psychology.* New York: Greenberg, 1950.

Dreikurs, R. *Psychology in the Classroom.* New York: Harper & Row, 1968.

Dreikurs, R. and Grey, L. *Logical Consequences.* New York: Meredith, 1968.

Festinger, L. A. *A Theory of Cognitive Dissonance.* Evanston, Illinois: Row, Peterson, 1957.

Frank, J. D. *Persuasion and Healing.* Baltimore: Johns Hopkins, 1961.

Frankl, V. *Man's Search for Meaning.* New York: Washington Square Press, 1963.

Galantier, E., Miller, G. and Pibram, K. *The Structure of Behavior.* New York: Holt, Rinehart & Winston, 1960.

Grubbe, T. E. "Adlerian Psychology as a Basic Framework for Elementary Counseling Services." *Elementary School Guidance and Counseling* 3 (1968): 20–26.

Hansen, J. "A Behavioral Approach to Elementary School Guidance." In *Elementary School Counseling: A Composite View,* edited by W. H. Van Hoose, J. J. Pietrofesa and J. Carlson. Boston: Houghton Mifflin, 1973.

Hillman, B. "The Elementary School Counseling Process: An Adlerian Model." *Elementary School Guidance and Counseling* 2 (1967): 102–113.

Homme, L. E. "Use of the Premack Principle in Controlling the Behavior of Nursery School Children." *Journal of the Experimental Analysis of Behavior* 6 (1963): 544.

Hosford, R. E. "Behavioral Counseling—A Contemporary Overview." *The Counseling Psychologist* 1 (1969): 1–33.

Kelley, E. C. *Education for What is Real.* New York: Harper & Row, 1947.

Kelly, G. *The Psychology of Personal Constucts. Vol. I. A Theory of Personality. Vol. II. Clinical, Diagnosis and Psychotherapy.* New York: Norton, 1955.

Kennedy, D. "Use of Learning Theory in Guidance and Consultation." *Elementary School Guidance and Counseling* 4 (1968): 49–56.

Kennedy, D. A. and Seidman, S. B. *Contingency Management and Human Relations Workshops: A School Intervention Program.* Unpublished manuscript, Broward County (Florida) Board of Public Instruction, 1971.

Krumboltz, J. D. *Revolution in Counseling: Implications for the Behavioral Sciences.* Boston: Houghton Mifflin, 1966.

Krumboltz, J. D. and Hosford, R. E. "Behavioral Counseling in the Elementary School." *Elementary School Guidance and Counseling* 1 (1967): 27–40.

Krumboltz, J. D. and Thoresen, C. E., eds. *Behavioral Counseling: Cases and Techniques.* New York: Holt, Rinehart & Winston, 1969.

Mayer, G. R. and Benoit, R. Contingency Analysis Chart. Los Angeles: California State College, 1972. (mimeo.)

Maslow, A. *Motivation and Personality.* 2nd ed. New York: Harper & Row, 1970.

McGehearty, L. "The Case for Consultation." *Personnel and Guidance Journal* 47 (1968): 247–262.

Parke, R. D., ed. *Readings in Social Development.* New York: Holt, Rinehart, & Winston, 1969.

Reese, E. P. *The Analysis of Human Operant Behavior.* Dubuque, Iowa: William C. Brown, 1966.

Rogers, C. *Client-Centered Therapy.* Boston: Houghton Mifflin, 1951.

Rotter, J. "Generalized Expectancies for Internal Versus External Control of Reinforcement." *Psychological Monographs* 80 (1966): 1–28.

Sinnott, E. *Cell and Psyche: The Biology of Purpose.* New York: Harper & Row, 1961.

Skinner, B. F. *Contingencies of Reinforcement.* New York: Appleton-Century-Crofts, 1969.

Sulzer, B., Mayer, G. R. and Cody, J. J. "Assisting Teachers with Managing Classroom Behavioral Problems." *Elementary School Guidance and Counseling* 3 (1968): 40–48.

Sulzer, B. and Mayer, G. R. *Behavior Modification Procedures for School Personnel.* Hinsdale, Illinois: Dryden Press, 1972.

6

Consultation Processes

We have depicted the current situation and the faulty assumptions about children and learning which limit the development of human potential. We have also presented a theory of learning and human behavior. However, it will be of little value to have a philosophy, a theory of learning and human behavior, and fail to be systematically organized to achieve one's purposes.

It is apparent from reading educational literature that there have been a number of authors who have spotted the critical lack of humaneness in the educational process. However, despite their theorizing and pleading, little change appears to have occurred.

CAN HUMANENESS BE DEVELOPED IN A
DEHUMANIZED SYSTEM?

It appears that the central problem in reorganizing schools to value persons before knowledge and value individuals as much as systems involves recognition of how dehumanized the educational system has become. We can document this dehumanization in many areas. The communication between administrative and supervisory levels and teaching staff is often reduced to the level of formalized memos. There is an increasing tendency to minimize informal, personalized contact between administration and staff. This is often illustrated by contacts between school boards, those who set policies for the institutions and staff. Board members often think of the staff in terms of statistics, the number of positions, and a specified amount of salary. But they have not had an opportunity to become personally acquainted with what the staff may have to offer as persons.

The development of formal reporting methods, and in some instances an increasing tendency towards departmentalization and team teaching, unfortunately has often developed into a reduced amount of parent-teacher contacts.

In some systems the teacher-child contact has also become less personal. Some schools, by departmentalizing at an early stage, bring the child into contact with a large number of teachers and hence reduce the possibility of him becoming identified as a person. The teacher does not know the student in terms of his uniqueness. This occasionally is observed in the data-processing approach which tends to deal with all individuals on the basis of numbers and statistics. It is our premise that education must be based on a belief in the dignity of all persons, and that if we develop a system that is basically dehumanized from the top to the bottom, neither the teacher, the parent, nor the child will have available a model which encourages them to function on a more personalized basis.

It would appear that we must clearly determine what it is we value and then implement programs which translate this into performance objectives that facilitate our priorities and values. If we value grades, authoritarianism, and content, we may desire a different system than if we value responsibility, independence, involvement, democratic participation, and an open and positive attitude towards learning. One of the goals of this book is to provide each child with a teacher who is concerned and interested in facilitating the human potential of every child. As a result of this concern, the teacher seeks to both understand and treat the child as an individual. The teacher organizes the classroom group to facilitate the development of both the individual and the total group. Anything less than this type of commitment on the part of the teacher results in a dehumanized system. It is our contention that humaneness has little chance of being developed in a system that is basically dehumanized. The teacher has little opportunity to be involved and concerned with the individualities of all of the children when he works in a system that provides no model which understands and empathizes with his own individuality and human needs.

FACTORS WHICH BLOCK HUMANENESS

There are a number of basic organizational factors in the school which really work to impede humane development. They exist in some of the following common problems.

Goals

There is a lack of mutually determined and aligned goals. The pretentious and inclusive goals set forth in many school handbooks are often remote from the yearly or daily plans of the teachers. The paper objectives bear little resemblance to actual classroom activity. Until teachers feel that they are taken into consideration in the planning for educational experiences of children, institutional goals will remain nothing more than paper objectives. Each teacher should be treated with the same respect that we would expect for ourselves. Then, as a professional, the teacher becomes engaged in the process of studying curriculum, the child, and the best methods for administering and organizing the educational experience. This approach would be considerably different from the current tendency to make changes that are closely aligned to educational innovation and fads, but have little to do with developing more effective, purposeful, and humane individuals.

Evaluation

Our current procedure for evaluating the child and the school's success looms as a major stumbling block. It too often focuses on development of the cognitive domain and functions as if educational objectives could be assessed solely through current achievement tests. It appears as though we really believe that if a child is reading, spelling, and doing arithmetic at a given level, he is truly an effective functioning human being. We must do something which ties together in a meaningful manner our educational philosophy, objectives, and methods of evaluation and measurement.

Administration

There must be a reexamination of the position of the school administrator and school principal. In many instances this role is not well defined. Although the administrator should serve as an educational leader who inspires greater productivity from staff and students, too often he is placed in the position of an "administrator of minutia," a "superclerk," or a disciplinarian. If schools are to become humanized and be administered effectively, we must develop school administrators who can inspire, lead, understand, and utilize group dynamics.

There also must be an increased emphasis on involving teachers in the planning of educational programs. If we want to develop professionals who are primarily concerned with their clientele (the students), then we must involve them continuously and in every stage of the planning process.

THE HUMANE TEACHER

It is our opinion that the humane teacher is one who is able to accept each child as he is, value him for his idiosyncrasy, relate to him as a unique human, and stimulate his creativity and spontaneity. The teacher can only be this humane if he accepts his own uniqueness and feels valued by staff and administration as a unique person. Unless teachers are free they will feel hindered in creating a humane climate. However, realistically, this often is exactly the opposite of what some supervisors and curriculum directors appear to communicate. Many curriculum guides and supervisory practices appear to focus on the development of automats in contrast to creative, spontaneous teachers who serve as facilitators and catalysts for the educational process.

If we honestly believe in the importance of placing each child in contact with a teacher who values his humaneness, then we must be much more selective in our current teacher education program. We should place more emphasis on the type of person coming out of the teacher education program and less emphasis on the kinds of courses which he has taken. This would also suggest the need for a continued emphasis on in-service education, institute days, and faculty-staff seminars which are designed to provide experiences to increase self-understanding and the human potential of the teacher.

The teacher must perceive and accept his own individuality first and must feel his uniqueness is valued by the school. Without this awareness there is the tendency for carbon-copy teachers to produce carbon-copy students. This would contrast with the current emphasis upon presentation in the content areas without attempting to involve the feelings and motives of the teachers. A close inspection of the data compiled by Combs in his study (1969) points to the importance of humanizing the teacher. The in-service process would focus on a continual upgrading of the humaneness and the personal awareness of the teacher.

One of our problems is that frequently our educational systems have been closed, in contrast to open, systems. By closed we mean systems that have emphasized the learning of facts, the following of directions, and the acquiring of the "one correct answer," which obviously has suppressed personal creativity and spontaneity on the part of both staff and children. We have not valued inquiry, discovery, independence, democratic problem solving, and human relations.

One wonders what has kept the schools from initiating more flexible, dynamic, humane programs. This is probably summarized most adequately by noting the values and expectations of the educational community, parents, and the general public. The experience of most adults with the schools unfortunately has been less than inspiring and stimulating. They have expected school to be a place where one is controlled, forced to learn, and expected to suppress his personal feelings and attitudes. As a result, they neither comprehend nor see much value in a different kind of educational process.

In some instances progress also has been hampered by the hostile attitude a lot of school staffs have toward people who have different values and attitudes. We talk of those who are from a different cultural background as "those people" and "they." We are impatient with their children and their lack of achievement. In some instances teachers even may be puzzled, frustrated, and annoyed with the gifted student who challenges their routines and rote type of lesson plan.

PLANNED ORGANIZATIONAL CHANGE

In order to change the educational system, one must have clearly in mind the imperative necessity of a humane school system. Once one has grasped the critical nature of humanizing and pluralizing our society, then the motivation for reorganization is present. This type of reorganization cannot occur haphazardly. It cannot come about by authoritative, autocratic orders. One does not develop a humane system by fiat or executive order. Those who would develop and implement the plans for organizational change must be models of humaneness. In some instances they will be in contact with people who disagree with their goals and aims for the school. A democratic change process suggests that all people must be heard and that their thinking must be considered in the general planning for the schools. The change agent will not be trapped into attempting to humanize the schools by authoritarian threats, pressure, and failure to communicate effectively—he is aware that his methods and message must be congruent.

If one earnestly seeks to bring about organizational change, he will consider four basic steps:

1. There must be an analysis of the total situation to determine the current relationship between all concerned—administration, staff, teachers, parents, and students. This analysis must be approached on a democratic basis, which means that those who serve as leaders must be less concerned with their personal status and prestige, and more concerned with the end product—a humane society. They cannot be caught in personal "hangups" about their own superiority or inferiority, their position and status. In contrast, all dealings within the organization must be done on the basis of complete and total equality. One cannot bring about humaneness unless there is mutual respect and trust. The concern and involvement of those who would provide leadership must be such that their desire to work together for the development of a more functional education is more important than self interest. This step basically involves developing a collaborative relationship characterized by mutual respect, mutual trust, and goal alignment.

2. The second step involves analysis of the problems that are keeping the schools from functioning effectively. This is not done by an outside set of experts, by a special committee, or by any other group. It becomes both the right and responsibility of all concerned—administration, supervisors, staff, parents, and teachers—to become involved in identifying the problems and establishing the priorities and hierarchies of problems. This must be accomplished on an equalitarian basis. One cannot ask for staff participation and then treat it in a perfunctory manner. However, when the staff becomes involved in pinpointing the real issues, one immediately gains an added benefit. Due to their participation they will take on a greater responsibility and involvement for bringing change.

3. To bring out organizational change necessitates that each person take on personal responsibility for bringing about this change. This involves being willing to change personal attitudes, values, and goals. We must be both willing and capable of looking at ourselves and the situation. It implies being fully aware of our personal biases and private logic.

4. The system works most effectively when all have equal rights and responsibilities for participating in decision making. This suggests that all will share in the decisions and in the rights and responsibilities which evolve from these decisions.

The humanized school system will have educational goals that can be described in specific terms and observed in the behavior, attitudes, and performances of the staff and students. This system also must have developed a process for interaction on an equal basis among all concerned. The organization must provide a procedure for processing communication which has both formal (committee) and informal (direct access to leaders) opportunities. No organization can be altered and humanized unless there is a systematic procedure for feedback. The goal in this type of organization is to increase the interaction within the work groups. It is also important to increase the interpersonal attractiveness of the group's interaction. The groups are selected carefully to produce maximum growth for the staff and the children. This opportunity to clarify their opinions on relevant issues increases the possibility of cohesiveness and real conformity and the acceptance of group norms and group expectations.

GROUP INFLUENCES AND FORCES

Those responsible for bringing about a change in the system always must consider the influential forces that exist within a group. Without an understanding of group forces, one cannot function effectively as a consultant. While it is apparent that autocratic leadership, on the surface at least, tends to produce more extensive quantitative results, it has been demonstrated that democratic group-centered leadership always produces better morale and qualitative results. This system is concerned with the quality of human relationships.

One of the most critical factors to consider is the factor of cohesiveness. Cohesiveness, for our purposes, is defined as the degree to which members of the group desire to remain in the group. When a group is cohesive, this factor contributes to the group's potency and vitality.

It is also important to recognize the value of a goal for the group. If the group has a distinctive goal or purpose, this usually serves to attract to the group people who share that unique motive. However, when the goals are nonspecific, it discourages those who are goal oriented. Thus, as a group becomes more cohesive, it has been demonstrated that the members will tend to conform more to the norms of the group. The greater the cohesiveness of a group, the greater the power of that group to influence its members. One of the basic requisites of a group leader is the skill to develop this most necessary group cohesiveness.

One must understand the complex process of motivation in groups. It is quite clear that members who are acceptant of group goals are more likely to cooperate in the attainment of objectives. However, when the individual does not clearly perceive the group goal or does not agree with it, he will more often function on the basis of his own personal references. Thus, to elicit change in a group, group members must be made aware of the purposes and must accept some responsibility for helping to bring about a change. Change is accomplished most effectively through utilizing group procedures. It is important to have available leaders to plan and organize the development of groups. The groups are developed from persons who are concerned and have a commitment to consider change. The groups should be heterogeneous so they represent a variety of opinion. When organizational training procedures are used, one will typically work with the presently organized groups.

IMPROVING GROUP LEADERSHIP

It has been demonstrated that if one is to train effective group leaders, he cannot be trained in the abstract by studying about groups. The improvement of leadership is most effectively developed not by improving leaders apart from their groups, but by modifying the relationships that exist between the leaders and their ongoing groups. An effective leader is one who is sensitive to group movement, the conditions that exist in the group, and can adapt to the changing psychological movement of the group. Our target is to help teachers to understand themselves through the group experience while becoming aware of the implications of group procedures for their classroom. By working with the staff's established groups, one can also improve relationships among the staff.

Perhaps the most crucial factor in group leadership is the personality of the leaders. Effective leaders cannot be developed simply by exposure to course work and lectures. While these experiences have value, participation in personal growth experiences is necessary to maximize human potential.

The effective group leader will be able to perform some of the following functions:

1. Structure the group so purposes and focus are apparent.
2. Promote cohesiveness, collaboration, and togetherness.
3. Be sensitive to affect, feelings that are stated, implied, or left unsaid.
4. Be able to perceive psychological movement and the meaning of transactions between the members.

5. Promote interaction among members of the group.
6. Help the group to focus on the "here and now" as well as the "there and then."
7. Help the members to resolve their conflicts, clarify issues, and provide the development of alternative action.
8. Link the attitudes, ideas, and feelings of members so they recognize the universal nature of their problems.
9. Provide support and be patient, so quiet members can participate verbally as well as through listening to others.
10. Enable teachers to make a commitment to action.
11. Summarize.

CONSULTATION PROCESSES

Development

The consultant must establish a procedure for communication between himself and the potential consultees in the institution. Without the proper channels for communication, there will be little opportunity to fully utilize the consultant techniques. The readiness phase, then, cannot be handled in a perfunctory manner but must be systematically developed in order to produce maximum gain for consultees and the clients. The consultee must experience a need for the help. The consultant must clearly think through the communication procedures, the human relationships, and the organizational structure, all basic to the delivery of his service—consultation.

The consultant must be aware of the total field of forces which exist in an institution. His cognizance of the role expectation that consultees and clients have for him and its dissonance from the role which he anticipates taking are important factors in the development of the consultant function. Institutions often have predetermined roles and images that they place upon their consultants. While originally he may have to meet their faulty expectations of him and become involved primarily in crisis-oriented remediation or the handling of didactic lectures, he must not lose sight of his eventual goal—the development of a complete consultation service.

In the beginning stages of consulting the members of the consulting institution who come to him are often representative of the total institution. In many instances they represent new staff members, inexperienced personnel, and occasionally, minority cliques who are dissatisfied with the general organization of the institution. Thus, while he must provide services to those who contact him, he must also be careful to not become identified solely as someone who services the inexperienced or dissident elements in the staff. If he is to build a strong consulting service, he cannot be classified as primarily peripheral. He must become involved with those who influence the decision-making processes in the institution.

New problems are always assessed in terms of their meaning for the particular consultee institution. The consultant should be able to readily identify environmental pressures that exist within the institution and clarify the pattern of problems which appear in this setting. This awareness enables him to see that a client problem presented by a consultee is often only symptomatic of a social system problem. The consultant should clarify the image that he holds in the eyes of the consultee. In many instances he is perceived as a specialist, a significant resource person for assisting individuals, or some type of a psychological examiner. He often is not seen as a vital part of a total educational team. Although he may provide diagnostic and therapeutic services, he must keep in mind long-range goals and the roles which will be most productive in a particular system.

The consultant will know that he has prepared the group for consultation effectively when teachers begin coming to him as a professional colleague and a collaborator in the central educational process. He must dispel any idea they have of him as an authority, one with special privileges and, perhaps, as only peripherally interested in the educational process. This is accomplished by refusing to become involved in supplying solutions. The only effective answers to educational problems are those developed in consultation with the consultee. Diagnosis and treatment must be fitted to the idiosyncrasies of the setting and to the teacher as well as the student. This cannot be accomplished by a written report which does not have the benefit of open communication between consultant and consultee.

The relationship of the consultant and the consultee should be similar to that of the counseling relationship, insofar as mutual trust and mutual respect are essential.

> In observing counselors at work, one fallacy becomes apparent. Even well-educated counselors tend to counsel students but advise parents or teachers. They attempt a collaborative relationship with students and an instructive role with teachers. When counselors try to work on problems with teachers, they often find themselves giving quick pseudo-expert opinions or vague generalizations (Dinkmeyer 1967, p. 295).

In contrast, the counselor must listen, be emphatic, and develop the necessary collaborative relationship. He cannot forget all the basic techniques necessary for formulating the helping relationship.

Principles and Procedures

Consultation should be by direct contact with the consultant and not through an intermediary. Indirect access to the consultant, which necessitates going through an administrator or filling out forms, tends to destroy immediate accessibility. It is fundamental that the consultant be available as close to the time of the problem as possible and that he and the administration avoid constructing any unnecessary barriers. His relationship with the principal should be made clear since some administrators may be concerned about outsiders learning about the ineffectiveness of the staff. The consultant should work to see that there is no feeling that he is there to "check the dirty linen," nor should he do anything which fosters a feeling of rivalry between him and central administration regarding expertise in human relationships.

By noting the arrangements which are made for the reception and development of his work, the consultant will be able to see the anticipations and expectations of both administration and staff. There is an advantage in allowing consultation to be planned by administration in order to understand the image administration holds of consultation. However, it is important to participate at an early date in the arrangments for the introduction of the consultant service. One can note the assumptions that are made about consulting during the planning phase, but it is essential to see to it that misunderstandings about role and image are not projected to the total staff.

It is our belief that the consultant process is subject to all of the basic principles involved in the necessary and sufficient conditions for a helping relationship (Carkhuff 1969).

The relationship in the consultation process always involves three persons: the consultant, the consultee (the one asking for help), and that consultee's client. The original contacts with the consultee will make it clear that the consultant's attitude is nonevaluative and that he has no administrative responsibilities. The consultant is not there to judge the teacher's effectiveness nor to make decisions regarding the kinds of problems he chooses to discuss. He has no standards to enforce, and his major role is to develop a relationship which facilitates the human potential of both the consultee and the client. He should originally accept the consultee and the institution on a nonevaluative basis. His job is not to become involved in teacher complaints about other staff members or central administration, nor is he to enter into any administrative wrangles or power politics. He is there to establish channels of communication based upon a need perceived by the consultee. The consultee, therefore, originally decides which problems are to be discussed.

The consultant is aware that the anxiety the consultee brings to the relationship sometimes serves as a motivating force, since it is a crisis or special need that brings the consultant and consultee together. The consultant avoids the use of ineffectual procedures such as reassurance or simple statements such as: "This is something we can solve easily." "I think I can give you that answer right now." Instead, he works for joint examination and clarification of the problem. The first session is involved in this type of investigative effort and at the conclusion of the session specific arrangements are made for a second meeting. Obtaining a commitment to a second meeting establishes a commitment and involvement on the part of the consultant and consultee. The second meeting enables the consultant and consultee to develop recommendations and check on the effectiveness of procedures agreed upon during the first meeting. The consulting relationship is enhanced by being available and accessible and by attempting to respond to requests promptly.

The consultant is an aid to the consultee by helping to dissipate stereotypes and set images that consultees have about the client. The consultant helps the consultee to drop his educational jargon, i.e., the use of psychological terminology or presentation of general recommendations. In contrast he collaborates with the consultee to fit recommendations to the uniqueness of both client and consultee.

Effective consultation occurs when certain types of cases are not referred again by a specific consultee. This indicates the consultee has learned and does not need help on this type of problem. When the consultant continues to get referrals of the same type from the same consultee, he knows that he has created dependency and is certainly not involved in helping facilitate the professional growth of the consultee. The goal is to develop human relationship skills in the consultee which are permanent. The consultee may seek help relating to new problems or different facets of a problem, but permanent learning should take place. For example, if one learns to stop reinforcing bids for attention for behavior that is not desirable and, instead, attends to active-constructive behavior with one child, he hopefully can generalize this procedure to other children.

COMMUNICATION IN CONSULTATION

The consultant is not only a specialist in human relationships but also in communication. He is aware that the messages which he sends and those that are sent by consultees and clients are always multi-faceted messages—they include words and affect or feeling. As an active and skilled listener, the consultant must hear both the words and the feelings in order to get the message from the consultee. He eventually helps the teacher to become a more effective listener by hearing the total message of the client. We must become aware that some messages are incongruent, i.e., the words are different from the feeling. For example, there are a variety of ways of saying "I am happy" or "I am angry" to make feelings incongruent with the words. One must note tone of voice, facial expression, and other nonverbal clues.

In his consultation work, the consultant is aware of various methods of dealing with stress. Virginia Satir has developed a format for analyzing the difference between manipulative and actualization response forms. The consultant's goal is to develop responses where the communication is characterized by hearing, listening, understanding, and mutual meaning.

The types of responses include:

1. *Placating:* response used by a person who always keeps himself safe. He attempts to placate or be the martyr. He crosses himself out as important and is willing to agree with anything the other person offers.

2. *Blaming:* response used by the person who is aggressive. He is suspicious that others take advantage of him and essentially believes only he is important. Others don't count, so he crosses them out. This has been classified as "the boss" response.

3. *Conniving and Reasonable:* response used by communicators who put an emphasis on being correct and in not letting anyone know their weaknesses. They speak as if they were computers and have no feelings.

4. *Avoiding and Irrelevant:* response used by the person who essentially talks as if he has no relationship to persons, almost as if he were "psychotic." He seems to be saying, "I am not here and you are not here." There is no attempt to communicate.

5. *Congruent:* response equaling real communication in which the affect and words are congruent. A person who makes a five-level response creates a relationship which is real and safe. The goal for consultees and clients is to reach this level of responding (Satir 1967).

Verbal messages in the classroom too often are destructive and do not facilitate growth. Communication is at times ineffective because we send ineffectual messages. Examples of these ineffective messages include procedures such as:

1. Ordering and commanding
2. Warning and admonishing

3. Exhorting and moralizing
4. Advising and providing solutions
5. Lecturing
6. Judging and criticizing
7. Praising and agreeing
8. Name calling and ridiculing
9. Interpreting and analyzing
10. Reassuring and sympathizing
11. Probing, questioning, and interrogating
12. Withdrawing, humoring, and diverting

Many of these types of responses between the consultant and the consultee are the type which will bring about ineffective communication. Because the consultant wants to develop congruent communication, he is alert to any ineffectual communication with the consultee. He also helps the consultee to become aware of how this ineffectual pattern of communication will affect his interaction with children.

CONSULTANT LEADS AND VERBAL TRANSACTIONS

Consultation in the past has been limited in its effectiveness. Too often the verbal communication and the nonverbal messages restricted open communication. The consultant's limited conception of his role placed him in the position of "Answer Man," and the staff accepted the image and therefore presented him with their problems. The process must be a collaborative one with total involvement of the consultee for the productive hypotheses to be generated and workable corrective procedures to be established.

Effective consulting is always tailored to the uniqueness of both the client and the consultee. This uniqueness can only be understood by establishing communication that is open and which deals with all of the messages, especially the feelings and personal meanings in the content which are often not understood in ordinary social conversations or communications between professionals.

These procedures must go beyond telling, lecturing, advising, and sharing "pedagogics." In contrast, one must establish an atmosphere which encourages sharing and exploring ideas. The communication includes messages which are positive and negative, and content and feeling oriented. Effective consulting engages the cognitive, affective, and actional domains. It seeks to examine and share ideas, openly exploring the feelings of all concerned, and to move toward commitments to action.

The relationship operates on the premise that emotional communication is two-way, insofar as it elicits feedback and processes the feedback continuously to clarify the messages that are being sent and their meanings.

The essence of consultation is communication. The consultant must be able to understand the messages being sent and be sensitive to the relationship with the consultee. This necessitates being aware of one's verbal and nonverbal communication and the impressions that are being developed in the transactions with staff.

During the educational process, the consultant should be involved in experiences which help him to understand how he is perceived by others. On the job it will continue to be important to establish the type of communication which processes this type of feedback.

A consultant lead is the initiation of a transaction or the response to the consultee. It involves the messages which the consultant sends which influence the responses of the consultee. Consultant leads may focus on:

1. Techniques which focus on content:

   Summarizing what has been explicitly stated

   Encouraging continuation, as "Tell me more about . . ."

   Verifying beliefs, as "You seem to believe . . ."

   Asking questions that systematically explore the transactions with the client, as:

   What did you do? What did the child do?

   How did he respond? How did you respond?

   How did you feel?

   What did you do about his response?

   What was the child's reaction to your response?

2. Techniques which elicit affect and encourage expression of feeling: (These facilitate the consultee becoming aware of his own feeling life and enable the consultant to express his comprehension of feelings and empathy. Eliciting affect gets the whole person involved in the consultation.)

   Restatement of feeling

   Reflection of feeling

   Silence

3. Techniques designed to facilitate self-understanding, awareness of one's own part in the transactions:

Clarification, as "You believe . . ."

Restatement of content

Restatement of content and its hidden message

Questions which enable the consultee to see the psychological movement in transactions with the client.

4. Techniques designed to analyze the purpose and dynamics of behavior to develop insight:

Confrontation

Tentative hypothesis

Exploration of feelings during client's actions

Definition and analysis of purpose

5. Techniques designed to facilitate new responses, procedures for improving the consultee-client relationship, and methods for modifying behavior:

Encouragement

Development of choices

Enlargment of consultee's view and presentation of alternatives

Establishment of goals

Establishment of procedures

Formulation of change strategies

Obviously the utilization of these leads must be accomplished with appropriate timing and sensitivity to the human relations involved. As Combs has indicated, the techniques must be integrated into the personality (Combs, Avila and Purkey 1971).

The leads which are utilized are a function of the personality and theoretical bias of the consultant. They cannot be used mechanically, as they are only effective when transcribed in a climate where threat and fear are minimized and the relationship is not perceived to be judgmental. The evaluation and diagnosis are always done collaboratively. The consultant cannot prescribe for the consultee, and even if he could, prescription without feedback and acceptance is nonefficacious. The written reports filed in most large pupil personnel psychologists' and administrators' files are testimony to the intellectual exercise performed in this one-way communication.

In contrast, goals are mutually aligned, and the consultee participates in terms of his perceptions, beliefs, values, and attitudes which
influence his assumptions about students and the educational process.
When the consultee comes, he listens closely since his leads will influence his relationship with the consultant, the probabilities of a
collaborative diagnosis and treatment, and the images, anticipation,
expectation, and roles that are assigned to the consultant. Thus, the
early transactions are crucial. They must create a climate, establish
communication, and set a pattern or model for ensuing contacts, while
at the same time, provide some help in understanding and dealing with
the current concern.

Consultants may err in terms of being highly directive, developing
ready answers or instant, pat solutions, e.g., "Give him more love,"
"Individualize the instruction," "Reinforce his good behavior." None
of these "solutions" are necessarily bad, but they must be designed to
fit the idiosyncratic assets and liabilities involved in the transactions
between consultant and consultee. In some instances such pat answers
cause the consultee to consider the consultant's idea as superficial.

It is important to recognize that the more active leads, such as dis-
closure, confrontation, and tentative hypotheses, may provoke resistance. When the consultant is involved in sharing his perceptions,
which come from an external frame of reference, he must be aware
that they may be perceived as judgments or authoritarian statements
and, therefore, occasionally will build resistance and eliminate any
possibility of a collaborative relationship. However, active leads do not
necessarily inhibit the consultation process if they are aligned with the
consultee's personal meaning.

Carkhuff and Berenson (1967) indicate that confrontation can serve
as a vehicle to bring the client in direct touch with his own experience
in order to allow him to move from a passive-reactive stance towards
an existence rooted in action and meaningful confrontation. Honest
confrontation can elicit constructive therapeutic process, movement,
and ultimately constructive gain or change. These power factors in
consultation, which elicit dissonance, help the consultee to become
aware of the lack of harmony among his goals, philosophy, and actions
or practises.

The diagnosis actually is facilitated by collaborative exploration of the
current life situation, the perceptions of both client and consultee, and
open and honest feedback about any and all impressions which are
generated. This phase of diagnosis is unique in its emphasis on searching for assets and strengths in the consultee and the client. The consultant must recognize that while the less active leads have less
potential for harm, they also have greater potential for being circular,

impotent, and unable to move the consultee towards awareness and new procedures.

KINDS AND TYPES OF CONSULTATION

For our purposes, we will consider consultation to be divided into that which is: 1) Consultee initiated, or 2) Other initiated, meaning initiated by someone other than the consultee.

Consultee-Initiated Consultation

Consultee-initiated contacts begin with a self-referral by the consultee. He obviously is motivated and has a felt need for assistance. This assistance focuses on external factors, and he may need help only with a type of information or some instruction regarding a procedure. In any instance, the consultee is helped with the concern that he brings to consultation.

Another type of consultee-initiated work deals more with the internal factors, or the feelings of the consultee which may be interfering with progress. This type of consultation develops as the relationship progresses and the consultee feels more comfortable with the consultant. It is increasingly apparent that one needs to consider these factors if consultation is to go beyond the superficial.

A third level we have titled the "C" approach, which is holistic and always involves consideration of both the external (client) and internal (consultee) factors. The beliefs, feelings, and actions of both the client and the consultee must be understood in order to ascertain the purpose and meaning of behavior. This kind of consulting is best done when the consultant is well accepted in the system.

Other-Initiated Consultation

Other-initiated consulting usually develops at the request of the administration of the institution. This type of consulting provides additional problems since one may be dealing with the resistance of the teacher. Many feel that this type of work is impossible because of the lack of a cooperative relationship. While it is more rewarding to work with a self-referred consultee, consultants must face the reality that at times administration and the institutions will want them to work with teachers who are not "ready" for consultation. This type of consulting requires that the consultant be available to help with whatever anxieties and needs are currently expressed by the consultee. Beginning with any current concern or attitude and working with that may be a bridge to getting into problems the consultee originally was not ready to discuss. Other-initiated consulting may also develop into the more holistic "C" approach, depending upon the consultee's needs.

This model differs from that presented by Munson (1970) in which, by utilizing the excellent work of Kaplan (1959), he suggests that the counselor can serve as both counselor and consultant. This is also differentiated from the position Faust has taken (1968).

Munson's consulting model talks about three levels:

1. First-level consulting relationships with teachers are usually teacher initiated and are concerned with needs that are external in nature. The consultant stays in the role of dealing with the external requests.

2. Second-level consulting relationships go beyond the safe and nonthreatening "to develop more personally significant relationships and enable teachers to feel capable of moving in areas where they are less secure" (Munson 1970, p. 124). Munson feels that it is only at this level that the more innovative practices may be encouraged.

3. Third-level consulting relationships are similar to the counseling relationship. They come after a long series of interviews and are both planned and designed to increase self-understanding on the part of the consultee.

We agree with Munson in suggesting that the consultant will not engage in psychotherapy, but that he should be available to work with the consultee's beliefs, feelings, and attitudes that are related to the educational process.

Faust refers to consulting as having a focus that is mostly external to the self of the consultee. While in counseling the central focus of the relationship is on the counselee, in his definition of consulting Faust does not see it containing the necessary factors that are part of the counseling relationship. He suggests this is why consultation, as it has been practised, has produced so little change in the schools. He advocates the counseling process for teachers as having the greatest potential for creating climates for learning (Faust 1971).

Our "C" group process combines the counseling and consulting functions. This holistic or "C" group approach may only occur with highly trained and skilled consultants, and even then, it won't be possible to facilitate a humane climate for learning unless the consultant is able to get to this level with a large number of the staff.

STRATEGIES IN CONSULTATION

The consultant is careful not to utilize reassurance or deal in incongruent, dishonest communication. He must serve as a model for the type of communication he wants to promote within the total institution. This involves developing the kinds of relationships which allow him to be accepted by a variety of staff members. It also highlights the importance of timing and being accessible at strategic moments to provide maximum assistance.

The consultant helps consultees to see psychological movement as it exists in the client, the consultee, and the institution. He creates awareness of the purposive nature of behavior and the meaning of transactions between persons. He enables the consultee eventually to become aware that his feelings about and responses to misbehavior can be used to identify the purpose of the behavior. By developing increased awareness of self and others, the consultant seeks to communicate and to translate human relationship principles so they become part of the consultee's style of life.

The meaning of the client's problem is always understood in terms of the total emotional, social life of the consultee's institution. The consultant must be aware of reasons for underlying attitudes and understand the factors that stimulate various environmental pressures.

The consultant must be sensitive to his own feelings as a part of a total field of forces. When he is feeling anxious he ascertains what it is that is anxiety provoking. He notes in the communication how the consultee has certain expectations and roles that he ascribes to people, including the consultant. He becomes aware of the faulty assumptions which interfere with effective consultee-client communication. However, his attitude is one of acceptance and nonevaluation as he searches for strengths and positive qualities existing in the consultee. These assets must be sincerely encouraged and valued.

The consultant eventually serves as an ego-ideal figure and a model for human relationships. His open, honest relationships with the consultee teach more than mere talk about the importance of this type of relationship with students. His attitude towards the consultee and the client provides a goal for the consultee-client relationship. This obviously only can be accomplished as he dissipates the stereotypic image that the consultee assigns to him. He focuses on the client's and consultee's strengths in the situation rather than their weaknesses. The consultant process originally is focused on the interpersonal relationship between the consultee and his client and on the client's difficulties. Consulting moves from the external to the internal frame of reference insofar as the consultee indicates a need, interest, and willingness. However, it is always clear that the client is the responsibility of the consultee, and that the consultant will not make decisions for the consultee.

PROCEDURES

1. The relationship is collaborative, not that of a "superior" supplying techniques to a consultee who is inadequately trained. Emphasis is placed on reducing psychological distance between consultant and consultee and avoiding stereotypes. They deal with each other as humans who have problems in human relationships and in improving professional skills.

2. The diagnostic and assessment phase involves total collaboration between consultant and consultee to develop tentative hypotheses and mutually acceptable courses of action. The diagnostic phase involves full utilization of consultant and consultee observations and perceptions. It involves looking at the client's situation, the consultee's responses, and the meaning of the transactions between the consultee and client. It is concerned with helping the consultee to make better use of his education and personal resources by heightening his awareness of ways to change the relationship or modify the client's behavior. The tentative hypothesis and plans are mutually formulated, and action is only attempted when the consultee is ready to change and act. The testing and reformulation of plans is a growth experience for both consultant and consultee, and both benefit from the feedback and interaction. Each consultee and client situation is unique and must be approached idiographically.

3. In the reorienting and modifying phase of consultation, the emphasis is upon developing specific procedures which bring about modification of client behavior. It is our experience that this can often best be accomplished in the "C" group. The presence of a group of teachers is a potent force for the consultant to utilize. It provides all of the benefits which accrue in a therapeutically designed group and is enhanced by the presence of the additional experience, perceptions, and education of the teachers in the group. The consultant has available the creative resources of teachers who can provide insights and procedures which may not occur to him or might be beyond his realm of experience.

COUNSELING WITH TEACHERS

In this facet of work the consultant is involved in a type of counseling relationship with the consultee. There have been many concerns about the implications of counseling with teachers. However, it seems that the consultant in the future will be available for counseling (not psychotherapy) with teachers when deemed appropriate by all concerned. It is apparent that if teachers' personal concerns affect the way they work with children in the classroom, then there is need for an additional type of assistance. The counseling relationship with teachers is an outgrowth of an effective consulting relationship.

While it is acknowledged that counseling with teachers will provide additional relationship problems for the consultant (Faust 1968), it is deemed necessary that there be available a resource to help to reorient teachers.

The counseling function with teachers may include a wide variety of concerns, but primarily it should be related to the educational setting. As Munson (1970) has suggested, they may be reduced to two types:

> First, teachers may bring to the guidance specialist personal problems that involve outside-of school concerns stemming from family, social or economic difficulties and conflicts. . . . In the second type, teachers may seek assistance in self-evaluation and self-examination (p. 118).

This type of mental health consultation helps the consultee to understand the interpersonal forces in the social system which bring stress and anxiety. The goals of this kind of service are to help the consultee to understand the client situation and the consultee's personal conflicts and problems which keep him from utilizing his professional skills and resources. The goal involves facilitating better use of self and the consultee's resources in the professional setting. As the Combs studies have indicated, the most significant resource available is the effective use of self (Combs, Avila, Purkey 1971). The client problems are originally discussed with an awareness of the implications for the consultee. In some instances, the client problem really is associated with a crisis which exists in the consultee. In other instances the problem exists in the social system and necessitates dealing with the total organization.

REFERENCES

Carkhuff, R. *Helping and Human Relations.* vol. II. New York: Holt, Rinehart & Winston, 1969.

Combs, A. et al. *Florida Studies in the Helping Professions.* Gainesville, Florida: University of Florida Press, 1969.

Combs, A., Avila, D. and Purkey, W. *Helping Relationships: Basic Concepts for the Helping Professions.* Boston: Allyn & Bacon, 1971.

Dinkmeyer, D. "The Counselor as Consultant to the Teacher." *The School Counselor* 14, no. 5 (May 1967): 295.

Faust, V. *The Counselor-Consultant in the Elementary School.* Boston: Houghton Mifflin, 1968.

Faust, V. "Consulting—What Is It All About?" American Personnel & Guidance Association, Atlantic City, April 1971.

Kaplan, G. *Concepts of Mental Health and Consultation.* Washington, D.C.: Children's Bureau, U. S. Dept. of Health, Education and Welfare, 1959.

Munson, H. *Elementary School Guidance: Concepts, Dimensions, and Practice.* Boston: Allyn & Bacon, 1970.

Satir, V. *Conjoint Family Therapy.* Rev. ed. Palo Alto, California: Science and Behavior Books, 1967.

7

Basic Procedures for Individual Consulting

The consultant must have a clear perception of his task and understand a rationale of human behavior if he is to be effective. He must be aware of the implications of his role as an agent for change and a facilitator of human potential. He is concerned with making the system more open, dynamic, and sensitive to feedback. The task is to help the teacher to become more aware of his own resources and more sensitive to beliefs which keep him from functioning and being open to new ideas. The consultant not only understands theories and specific procedures, but must be able to develop a collaborative relationship with the staff members. The consulting process is similar to the counseling process, insofar as it is another format for the helping relationship. It is different in its original focus on the consultee's concern with the client, but if consulting is to be effective, it will be based upon empathy, open communication, commitment, encouragement, and all of the essential components of counseling.

The collaborative relationship is based upon certain fundamental beliefs about people and how one facilitates change in behavior, attitudes, and beliefs. The relationship must be based upon a belief that consultation is enhanced by cooperative problem-solving approaches and always impeded by specialist-teacher or superior-inferior methods of relating. The teacher is not someone who needs to be "advised," but rather collaborated with in the consultation process. The consultee's concern can never be solved by any superficial approach which suggests that the consultant has all of the answers and the task of the consultee is to listen attentively and apply his knowledge. Teachers need more than ideas. If they are to change, the consultant must help them to integrate new ideas with their beliefs, emotions, and values.

It must be recognized that the consultant is not hired to "play expert," even though this may be very ego-inflating. Pupil personnel specialists who are always engaged in "crises" are often those whose life styles seek excitement and who are concerned with being important and keeping others dependent. It is vital that the consultant be aware of his own beliefs and values if he is to facilitate this awareness in others.

Instead, the consultant should transfer his "expertise" into the working repertoire of other staff members. His expertise is in the understanding of human behavior and group dynamics, and his skills are in communication and human relations. These skills must be internalized by administration, teachers, and parents if education is to facilitate human potential and promote social responsibility. It is always flattering to have a request from another professional that indicates he has a problem which appears to be beyond his competence. It is exhilerating to think that we might be able to provide a ready answer and solve the problem for him. This is a trap the consultant must avoid. The specialist who provides all of the answers is like the traditional teacher. He will frequently promote resistance, and even when his "answer" is accepted, it will not be internalized and acted upon.

However, it is obvious that if teachers enter the consultant relationship passively, waiting for the specialist to solve the problem, little that is productive will occur. The teacher is a critical resource in consultation. The teacher is not incidental to the problem situation, but certainly a part of it. It is only as the consultant becomes aware of the teacher's role in the total situation that there is a possibility of bringing about change.

The teacher brings to the consultant situation certain unique contributions. He is the only one who can provide a detailed picture of the interaction that has been going on between him and the child. The teacher is in the classroom on a daily basis and has access to the situation where the action and interaction are occurring. He obviously is the only one who can provide the consultant with his perception of the causal factors. The consultant must be aware of how the teacher sees the problem if he is to be effective. Eventually, the teacher is also the only one who can provide feedback to the consultant regarding the effectiveness of his recommendations.

Thus, we are suggesting that the day of written reports describing the results of child diagnosis and suggesting specific recommendations developed without dialogue with the teacher will not effect change, but only accumulate reports. Nomothetic solutions developed to describe how to handle the average child and concerned with the "average teacher" are no longer efficacious, if they ever were.

> Summary Report on Harry Jones to Mrs. Smith
>
> Harry is a child who needs more love and acceptance. He feels left out and discouraged. It will be important to give him understanding and individual attention.

This type of written report with its generalizations and submitted without specific recommendations mutually developed and agreed upon by teacher and consultant has little value.

The lack of effective consultation procedures usually has been based upon a failure to recognize that the teacher, himself, must become involved and make decisions about the kinds of recommendations which are appropriate not only for the child, but which are possible for him to utilize. Teachers cannot utilize certain recommendations effectively because of their own beliefs and attitudes.

The following is an excerpt from an individual consulting session in which the consultant is helping a teacher to explore his beliefs and to start considering alternatives:

Consultant: "Could you give me a specific instance to illustrate Melvin's behavior?"

Consultee: "First of all, it strikes me that Melvin is somehow putting up some kind of a front. He comes to school very nicely dressed. He has impeccable taste in clothes. He always has the latest style, and he wants me to notice what he is wearing. Yet, when he's in class and we're at work, I notice Melvin staring at me very coldly, almost a contemptible stare, daring me to either call on him or remind him that he is there to work. The times that I've said to him, 'Melvin, you do have some work to do. I'd like to see you doing it,' he mutters something and continues to stare at me."

Consultant: "How do you feel when you look up and see him staring at you with what you call an angry or hateful kind of stare? What goes through your mind?"

Consultee: "Well, I'm not sure. I'm not afraid of him, but yet I guess I feel somewhat threatened because I really don't know how to handle him. I don't want to be cruel to him, or to any of my students, but at the same time, I don't appreciate the tensions that he creates in my classroom."

Consultant: "You feel a challenge to your authority."

Consultee: "Well, yes, I guess I never thought of it that way."

Consultant: "When you speak of tensions, have you noticed that it's with other children, or are you speaking of tensions between just yourself and Melvin?"

Consultee: "Well, it isn't that he's created any tensions between himself and other students so much as it is that the other students in the class realize that there is a tension building between Melvin and myself. I think they expect eventually things are going to come to a head as they have in other classes."

Consultant: "You mean with other teachers?"

Consultee: "Yes. It seems that the past two years—I know the teachers who have taught Melvin—have been a real struggle and battle."

Consultant: "Did you know things about Melvin before you got him in your class this year?"

Consultee: "Well, I'm somewhat friendly with his last year's homeroom teacher who taught him math. When the class lists came out and she was going down the list, she came to Melvin's name and said, 'You have won the prize before the game has even started!' I asked her what she meant. She pointed to Melvin's name and said, 'Honestly, this is the worst yet, so get ready!' "

Consultant: "Is it possible that her initial warning to you that this boy was coming may have had something to do with your present attitude towards him?"

Consultee: "Exactly. I really believe that there was a prejudice toward him set up in my own mind before he came in the class. The very first day when he walked into the room, my first urge was to nail him against the back wall and say, 'Jax (his last name), I know what you're up to. Don't think you're going to pull anything in this room, because you aren't going to get away with it.' However, I realize that such behavior on my part wouldn't have even granted the fact that he may have grown up over the summer or that he may be struggling with some problems."

Consultant: "You recognized that you might be expecting him to misbehave?"

Consultee: "Yes. One thing that I forgot to add which I think is probably very important here is that, according to his medical records, the surgeon that operated on Melvin has apparently stated that his leg will stop growing. Eighth graders age fifteen or sixteen, and some fourteen year olds, are extremely body conscious. I would consider that a serious problem for him and something that he has to try to overcome."

Consultant: "Could it be possible that Melvin's awareness of his physical incapacities makes him have to show his capabilities in other areas, for example, in his dress, and in his ability to overpower you by simply not doing what you want him to do?"

Consultee: "It is possible. I remember one time earlier in the school year when a salesman from the NCAA demonstrated physical fitness to the students and asked if he could come to my class. I said, 'By all means.' He brought trampoline equipment. In the course of his demonstration, he wanted to play a game with several of the students. You pass a ball back and forth through a netted hoop by jumping up and down on the trampoline. It's not a very involved thing, but he was trying to prove it is difficult to keep motion going in two different directions. He asked Melvin to try. Melvin was the only one who was able to successfully play the game. In fact, he even beat the salesman at his own game! I found this to be wonderful for Melvin, and I praised and applauded him."

Consultant: "Following this opportunity to excel, did you notice any change in him the rest of the day or the rest of the week in other areas, like his scholastic achievements?"

Consultee: "I noticed that he seemed to be uplifted the rest of the week and this had happened on Wednesday or Thursday."

Consultant: "Hmmm! Do you have any ideas of what you could do to change this relationship with him? "

Consultee: "Well, I know he likes to tell about his travel experiences in Geography, but I haven't listened."

This consultant incident is an illustration of one way to help the consultee to become aware of his beliefs and find new ways to relate. Recommendations must be tailored to the uniqueness of the teacher as well as the child. They can only be developed in a relationship that is clearly based upon collaboration—working together—and is not a relationship which assumes that one of the parties has all of the skills and answers, and hence, needs only to supply the less adequately trained individual with the necessary information.

THE RELATIONSHIP

A collaborative relationship suggests that the counselor must pay more than cursory attention to the method by which he establishes contact with other professional members of the staff. It is important that he be perceived by all who are concerned as a helping partner in the educational milieu. His specialty involves understanding the dynamics of human behavior and the feelings, attitudes, and purposes of children, as well as adults. He is a skilled listener who is able to help persons concerned to clarify their own beliefs, attitudes, and goals. In order to establish this type of relationship, it is important that the consultant be perceived by central administration as one who is available to help the significant adults, as well as the children, in the educational setting.

There must be administrative support which clearly accepts the consultant function with teachers as a high priority item, and thereby, develops a milieu which fosters this relationship. The consultant is specifically introduced to the staff by administration in terms of this role. The administration realizes that, in order to establish this kind of role with staff, it is necessary to allow time to establish the necessary and sufficient conditions for consultation. The consultant must be not only capable of analyzing concerns and developing recommendations, but he must be capable of assessing teacher strengths and providing encouragement which builds the teacher's self-esteem.

The consultant may well spend a good part of the first month of the school year becoming acquainted with the teachers both formally and informally. He becomes aware of their perceptions of their classroom situations and their specific problems. The opportunity to visit classrooms and assess the climate for learning helps him to become aware of the factors in a school setting that seem to impede learning. The consultant also identifies the strengths in the system upon which he can build.

The consultant must plan his daily schedule so that he avoids being continually manipulated by "the crisis situation." He must perceive that the real crisis situation for him is the development of a relationship with teachers which makes it both possible and probable that they will seek him out as a helper in connection with problems in the pupil personnel and guidance area. It is easy to be seduced into responding rapidly to every "crisis." However, the history of special services indicates that this is generally highly unproductive. A collaborative relationship with staff must precede all other efforts.

This may necessitate being available and accessible in the areas where teachers are usually found, e.g., the teachers' lounge. Obviously, the teachers' lounge is not the place to conduct professional consultation. However, it may be the place where one can break down the artificial barriers that are sometimes established between the specialist and the teacher. It must become readily apparent that the consultant shares the professional concerns of teachers. He is interested in them as persons, not as objects to be manipulated. He is not to be seen only as an advocate for the child. He must develop a relationship which makes it apparent to the teachers that he is there to help them to accomplish their tasks with less personal stress and tension. Too often the consultant is perceived as someone who comes implicitly to suggest that the teacher's procedures are ineffective and that treating the child as an individual, or providing more love, will resolve all problems. Teachers often feel that there is little understanding of the problems that they have in trying to deal with loving a revengeful child, or providing individualized instruction when both the size of the class and available materials makes this an impossibility. The consultant, therefore, must be able to enter the perceptual field of the teacher. He must be able to understand the teacher's frame of reference. By "walking a mile in his shoes" he can truly empathize. If he has taught, he will know the challenge and have experienced the frustration. He must come to recognize that the teacher's beliefs of "I must be in control," or "I know what is best for children" may be major deterrents to the change process.

Perhaps Krumboltz and Thoresen (1969) have posed the question most clearly when they state some fundamental propositions regarding accepting referrals from teachers: "The first question a consultant must ask is, 'Who is my client?' In almost all cases the answer should be, 'My client is the person who brought me the problem'" (p. 9). The consultant helps the consultee, who is his client, to recognize problem ownership. Though the consultee might like to "turn the case over" to the consultant, the consultant helps the consultee see his part in the interaction and makes him aware of the elements which he will eventually need to change.

Thus, in many situations, the client is actually the teacher, and he is the one who has access to the situation in which the child's behavior can be changed. It is obviously essential that the consultant does not operate as if the child is the one who is concerned about the problem. In many instances the child does not even perceive the situation as a problem. Indicating in this instance that the teacher is the client is not derogatory, but only acknowledges the reality that it is only through working with the teacher that the teacher's specific concerns can be handled. The unmotivated child will not be likely to be concerned about the teacher's goals.

Pupil personnel services have traditionally confused the issue and have been ineffectual because they have been interpreted as having the power to change through diagnosis. Hence, the classic story: "I sent Johnny to get a Binet or WISC a month ago, and he still isn't any better."

Jerry seldom gets his arithmetic finished and spends the time talking with another child. This is not something he may readily desire to change. Thus, when the teacher makes the contact about the child, it is important to recognize that this is a real problem. Although it may not be the same problem the teacher perceives, it is a problem that can only be solved if the consultant and the teacher work together. It must be made clear that one can only change his own behavior. If Jerry is to change, the teacher himself must do some things differently. As he functions differently, Jerry starts to develop a different perception of the teacher and the situation which has brought forth the problem. This does not imply that the teacher is at fault. Instead, it merely deals with the reality that the teacher must change something about his approach if he is to succeed with the child. This approach recognizes that the teacher is in discomfort, experiencing dissonance, and is therefore ready to change.

Thus, change involves changing both teacher and child perceptions. Contacts with staff members can be developed through some formalized procedures, such as presentations at faculty meetings relevant to the consultant role, role-playing demonstrations with teachers which provide some insight into the way in which the consultant functions, and through newsletters from the consultant. It has been demonstrated that the utilization of a newsletter can provide an unusually fine opportunity for in-service contact with faculty. This newsletter could include material about identifying emotional problems, detecting guidance needs, implementing group discussion procedures, handling discipline, or conducting parent interviews (Heisey 1967).

THE HELPING RELATIONSHIP

Before attempting to discuss any specific procedures related to data collection or therapeutic intervention, it is important to begin by considering the nature of the helping relationship. Perhaps the most extensive study of the helping professions has been accomplished by Arthur Combs and his staff at the University of Florida (Combs et al. 1969).

It is recognized that the helping professions are based upon the capacity of the helper to be a problem-solving person who is able to engage in dialogue which requires *immediate*, not delayed, responses. The necessity for communication and human relations skills that process dialogue instantly and meaningfully is at the core of the consulting process. The consultant must be able to really listen to the whole message (cognitive-affective-actional) and facilitate the potential of the consultee so that growth occurs in both the child and the consultee.

Research by Combs et al. indicates that the basic tool with which the helper works is himself. Daniel Soper, a member of the research team, thus developed the concept of "Self as Instrument."

In the effective consultant relationship the teacher presents a problem as he perceives it. The teacher interacts with the child according to how things seem to him. His typical set of responses arise from his own values, beliefs, purposes, and perceptions. These belief systems he may be aware of, but more often, they are in the unconscious responses which he utilizes as automatically as the decision to put which shoe on first in the morning.

The consultee can only function on the basis of the perceptions that are currently available to him. If he believes that Johnny behaves a certain way out of "meanness" or "stupidity," then he treats Johnny as if he were mean or stupid. It is only as the consultant helps the teacher to develop alternative perceptions and become aware of his resources that the teacher can thus be free to develop new methods of interacting and responding. The consultant facilitates perception change by emphatically relating to the consultee his beliefs and attitudes as they come across in his transactions with children. This facilitative confrontation creates awareness and insight. He helps the consultee to see he is free to change his beliefs and perceptions.

In many instances the teacher is in the same position as the computer. He is completely dependent upon the data available to him. One of the functions of the consultant is to increase the consultee's understanding and acceptance of new hypotheses and new perceptions, or to make new data available to the consultee. The consultant helps to generate tentative hypotheses and explore alternatives.

From the perceptual framework, behavior is always understood as a consequence of the perceptions one has about the world and the perceptions one has about himself (Combs and Snygg 1959). If one is familiar with the history of the helping professions in the fields of counseling, psychology, and social work, it is apparent that they have frequently tried to change the behavior of significant adults by providing them with additional information. This has traditionally occurred in in-service programs which present new theories, additional observations, or the results of research related to human behavior. For most teachers, this type of approach remains on the periphery of their consciousness. They hear about new ideas, they even consider them as exciting, possible or plausible, but it is infrequent that they make an attempt to change. The reason is clear. Knowledge alone will not produce a change in behavior! It is only as the knowledge is experienced in terms of its personal meaning, and as the knowledge is presented in a manner that involves the teacher's feelings and attitudes as well as cognitive acceptance, that the new approach can start to be meaningful for the teacher.

Only as knowledge takes on the quality of a belief and becomes central to one's experience is it liable to produce a change in behavior. The teacher cannot hear about a new approach and be expected to change. He has to consider this approach in the light of his present perceptions, beliefs, and attitudes. It is not until we help the teacher explore what it is about his "self as instrument" which is preventing him from utilizing this approach that we begin to have a chance to affect the interaction between the teacher and the child.

In the case of consultation, the problem is obviously compounded. Our beliefs, once they have been established and have become a part of our life style, tend to have an organizing or directing effect upon all of our perceptions. The established beliefs appearing in the form of selective perceptions limit the capacity of the individual to change his behavior. It is only as we deal with what it is that the teacher believes, feels, and perceives that we can facilitate a change.

Thus, consulting involves becoming concerned with the internal frame of reference of both the teacher and the child. Too often we have emphasized the importance of understanding the child's perceptual field and have even suggested that, if the teacher understood the child's perceptions, things would change. This understanding by itself will not bring about change. In many instances the teacher is restricted from changing his perceptions of the child because his set of established beliefs about children, classrooms, the nature of learning, and the implicit goals of education are limited.

One of the most interesting aspects of the research conducted by Combs is the recognition that much of the previous research on the helping professions failed to be productive in distinguishing efficacious helpers because it was concentrated on symptoms and not causes. The Combs' research was concerned with getting into the internal frame of reference of the helper. It is only when the consultant is able to enter the internal frame of reference of the consultee that he has an opportunity to be of assistance.

In the training of helping professionals we must be concerned with making them more people-oriented and less thing-oriented. They need to be more concerned about their relationship with the teachers and less concerned with the technical aspects of diagnosis. It was established in the Combs' research that it made considerable difference whether the helper perceived the client as able or unable. The consultant must value the teacher. He must understand and value the educational process. He must also be able to communicate that he feels the teacher is a person of worth who is truly concerned with improving the present situation.

This relationship is contrasted with the attitude of professional superiority which some consultants transmit. Consultants often convey indirectly or nonverbally the message, "Teachers don't understand children," "Education courses are irrelevant to helping children," or other attitudes which devalue and degrade teachers. An effective helper always begins by seeing persons in essentially a positive way.

He must see the teacher as dependable, able, and of worth. The consultant and consultee truly are collaborators in bringing about change. The relationship is one of equals (Dreikurs 1971).

The Combs' study indicates that two characteristics stand out in terms of the helper's perception of self. Effective helpers appear (1) to see themselves as identified and involved with persons, and (2) to have a positive view of self.

Combs et al. (1969) suggest why these characteristics are important when they state:

A positive view of self provides the kind of internal security which makes it possible for persons who possess such views of self to behave with much more assurance, dignity, and straightforwardness. With a firm base of operations to work from, such persons can be much more daring and creative in respect to their approach to the world and more able to give of themselves to others as well (p. 74).

The person who sees himself as capable conveys this confidence to others and thus is enabled to be more spontaneous and creative in his approach to problem solving. He knows that he is worthy, but does not have to be perfect. He recognizes that he is working in a collaborative relationship in this approach to problem solving. He refuses to accept or participate in any myth which appears to assume that it is up to the teacher to provide the problem, and it is up to him to provide the solution.

Thus, Combs et al. (1969) suggest that we discontinue any attempt to find the common method that will be effective for all persons. They state:

The question of methods in the helping professions is not a matter of adopting the "right" method, but a question of the helper discovering the right method for him. That is to say, the crucial question is not "what" method, but the "fit" of the method, its appropriateness to the self of the helper, to his purposes, his subjects, the situation, and so forth. We now believe the important distinction between the good and poor helper with respect to methods is not a matter of his perceptions of methods, per se, but the authenticity of whatever methods he uses (p. 75).

This research obviously has considerable implication for the type of person the consultant must be and the nature of the helping relationship. The education of the consultant must focus on and be concerned with the type of person who is developed as much as with the cognitive knowledge that is acquired. The consultant also must be aware that if he is to have an impact on the school setting, he must be able to deal with the internal frame of reference and uniqueness of each client, including the teachers. This ends an era of futility characterized by generalizations and pat recommendations for behavioral difficulties. The consultant will consider the uniqueness of the child, the teacher, the setting, and the relationships which are produced in this set of transactions, thereby facilitating growth in all of these areas.

A major problem of the helpers who are ineffective involves the fact that their methods are unauthentic and contrived, "put on" for a certain situation. They have not been internalized as genuine beliefs about self and others. This is communicated to the teacher as incongruent and confusing; hence, the teacher is seldom convinced by someone who suggests the importance of listening, understanding, and accepting the child, but who demonstrates (in the consultant relationship) a telling procedure that fails to listen, understand, and accept his perceptual field.

To summarize Combs and his colleagues' research, we would suggest that there is a statistically significant difference between effective and ineffective helpers in the following dimensions. The effective helpers were characterized by the following perceptual organization:

A. The general frame of reference of effective teachers tends to be one which emphasizes:
1. An internal rather than an external frame of reference.
2. Concern with people rather than things.
3. Concern with perpetual meanings rather than facts and events.
4. An immediate rather than a historical view of causes of behavior.

B. Effective teachers tend to perceive other people and their behavior as:
1. Able rather than unable.
2. Friendly rather than unfriendly.
3. Worthy rather than unworthy.
4. Internally rather than externally motivated.
5. Dependable rather than undependable.
6. Helpful rather than hindering.

C. Effective teachers tend to perceive themselves as:
1. With people rather than apart from people.
2. Able rather than unable.
3. Dependable rather than undependable.

    4. Worthy rather than unworthy.

    5. Wanted rather than unwanted.

  D. Effective teachers tend to perceive the task as:

    1. Freeing rather than controlling.

    2. Larger rather than smaller.

    3. Revealing rather than concealing.

    4. Involved rather than uninvolved.

    5. Encouraging process rather than achieving goals.

(Combs et al. 1969, pp. 32–33).

SELF-REFERRAL

The following conditions tend to increase self-referral:

1. An orientation, through faculty meetings, newsletters, and personal visitations, gives the entire staff the opportunity to be fully aware of the services the consultant can provide.

2. The consultant should make himself available and accessible at locations where teachers frequent. He should not wait in the office only for scheduled appointments. His schedule should be organized flexibly so he is available as soon after a request for assistance as possible.

3. The administration must believe in consultation and direct teachers to the consultant, not see consultation as a threat.

The best methods for consulting in a given situation will always depend upon the uniqueness of the individuals to be considered and the setting. It is important that the consultant establish a procedure that makes consultation visible and readily accessible. Policy should be established with the administration so that the consultee is not required to first inform the administrator before seeking consultation. If the goal is to establish an atmosphere whereby it is normal to recognize one's deficiencies in certain relationships, then one must be cautious about going through a procedure which necessitates that the teacher indicate to the administration that he is having problems. Experienced administrators will recognize that consultation is much more effective when the teacher can feel free to talk with a person who has no supervisory or administrative responsibility over his professional position.

The consultant can often be most available and accessible by being around places where teachers gather before school, during recess, and after school. However, he must also recognize that this may not be the best setting for many teachers to reveal their concerns and problems. Thus, he will also establish a schedule indicating office hours. This, combined with regular routine observations in the classroom, helps to establish his availability.

COLLECTING INFORMATION

Since it is important to collect information systematically, we are suggesting the basic outline presented on page 179 for the consultant referral form. This form provides an opportunity for the teacher to list the times when he is available for consultation. It also helps him to categorize the primary reasons for developing the referral.

It is vital in working with teachers to develop some skills in collecting anecdotes. These anecdotes will provide insight into both the child and the teacher's reactions to the problem situation. They should be developed so that they give a complete picture of a transaction. The consultant should help teachers to clarify the difference between an anecdote and a biased report. "Johnny is an underachiever" is not an anecdote. However, "Johnny gives considerable evidence of verbal ability in spelling during informal recitations, but for the past two weeks it seems he hasn't been studying as he has scored a 20 and a 30 on spelling tests" is an anecdote. The latter starts to give us some insight into what it is that Johnny is doing. Admittedly, the anecdote is limited, but it reveals specific behavior. Such an anecdote would be enhanced considerably if we knew how Johnny felt and behaved, and how the teacher responded to his behavior at that time.

It is important to ask the teacher his tentative hypotheses about the reason for the behavior. This helps the consultant to get into the teacher's internal frame of reference. While he may not agree with the teacher's approach to explaining the child's behavior, he can become aware of the teacher's beliefs about children. The consultant begins at the point where the staff member presently is in terms of psychological knowledge.

The consultant should have the teacher list the child's assets and strengths. They are the basis upon which a more effective relationship can be built. If the consultant can know the ways in which the teacher sees the child as being adequate, then he has an entry into a more effective way to relate—by emphasizing and utilizing these assets. The consultant should determine what efforts and actions have been tried

CONSULTANT REFERRAL FORM

Child's name _____ Grade _____ Age _____

Teacher _____ Time available for consultation _____

Family constellation (by age) _____

Family atmosphere _____

Specific description of learning difficulty or behavioral difficulty:

Is the problem you are concerned with focused primarily on one of the following 5 areas? Please circle. These areas are listed only to suggest classifications at the moment. Obviously many problems will overlap.

1. Intellectual deficiency
2. Learning problems, educational adjustment, questions regarding placement
3. Emotional problem, personality maladjustment, social adjustment
4. Discipline
5. Delinquent tendencies

Please describe the problem briefly. Anecdotal observations would be particularly appropriate. The anecdotes should include the child's behavior, your response or reaction, and his response to corrective efforts (antecedent event, behavior, consequence).

Tentative ideas regarding reasons for the behavior:

Child's assets, strengths:

Corrective actions utilized to this point:

Procedures which work with this child:

Mutually acceptable recommendations:

and what has worked with the child. This is invaluable. He should not hesitate to ask about procedures which are effective with the child. The teacher is often doing many things which work quite well, but his discouragement over those that fail may cause him to forget his own effectiveness. The consultant relationship values the teacher and encourages him to see his strengths and to become aware of his abilities. The final section of the form provides space for listing recommendations that have been mutually developed.

The form that is included in this chapter is only a suggested form. Forms should always be developed with a specific staff in mind, and preferably, it is the product of work by a guidance committee which helps the consultant to know the kinds of information which teachers have and are willing to take the time to supply. The form must be mutually satisfactory.

THE TEACHER INTERVIEW

One would presume that the teacher interview would be a simple procedure for the consultant trained in counseling procedures. However, too often one forgets the fundamentals of effective communication in the counseling process and is trapped into advice giving. Communication in the consultation process is purposeful and must be more than social conversation.

The consultant must avoid playing the role of the specialist who is geared to providing answers. Instead, he focuses on utilizing the full range of counseling leads and procedures. The communication will involve procedures designed to elicit feelings, develop self-understanding, extend knowledge, and facilitate action. At times the consultant will concentrate on listening and provide an opportunity for the teacher's feelings to be heard. He may reflect or restate both content and feelings. The consultant also will be engaged in helping the teacher to summarize where he presently stands in his understanding of the child and himself. This may involve helping him to clarify his convictions, beliefs, and attitudes. In other instances it will involve making a tentative analysis or developing possible hypotheses about the behavior and attitudes of the child as well as the teacher.

The consultant must be aware of the importance of providing information that enables the teacher to reevaluate the situation. However, he will try to present the information in such a way that the teacher is encouraged to bring forth his own ideas relative to the source of the difficulty.

The teacher has had previous training in child and educational psychology. The interview should help him to understand how these general principles can be applied in a specific situation. At times the consultant will supply encouragement. At other times he will enlarge the teacher's horizon and help him to consider a variety of alternatives.

Consultant: "I'm here to do what I can to help you, Pat. Would you like to tell me about the child you are having a problem with?"

Consultee: "In these past three months I've been doing some observations of him. I'm kind of disappointed because he isn't producing any work that is worthwhile in any way. He is becoming a problem on the playground so that the children are complaining that he always steals their chips."

Consultant: "Could you give me one specific example of misbehavior?"

Consultee: "Well, the children take their snacks out at lunch, and they come in and complain that Douglas stole their Fritos. But it's his paper work that bothers me. He doesn't follow any directions—he just scribbles, and I've mentioned it to him."

Consultant: "Could you give me an example of his paper work?"

Consultee: "It's the regular work we give the children that goes along with the reader. They're supposed to fill in the missing words or do the comprehension and color the pictures. Well, he would just as soon scribble the whole page instead of putting the answers down. They are either incomplete or so poorly printed that I can hardly read it."

Consultant: "How do you feel when this happens? How does it affect you?"

Consultee: "Well, it affects me in that it bothers me that he isn't doing the normal work of a first grader."

Consultant: When you say it bothers you, could you describe the feeling that you have?"

Consultee: "It's not so much that he as a person bothers me. It bothers me because I feel that he is the loser, not myself."

Consultant: "What do you do in a situation when you feel he is wasting his time?"

Consultee: "I try to isolate him and put him in a place where I feel he won't have so many distractions. He watches others at their work, and he can tell me what somebody in the back of the room is doing when he is sitting in the front. He is a very lovable child. He just looks at you and you melt; this is how he catches people. His mother says he does only what he wants to do."

Consultant: "Then, you feel that he gets along socially. He just doesn't act responsible when it comes to performing these certain work tasks that you assign. You mentioned that you have isolated him in certain situations. Has that helped at all?"

Consultee: "No, not really, because he can divert his own mind even in an isolated situation. He will find someone he can pester in some way."

Consultant: "Do you feel he is trying to get attention?"

Consultee: "Oh, definitely. There's no doubt about that at all."

Consultant: "Have you found other ways to give him attention, or some things that he has done well? Can you think of any situations where you might have given him attention when he wasn't looking for it?"

Consultee: "I usually praise him for any work he does well."

Consulant: "I am thinking more of encouraging any positive effort instead of rewarding him for functioning. What about his class participation?

Consultee: "He will participate at times, but you always have to initiate his answers. He doesn't volunteer."

Consultant: "In other words, he finds that he will get more attention from you if he is reticent to speak. This could be another way of attention getting."

Consultee: "Yes."

Consultant: "On the playground he does things to get you to notice him so you have to correct him."

Consultee: "Yes."

This segment of the interview helped the consultant and consultee to explore the concern and identify some possible purposes for the child's behavior. The consultant was concerned with:

1. Establishing a cooperative relationship.
2. Obtaining *specific* examples of the behavior.
3. Determining the teacher's feeling and reactions to the behavior.

The consultant will eventually help the consultee to establish specific commitments to new ways of interacting with the child. The critical part of the interview, assuming the relationship and analysis have been established, involves obtaining a commitment to make a specific change. The interview never is successfully accomplished until a decision is made by the consultee to take some positive action.

This interview, then, necessitates that the consultant develop a relationship characterized by mutual trust and respect for the teacher's skills. He shows the teacher that he cares and that he believes that through cooperative problem solving a solution will be found. It is most important that the consultant show an empathic attitude for the teacher's concerns. He does this by being prompt in connection with the request for help. In his original contacts with teachers, no problem is too small for his consideration. He needs to show his interest, concern, and involvement. He starts wherever the teacher is in terms of his understanding of psychology and human behavior. The consultant provides an opportunity for the teacher to work with someone who listens, who helps him to explore alternatives, and who clarifies his own thinking about a specific problem. The consultant must be able to see the teacher's point of view. It is imperative that he is aware of the necessity of reducing "psychological distance." The teacher may perceive the consultant as the expert who will provide all the answers, or he may perceive him as someone who will be critical.

Basic acceptance, which reduces distance, should be conveyed to the teacher early in the interview. The teacher interview is best conducted in a private setting, e.g., the counselor's office or the teacher's room, at a time when the children are not present. Consulting can be accomplished in informal public settings, but seclusiveness usually helps to establish a confidential and collaborative relationship.

The teacher should be helped to understand that behavior is usually a result of its consequences. As the consultant explores specific classroom situations, he can start to develop insight into what produces and maintains this dysfunctional behavior. He indicates to the teacher that some behavior can best be understood by looking at the paradigm of the ABCs of behavior.

"A" equals the antecedent event that stimulates behavior by another. In a teacher-child relationship, the antecedent can be an action by either the child or the teacher, which produces a response.

"B" is the behavior and response to the antecedent event; in other words, the action of the other party.

"C" equals the consequence of the interaction, or the action which is taken by the originator of the interaction.

The feelings which accompany each element of the ABCs help the consultant in diagnosis. Determining that the consultee feels annoyed, angry, vengeful, or defeated helps to point to the possible purpose of the client's behavior. Once the consultee is aware that the consultant hears his feeling and understands his point of view, the consultant may proceed to have the teacher talk about the specific situations illustrating problem behavior.

A practical format for anecdotal recording would involve:

Holistic Observational Format

I. Situation or setting: Math period

II. 1. Antecedent: Billy is not working and
                       I noticed him.

2. Behavior: I came over and coaxed
                       him to no avail.

II. 3. Consequence: He works only when
                       I stand over him and
                       then very little.

4. Feeling: Discouraged
                       Defeated
                       Nothing will work.

The original interview establishes the collaborative relationship, and provides for the teacher someone who listens, cares, helps to clarify, and gives support. This atmosphere increases the teacher's security, enabling him to have greater access to his resources. As threat is reduced, he becomes free to explore solutions.

While all of the important data may not be available in the first interview, if the consultant is able to help the teacher to explore some tentative hypotheses about the dysfunctional behavior, the interview has been extremely helpful. Together, they might suggest the tentative reason for the child's behavior. Some tentative suggestions about ways to respond to this type of behavior might be made. These recommendations always must be developed with a full awareness of the personality structure of the teacher and his readiness to accept such recommendations. The consultant must be sure to remember that this is a first interview and that a number of steps still remain if satisfactory attention is to be given to the problematic situation. By beginning to explore and mutually develop recommendations, the teacher and consultant have the opportunity to check out hypotheses about the client. Frequently a change in perception of the client or in one's response to the client will modify the client's behavior, thereby permitting the teacher to verify or reject ideas.

The consultant utilizes his understanding of human behavior and communication so that each sentence and each transaction provides data for consideration. Thus, he must schedule a follow-up meeting which will occur within one week. In the interim, he requests that the teacher keep some anecdotal records. These anecdotes are designed to record specific situations. They help both the teacher and consultant to understand the meaning of the child's experiences and how these experiences formulate the child's approach to life. Anecdotes are helpful in enabling the teacher to see the child's situation through the child's eyes. One can infer the child's perceptual field through carefully acquired anecdotal records. However, the anecdotes must not be biased reports. They must be representative of the general behavior of the child.

Daniel Prescott (1957, pp. 151–152) lists seven sources for obtaining anecdotal information about the behavior pattern in order to establish procedures to modify the pattern:

1. Observing the child in action in the classroom, on the playground, and elsewhere in and around the school and writing descriptive anecdotes about characteristic and routine bits of behavior, as well as about unusually significant or revealing episodes.

2. Studying the child's accumulating records at school and entering significant data from them into his own written record about the child.

3. Making visits to the child's home, conferring with the parents both at home and at school, and recording descriptions of what he observed in the home and significant portions of the conversations with the parent or parents.

4. Observing the child's life space, recording descriptions of it and of things going on in it, and making notes of the child's references to his own life space in his classroom functioning.

5. Conferring with colleagues who have taught the child in the past or are currently teaching him or who have special opportunities for observing him in action, and recording the facts they can give rather than their evaluations of or opinions about the child.

6. Collecting and examining samples of the child's classroom work, including written work done in each subject of study or unit of work, drawings, paintings, and other products of manual or creative activity, and saying characteristic samples of these for inclusion in the study record.

7. Conversing with the child individually and informally after school, at recess, or during free time and recording significant bits of these conversations.

Anecdotes must report behavior accurately and without personal interpretation. Insofar as possible they should replay, almost as the video-tape camera, the moment of observation. Prescott (1957, pp. 153–154) has developed the following characteristics for a good anecdote:

1. It gives the date, the place, and the situation in which the action occurred. We call this the setting.

2. It describes the actions of the child, the reactions of the other people involved, and the response of the child to these reactions.

3. It quotes what is said to the child and by the child during the action.

4. It supplies "mood cues"—posture, gestures, voice qualities, and facial expressions that give cues to how the child felt. It does not provide interpretations of his feelings, but only the cues by which a reader may judge what they were.

5. The description is extensive enough to cover the episode. The action or conversation is not left incomplete and unfinished but is followed through to the point where a little vignette of a behavioral moment in the life of the child is supplied.

It is important to supply the teacher with some training in acquiring anecdotes. This can be accomplished through in-service workshops which convey the value and meaningfulness of anecdotes. In other instances this is best done by visiting the classroom upon the teacher's invitation and recording anecdotes.

If the teacher already has available sociometric data, autobiographies, results of a pupil-interest inventory, or samples of creative art work, the consultant might request the teacher to have this available in the pupil's folder for his classroom observation visit (Dinkmeyer and Caldwell 1970). If this data has not been collected and the teacher has an interest in classroom guidance procedures, they might jointly decide how best to collect this information.

The consultant increases his understanding by scheduling a classroom observation. The teacher advises him regarding times when the specific behavioral difficulty is most likely to occur. The consultant makes certain that the teacher arranges to call on or involve the child during his visitation. The observation period is mutually agreed upon. He asks that the child's cumulative record, including any work samples, autobiography, or personal-social data be available at the time of the visitation. When he comes to the room, he acquires the cumulative record so it can be studied during the visitation. Experience indicates that it takes some time and patience to observe the child in situations which produce material that helps to clarify his motives and purposes. Thus, it is valuable to have cumulative data available to assist in generating hypotheses. The consultant takes a seat in the back of the room, and because he visits classrooms regularly, his presence does not create an artificial tone to the interaction between teacher and child.

During the observation, the consultant must concentrate on observing, as unobtrusively as possible, the interactions and transactions which occur between this child and the teacher. He will be noting what is said and not said. He will be alert to nonverbal cues which are exchanged between the teacher and child, such as a facial expression, posture, or tone of voice (Fast 1970). The consultant is aware that messages are conveyed through words, feelings, and actions, but that often the message is neither heard nor received. He strives to improve the communication system. While observing the transactions, the consultant is always asking himself: What is the purpose of this type of interaction? What is the social meaning of this behavior? What has happened as a consequence of the transaction between the teacher and the child? He will be interested in recording his perceptions of the child's approach to both work and social tasks, and how he goes about dealing with school assignments. Does he participate readily or is he easily discouraged? How does he get along with the other children in the room? How do they perceive him? The consultant should leave the classroom with some hunches about the image that the child is trying to project to both the teacher and his peers, and the reputation that he is seeking to enhance.

Observation should also supply the consultant with some specific information in regard to the following details:

1. The child's physical size in relationship to the group.
2. The child's general coordination.
3. The way in which the child uses his body to express his feelings.
4. His ability to follow directions.
5. The things which appear to interest him and the things which appear to bore him.
6. The type of relationship he has with other children, the ways in which he relates with them and the way that they appear to value or devalue him.
7. The child's control over his feelings, the way in which he expresses joy or anger, his reactions to frustration, his dependency on or independence from personal approval.

The observer focuses on the child but is aware of all the action occurring around the child and the child's interaction with the general group. The child is a social being best understood in his social context.

The consultant in many instances will want to observe the child in connection with classroom situations that permit more freedom—perhaps art, music, or physical education. If the child has additional teachers, he will want to know how the child behaves in a variety of situations.

THE DIAGNOSTIC CLIENT INTERVIEW

This type of interview does not involve a lengthy contact with the pupil. The purpose is to establish some impressions about how the pupil sees the world. It also enables the consultant to check his tentative hypotheses about the reasons for the dysfunctional behavior. Thus, while it is important to establish a relationship which indicates that the consultant is willing to listen and is empathic, at the same time much less emphasis is placed on developing a counseling relationship. This is an interview designed to gather information and check impressions. It does not have therapeutic intentions. The consultant must convey to the child that he is interested in him as a person and in his progress in the school setting. Opportunities should be presented for him to talk about himself and how he sees his relationships with the teacher, his peers, and school tasks.

The diagnostic client interview is structured to understand the child's perceptions, and the skilled interviewer will obtain insight into the life style from each transaction. Thus, although we provide suggested topics or questions, the interviewer will be free in the sense that the answers or responses will provide clues as to the most productive areas for investigation.

Some questions that have been found to be particularly useful include:

1. Which of your brothers or sisters behaves most like you? How?
2. Which of your brothers or sisters behaves most differently from you? How?

   (*These questions provide some insight into how the child sees his behavior. They give some understanding of his perceptual field. By telling how his siblings are alike or different by implication, he is telling a good deal about himself.*)

3. What do you like about school? Why?
4. What do you dislike about school? Why?
5. Are there any subjects you particularly like or dislike?

   (*These questions provide some insight into how the child perceives school and its requirements.*)

6. What do you particularly enjoy doing with mother or father? Why? When you misbehave, who disciplines you, mother or father? How?
7. What do you like to do least with mother or father? Why?
8. Do you have jobs to do at home? Do you usually do them without being reminded?

(These provide some insight into the family atmosphere and the type of relationship that exists in the home.)
9. How do you spend your time when you can do just as you please?

If the relationship with the child is a good one—if he is interested and involved in the interview—sometimes additional diagnostic clues can be obtained by asking him the following questions:

1. If you were going to be in a play or show, what kind of person would you like to pretend to be? Why?
2. If you were going to pretend to be an animal, what animal would you like to be? Why?
3. Which kind of animal would you not like to be? Why?
4. If you had three wishes, and only three, what would you wish for first, second, and third?

These kinds of questions will give some insight into the fantasy life and wishes of the child. The kind of person he chooses may not be significant, but the reasons that he chooses a person may provide some clues. One must determine why the person or animal is chosen. For example, if he chooses a policeman, we don't know anything about his value structure, but if he tells us he chooses a policeman because he would like to boss others around instead of because he would like to help others, it gives us some idea of the value structure.

The selection of an animal also attains significance only after we have ascertained the reason. A child may choose an alligator, but we should not attempt to guess his reason because some children may choose alligators because they are vicious and can "get even" while others choose them because they lie in the sun and sleep all day. The consultant must ask the child why he chose a particular animal in order to avoid projecting his ideas upon the child. The kinds of wishes that are selected will also give some idea of how the child values people and things.

When the consultant has had special training in understanding the use of early recollections, he may find them particularly helpful in gaining an impression of the way in which the child views the world. When a child is asked to recall one of the first things he can remember happening to him, either before or after school or during his first years of school, these recollections provide some indication of his assumptions about life (Mosak 1958, Ferguson 1964, Dinkmeyer 1964).

The following is an example of a particularly meaningful recollection taken from the case records of an eleven-year-old child who was referred because, although he had above average IQ, he seldom produced in the classroom in line with the teacher's expectations. The consultant asks, "Tell me about the first things you can recall that happened to you, and how you felt about them." The child replied, "I remember when I was five my friends could ride a two-wheeler, but I could only ride a tricycle. I tried to catch up to them but I couldn't. I felt very bad about this." Another recollection: "I remember when I was in the first grade, the teacher told me I would have to do all of my work over. My parents felt I was too small. I felt very unhappy." These recollections give us some insight into some faulty assumptions, such as:

1. I am not as much as others my age.
2. People don't believe I can function as well as I should.

The interview provides the consultant with an opportunity to establish some tentative hypotheses about child behavior. He attempts to ascertain the purpose of the behavior. He uses this interview to pose some tentative hypotheses to the child, such as: "Could it be you are behaving the way you are because it keeps the teacher very busy with you?" "Is it possible you don't do your work in school so you can be excused from all requirements?" While the answer the child gives may be significant and often an indication of his awareness of the reason for his behavior, they are not all determining. One must look closely for nonverbal signs such as tone of voice, nervous movement of the eyes, facial expressions, and of course, a roguish smile or twinkle of the eyes which Dreikurs (1968) describes as the "recognition reflex."

PLANNING AND DEVELOPING RECOMMENDATIONS

The consultant has an opportunity to talk with the teacher, review the cumulative folder, observe the child in the class, and conduct the diagnostic interview with the child. In some instances he may feel that it is important to consult with other pupil personnel specialists, the child's other teachers, or the parents.

The interview, which is designed to formulate recommendations, should always occur within close proximity of the original requests for assistance. Consultants must develop a schedule and an appropriate teacher consultant load that enable them to follow up promptly on original requests for assistance. Teachers too frequently have been the victims of remote services which promised much while in practise afforded little. In particular, the consultant's recommendations must be designed to incorporate his understanding of the uniqueness of the consultee (his original client), the problem, and the child. By the time recommendations are offered, the consultant has had an opportunity to clarify how the consultee and client perceive their situation. He has already established an atmosphere which makes the teacher aware that it is critical that he modify his behavior if the child is to change. The modification may be slight, but obviously whatever has been happening in the past necessitates a new approach.

The consultant begins the interview by ascertaining how things have gone with the child since he developed some tentative hypotheses and he and the teacher mutually formulated some slight changes in teacher behavior. This enables him to check how things have been going during the past week and to determine if any of their speculations or tentative hypotheses were on target. The original suggestions thus provide an opportunity to judge whether the hunches about the interaction are accurate.

The final recommendations are always developed jointly. They arise from the ideas of both the teacher and the consultant. Recommendations must always be related to the teacher's personality and his ability to carry out the recommendations. If the teacher is impatient or sets excessively high standards, the consultant cannot expect to change these traits through the limited contact he has had at this point. This type of change is a more sophisticated change and may come out of the teacher's membership in a "C" group or through some extended contacts which merge into teacher counseling. This type of change obviously involves certain kinds or reorganization of the teacher's perceptions, attitudes, feelings, and beliefs. The consultant helps the teacher to recognize that through his own personal change he can influence the child to change.

The recommendations would not necessitate basic changes in teacher personality, but might encourage the teacher to be somewhat more patient or less demanding. It is important that the recommendations be developed through open dialogue in which the teacher participates as a colleague and equal. The consultant's job is to help the teacher to become aware of all the alternatives. Once the varied courses of action have been studied, he must be certain that the teacher is in full agreement with the recommendations and the recommendations are realistic. He must always be aware that the decision to use or reject an idea remains with the consultee. It will do little good to obtain verbal agreement when personally the teacher is skeptical about the reasons for the behavior or the rationale for the changes that are being suggested. It is important to check out specifically what the consultee believes and feels in his verbal assent, as, "I'll try that," "O.K., it sounds good," etc.

The consultant must be well grounded in his understanding of the psychology of human behavior and the dynamics of classroom interaction. This enables him to provide a variety of corrective techniques which can be tailored to the uniqueness of both the child and the teacher. Some general suggestions which have been found to be very helpful when applied idiographically include:

1. Helping the teacher to be aware of the importance of the relationship between himself and the child. The consultant could suggest a specific way in which the teacher might change the relationship and indicate how this change, if it is done consistently, may influence the child. The encouragement relationship is basic to the consultation process (Dinkmeyer and Dreikurs 1963).

2. Helping the teacher to understand the efficacy of logical consequences, in contrast to punishment. For example, the consultant can help him to recognize, that if the tardy child does not have the assignment reviewed for him, he may learn to come on time. In the same manner, if the child who acts out during instruction is given his instruction after the class, he may learn to be more cooperative (Dreikurs and Grey 1968).

3. Helping the teacher to avoid rewarding misbehavior. Frequently, the teacher unconsciously helps to maintain the misbehavior. For example, if a child is acting up and disturbing the class, instead of removing the child, which may involve the teacher in a power struggle and may be just what the child is interested in, the teacher should refuse to fight with the student. He could, instead, dismiss the child at this time and arrange a private session with him at a later date (Dreikurs 1968).

4. Helping the teacher to be aware of the nature of his relationship with the children. Some teachers are too kind, and the children run all over them. Other teachers try to be too firm and too tough, and the children only rebel. The consultant can provide the teacher with a more objective observation of the nature of his relationships with children. He can help him to see how each relationship must be composed of both kindness and firmness. The kindness will indicate to the children that he really cares and respects them, while the firmness will indicate that he has some respect for himself, which in turn elicits the children's respect.

5. Helping the teacher to become aware of the power of the group and group discussion. Since all behavior has a social purpose, behavior can often best be influenced through group discussion. The group can often serve as an excellent diagnostic tool. When the teacher does not know why the child is misbehaving during a group discussion, he may ask the class, "Why do you think Johnny is acting as he is?" Frequently the peers will be very sensitive to the purpose of this misbehavior.

6. Helping the teacher to become more aware of the way in which the child reveals his life style through his interactions with him and peers. Nonverbal behavior (smiles, signals, and other facial expressions) may help to see the child's psychological movement and the way in which he seeks to become significant in the group. It is only as the teacher becomes aware of each child's unique life style that he has access to procedures for modifying his behavior.

7. Helping the teacher to recognize that one of his most powerful tools for change is the proper utilization of responsibility. Too often teachers give responsibility to the child who has demonstrated responsibility. It is much more useful therapeutically to give responsibility to a child who needs the responsibility to enhance his development.

8. Helping the teacher to free himself from outmoded approaches for dealing with difficult children. He should be particularly cautious of using schoolwork or assignments as a punishment and should refuse to become involved in the client's attempts to manipulate him. The teacher must become competent in understanding human behavior and motivation.

9. Helping the teacher to understand the child's style of life and to learn to anticipate the child's actions. Often when the teacher is confused, his best response is to do exactly the opposite of what the child expects.

10. Helping the teacher to recognize that talking at the child will not change his behavior. It is often observed that teachers tend to talk too much and act too little. The consultant should help the teacher to see how a new relationship and logical consequences are more efficacious.

11. Helping the teacher to develop a classroom council. When there is considerable difficulty within a room, a classroom council can help set limits and rules which will be more acceptable to the total group. The council is an extension of the ideas of Dreikurs

(1968) and Glasser (1969) regarding classroom group discussions.

The above recommendations obviously should not be implied as general solutions to all problems. However, in many instances, when they are tailored to meet specific problems, they may bring about significant changes.

Once there has been some agreement about the recommendations, which have been recorded on the consultant form, the consultant arranges to return in another week or as a follow-up in order to ascertain progress and to enable him to check the quality and validity of the type of recommendations he is making. The teacher serves as a real source of professional growth for the consultant insofar as he helps the consultant to become more specific and precise in his recommendations.

It is important that consultants be aware that often the major contribution they make is not bringing a special knowledge of psychology, learning disabilities, or special approaches to the situation. In contrast, it is often the quality of the relationship which develops between the teacher and the consultant that is really significant. Teachers need the opportunity to discuss educational problems with a colleague who understands human behavior in a nonevaluative setting which facilitates the development of new approaches and new hypotheses. Thus, it is the quality of the emotional support and encouragement the consultant provides that may be most significant in facilitating change.

Individual consulting requires a number of skills and an awareness of procedures, but it is always based upon the capacity to develop an effective, problem-solving approach with the teacher. The following example illustrates some of the problems encountered in helping teachers to focus on the specific problem and to become aware of their feelings and reasons for behavior. Each of the consultant's carefully selected leads and responses has a specific purpose.

T = teacher	C = consultant	*Purpose*

C^1: "Could you tell me something about this boy Phil?"

T^1: "Yes, he's in my eighth-grade science class, and he drives me insane."

C^2: "He really bothers you." *Hears the feeling*

T^2: "The worst I've ever had."

C^3: "Tell me about a specific time."

T³: "Every time I start to teach he gets up and walks around the room. Sometimes he just leaves the classroom."

C⁴: "Can you think of one specific incident recently that you could describe?"

Aims to get away from generalizations

T⁴: "Yes, I was teaching science, and I thought I had a pretty good science lesson prepared. The boys and girls were sitting in a group when all of a sudden Phil starts to cough real loud. I thought maybe he needed to get a drink so I said, 'Phil, if you want to get a drink, go ahead.' He answered, 'Oh no, that's OK.' I proceeded to teach, when suddenly he just gets up and leaves my classroom. I asked him, 'Where are you going?' He said, 'I'm going to get a drink. You said I could.' But this was twenty-five minutes later."

C⁵: "How did you feel when he did this?"

Attempts to see how behavior affects teacher

T⁵: "I'm always angry whenever he does something like this. He really makes me mad."

C⁶: "What do you do?"

Attempts to identify teacher's response

T⁶: "I told him to get back to his seat. Sometimes I try to ignore him."

C⁷: "When you tell him to go back, does he go right away?"

T⁷: "Oh yes, he's usually pretty good. He might look out the window a few minutes, but he eventually strolls back to his place. I mean he's not bold or anything."

C⁸: Do you have any idea why he does this?"

Investigates teacher's perception of purpose of behavior

T⁸: "I think he does it to get my attention. He knows every time he walks around or leaves the classroom I'm going to stop whatever I'm doing and ask him, 'What's wrong?' I think he's really a boy who craves attention." (Here the teacher describes his home situation, stressing the fact that he has a very tough father.)

C⁹: "What kind of attention do you give him?"

T⁹: "Well, I try to spend time with him. I spend time after school. He's on the basketball team, and he's got tremendous potential, but he drives the coaches insane. He doesn't pay attention to what he's doing."

C¹⁰: "Could we just go back for a minute? You said that when he does this sort of thing you get really mad, and you also said at one point that you ignore him. What would you say is your usual reaction to what he does?"

T¹⁰: "I think he's aware of the fact that he makes me mad."

C¹¹: "Do you think he knows he's going to get you angry?"

Attempts to see how child perceives his response

T¹¹: "Well, I don't know if he can see my anger, because I don't ever really yell at him, or scream."

C¹²: "I was thinking that sometimes children, if they know they can get you angry, are really trying to control you. You know, they want to be in charge."

Poses a tentative hypothesis so teacher can see the relationship between his feelings and child's purpose.

T¹²: "I really think he's a smart boy. He's got a high IQ, and I feel he could do much better in school. I'll give him five or ten science problems, and he'll do maybe two of them for homework. (She then describes his work on similar assignments.) I think he deliberately doesn't do the problems."

C¹³: "And you think he does this to get your attention?"

T¹³: "Oh, I think so. If I keep him after school, he's really happy."

C¹⁴: "And yet the problem seems to be mostly in school. Are there ever times that you think that maybe you give him a little encouragement?"

Attempts to focus on school situation where teacher had problem

T¹⁴: "I don't know. I think maybe I'm just very negative against him. I don't see him doing too many things I could praise him for. I can't praise him for burning a kid's hair, or leaving the room, etc. I could try that, though."

C¹⁵: "It would almost seem that if he wants attention, he could get it another way. He seems to want your attention."

Creates awareness of how child gets attention

T¹⁵: "I could maybe try looking for things. I don't know if I'll find anything, but I could at least try."

C¹⁶: "I think maybe for the next few days you should give it a try, even if it's just a small thing."

T¹⁶: "Yes, I really never thought of that. It might be what he needs."

C^{17}: "If he could get your attention another way, he wouldn't have to resort to these other things."

In this example it appears that the child was involved in a power struggle with the teacher, but the consultant focused on attention getting as the purpose of misbehavior. The consultant's lead were appropriate, but at C^5 and T^5 he should have caught the teacher's feeling of anger and explored the possibility of the child's desire to obtain power.

The following example illustrates how the consultant helps the consultee to explore his own beliefs:

T: "I sent for you to get your help on my friend, Ricky."

C: "Yes."

T: "He appears to be a child who needs some kind of affirmation. He just slugs anybody, anytime, and then chuckles to himself. Basically he appears to be tenderhearted. I really like him a great deal. I want him to be accepted by the other kids. He really wants to be accepted, and it appears to me that he does all these things to get the attention he is looking for. Do you think that is correct, or am I beating at straws?"

C: "Do you mean that he wants to be accepted and doesn't know how to go about it?"   *Clarifies teacher's belief*

T: "Yes, to get this attention without using diabolical means."

C: "Sure. Can you give me anything specific that he has done?"

T: "Somebody goes past his desk, and he takes a lunge at him, no matter who it might be."

C: "How do you feel when this happens?"   *Determines feeling in order to clarify purpose of behavior*

T: "Well, I feel kind of sorry for the kid. I'd like to see him get along with the others. I've talked to others to see what the problem is, but they can't seem to pinpoint it. They want nothing to do with him."

C. "Tell me more about how you feel?"

T: "I suppose basically I feel sympathetic toward him as he has so many good things about him. He really is tenderhearted. I would like him to be accepted. When we had our first parent-teacher-child conference, he was very quiet."

C: "Did you tell the parents why he was so unpopular?"

Fails to explore
teacher's belief
about Ricky

T: "Yes. His mother was constantly at his defense. This greatly bothered me. The father didn't have much to say. The mother talked all the while. The father seemed to approve of my attitude. I felt I got nowhere with the mother. Later on we had another conference, this time only with the mother. She told me the father beats Ricky all the time. I began thinking his actions toward his peers might be revenge."

C: "When he acts this way, what do the other children do? What are the consequences of his behavior?"

T: "They are varied. There's some laughter, girls feel defenseless, and boys generally ignore him or tolerate him. The girls complain when they have to sit near him."

C: "How does he react when he hears these complaints? Does he look satisfied or happy?"

Tries to establish
a purpose for
action.

T: "I think he is perplexed. Outwardly he shows little emotion."

C: "Has he ever been mean to you?"

T: "No, he never turns on me. I give him plenty to do."

Clarifies idea
about Ricky's
behavior

C: "From what you have said, he seems to tyrannize only those who are weaker than he is, more or less as his father does to him. I agree with you in thinking his goal is revenge. Do you ever punish him?"

T: "Sometimes if he is annoying someone near him, I move him away."

C: "That really isn't a punishment, just a result of his action. Have you ever talked to him about this?"

Clarifies
distinction
between logical
consequences and
punishment

T: "I've said to him, 'Tell me about how you act.'"

C: "What did he say?"

T: "He wants to be accepted. He knows how he acts. Sometimes he says he doesn't know why he acts the way he does."

C: "I'd like to make a few suggestions. On one of the better days, talk with him and hypothesize about revenge being his goal of behavior. See what he says and what his reaction might be. See if you can encourage him as you have been doing. Make some observations, and we will discuss Ricky again in a week. What do you think you could do differently with him?"

Attempts to accomplish too much in one lead

T: "I guess I could start to be more aware of my feelings about him."

C: "Your feelings, tell me more."

T: "I really feel very angry at times, but it is only now that I've recognized it."

C: "It's hard to admit this anger towards a child, but it will help us understand the interaction. Do you think you could find some small thing to encourage?"

T: "He is very helpful during math, and I could notice it."

Individual consulting involves putting counseling skills to use with the consultee to develop awareness, understanding, new relationships, and commitment to new procedures.

REFERENCES

Boy, A. and Pine, G. *Expanding the Self: Personal Growth for Teachers.* Dubuque, Iowa: Wm. C. Brown, 1971.

Combs, A. et al. *Florida Studies in the Helping Professions.* University of Florida Monographs, Social Sciences No. 37, Gainesville, Florida: University of Florida Press, 1969.

Combs, A. and Snygg, D. *Individual Behavior: A Perceptual Approach to Behavior.* Boston: Harper & Row, 1959.

Dinkmeyer, D. "Conceptual Foundations of Counseling." *The School Counselor* 2, no. 3 (1964): 174–178.

Dinkmeyer, D. and Caldwell, E. *Developmental Counseling and Guidance: A Comprehensive School Approach.* New York: McGraw-Hill, 1970.

Dinkmeyer, D. and Dreikurs, R. *Encouraging Children to Learn: The Encouragement Process.* Englewood Cliffs, New Jersey: Prentice-Hall, 1963.

Dreikurs, R. *Psychology in the Classroom.* 2nd ed. New York: Harper & Row, 1968.

Dreikurs, R. *Social Equality.* Chicago: Henry Regnery, 1971.

Dreikurs, R. and Grey, L. *Logical Consequences.* New York: Meredith Press, 1968.

Fast, J. *Body Language.* New York: Simon & Schuster, 1970.

Ferguson, E. D. "The Use of Early Recollections for Assessing Life Style and Diagnosing Psychopathology." *Journal of Protective Techniques* 28 (1964): 403–412.

Glasser, W. *Schools Without Failure.* New York: Harper & Row, 1969.

Heisey, M. "A Review of Literature as a Service to Teachers." *Elementary School Guidance and Counseling* 2, no. 2 (December 1967): 127–134.

Krumboltz, J. and Thoresen, C. *Behavioral Counseling: Cases and Techniques.* New York: Holt, Rinehart & Winston, 1969.

Mosak, H. "Early Recollections as a Protective Technique." *Journal of Protective Techniques* 22 (1958): 302–311.

Prescott, D. *The Child in the Educative Process.* New York: McGraw-Hill, 1957.

8

Group Consulting and Counseling with Teachers

The consultant who has a developmental emphasis in his work will be cognizant of the school milieu. If he is to influence this learning climate most effectively, he will work with teachers.

The pupil personnel specialist has often considered the child to be his major concern and has functioned as if direct work with children in diagnosis and counseling were the top priority. However, the history of guidance services has not been dramatically productive in the realm of changing behaviors and beliefs. It has become increasingly apparent that in many instances we are working with the wrong client. When the teacher has discussed a problem with a child, we have reacted as if the child were requesting the help. This has resulted in many referred clients who are unmotivated, unconcerned, and hence uninvolved in the process. There has been difficulty in trying to transfer counseling theories into effective procedures with children and adolescents. Given the additional handicap of working with the wrong client, the counselor has had little hope of being effective.

If the specialist is to be effective, he must become competent in procedures for working with adults. The original focus in consultation has been on working with individual teachers, but individual consulting has been hampered by several considerations:

1. There is a tendency for consultants to counsel students, hearing their feeings and helping them to explore alternatives, but to advise

staff members. This acting as an answer man by producing simple solutions for complex problems has tended to put the guidance worker into the category of "medicine man."

2. One cannot consult effectively unless he can get into the internal frame of reference of the consultee. It is basic to become aware of his perceptions and beliefs. We must become sensitive to his beliefs about persons, human relationships, and to how to effect change in behavior (Combs et al. 1969).

3. Often in individual consulting the questions that might attempt to explore the teacher's feelings and attitudes come across as threatening and therefore produce defensiveness. The consultant's suggestions may be responded to with, "I've tried that," "I have too many children in the room to do that," "Nobody could do that and still teach," or other responses which block communication.

4. Most significant, though, is the fact that the consultant is "stuck" with his limited resources—self. His education, experience, and perceptions can never embrace all the types of situations which teachers will present. However, as leader of a group of five teachers, he has access to the experiences, insights, hypotheses, and possible procedures which can be developed by the group. Also, he can observe how the teacher operates in this social field and can develop an awareness of the teacher's style of life and methods of relating.

It is important to understand the rationale for working with teachers in groups. Unless one is aware of the potential benefits in this didactic-experiential group, he will not be able to see its possibilities.

RATIONALE

Working in groups is more meaningful when we recognize that man is best understood as an indivisible, social, decision-making being whose actions have a social purpose (Dreikurs and Sonstegard 1968). This view of man as a social being develops new awareness and gives meaning to all of his verbal and nonverbal interactions and transactions.

Placing teachers in a group recognizes that most problems basically are interpersonal and social. The problem that the teacher presents originated in a group interaction with the children. The teacher needs to become aware of the necessity of understanding behavior in its social context. The teacher group then has the opportunity to analyze the child's life style as it is expressed in his social transactions and psychological interaction with the teacher. The child's unique approach to the tasks of life will be consistent with his concept of self and his assumptions about life. More important, the consultant and the group have an opportunity to observe the teacher's life style and his characteristic pattern of response to children and members of the group.

The group setting, then, provides the leader—the consultant—and the members of the group with an extremely valuable social laboratory, a miniature society or micro-community. As the teacher learns to function as a member of the group, he will begin to develop some insights into how children respond in a group; therefore, he probably will develop some skills that will allow him to work more effectively with his students. The group setting has both diagnostic and therapeutic values. Certain behaviors can only be observed in the group setting. There is considerable difference between telling how you relate to others and the child and becoming involved in relating to others, which reveals your characteristic approach to life's problems.

There are also a number of therapeutic effects which can be best processed in the group setting. The group provides the opportunity for a unique type of acceptance. This is a setting in which the teachers can experience the empathy which comes from their peers. It also provides the opportunity to ventilate and express how they feel. In the group one can try out some behaviors and ideas and at the same time process the feedback from members of the group. This type of group also helps the teachers to realize that their problems with children are universal. Recognizing that there are others with similar problems can cohese the group. This can stimulate one's altruism and desire to help fellow professionals become more effective persons. Each member can be a therapeutic agent for every other member.

The group provides teachers with a special opportunity to occasionally hear about another's problem and develop some ideas about how to handle a situation which, to this point, they have not even encountered. Spectator therapy, learning from another's experience, is a major benefit.

It has been demonstrated that the group process helps the members to become more aware of the fact that most of their concerns are social and interpersonal. These challenges are a product of interaction with the child and, in some instances, failure to understand the child's goals and purposes. This unique setting provides the opportunity not only to talk and release one's feelings about the problem, but to investigate some new ways of handling it. There is a unique opportunity to get the kind of assistance from a colleague which is often not available in any other setting. Schools have not devised effective ways for teachers to share with each other effective teaching procedures. The "C" group is a channel for this kind of communication.

Because the significance of behavior always lies in its social consequences, one is able both to explain the transaction that occurred with the child and become more aware of his own investment in the interaction with the child. Teachers can become more aware of their traditional methods of responding to children who are difficult to teach.

The group setting provides a new way to see the life style, faulty assumptions, and mistaken ideas of both child and teacher. It is essentially a holistic approach in the sense that it takes into consideration not only the intellect, feelings, and behavior of the child, but also the teacher. It creates an experience in which the teacher enters into a supporting, caring, accepting atmosphere. He has access to feedback about his behavior, feelings, and attitudes, and through this, he can develop a new perspective on human relationships and more effective procedures for working with children. The group also benefits teachers who do not have difficulties with children because it gives them an opportunity to contribute, and feel needed and accepted.

In order to understand group dynamics of children in groups, teachers must experience being a member of a group. Often teacher education has not permitted them to have an experience either as a group member or a group leader. If we are going to deal with the whole child, we must engage teachers in situations in which they participate as "whole teachers" and can express their feelings, attitudes, purposes, and values. They must be able not only to talk about the child, but to become aware of their own feelings. As the teacher becomes able to recognize and verbalize, "He makes me mad," or "I'd really like to get even but know I can't," he has access to diagnostic procedures and therapeutic resources which were formerly blocked in the strictly intellectual problem-solving approach. The opportunity to be in a group with didactic and experiential components enables teachers to not only learn about universalization, belonging, commitment, and leadership competencies, but also to *experience* them.

Group work with teachers is a holistic approach that takes into consideration the intellect, feelings, and behavior of both the teacher and the child. This didactic-experiential group is much different than traditional in-service training. In contrast, it emphasizes that if we are to help teachers to become skillful in dealing with "the whole child," then we must give them experiences in which they participate as "whole teachers." In-service training that is to be efficacious will create situations in which the teacher becomes part of a group in which the climate is one that shows care and concern and provides support, but at the same time, enables him to benefit from the feedback of the group about his behavior, feelings, and attitudes.

The group is also an especially unique opportunity for the consultant. It permits him to work with several teachers at one time and utilize the resources of the total staff in attendance. Often, in individual consultation, the consultant is "stuck." He does not have a good idea or procedure for helping to modify the behavior or attitudes of a specific child. In almost every instance, a group of teachers, with their varied backgrounds of educational and practical experiences, will be able to help him to develop alternatives.

Thus, the group provides the opportunity for teachers to help each other to grow professionally and personally. There is a unique opportunity for the teacher to experience the acceptance and belonging which comes from being part of a staff which is concerned with helping each other.

It cannot be overemphasized that group work with teachers provides a new channel for communication which permits both the beginning and experienced teacher to share their ideas about human behavior and their approaches to understanding children. The group provides for meaningful interaction among educators (consultants and teachers) and has the potential to stimulate the professional and personal development of the total staff. It has also been observed that when group programs are developed in an effective manner, the faculty becomes much more cohesive.

THE SETTING AND THE SITUATION

The history of teacher education and in-service education points to the critical need for new procedures for consultants in the area of human behavior. There is a great gap between the course work in child and educational psychology and teachers' educational practises. The consultant serves as a translator of "psychological theory into practise." The teacher must be able to utilize psychological principles in working with individual behavior and the dynamics that occur within the group.

The record of past efforts at in-service education indicates that we will only be effective in changing the course of the educational profession insofar as we provide professional educational experiences that involve the "whole teacher." Teacher education experiences, both pre-service and in-service, must involve the affective and cognitive domain and result in specific changes in perceptions, attitudes, and behavior. Anything less than a dynamic approach will only result in talk about more humane classrooms and individualized attention, with little implementation.

The National Education Association reviewed all of the research presently available on good and poor teaching and arrived at the conclusion, "There is no method of teaching which can be clearly shown to be associated with either good or poor teaching" (Ellena, Stevenson and Webb 1961). The nature of effective helping relationships cannot be found in what the teachers know or their methods, but is involved in their understanding and application of the communication and motivational processes.

Analysis of teaching behavior indicates the critical nature of communication. Teachers must possess the capacity to respond immediately and in an effective manner. When they encounter attention-getting behavior, rebellion, apathy, and an unwillingness to try, they must be capable of facilitating communication. Skills in creating a climate of openness, trust, and mutual purpose are basic to the teaching task. This type of competency cannot be acquired through memorization or course work. It is a product of a person who understands himself and uses "Self as Instrument" in facilitating a helping relationship (Combs et al. 1969). Teachers must be helped to develop empathic understanding, spontaneity, flexibility, and openness, the interpersonal and communication skills which facilitate growth (Berenson and Carkhuff 1967).

The teacher, then, is not a dispenser of knowledge, nor is he a walking encyclopedia. Although considerable emphasis is placed upon actual knowledge, cognitive skills, and academic grades both in teacher education and in the public schools, we know that one's intellectual competence does not guarantee his ability to facilitate learning. The teacher may know the material, but he cannot be effective unless he is able to communicate, inspire, motivate, and involve learners.

Combs and his colleagues at the University of Florida (1969) published the results of ten years of exploration into the nature of the helping relationship. They hypothesized that the primary tool with which teachers work is the self. This concept in the study, as previously stated, is referred to as "Self as Instrument." Effectiveness is a function of the way in which the teacher is able to combine his knowledge and understanding with his own unique way of utilizing the knowledge so that it is helpful to others.

This research clarifies why our investigation of knowledge, skills, methods, and other procedures has been discouraging and confusing. It is now apparent that it is not as important to know what the teacher has been taught as it is to know the way in which the knowledge, attitudes, beliefs, and feelings have been internalized. Persons behave on the basis of how they perceive, and their perceptions are always a product of their psychological experiences. The stimulus which comes from the professor's lecture eventually must be modified and translated by the filter of the student's perceptual field. Teachers most often teach as they have been taught. They learn more from what they experience than from what they are told.

Knowledge seldom produces change in behavior. It is fruitless to be overly concerned about the addition or subtraction of courses in educational methodology or the development of other special competencies. Any surface manipulation has little possibility of affecting teacher effectiveness. It is more critical that we deal with the meanings and beliefs which organize the perception of teachers and influence their behavior.

CHARACTERISTICS OF EFFECTIVE TEACHERS

The teacher must be able to interrelate his attitudes, perceptions, feelings, and values with his developing skills and knowledge. Teachers' real beliefs and feelings—their emotional life—are often denied and suppressed by "professional education" and their own faulty assumptions about membership in the teaching profession. One of the functions of the teacher group is to help the teacher to recognize that his feelings and beliefs may be his most significant resource. He needs to become aware of these feelings so that they can be utilized to:

1. diagnose the purpose of behavior.
2. help them to know what keeps or prevents him from improving his relationship with a specific child.
3. free him to find solutions and see new alternatives.

THE COUNSELOR AND THE ADMINISTRATOR

The development of teacher groups requires that the leader spend considerable time in establishing the climate and setting for the group. The original contact is made with the administrator. It is imperative that administrators understand how "C" groups can help them to accomplish their objectives in staff and student development. The teacher group is a dynamic in-service procedure which helps teachers to understand and modify specific children's behavior, while providing them with an experience which helps them to become aware of how their feelings, perceptions, and beliefs affect their interaction with children on the whole.

It is apparent that in-service education which stays at the cognitive level and does not engage or involve the "whole teacher" cannot be efficacious in affecting practise. Teachers may come from the meetings with more ideas, but without any commitment to personal change. The administrator who is interested in affecting the learning climate of the school can accomplish this best through the teacher group. Through teacher groups the guidance worker and administrator can collaborate. Consulting becomes a significant resource for administration, not merely an ancillary service.

It is the administrator who can supply the encouragement, space, and facilities necessary for group work. His enthusiastic public support of the concept and his efforts to develop schedules which make it convenient for teachers to participate in the group are critical in the establishment of the program.

The consultant will make the teacher group program known to the staff through varied media. During an early faculty meeting or formal in-service session he can describe the program. He will also supply the teachers with printed material which clarifies the purposes, activities, and benefits. As he is engaged in individual consulting and identifies teachers who are good candidates for a teacher group, he will encourage their participation in the development of a group.

THE CONSULTANT AS A LEADER OF TEACHER GROUPS

If the consultant is to serve as an agent of change and a motivating force to help teachers to become more aware of themselves and their behavior, he often can accomplish this best through the teacher group. The group provides the opportunity to investigate the purposes of behavior, became aware of reasons for failure to function, and at the same time, enables all the members of the group to have an experience through which they can learn to communicate openly with each other. The most potent aspect of the group is involved in the concept of commitment. As the counselor utilizes group dynamics and involves the teachers in commitment, he moves the teachers towards significant changes.

The consultant has special competencies in human relations and group work. He has had theoretical work which enables him to understand human behavior, classroom procedures, and group dynamics. His professional education includes course work in the theory and practise of group procedures with both children and adults. The training program also will have required that he has been a part of a learning efficiency process experience where he, as a member of the group, became more aware of himself and others. This advanced training enables him to take his skills in group dynamics and group counseling and apply them to work with the staff.

The leader of an effective teacher group performs the following functions:

1. He structures the group from its inception so that the purposes and focus are clear. The group is didactic in the sense that it translates the psychology of human behavior into practise, and experiential, insofar as it makes the teachers aware of themselves. The leader establishes and structures the group in such a manner that the purposes of the "C" group are accomplished.

2. He is sensitive to feelings which are expressed and unexpressed. His skills in dealing with nonverbal cues, such as tone of voice, facial expressions, and gestures, are essential.

3. He focuses on linking the ideas of group members. He helps the members to see how their thinking is alike and also how it is different. Linking helps group members to recognize the similarities in their problems and the universality of most human problems. This is basic to the development of a cohesive group.

4. He is alert to signs from less verbal group members indicating they want to participate. He recognizes that members may learn through listening and spectator therapy, but if any indicate an interest in verbal participation, he is sure to facilitate this entrance into group activity.

5. He keeps the focus of the group on the here and now, so that members are aware of the interpersonal relationships among themselves. Enabling them to become aware of the human relationships in groups serves as a model for an understanding of the interpersonal transactions which occur with children.

6. The leader is concerned with helping group members to become aware of their strengths and assets, in order to develop their feelings of adequacy. This type of group experience is concerned with facilitating feelings of competency and encouraging group members to utilize their personal strengths as well as the strengths that exist in the entire group.

7. The leader helps the group to clarify and focus on their primary concerns and investigates alternate ways of solving these challenges. Progress is best facilitated through this type of group since the varied education and experiences of the teachers enable them to contribute a rich resource of diagnostic and therapeutic skills.

8. The leader is a resource who enables teachers to recognize that they can change children best by changing their own pattern of interaction with children. The leader helps group members to make specific commitments to action to change their behavior patterns.

ORGANIZATION AND ADMINISTRATION OF TEACHER GROUPS

Goals

Teacher groups are concerned with the following goals:

1. Developing an understanding of the practical application of the dynamics of human behavior, and helping the teachers to comprehend how a social-psychological theory and practise of human behavior can help them to relate more effectively with children.

2. Acquiring an understanding of self and developing awareness on the part of teachers of their role in the teacher-child conflict. The teacher develops not only an intellectual comprehension of why children function as they do, but gets into touch with his own motives and feelings and becomes aware of the way in which they influence his interaction with children.

3. Developing an understanding of new concepts and procedures, while integrating them into one's own value system. One derives the benefits which come from group thinking.

Organizational Details

The establishment of teacher groups, just like the establishment of group counseling with students, requires careful attention to a number of organizational details. The total staff must be orientated to the purposes and directions of the teacher group program. The first teacher group preferably will be people who have social and professional power within the staff. They will be people who are valued and respected by the staff members. It will be important to dispel any faulty assumptions that members may have about the group, i.e., group psychotherapy or sensitivity training. In some instances it will be valuable to use some faculty meeting time to demonstrate the way in which the group actually proceeds.

A basic problem involves developing appropriate meeting arrangements. These groups function best when they meet on a weekly basis, preferably for at least one hour. The teachers should make a commitment to continue this type of activity for a minimum of six to eight weeks. "C" groups can meet at a variety of times and places. In some instances the "C" group will meet before the school day, during the lunch hour, or immediately after school. Where it is possible, a group of teachers may arrange their schedules so specialists (instructors in physical education, music, art, etc.) take over their classes during the meeting. Some school districts arrange to have parents supervise a study period while the "C" group is in session. In some instances teachers who have felt the value of this type of procedure have made arrangements within the staff whereby they divide their classes by five and send each group for a study period in other teachers' rooms, thereby engaging five teachers in the supervision of their class while they engage in the "C" group. Of course the courtesy is exchanged.

The possibilities for effective ways to utilize the "C" group within the professional development of an educational staff are unlimited once we think creatively about the advantages. It is usually important to establish some ground rules about group membership. It is preferable to have the group a closed group, meaning that no one joins the group once it has started. When additional teachers become interested in the group process, another group is formed. This provides for better continuity.

The group should meet in a physically comfortable setting which permits them to sit in a circle. The arrangement should be such that the room is pleasantly furnished and creates a confidential atmosphere.

Group Composition

Experience dictates that it is important to have a heterogeneous type of group in the sense that it represents experienced as well as inexperienced teachers, older as well as younger staff members, and people with different ideas about and experiences with the educational process. It is usually best to work with staff members who are able to share some similar interests, e.g., all primary grade teachers or all junior high staff. Frequently a great discrepancy in the age level of the children being discussed will serve as a handicap in terms of the concerns of the teachers in attendance.

In developing his first group, the consultant must consider obtaining at least two experienced teachers who can contribute to the professional growth of the group, as well as several young teachers who can bring their new ideas about educational procedures. The focus is on improving communication; hence, the necessity of this type of diversity.

Experience also indicates that teacher groups work best when they are restricted to five members plus the leader. This allows each member of the group to become easily involved at each meeting. This is more effective than developing a case study approach which focuses strictly on one child or one teacher and his problems. The value in the process comes as members recognize that they all have problems and can benefit from the mutual opportunity to share and discuss ideas.

Membership in the group is always voluntary, never by recommendation of others. Before becoming a member of the group, each teacher will have a brief interview with the leader to clarify the goals of the group in general and to establish some concrete, individual goals which that teacher hopes to accomplish through participation. Teachers qualify for membership by meeting three conditions: having (1) a concern to discuss, (2) a willingness to discuss that concern, and (3) a real interest in being helpful to other staff members. They must recognize that they are making a contract which involves their willingness to present their concerns as well as to be of assistance to others.

Getting Started

Even though the consultant will have explained through verbal as well as written material the purposes of the group, and will have held an individual interview with each group member, he must remember that the first session of the group is likely to produce a degree of anxiety on the part of both the leader and the group members. This is a new experience for all, and there will be some preliminary attempts to clarify roles and purposes. It will be important that the consultant set the stage by restructuring the purpose of the group and by seeing to it that while the anxiety level of members is being reduced, the primary purposes of the group are being adhered to.

Experience indicates that the group members need to become better acquainted with each other. Exercises which facilitate an awareness of verbal and nonverbal communication are helpful. Some productive assignments involve having half of the group become concerned with a topic such as "Become a Group" or "Make Yourself Known to Each Other." The other half of the group observes how this procedure is processed and then gives specific feedback to group members about what they liked about what they saw and what they didn't like in terms of that individual's interactions and communications.

One of the most effective procedures for breaking down interpersonal estrangement is Dr. Herbert Otto's Depth-Unfoldment Experience (1967). In this procedure the leader tells the group that the first task is to get to know each other better. Members are then given some possibilities of exploring various ways to get to know each other better. The leader then introduces the DUE method, suggesting that it is an approach which requires a deeper sharing of self and courage. He suggests that while it may produce tension, the benefits are distinctly worthwhile. He only utilizes the approach if all members of the group are willing to cooperate. In the procedure, each individual has a set period of time (five or six minutes) to share himself. He uses the first part of the period to tell about key experiences in his life that he believes made him the person that he is. The final minute is used to describe the happiest moment of his life. If the group member doesn't use all of his time, the other participants may ask him questions. The leader always begins this method by sharing himself with the group, thereby setting the tone and establishing the depth of the experience.

PSYCHOLOGICAL FOUNDATIONS FOR GROUP APPROACHES

This approach to group work requires training in group dynamics and group procedures. It is most effective when the leader understands certain basic assumptions about the nature of human behavior. These groups are formulated and organized on the basis of the following socio-teleological constructs:

1. Behavior is understood on a holistic basis and comprehended in terms of its unity and pattern. The holistic understanding of human behavior places an emphasis on the pattern of behavior in contrast to the details or specific units of behavior. The group leader is always aware of the patterns of behavior which are revealed in the classroom and among group members. Psychological movement and the transactions between teacher and child or teacher and teacher clarify the purposive nature of the behavior.

2. The significance of behavior lies in its social consequences. Because behavior is influenced by interpersonal relationships, the group provides an excellent setting for understanding the meaning of behavior.

3. Man is understood as a social being whose behavior makes sense in terms of its social context. The interactions and transactions between people (teacher-child, teacher-teacher) help to clarify the meaning of behavior. Since all behavior has social meaning, the group provides a significant setting for creating awareness of the meaning of behavior.

4. Motivation is best comprehended by observing ways in which the individual seeks to be known or become significant. Striving for significance is the result of the individual's subjectively, sometimes

unconsciously, conceived self-ideal. However, the striving emerges as the individual experiences a feeling of being less than others and compensates by attempting to become more. The group, then, is concerned with helping the individual to understand his central purpose or master motive. Group experiences enable people to observe the way in which the individual seeks to be known and to understand the forces which direct his behavior.

5. Behavior is goal-directed and purposive. Psychological movement has a purpose, and the goals are more clearly revealed in group interaction. Psychological transactions and the consultee's response and feelings about the interaction reveal possible purposes of misbehavior, i.e., attention getting, power seeking, revenge, and display of inadequacy (Dreikurs 1968).

6. Belonging is a basic requisite for human development. The group helps teachers to recognize they have common problems and can grow from participating in the give-and-take of group consultation. The group provides a caring and concerned environment and a special setting for growth through the feeling of belonging and a commitment to change.

7. The phenomenological point of view emphasizes that man is understood in terms of his perceptions. The group helps the individual to explore his phenomenological field, and the interaction provides him with new data regarding his feelings, attitudes, and values. The group experience enables him to reevaluate and change his perceptions.

8. The group experience is a unique opportunity to develop a feeling of belonging and to create social interest that is basic to the development of mental health. The individual has the opportunity to develop his social interest, his capacity to give and to take, and to become concerned about others. The development of social interest, then, makes for more effective staff relationships.

The leader supplies didactic material which he shares with the group so that they become acquainted with the socio-teleological approach. This material is discussed with the group in order to clarify the psychological principles used in understanding behavior. The didactic material supplied usually includes:

a. A brief handout—the "C" Group

b. An explanation of the Adlerian or socio-teleological approach

c. A chart, "Identifying the Goals of Children's Misbehavior"

These are presented on the following seven pages.

THE "C" GROUP

Purpose:

1. To develop an understanding of the practical applications of the dynamics of human behavior. To enable participants to develop hypotheses regarding behavior and specific recommendations.
2. To become aware of the interrelationship between patterns of child behavior and one's own life style. To experience the benefits of group learning.
3. To help teachers to see patterns of behavior in children and to develop procedures for improving relationships and behavior.
4. To provide a channel for open communication so members can share experiences and insights.

Practical Value for Teachers:

1. Sharing of similar concerns about children and the learning process.
2. Learning how to deal more effectively with children's misbehavior.
3. Becoming acquainted with skills in leading classroom discussions concerned with pupil attitudes, behavior beliefs, and perceptions.
4. Becoming aware of our methods of relating to others and receiving feedback on how we come over to others.

Rationale:

Most problems are interpersonal and social. Problems with children originate in group interactions and can be best solved by the teachers participating in a teacher group. The "C" group developed because of the mounting evidence that lectures, discussion, and telling would not help change the basic attitudes of teachers, parents, and students.

Schools have not devised effective ways for teachers to share with each other effective procedures. The "C" group is a channel for communication. The group provides support, a chance to express personal feelings and to share common problems and solutions for those problems, and a chance to gain feedback for oneself.

What Does "C" Stand For?

The group has been titled "C" group because the dynamic forces which operate in the group all begin with the letter "C": collaboration, consultation, clarification, confrontation, communication, concern and caring, confidentiality, commitment, change, and cohesion.

Possible Organizational Format:

1. Meet once a week for one hour.
2. Meet at least six to eight times.
3. Meet at a time convenient for the four to six teachers involved.

BASIC ASSUMPTIONS UNDERLYING THE DEVELOPMENT
OF PERSONALITY ACCORDING TO ALFRED ADLER

*This brief overview of Adler's socio-teleological approach was developed
by advanced students in a workshop at the University of British Columbia
the summer of 1971. It is designed to introduce teachers to Adlerian psychology.*

People who are concerned with the task of understanding and influencing
behavior generally operate on some basic assumptions about the nature of
man. The Adlerian (Individual Psychology) model of personality development states that man determines his own behavior, that he is active and
responsible and is, indeed, both "the artist and the painting."

The following assumptions are basic to Adler's model of man:

1. *Man is Primarily a Social Being.*

Adler said that all behavior takes place in a social field. Hence, man's behavior can be understood only if one considers him in the social situation. It
is in his social interaction that conflicts arise. That is, his struggles are interpersonal rather than intrapersonal. Adler believes that normality equals
social interest and that this social interest is the key concept to understanding
human behavior. The more the social interest of an individual is developed,
the more harmonious his relationship is with his fellow man, and "the more
successful he will be in fulfilling his three[1] life tasks of work, love and
friendship and the better balanced his character and personality will be."

"The social interest has no fixed objectives. Much more truly it can be said
to create an attitude to life, a desire to co-operate with others in some way
and to master the situations of life. *Social interest* is the expression of our
capacity to give and take."[2]

2. *Man is Self-determined.*

Man is not a victim of heredity, societal conditions, or impulses. He makes
choices. His uniqueness is the result of what he perceives and how he
chooses to perceive it.

---

[1] Dreikurs and Mosak have added two more tasks: (a) to get along with self and
(b) to establish relations with the universe and religion.
[2] Rudolf Dreikurs, *Fundamentals of Adlerian Psychology* (New York: Greenberg,
1950), p. 9.

"It is obvious from everything that a human being does that he has the power to orientate towards a certain environment, for ultimately his action and inaction are decided solely by the question of 'which way?' or 'for what purpose?' He is not driven through life by his past, but impelled to go forward into the future and the force that impels him is not an external force. He moves of his own accord. All his actions, emotions, qualities and characteristics serve the same purpose."[3]

3. *Man's Behavior is Purposive.*

Dreikurs speaks about the teleoanalytical approach (goal striving) in understanding human behavior. Adlerians believe that all behavior is part of a movement toward a goal (what Adler calls "finality"). For man, this goal is to have a place. Man's purpose is the means by which he achieves his goal (his place).

"The psychic life of man is determined by his goal. No human being can think, feel, will, dream, without all these activities being determined, continued, modified and directed toward an ever-present objective".[4]

Adler emphasizes that the significance of behavior lies in its consequences.

"Knowing the goal of an individual and knowing, also, something of the world, we must understand what the movements and expressions of his life mean, and what their value is as a preparation for his goal".[5]

4. *Man Must Be Viewed Subjectively.*

Adler states that man shouldn't try to be objective about man since objectivity does not exist. When there are two explanations for one phenomenon, both are right and both are necessary to understand it. Truth is only from the point of view of the observer; one's subjective view of life—one's "private logic"—is extremely important to the understanding of behavior. The significance of man's past experience depends not so much on the experience but on how he has come to interpret it (life style), e.g., children who have a mistaken concept of life are as if they are standing in one corner and unable to move. Unless shown that they can move—can change positions in life—they may go through life this way.

5. *Man is Holistic.*

All of man's functions co-operate. He is an indivisible whole. Just as a mosaic which consists of a variety of separate tiles is meaningless unless

---

[3] Dreikurs, *Fundamentals of Alderian Psychology,* p. 13.
[4] Alfred Adler, *Understanding Human Nature* (Greenwich, Connecticut: Fawcett, 1968), p. 29.
[5] Ibid., p. 29.

we can see the whole of the pattern, so man must be seen as a whole—as indivisible.

"The whole individual, in all his aspects, reveals himself through his movements".[6]

"Behavior is the movement of an 'individual as a whole' asserting himself in his social context. All his decisions and movements reflect his guiding principles and assumptions. While specific actions may differ when the individual meets new and different situations, they remain consistent with the specific life style."[7]

Making Hypotheses About a Child's Mistaken Goals

One of the ways to guess the goal of a child is to see how you feel when he does something.

If you feel *annoyed,* his goal is probably to get *attention.*
If you feel *defeated,* the goal is probably *power.* (He wants to defeat you.)
If you feel deeply *hurt,* the goal is probably *revenge.*
If you feel utterly *hopeless,* he wants to be left alone. He is discouraged and wishes to *withdraw.*

Another way of identifying goals is to observe the reaction of the child when he is corrected. If his goal is to get attention, he may stop misbehaving—but not for long—and will try another form of misbehavior of equal intensity to keep the adult busy. If the goal is power, any attempt to stop the behavior will increase it. If it is revenge, he will continue his misbehavior and become more violent. If the goal is inadequacy, the child will likely become slower with very little movement to complete the task.

Adler believes that all men feel a basic inferiority. Since the basic need is to find one's place, the individual seeks ways of overcoming his inferiority feelings. These feelings are based on his perception of where he stands in relation to others. This stems from the transactions made within the family constellation and results in mistaken ideas about how he may find his place.

All misbehavior of children is directed towards four possible goals—mistaken goals, which a child thinks will enable him to find his place, and which reflect his discouragement.

---

[6] Don Dinkmeyer and Rudolf Dreikurs, *Encouraging Children to Learn: The Encouragement Process* (Englewood Cliffs, New Jersey: Prentice-Hall, 1963), p. 14.
[7] Ibid., p. 14.

Chart 1 (pages 220–221) indicates what these four goals are and shows them in relation to a continuum of useful to useless behavior, or behavior which shows social interest to that which lacks social interest. The degree of discouragement felt by the child will also have a bearing on his choice of goal.

IDENTIFYING THE GOALS

INCREASED SOCIAL INTEREST ◄──────► DIMINISHED SOCIAL INTEREST

MINOR DISCOURAGEMENT ─── DEEP DISCOURAGEMENT

	USEFUL		USELESS		
	Active Constructive	*Passive Constructive*	*Active Destructive*	*Passive Destructive*	*Child's Action & The Message*
	"Success" Cute remarks Seeks praise and recognition Performs for attention Stunts Overambition Impression of excellence (may seem to be an "ideal" student, but goal is self-elevation not learning)	"Charm" Excess pleasantness and charm "Model" child Bright sayings, often not original Little initiative Exaggerated con-scientiousness "Southern belle," (are often the "teacher's pets")	"Nuisance" Show off Clown Restless Talks out of turn "The brat" Makes minor mischief "Walking question mark" (questions not for information but for notoriety) Speech impediments Self-indulgence	"Laziness" Clumsiness, ineptness Lack of ability Lack of stamina Untidiness Fearfulness Bashfulness Anxiety Frivolity Performance and reading difficulties	"Nuisance" Show off Clown Lazy Puts others in his ser▮ keeps teacher busy I only count when I ▮ being noticed or se▮
	A Criterion of Social-Emotional Maturing is "Social Interest" Respects the rights of others Is tolerant of others Is interested in others Co-operates with others Encourages others Is courageous Has a true sense of his own worth Has a feeling of belonging Has socially acceptable goals Puts forth genuine effort Meets the needs of the situation Is willing to share rather than "How much can I get?" Thinks of "We" rather than just "I"		"Rebel" Argues and contradicts Openly disobedient Refuses to do work Defies authority Continues for-bidden acts Aggressive May be truant	"Stubborn" Extreme laziness Stubbornness Disobedience (passive) Forgetting	"Stubborn" Argues Temper tantrums Tells lies Disobedient Does opposite to instr▮ Does little or no work Says "If you don't let do what I want you▮ don't love me." I only count when I a▮ dominating.
			"Vicious" Violent Brutal Steals (Leader of juvenile delinquent gangs)	"Violent passivity" Sullen Defiant	"Vicious" Steals Sullen Defiant Will hurt animals, peers and adults Kicks, bites, scratches Sore loser Potential delinquent I can't be liked and I count if I can hurt ▮
	Presented by Dr. Don Dinkmeyer Adapted from Edith A. Dewey, January, 1970 Adaptation of charts by Dr. Rudolf Dreikurs, M. L. Bullard and Pearl Cassel		"Hopeless" Stupidity Indolence Inaptitude (Pseudo feeble-minded) (Inferiority complex)		"Feels hopeless" Stupid actions Inferiority complex Gives up Rarely participates Says "leave me alone, can't do anything w▮ I can't do anything rig▮ I don't ever try. I am no good, and inc▮

This chart first appeared in: Don Dinkmeyer, "The 'C' Group: Integrating Knowledge and

CORRECTIONS OF MISBEHAVIOR

eacher's Reaction	The Child's Probable Goal And His "Faulty Logic"	Teacher's Corrective Procedures	Teacher's Interpretations Of Child's Goal To Him All questions must be asked in a friendly non-judgmental way and NOT at times of conflict.
‍t busy by child. ‍emind, scold, coax e child extra service. ‍ed by constructive hild. ‍d. ‍pies too much ‍ime." ‍e would ‍ie alone."	GOAL I. (AGM) ATTENTION-GETTING Child seeks proof of his acceptance and approval. He puts others in his service, seeks help. "Only when people pay attention to me do I feel I have a place."	Give attention when child is not making a bid for it. Ignore the misbehaving child. Be firm. Realize that punishing, rewarding, coaxing, scolding and giving service are attention.	"Could it be that you want me to notice you?" "Could it be that you want me to do special things for you?" ". . . keep me busy with you?"
‍dership of the threatened. ‍eated. ‍running this ‍He or I?" ‍let him get ‍vith this."	GOAL II. POWER Wants to be the boss. "I only count if you do what I want." "If you don't let me do what I want you don't love me."	Withdraw from the conflict. "Take your sail out of his wind." Recognize and admit that the child has power. Appeal for child's help, enlist his cooperation, give him responsibility.	"Could it be that you want to show me that you can do what you want and no one can stop you? "Could it be that you want to be the boss?" ". . . get me to do what you want?"
‍he child. ‍eply hurt. ‍ed by child. ‍ get even. ‍n he be so mean?"	GOAL III. REVENGE Tries to hurt as he feels hurt by others. "My only hope is to get even with them."	Avoid punishment. Win the child. Try to convince him that he is liked. Do not become hurt. Enlist a "buddy" for him. Use group encouragement.	"Could it be that you want to hurt me and/or the children?" "Could it be that you want to get even?"
‍pless. ‍know what to do. ‍do anything ‍im!" ‍p!"	GOAL IV. DISPLAY OF INADEQUACY Tries to be left alone. Feels hopeless. "I don't want anyone to know how stupid I am."	Avoid discouragement yourself. Don't give up. Show faith in child. Lots of encouragement. Use constructive approach.	"Could it be that you want to be left alone." ". . . you feel stupid and don't want people to know?"

Experience to Change Behavior." *The Counseling Psychologist* 3, no. 1 (1971): 68–69.

GROUP MECHANISMS

The group leader must be aware of the mechanisms which occur in the group and their effect upon the members. He is aware that it is his responsibility to create a climate and develop interactions which promote personal-social growth, self-understanding, and eventually change. Through utilization of therapeutic forces in the group, he facilitates a climate for change and more effective communications.

Group mechanisms are processes that occur within a therapeutic group. They have considerable potential for increasing communication and facilitating development. However, they do not occur without some effort on the part of the group leader. The mechanisms provide the catalyst for the development of individuals within the group as well as the total group. The mechanisms that are particularly important for the teacher groups are those originally identified by Corsini and Rosenberg (1955). These mechanisms, briefly described, include:

1. *Acceptance*—the respect and empathy which each individual in the group receives as a person of value. Acceptance involves group identification and a strong communal feeling which is the opposite of alienation. These strong feelings of belonging are basic to developing a group atmosphere.

2. *Ventilation*—the opportunity for group members to express feelings which previously have been internalized. The group permits members to expose their inner selves, their feelings, thoughts, and values, whether they be negative and hostile, or positive and accepting.

3. *Reality Testing*—the opportunity to experience a set of social relationships in which one can test his attitudes, values, actions, and relationship skills, and find ways to see his behavior more accurately. This type of testing also provides opportunities for the member to experiment with new social relationship skills.

4. *Transference*—the development of a strong emotional attachment, which may involve either positive or negative feelings, but which tends to cement the group into a cohesive group. Transference suggests that the group provides considerable opportunities for emotional support.

5. *Intellectualization and Feedback*—the concern of the group with learning that is both cognitive and affective, which occurs in the group. Feedback from group members, when properly processed, eventually develops new information and helps to create insight. Group members become aware of themselves and are able to learn about their feelings, values, purposes, and perceptions; hence, to reevaluate all of their assumptions and attitudes about life.

6. *Interaction*—the relationships that occur within the group which enable the consultant and group members to see the individual's purposes. Group interaction enables the consultant not only to depend on what the person says he does, but on his behavior that can be clearly observed in the group transactions.

7. *Universalization*—the realization that one is not unique, and that others have similar problems. This awareness reduces alienation, breaks down isolation, and stimulates communication by creating a climate of mutuality.

8. *Altruism*—the positive desire in man to help others, to lose oneself in service and mutual assistance. This is best facilitated in a group which provides the opportunity to be of mutual service. The leader, as a model of altruism, encourages this attitude and behavior.

9. *Spectator Therapy*—the helping of group members to achieve an understanding of self by hearing about the concerns of others. This opportunity to listen to problems often puts their own problems into better focus, and although it is a passive kind of participation, it often brings considerable change.

Group mechanisms are dynamic processes that occur within a therapeutic group which have potentiality for serving as a catalyst for developing the individual. The group may be the only situation where a member can experience some of these processes. The consultant uses these mechanisms as therapeutic forces to promote change.

THE "C" GROUP

There is considerable evidence and experience to indicate that teachers are not helped significantly through lectures, discussions, or by merely being told about new methods of understanding children. Unless there is personal involvement and opportunity to test out ideas, match them to one's style of life, internalize the new concepts, and then exchange results with other professionals, little change will occur. Schools have neglected a significant resource—the cross fertilization of ideas between experienced and inexperienced teachers led by a specialist in human behavior and group dynamics. This approach develops a new channel of communication whereby teachers can share their ideas and experiences. It also provides a model for improved communication procedures in their own classrooms.

Without the opportunity for some exchange of ideas, each teacher becomes an isolated autocrat in his own castle, succeeding or failing on the basis of his present capacities. If he is successful, he is not concerned about the incapabilities of other teachers. If he is not effective in his relationships with children, he can expect little assistance from his colleagues. Educators often do not have a systematic way whereby they can exchange ideas and assist each other in becoming more effective in the profession. Opportunities for professional growth in education are limited as compared with the sharing of ideas and procedures that occurs in professions such as medicine and psychology.

Teacher groups are concerned with helping each teacher to become more aware of his strengths and his capabilities for coping with the challenges of teaching. In this sense the groups are organized upon the principles of achievement motivation seminars insofar as they focus on strengths of individuals and seek to help them to develop meaningful personal goals (Sharp 1968a). The group is an important resource for teachers. The members may approach the group with real ambivalence, recognizing they have been unsuccessful, are eager to learn, but frightened that what they discover about themselves may be disturbing. Other members may join in a condescending sense, not aware of their part in teacher-child problems. In either situation, it is crucial to obtain full involvement, and this usually is best accomplished by helping them to identify each other's strengths and to internalize procedures for using strengths.

The "C" group is based upon a very basic principle of learning. In order to facilitate learning and change, there must be a holistic experience which involves access to the affective, cognitive, and psychomotor domains. Feelings, values, beliefs, attitudes, and behaviors must be openly revealed and considered. The false dichotomy between emotions and intellect, which is too often present in in-service education, cannot be permitted in the "C" group. This group enables the teacher to become aware of the factors that keep him from functioning more effectively.

The group is concerned about improving conditions which facilitate human potential and learning. It recognizes that the learner is a social being who must be understood in terms of the sociometrics and dynamics of the classroom group. The teacher group considers how to help students, but at the same time, considers factors which keep teachers from utilizing the understandings they already possess. Obviously, many teachers understand much more about human behavior than they are able to put into action. Moving from theory into practise is best facilitated through a group experience where one becomes more aware of the effect of feelings and beliefs upon behavior (Dinkmeyer 1971b).

This new approach has been labeled the "C" group because factors which make it effective begin with a "C." They include: collaborating, consulting, clarifying, communicating, being cohesive, confronting, being concerned, caring, being confidential, being committed and being willing to change. This approach is not to be confused with the T group, for it goes beyond consideration of the process and self and examines actual transactions between teacher and child and develops specific procedures for new relationships.

However, the process also confronts the teacher with how his own attitudes and feelings often keep him from developing new relationships or changing his behavior. The process thereby is a combination of the didactic and experiential.

The specific components of the "C" group are:

1. The group collaborates and works together on mutual concerns. The leader has an equal position; there are no superior-inferior relationships between him and the group or between members of the group. They are all in the group for the purpose of mutual help.

2. Consultation is both received and provided by the teachers. The interaction that occurs within the group between the leader and the members helps group members to become aware of new approaches with children.

3. The group clarifies for each member his belief systems, his feelings, and the congruency or incongruency between his behavior, his beliefs, and his feelings.

4. Confrontation makes the group more productive insofar as it produces more realistic and honest feedback. There is an expectation that each individual will see himself, his purposes, his attitudes, his beliefs, and will be willing to confront other members about *their* psychological make-up. Members in the group confront each other because they want to help each member to become more effective.

5. The group is concerned and shows that it cares. This concern leads members to collaborate, consult, clarify, and confront, in order to develop the human potential of both children and group members.

6. The group is confidential in the sense that whatever is discussed within the group stays within the group. The purpose is to be mutually helpful, not to generate gossip.

7. The group helps individuals to develop a commitment to change. Participants in the group become involved in helping members to recognize that they really can change only them-

selves. They may come to the group expecting to change children, but they soon learn that *they* must develop a specific commitment to take an action before the next "C" group that will attempt to change their approach to the problem.

8. The group is a new channel for communication insofar as it communicates not only ideas but feelings, attitudes, and beliefs. Members become involved with each other as persons.

9. The group members recognize that changing children's behavior often requires that they change their beliefs, attitudes, and procedures.

10. The group is most effective when there is cohesion and the members work together as a team.

"C" groups usually are developed or formed from teachers who have similar concerns or who work with the same children. They may be at the same grade level or part of a team of teachers. Groups are most effective when they are heterogeneous in terms of teacher personality and experience, but are concerned with a similar set of behavioral or developmental problems. However, small schools have found that "C" groups can be formed from any group of teachers who have an interest in human behavior and are willing to work together. The basic criterion is that they are concerned with helping each other to gain a new perception of both child behavior and themselves in order truly to see the transactions that are occurring in the classroom.

The specific procedures are similar to those utilized in group work. The leader is aware of group mechanisms and procedures which develop interaction. However, he has a special purpose and that is to help the group to accomplish both a didactic and affective experience. The authors have found it common that beginning "C" groups become involved with trivia and operate as if they were extensions of the teachers' lounge. Early themes may focus on mere ventilation and complaining: "Isn't it awful . . . ," "That type of child . . . ," "Those parents . . . ," and similar unproductive themes. The members of the group, similar to other groups, are often anxious, self-conscious, frustrated, and confused. They are not clear about their purposes nor the purposes of the group. The confused pattern of talk often is really asking a basic question: "What do we do in the 'C' group?" "What can we expect to happen here?" This is the point at which the leader must be certain that he structures the group in such a way that he models empathy, caring, understanding, accepting, clarifying, and confronting behavior. He helps to set a model and pace for the group by exemplifying the types of behavior, attitudes, and feelings which are expected to be norms for this group.

The consultant surveys the group to determine the type of children that are of concern at the moment. He helps the teachers to select a child who represents a mutual concern. It is important to find a problem that is universal, since this will help to develop a cohesive group. As soon as the teachers recognize many of them have the same type of problems, they will be more willing to cooperate and collaborate.

The group develops other mechanisms, such as the feeling of acceptance, altruism, and the willingness to give as well as receive help. The leader is aware that it is his responsibility to use the mechanisms to promote growth. Mechanisms do not occur automatically, and the leader must be alert to methods which facilitate interactions that increase communication and personal and group development. There is also an opportunity for reality testing, testing of new ideas, and developing alternate approaches. The group begins by selecting a child and looking at four factors in connection with the teacher-child situation:

1. What did the child do?
2. How did you (the teacher) respond to his action?
3. How did you feel when the child was misbehaving and you were responding?
4. How did the child respond to your corrective efforts?

By going through the four steps, one is able to see the pattern in the behavior and to become more conscious of the purpose of the behavior. Insofar as the group helps teachers to develop insight and take action, they facilitate the making of commitments to new kinds of behavior.

Some groups need communication exercises which help them to become more willing to share and more committed to change. If readiness for honest and open interaction does not exist in the group, it must be established. We have found that it is often helpful to use a group exercise such as Herbert Otto's DUE Experience (Otto 1967), which was discussed earlier. The DUE Experience encourages members to become better acquainted. They talk about experiences that have been formative in the development of their personalities, and they share events they consider to be most significant in their development. They also tell about the happiest moments in their life. This experience generally stimulates feelings of mutuality, belonging, and caring. The alienation apparent in many groups is diminished when group members appear as real persons with real problems, committed to helping each other.

Group members are helpful to each other insofar as they process feedback on their perceptions of each member's behavior, attitudes, and feelings. This is accomplished through clarifying, confronting, and reflecting procedures. The members provide new approaches to the problem, which were developed from their experiences with such children or their professional training. Teachers also are able to supply practical procedures in behavior modification, logical consequences, and other specific procedures to help children to develop in a more positive direction.

Ideas are discussed in relationship to a specific child, never in the abstract. The procedures must be able to be accepted and internalized and blend with the personality of the teacher. Effective procedures often do not work because the teacher's perceptions, beliefs, and feelings keep him from implementation. However, each teacher must decide on the kinds of ideas which he is willing to accept and which he will utilize and institute before the next meeting. The discussion is usually concluded by the leader helping each member to make a commitment to change.

The leader of the "C" group is concerned with involving as many members as possible in presenting their concerns. The group focuses on a particular teacher-child interaction to the extent that tentative hypotheses and plans are made, including a teacher commitment. It is a goal to go all around the group so that all may be involved in helping each other, as well as in being consultees. The group's development is generally impaired by regressing to a case-study approach wherein time permits assisting but one or two teachers.

The following is an excerpt from a teacher group in its eighth session. The consultant helps the teachers to become aware of their beliefs and methods of communication.

C: "I wonder what would happen if you noticed something positive he is doing."

T-1:   "Well, with Jeff, I have tried complimenting him when he does good work, but I have never had a good result. It's as if he feels, 'Well, OK, I've done it. Now I'm through and I can go back again and not do any work.'"

C: "I mean working with him when he hasn't finished his work, or finding some asset in his personality."

T-1:   "Sometimes . . I'll be walking by, like this morning, as he was starting his work. I said, 'That's very good work. Keep it up and finish the rest of it.' He didn't do any more after that."

C: "I wonder what happened there. Does anybody have an idea?"

T-2:   "You should have waited until he was finished, a complete paper, and then . . ."

T-3   "I think he is fighting her. Whatever she says, he is going to do the opposite."

C: "You believe it is his need to be in control?"

T-3:   "Yes, some think they are in charge."

C: "You feel challenged by these students?"

T-3:   "Right. I can't let them get by with anything."

C: "What do some of you think about that?"

T-4:   "I recognize I have the same problem about wanting to be in control."

C: "If it's important for you to have the power, what do you think the child experiences?"

T-1:   "I imagine our real problem is getting involved in fighting with them."

T-2:   "I've found things go better when I refuse to become involved in power contests."

C: "Let's look at this in another way. What if you're busy writing and somebody comes by and says, 'That's really good work. Now I hope you keep that up.' "

T-4:   "No, I don't think I would like that . ."

T-5:   "You're not satisfied with it." (laughter)

C: "Yes, what is the implication?"

T-4:   "Well, I don't expect you to really finish."

T-1:   ". . that he won't cooperate."

T-4:   "It's like a backhand slap."

T-1:   "That's really true, because I don't expect him to finish and I gave him the clue."

T-2:   "I can do that with the brighter children and say, 'Oh, that sounds like a good story,' or 'Oh, that sounds like it's going to be exciting; go on and finish it.' That excites them to want to go on. With the slower children, or the child who needs discipline, why should it work in a reverse order?"

T-4:   "Because of your attitude and expectations."

T-5:   "It's negative."
       (Begin talking all at once, explaining to each other)

T-4:   "This is great, but if you say, 'That floor you're washing looks much cleaner; I hope you are going to finish it,' they look at you and say, 'Finish it yourself.' "

T-2:   ". . . if you add that one sentence, you seem to spoil the communication."

T-4:   "That's where we have to watch our words. How important a word is! So often we say it like that; I didn't even catch it when she first said it."

T-2:   "No, I didn't either."

T-4:   "We have to learn to be more aware of our communication and the messages we send."

C: "It seems difficult to understand, but our communication does affect the child's motivation."

T-2:   "It really has to be a habit, where you have to be able to do it unconsciously, always positive."

C: "And I think that you are right about a habit. It takes a long time to get to that because you're so used to doing it the other way."

T-4:   "One thing, I don't know whether I mentioned it here, but I have found it is a tremendous help if I really take some time out when the children come in and call five or six of them out in the hall and say to each, 'Robert, I'm so thrilled that you are here because you were such a good boy this morning and it was so nice to have you in my room.' I suppose it would be like the boss coming along and saying to you he's proud of your work. I reflect on that and my afternoons go ten times better!"

T-2:   "I have got to try that. That sounds good."

T-4:   "But a lot of times I come in and begin spelling and say, 'Sit down, be quiet.' This is like throwing the monkey wrench into the machinery."

C: "Or, when you come in you could say something like, 'I noticed that you were really working at that math this morning.' . . . just some little encouragement."

To summarize, the original focus in the "C" group is on an external unit, the child. As the group develops mutual trust, the leader helps members to clarify, reflect, and confront their own feelings, attitudes, and beliefs. The purpose at this point is not group therapy, nor is it to study about children, but instead to focus on the transactions and their meaning for the teacher and the child. This is a holistic approach that involves treating the purposes, values, attitudes, beliefs, and behaviors of the children and the teacher.

ACHIEVEMENT MOTIVATION PROGRAMS

The achievement motivation programs were originated by the Stone Brandel Foundation of Chicago. This type of program is concerned with increasing human potential by emphasizing presently unidentified and unused strengths in the person. The program operates on the basic principle that individuals, regardless of their current situation, have meaningful personal goals and objectives with the capacity and desire to change and grow. The program provides a creative opportunity for individuals to design their own growth, and through the use of the group, they are encouraged to reinforce and explore constructive change (Sharp 1968b).

The objectives of the six phases of A.M.P. are:

1. Sharing through establishing group rapport which permits meaningful experiences to be shared.
2. Identifying successes and establishing positive feelings about self.
3. Identifying strengths, seeing one's uniqueness and putting these strengths into action.
4. Identifying and accepting values, developing a rank order of one's preferred values and making a commitment to action.
5. Managing conflict through identification of conflict styles and learning more positive ways of conflict management.
6. Reinforcing internal motivation via goal setting.

The Achievement Motivation Program has had considerable success in helping to facilitate the personal growth of teacher personnel. The consultant should be acquainted with these group procedures which focus on identifying strengths and successes (Otto 1967).

REFERENCES

Berenson, B. and Carkhuff, R., *Sources of Gain in Counseling and Psychotherapy: Readings and Commentary*. New York: Holt, Rinehart & Winston, 1967.

Combs, A. W. et al. *Florida Studies in the Helping Professions*. University of Florida Monographs, Social Sciences No. 37. Gainesville, Florida: University of Florida Press, 1969.

Corsini, R. and Rosenberg, B. "Mechanisms of Group Psychotherapy." *Journal of Abnormal Social Psychology* 51 (1955): 406–411.

Dinkmeyer, D. "The 'C' Group: Focus on Self as Instrument." *Phi Delta Kappan* 52, no. 10 (June 1971a): 617–619.

Dinkmeyer, D. "The 'C' Group: Integrating Knowledge and Experience to Change Behavior." *The Counseling Psychologist* 3, No. 1 (1971b).

Dreikurs, R. *Psychology in the Classroom*. 2nd ed. New York: Harper & Row, 1968.

Dreikurs, R. and Sonstegard, M. "Rationale of Group Counseling." In *Guidance and Counseling in the Elementary School: Readings in Theory and Practice*, edited by Don Dinkmeyer, pp. 278–287. New York: Holt, Rinehart & Winston, 1968.

Ellena, W. J., Stevenson, M. and Webb, H. V. "Who's a Good Teacher?" Washington, D.C.: American Association of School Administrators, NEA, 1961.

Faust, V. *The Counselor-Consultant in the Elementary School*. Boston: Houghton Mifflin, 1968.

Otto, H. *Group Methods Designed to Actualize Human Potential: A Handbook*. Chicago: Stone Brandel Center, 1967.

Sharp, B. "Within Every Student Is a Gifted Student." Achievement Motivation Seminars. Chicago: W. Clement and Jessie V. Stone Foundation, 1968a.

Sharp, B. "Every Adult Is a Gifted Adult." Achievement Motivation Seminars. Chicago: W. Clement and Jessie V. Stone Foundation, 1968b.

9

Promoting Human Potential in the Classroom

> Every child, every person can delight in learning. A new education is already here, thrusting up in spite of every barrier we have been able to build. Why not help it happen? (Leonard 1968, p. 239)

The consultant is in a unique position to do just this. It already should be apparent that a most appropriate role for the consultant is to facilitate and encourage individuals to learn and to assist them in effectively applying their learning to life. The consultant is concerned with the total learning environment that promotes or interferes with learning and with the learner's ability to make maximum use of this newly acquired skill or knowledge. In order to make this vision a reality, it seems logical to assume that the consultant will need to work with the significant adults in the individual's life, i.e., parents and teachers.

In contemplating the promotion of humaneness in the classroom, three basic assumptions put forth by Leonard (1968) need to be recognized:

1. The potential of man is much greater than we have been led to believe. When we act upon this assumption, we find that minor efforts yield major gains. This is as in G. B. Shaw's *Pygmalion,* in which the difference between a lady and a flower girl was the way she was treated, not in how she behaved.
2. Learning is enjoyable and pleasing.
3. Life's ultimate purpose is learning itself.

Literature is becoming replete with documents that testify to the failure of the school to educate people in a manner that allows them to acquire a feeling of dignity and an understanding of their world. The school is identified as being a "non" lifelike environment, and the goal of educational reform is to knock holes in the wall of the school in order to let life inside.

The culture of today seems to be changing man in a potentially harmful or dangerous way (Cox 1969, Michael 1968, Reich 1970, Roszak 1968). Environments have been developed which seem to deprive man of many experiences that are necessary for his well-being as a human being. The so-called "successful" man of today leads a meaningless, alienated, and confused existence. Man must begin to assume responsibility for the wrath that technology and industrialization have done to the culture. Each individual needs (1) to assess himself, and (2) to change the many environments that confront him (Thoresen 1971).

Erich Fromm (1968) feels that man now has three options. He can continue in his current fashion, which will result in a disturbance of the total life system (e.g., war or mental illness). He could choose to alter the course of mankind through violent revolution, which would also disrupt the whole system. His third choice would be to humanize the system in order to serve the purposes of man.

Humanistic observers believe that the responsibility for the realization of the third possibility must begin with the personal development of each individual, with the goal being to bring man into congruence with himself and his natural environment. A summary of the major concerns in creating this change is as follows:

1. Concern with the search for unity in human experience, the recognition that man must exist in harmony with nature, i.e., an ecological systems perspective.

2. Concern with awareness and awakening, with expanding the conscious range of man's behavior, especially his own internal behavior.

3. Concern with the need for compassionate persons, individuals who can communicate personally and intimately with others and who can help others experience life more positively.

4. Concern with diversity and pluralism, a reverence for the idiosyncratic and the unique in individuals.

5. Concern that formal education must seek to engage the individual in a comprehensive sense, involving the social, the emotional, the sensual as well as the academic (Thoresen 1971, pp. 2–3).

The work of family therapists and researchers is pointing more conclusively to the opinion that mental and emotional problems are not interior disorders of the "psyche" but derive from the set of relationships a person moves in daily, or from the conflict between different sets (Satir 1967). From this we can see the importance of the school environment in the development of the personality of the individual. (This is not to disregard the influences of the family, peer group, neighborhood, and the community.)

Perhaps people drop out of school, refuse to get work, or behave as they do because of defective social environments in homes, schools, and factories, and not because they are mentally ill. The environment or system could be defective in that it fails to make positive behavior pay off.

WHAT IS A CLASSROOM?

The classroom is the arena where the child and formal schooling meet. The result is a conflict between educating and socializing. Human potential is lost as creativity is legislated out and conformity mandated. In this confusion, the individual becomes lost and the classroom becomes concerned with socializing *rather than educating*. However, it is in the classroom that the consultant has his greatest resource and can make his major contribution. He is very aware that learning can be improved by enhancing the psychological setting and therefore realizes the potential value of focusing on the climate of the classroom. The consultant needs to get involved with the learning climate which includes just about anything that happens to an individual at school (Faust 1968).

As we enter the classroom, we see thirty different heads! How can the consultant help the teacher to reach each one? Perhaps he can begin by helping the teacher to see thirty different children and to let them be thirty different persons without trying to make them all alike. By using group dynamics, the teacher can help the children to learn to cooperate with one another. They can learn to value the unique contribution of each individual to the development of the group. Secondly, the teacher could stop seeing himself as different and begin to realize the similarities he shares with other teachers. Fundamental to accepting and facilitating another's uniqueness is the realization and acceptance of one's own. Teachers gain a great deal from discovering the similarities that they share with other teachers. The teacher is relieved and enlightened when he discovers that others experience the same feelings. The teacher makes even greater gains through the process of self-encounter. Through this process, he is able to realize his uniqueness and special place in the world (Greenberg 1969).

Each classroom seems to be made up of essentially opposing forces with the teacher standing in the middle. The *challenge*, then, appears to be to help the teacher amalgamate these heterogenous elements and to guide the children into reasonably harmonious collaboration with regard to the work of the school. In view of this challenge, the *goal* is to get the leaders and the followers, the builders and the destroyers, the placaters and the blamers all to work in a collaborative fashion.

It is the teacher who would like to see this situation rectified. Teachers are not able merely to observe the psychological manifestations of children and then retire quietly to their studies to work out ingenious theories. It is of little practical value that the similarity of so many cases makes it possible to categorize children according to types. With each lesson comes another demand for immediate practical action. Teaching is a profession that requires an instantaneous response and the use of the Self as Instrument (Combs et al. 1969).

It seems as though the "open classroom" is what is needed.

> It is difficult to say exactly what an open classroom is. One almost has to have been in one to feel what it is. However, there are certain things that it is not. It is important not to equate an open classroom with a "permissive" environment. In an open classroom the teacher must be as much himself as the pupils are themselves. This means that if the teacher is angry he ought to express his anger, and if he is annoyed at someone's behavior he ought to express that too. In an authoritarian classroom annoying behavior is legislated out of existence. In a "permissive" classroom the teacher pretends it isn't annoying. He also permits students to behave in certain ways, thereby retaining the authority over their behavior he pretends to be giving up. In an open situation the teacher tries to express what he feels and to deal with each situation as a communal problem (Kohl 1969, p. 15).

A. S. Neill (1960) ran his now famous school, Summerhill, on these same principles. He felt that in the disciplined home or school the children have *no* rights. In the spoiled home or school they have *all* rights. The proper school or home is one in which children and adults have *equal* rights. (It is important to distinguish that freedom is a great privilege that is accompanied by responsibility.) Gordon (1970) refers to this latter type as the "no lose" method and Dreikurs (1971) as conflict-solving procedures for "social equality."

This method is best conducted in the form of free or open discussion in which all the members of the class can take part. The group discussion takes place when a group of individuals talk and think together about a common problem or topic. The process differs from mere conversation in that it has direction, examines problems, and faces many of the unpleasant details that are normally avoided. In the problem-solving process, a democratic interchange of ideas, guided by the needs of the group, is evident (Dreikurs, Grunwald and Pepper 1971). In this process, the individual deals not only with the problems set by the lesson but also the problems of relating and communicating with his classmates. As Spiel (1962) states, "the child is being trained at one and the same time for his work in the world and for his place in the community" (p. 47).

The following example taken from Dreikurs, Grunwald and Pepper (1971, p. 104), demonstrates how many teachers mistakenly use "group discussions" to lecture and talk at pupils.

Teacher: I'd like to talk to you about our basketball. I repeat, "a basketball," not "a football." I am sure all of you know the difference. A basketball is meant to be thrown into a basket. That's why it is called "basketball." This afternoon I saw some of you kicking it. Do you know what may happen when you kick it? It may get a hole in it and then we'd have to have it repaired. Do you know how much it costs to have such a ball repaired? It's not cheap, and the school will not pay for it. You know who will have to pay for it? You will. I know that you enjoy that basketball and wouldn't want anything to happen to it, so let's all be very careful how we use it. All right? (Children nod their heads.) I knew you'd see it my way, and I'm very proud of you.

This teacher is trying to convey friendliness and confidence in the children. However, she still resorts to "preaching." Chances are that the children pay little attention to what she is saying. She might have said:

Teacher: I must talk to you about our basketball. I know that you enjoy playing with it, but before we can take it out again, we'll have to make some decisions. Whose ball is it?
Child: Ours.
Teacher: I am afraid it is not.
Child: It belongs to the school.
Teacher: That's right. We may use it, but we are responsible if anything were to happen to it. How can we prevent this? (The children will now discuss various possibilities of how to use the ball so that no damage should occur.)
Teacher: What should we do if any of the children should kick it?

Children will then suggest a number of consequences that will make sense to the possible offenders. They may suggest that these children not be permitted to play basketball for a week or two. They may suggest that these children should pay for any damage they have done. The important thing is that the students need to be involved in the discussion and decision making.

Children are encouraged in this process to learn by finding out things for themselves. This may be called the "active" method. It can be contrasted with the "passive" method, which forces the learner to absorb what the teacher and textbooks present for him. Because the individual needs to do the work for *his* own education, other people can only help him. *Education is a do-it-yourself job.* The "active" method facilitates independent thought, which is a precursor to the development of an *independent* human being.

The classroom should provide conditions which promote the authentic growth of each individual. Variety and diversity in the environment provide the best opportunity for free exploration and experimentation. Teachers can facilitate the "authentic" development of the individual in the following ways:

1. They can confirm for the child his uniqueness, which therefore encourages further development of the self.
2. They can be authentically present, therefore becoming sources of life for the child to emulate. They can then stimulate and challenge children and enable them to further establish and clarify their own self-identity and deepen and extend their relations with others.
3. They may provide opportunities and resources which children need to actualize their potentialities and to gain new perceptions and insights of man, nature, and the universe.

THE TARGET: A LEARNING ENVIRONMENT THAT PROMOTES HUMANENESS

Education must go beyond the acquisition of a few facts and a faster reading rate. People need help in using and developing their innate creative potential. We need to go beyond our current level and help to create a truly humanistic education. This involves helping our young to develop compassion, concern for others, faith in themselves, the ability to think creatively, the ability to love, the ability to cooperate with others, the ability to maintain good health, and, above all, the ability to remain open to other people and new experiences at all times (Blume 1971).

The *context* in which an activity takes place becomes crucial for learning. The positive or negative feelings that tend to accompany an activity determine the learning involved. An individual's achievement in school, personality, and behavior is recognized as being at least partially related to the environmental influences of the school, community, and home. What the individual is and what he is to become seem to be a function of his total environment. Recently, specific study and research have been investigating school climates and learning environments. The results seem to indicate that the consultant needs to know the sociological and psychological conditions which effect the school climate in order to be productive.

The consultant's basic function in the classroom is to facilitate learning. His goal is to maximize the educational potential of each individual by helping to supply a learning climate which personalizes and humanizes. Some activities which facilitate the humanization process and corresponding dehumanizing practises are as follows:

Humanizing Practises	*Dehumanizing Practises*
Open dialogue	Lack of communication
Participation in decision making	Authoritarianism
Acceptance and facilitation	Rejection and frustration
Involvement and sharing	Isolation and alienation
Authentic and honest relationships	Artificiality and dishonesty
Respect and trust	Distrust and disrespect
Capacity for joy	Continuous stress and pressure
Openness to experience	Closing of environment
Appreciation and warmth	Depreciation and coldness
Personal responsibility	Personal irresponsibility
Prevailing successes	Prevailing failures
Freedom to disengage	Compulsion to engage
Positive expectations	Negative expectations
Stimulation of imagination	Prescribed reality
Individualized education	Groups standards and comparisons
Enriched and responsive environment	Impoverished and unresponsive environment
Reasonable guidance	Domination and license
Continuous progress	Stagnation
Flexibility and tolerance	Rigidity and fear of change

Consideration and politeness	Sarcasm and ridicule
Encouragement of expression	Discouragement of expression
Commitment to absolute human value	Rejection of human worth

(Purkey 1971)

Some of the important principles that the consultant can help the teacher to acquire include:

1. People do only what they would prefer to do.
2. The two aspects of learning are: 1) acquiring new information, and 2) discovering the *personal meaning* of that information. Information in itself is useless.
3. It is more appropriate for people to learn a few concepts or principles rather than many facts.
4. Learning is much more efficient if the learner first feels a need to know that which is to be learned.
5. People learn more easily and rapidly if they are involved in making the important decisions about their learning.
6. People learn and grow more quickly if they are not afraid to make mistakes.
7. Objectivity is not very useful for teachers.
8. Teachers teach the way they have been taught—not the way they have been trained to teach.
9. Pressure on students produces negative behaviors, such as cheating, avoidance, fearfulness, and psychosomatic illness.
10. Teachers would be more effective if they were self-actualizers.

(Blume 1971)

The consultant can also help the teacher to overcome the myths that have permeated education and tend to corrupt our contacts with children. Dwight Allen (1971) believes that if we can overcome this difficult task, we can reform the educational system from within. He lists seven of these deadly myths.

1. Children are stupid until the teacher makes them smart.
2. Rationality is good, and the body and the emotions are inherently dangerous and must at all times be under strict control.

3. There is one best or perfect way to solve a problem.
4. Knowledge is sacred, certain, and fixed.
5. The teaching machine is most effective because education is a mechanical rather than organic process.
6. Learning takes place in school and nowhere else.
7. The teacher is an interchangeable part in the educational machine.

The classroom should be a place where individualized and personally meaningful instruction flourishes. Students should be released from the closed, desk-bound classroom. Each individual pupil has unique needs that should be met. A situation that is stimulating, life-like, safe, and provides success will reach this goal more effectively.

The teacher's job is to arrange the external conditions of learning, provide a set of experiences that are likely to produce certain learnings. The consultant should be able to arrange growth-inducing experiences from which the teacher is likely to learn those attitudes and skills useful in dealing with his environment. The consultant realizes that when attempting to assist individuals in making personally satisfying decisions, these decisions are heavily influenced by feelings and attitudes learned from life experiences.

It appears crucial for the consultant to help the teacher to arrange learning experiences in ways that strengthen each individual's self-esteem and meet each child's social, emotional, and academic needs. These experiences can best be accomplished in an atmosphere characterized by:

1. A mutual respect and trust by teacher and child.
2. A focus on mutual alignment of purposes by teacher and child.
3. A feeling on the part of pupils that they belong to the group.
4. An environment where it is safe for the child to look at inner needs, hopes, and wishes.
5. An opportunity to express needs which, if not articulated and clarified, hamper the learning process.
6. An emphasis on the importance of self-evaluation in contrast to evaluation by others.
7. A climate marked by identification, recognition, acceptance, and appreciation of individual differences.
8. An emphasis on growth from dependence to independence.
9. Situations in which limits are most often a result of natural and logical consequences and not merely a reflection of the personal needs of the teacher.

(Dinkmeyer 1970a, p. 10)

The feelings which accompany learning activities have a significant effect upon the results. If a child has positive feelings, he tends to be motivated toward the task, to participate with a high degree of involvement, and be more likely to derive permanent gains from his efforts. Conversely, if his feelings are negative, he is poorly motivated, participates on a minimal basis, and is less likely to derive permanent gains from his efforts (Dinkmeyer 1970b).

Maxwell Maltz (1966) demonstrated how one can utilize the feelings of success to develop the success syndrome. Glasser (1969) in his book *Schools Without Failure* indicated how we can use choice to build better behavior. There are a number of indications that the teacher can no longer act as if the psychological relationship with the child is insignificant (Dinkmeyer 1970c).

Furthermore, there are numerous studies (Gibby 1967, Stotland and Zander 1958) supporting the conclusion that failure reduces ambition, lowers self-esteem, and is generally disruptive to learning (Carlson, Rotter and Dinkmeyer 1971). In the final analysis, most failure experienced by children in the school is created. Such devices as grades, report cards, groupings, and retentions are contrived for the benefit of the educational institution (Purkey and Harriff 1970). The likelihood that the individual will experience success cannot be left to chance. As Matheny (1971) feels, "The teacher's cooperation in adjusting demands to the student's current capabilities, in providing liberal rewards for the student's efforts, and in minimizing the consequences of failure is an absolute necessity" (p. 442).

The social process of learning cannot be ignored. The fact that most classroom learning occurs in a social setting in which interaction with one's peers is significant. Teachers should be acquainted with the practical implementation of sociometrics, group dynamics, and group procedures (Dinkmeyer and Caldwell 1970).

A teacher may work and plan carefully to carry out what he regards as an exceptional learning experience, but what each pupil learns depends upon his perception of the meaning, worth, and purpose of the activity. The classroom should focus on aligning teacher-pupil purposes. If this is to be accomplished pupil involvement must be utilized. As the teacher and the learner begin to perceive the purposes and goals of their behavior, the more likely they will recognize the basis of their faulty relationships with others.

The child has social and emotional needs which frequently take precedence over his academic needs. These needs must be satisfied first if his time and energies are to be available for academic attainment (Prescott 1957). Despite the many problem behaviors that children show, the main factor that is found in underachievement, lack of motivation, and unproductive conduct is low self-esteem. This low self-esteem is a result of our traditional ways of presenting learning opportunities (Randolph and Howe 1966).

The individual's self-concept is a primary source of motivation. It is derived in part from attitudes toward him expressed by the significant adults in his life (Cooley 1902). If he is loved and accepted, then he is more likely to possess self-confidence and courage, enabling him to develop an active-constructive approach to life.

Learning experiences are not merely cognitive but also affective and attitudinal, showing concern for attitudes, values, purposes, and feelings. This is mandatory in order to make meaningful instruction a reality. When this occurs, the following results:

1. Provision for maximum flexibility in the curriculum is made.
2. Each individual is understood and permitted to progress at his own rate.
3. Individualized teaching procedures are implemented.
4. Assets and successes are emphasized.
5. Each child is permitted to proceed in terms of the greatest acceleration possible for him.
6. Each child is helped to realize his greatest potential and to develop a more realistic self-concept.
7. Independent study in those areas in which the child has a genuine interest is provided.
8. The ultimate goals of education and, therefore, self-discipline are emphasized.
9. The enhancement of the individual's worth is a genuine concern.

(Dinkmeyer 1968)

This active method allows the pupil to think for himself and to develop into an independent human being. This involves making personal decisions and accepting the corresponding consequences. This type of program not only acknowledges, but *gives* students the right to make choices concerning their own destinies.

The classroom experience needs to be built around the unique needs of each student in terms of his purposes, self-concept, style of life, and ultimate potentiality for positive growth. The teacher needs to be able to diagnose the individual's needs and help him to reach an appropriate developmental level. The consultant can help the teacher to gain competency in these areas through the following identification procedures:

1. The utilization of tests for diagnostic purposes. The child, however, should not just be an object of study but a participant in self-study.
2. The recording of anecdotes to show the child's psychological movement and the consequences of his behavior.
3. A sociometric study of the group dynamics. This will help in discovering an individual's purposes.

Possibilities abound for the consultant to help the teacher in enhancing the individual's development. For example, in the area of emotional development, individual goal cards signed by the child can establish specific commitments, developmental contracts of tasks the child agrees to accomplish.

Education of the type being advocated by the consultant is centered around several assumptions. The teacher needs to become aware of these assumptions in order to approach education from this perspective:

1. Education is directed at human effectiveness, helping each individual to develop his human potential.
2. Personal meaning is the most important ingredient in learning. Knowledge, facts, and other types of objective or abstract meaning are secondary.
3. Involvement of the total organismic reaction (thoughts, feelings, and actions) is more effective in learning than isolation of intellectual or affective reactions.
4. Complete human development is not possible without human interaction.
5. It is the teacher's responsibility to provide a psychologically secure environment with suitable resources and *not* to provide information.

The teacher must then be willing to be himself, a person, rather than to assume the role of authority or teacher. The teacher will need to respond on a personal level or to begin to use his Self as Instrument in working with others. Perhaps the most challenging aspect of this task will be to allow the students to become truly independent—to teach children *how* to choose rather than *what* to choose. The imperative nature of allowing children to become responsible in our rapidly changing world has been documented by Toffler (1970). The world is rapidly changing, and it is apparent that individuals will be required to make innumerable important choices over a lifetime; therefore, each person should learn the process by which decisions are made. The decision-making process centers around learning how to (1) estimate one's values, interests, and abilities, (2) identify alternatives and corresponding resources, (3) predict one's success in each alternative, and (4) construct a plan of action. Materials that provide simulated avenues for learning these procedures are available (Boocock and Schild 1968, Gelatt 1967, Magoon 1969).

Self-exploration, the assuming of responsibility for one's life, and the development of satisfactory interpersonal relationships can be enhanced through exposure to select experiences. Membership in peer groups, acquaintance with representative work settings, guided role playing, participation in games or other activities which simulate life conditions, and the observation of social models are examples of experiences that may contribute to individual development. The consultant and the teacher need to help the learner to overcome his timidity about engaging in his classroom environment, to support him as he learns to thumb his nose at failure and perk up his ears at success, and to arrange for him to see, hear, smell, taste, and feel the variety of options which are actually within his grasp.

EXPERIENTIAL AND PROCESS LEARNING

In order to facilitate the individual's personal development, we need to become involved with the child's total being: intellect, feelings, purposes, and behavior. Failure to plan for experiences which are designed to produce the fully functioning person can only promote educational bankruptcy. This is currently seen in the lack of response to real needs and the lack of answers for real questions. We are proposing classroom learning that helps each individual to learn the process of learning, not the facts but how one learns, and to help him to use this in life.

The tremendous power of the computer has made it clear that intellectual knowledge is not in data, but in the process of handling data. A new kind of curriculum, therefore, is being developed, one that does not concentrate on any particular subject, content, or basic concepts, but instead defines and teaches the *process* of an educated mind —the ways of gathering, evaluating, and acting upon information.

These processes (methods, skills, purposive behaviors) cut across subject disciplines and are of such fundamental applicability that once a student learns them he can apply them constantly for the rest of his life (Borton 1970, p. 69).

Process education is different from what most of us are familiar with. We grew up in a system that required we learn what was taught, and we rarely helped one to understand what was happening. Thus, we have come to believe that learning how to learn, or how to think, or how to be, is either impossible or accidental. The educated mind can no longer be left to chance.

The process as described by Borton (1970) is illustrated in the graph below.

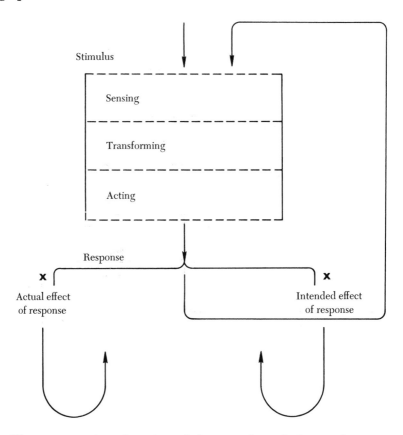

The response is a function of the stimulus, of the reinforcement, and of the intermediate processes. The intermediate processes, or the three basic information-processing functions, indicate more interaction with the environment. They are as follows:

1. A sensing or perceptual function which intuitively picks up transformation or stimuli. It provides data to answer the colloquial question "What?"

2. A transforming function which conceptualizes, abstracts, evaluates, and gives meaning and value to the sensed information. It deals with the "So What?"

3. An acting function that rehearses possible actions and picks one to put out into the world as an overt response. This is the learner's "Now What?"

Once the response is given, an awareness of the difference between his response, its actual effect, and the intended effect, forms feedback which can be used to modify behavior. The following is a lesson that has been expanded according to the What, So What, and Now What model:

Explanation of Sequence	*Class Activity*
What	
Immersion in new experience by reorienting the perspective.	Have class write about what it would be like to be a worm coming up in a city, on a drag strip, etc.
So What	
Analysis of the meaning of physical and psychological perspective.	Discuss papers. Why do the worms see as they do? What can they see that we can't?
Contemplation through imagination.	Sit for a few minutes and imagine that you are a worm. What is your life like? What do we mean when we say of someone that "he's nothing but a worm?" What would it feel like to be such a person? Would a giant lying down have a worm's-eye view?
Now What	
Reorienting and analysis by repeating the first phases in a more immediate setting.	Write about what a human worm would see in this school. How would things seem to him?
Experiment with personal behavior.	Spend a day pretending that you are a human worm. What difference does it make? What

	things can you do that you could not do before? What things are you not able to do?
Reapplication, choice, and recognition of consequences.	Go through the What, So What, Now What processes above for a human eagle. What is the difference between a human eagle and a human worm? How much choice do you have as to what you are going to be? Try behaving first as one and then as the other. Do your actions make you, or do you make your actions?

(Borton 1970, pp. 128–129)

The procedure is experiential with an emphasis upon learning through the involvement of the total being (intellect—affect—behavior). There is interaction and dialogue that reveal to self and others not only what is known but how one feels, and how his personal beliefs, purposes, and values are developed.

This approach begins with experiences which come before discussion and generalization and stresses the process rather than the content at hand. The behavior of the children reacting openly, honestly, authentically, and personally to the experiences becomes the content. A situation or experience is presented, e.g., open-ended story, role playing, puppetry, a picture designed to facilitate discussion, etc., and whatever the children produce is used. Their beliefs, feelings, attitudes, perceptions, and values make up the content of the course. The direction is determined by their perceptions, feelings, and values (Dinkmeyer 1970b).

In this type of learning there is no planned or right answer. Instead there is the opportunity to explore and consider hypotheses and alternative courses of action. The lack of one correct answer adds excitement, involvement, and challenge as well as facilitates the development of wisdom, spontaneity, and *creativity*. It encourages listening to others in order to stimulate one's own thinking and ideas. The opportunity to evaluate one's position in life (beliefs, attitudes, and values) is constantly present. Because the contribution of each child is valued, children become involved with each other as partners and not merely with the teacher.

The teacher is not cast in the role of dispenser of knowledge, but rather as a catalyst, skilled in promoting self-discovery and interaction. This role of facilitator is one that seeks to initiate interaction, feedback, and genuine dialogue. The goal is to increase contact among individual

children and their whole selves rather than contact with subject matter
or a limited type of teacher-child communication. When the children
are communicating with each other, the joy of communication and
the support and acceptance of the group rather than the teacher provide the reinforcement. This type of learning, then, is intrinsically
inspired, in contrast to being contrived for reward, and therefore,
becomes internalized, relevant, and permanent.

Experiential learning focuses on helping the individual to become
more aware of self, others, and able to generate hypotheses and questions. The classroom provides experiences which can lead to a myriad
of possible actions, reactions, and interactions. It is our belief that
the psychological balance of the organism knows best what facilitates
personal and social development (Maslow 1970). The teacher's sensitivity to individuals and the group helps him to establish a climate
for real learning. The focus is placed on the eight developmental tasks
that each individual is concerned with during the course of his development. The individual needs to learn:

1. A sense of self-identity and to develop an adequate self-image.
2. A giving-receiving pattern of affection.
3. To develop mutuality or to move from being self-centered to
   having effective peer relationships.
4. To become reasonably independent and to develop self-control.
5. To become purposeful, to become involved and seek the resources and responsibilities of the world.
6. To become competent, to achieve, and to think of self as capable of mastery.
7. To become emotionally flexible and resourceful.
8. To make value judgments, choices, and to accept the consequences of one's decisions.

(Dinkmeyer 1970c).

The teacher does not preach or moralize, but by involving the individual's feelings, beliefs, and values, encourages him to draw his own
conclusions. The course content is not something to be returned to
teachers or stored, but rather to be *used!* This type of learning is valued
and internalized.

GROUP DYNAMICS

The consultant realizes that productive interaction in the classroom
will not come about by chance. The teacher needs to gain the skills of
group discussion leadership. It is necessary to be able to observe psy-

chological interaction and hear not only what is said but to understand the affect, perceptions, purposes, and values implicit in the dialogue. It is important for the teacher to recognize that what is not said may be as important as what *is* said. The nonverbal messages presented in facial expressions, the eyes, posture, and by other gestures will certainly be helpful in understanding the individual.

The teacher's verbal leads may not focus on the stated content only. They could also deal with feelings accompanying the expression of a belief. Leads should be *open,* for example, "Tell me more about it," rather than "What is the . . . (eliciting a fact)?" The consultant needs to help the teacher to acquire the ability to restate or reflect feelings— "You are rather upset. It seems there is no change." The reflection of feeling may come from the restatement of what has been said or may emerge from an attitude that is present, but not verbally stated. At times the teacher also may develop tentative hypotheses as, "Could it be that we do that to keep people busy with us?" or "Is it possible he does that to be exempt from work?" Both of these hypotheses are tentative and are always stated as guesses or hunches.

Randolph, Howe, and Achterman (1968) found that we traditionally respond to messages with the following types of ineffective responses:

Ordering or commanding
Admonishing
Warning
Advising
Instructing
Criticizing and disagreeing
Praising and agreeing
Name calling and interpreting
Reassuring and sympathizing
Probing and questioning or dwelling

These responses deny the student the right to have a feeling, and they close channels to communication and understanding. The teacher who tries to lead through authoritarian procedures will only produce rebellion and resistance, both active and passive. According to Dinkmeyer and Muro (1971), "if the teacher is going to succeed in developing a cooperative effort among the members of the class, she must be acquainted with group procedures. It is her responsibility to develop a cohesiveness and to recognize both the individual and group needs of her students" (p. 248).

The importance of group dynamics for the teacher stems from our awareness that man is a social being and that all of his social transactions and social movements express his personality, character, and style of life (Dreikurs 1971). The teacher must develop the ability to understand the pattern of psychological movement and to be aware of the social purpose and consequences of behavior. Understanding and awareness, however, are not enough; the teacher needs to put this knowledge into action. The following list of competencies developed by Dinkmeyer and Muro (1971) seems appropriate:

1. Show the group you care and are concerned with developing a relationship of mutual respect. Demonstrate your interest, concern and kindness, but be committed to meaningful discussion and do not hesitate to be firm, showing respect for yourself as well as the children. Help the children comprehend how the teacher hears by reflective listening to each input. Be sure to hear not only the words, but the meanings and feelings of what is said.

2. Structure the group so the members understand the purpose of the group discussion and establish their own limits. Members must be ready to share their concerns and willing to listen closely to others. A spirit of give-and-take and honest, open feedback should pervade.

3. Sense the group atmosphere and be willing to discuss it. Be sensitive to the feelings of the individual in the group and help him feel understood—i.e. "I am getting a message that you are unhappy," or "I feel you really care!"

4. Link the thoughts and feelings of group members. Point out the similarities and differences in the concepts, attitudes, and feelings being discussed. The leader especially must be able to show the relationship between what two children are talking about to help them recognize common problems, and clarify differences and commonalities.

5. Encourage silent members to participate when they feel ready. This usually involves being aware of nonverbal clues such as a facial gesture, glance, or halting attempt to enter the group.

6. The children are learning a new process of cooperation in contrast to competition. The leader must observe any tendencies of children to be empathic or to link or supply alternative solutions to problems. These attempts should be immediately encouraged and reinforced.

7. Group discussion can take a negative turn if the leader is not perceptive of the interaction. We are interested in fostering personal development, hence the interaction should be concerned with topics which permit interpersonal exploration. Group members should be assisted to see both the strengths and assets in individuals. Emphasis is placed on positive as well as negative feedback. The leader helps the group see the value of feedback by modeling it and encouraging its utilization.

8. The leader must be alert to detect feelings and attitudes which are implied but not expressed. He helps the group develop tentative analyses of the purpose of behavior. He might say, "Is it possible?" or "Could

it be?" and state his hunch about the purpose in a tentative manner. He helps the group learn to formulate hypotheses and make guesses about the purposes of each other's behavior.

9. The effective group leader is able to help the children express more clearly their thoughts, feelings, and attitudes. He does this through clarifying, restating, and summarizing.

10. The leader helps the members summarize and evaluate what they have learned. About five minutes before the close of the session he asks, "What do you think you learned about yourself and others today?" He tries to involve each child in considering his personal learning. Helping the group consider what is happening accelerates and facilitates the group process.

(pp. 252-254)

In conclusion, a rationale and role statement for the consultant to facilitate human potential in the classroom has been presented. The uniqueness of the consultant's skills to produce a psychologically healthy and meaningful environment was stressed. In the next chapter, we will zero in on some specific techniques that the consultant can utilize to reach these ends.

REFERENCES

Allen, D. "The Seven Deadly Myths of Education." *Psychology Today* 4 (1971): 70–72+.

Blume, R. "Humanizing Teacher Education." *Phi Delta Kappan* 52 (1971): 411–415.

Boocock, S. S. and Schild, E. O., eds. *Simulation Games in Learning*. Beverly Hills, California: Sage Publications, 1968.

Borton, T. *Reach, Touch, and Teach*. New York: McGraw-Hill, 1970.

Carlson, J., Rotter, J. and Dinkmeyer, D. "The Power of Negative Teaching." *Teachers Voice* 48 (1971): 10.

Combs, A. W. et al. *Florida Studies in the Helping Professions*. Gainesville, Florida: University of Florida Press, 1969.

Cooley, C. H. *Human Nature and the Social Order*. New York: Scribner, 1902.

Cox, H. *The Feast of Fools*. Cambridge: Harvard University Press, 1969.

Dinkmeyer, D. "When Guidance and Curriculum Collaborate." *Journal of Educational Leadership* 25 (1968): 443–448.

Dinkmeyer, D. *DUSO Manual* (Developing Understanding of Self and Others). Circle Pines, Minnesota: American Guidance Service, 1970a.

Dinkmeyer, D. "Humanizing the Educational Process through Guidance Procedures." *Lutheran Education*, 105, no. 5 (1970b): 237–242.

Dinkmeyer, D. "The Teacher as Counselor: Therapeutic Approaches to Understanding Self and Others." *Childhood Education*, 46, no. 6 (1970c): 314–317.

Dinkmeyer, D. and Caldwell, E. *Developmental Counseling and Guidance.* New York: McGraw-Hill, 1970.

Dinkmeyer, D. and Dreikurs, R. *Encouraging Children to Learn: The Encouragement Process.* Englewood Cliffs, New Jersey: Prentice-Hall, 1963.

Dinkmeyer, D. C. and Muro, J. J. *Group Counseling: Theory and Practice.* Itasca, Illinois: F. E. Peacock, 1971.

Dreikurs, R. *Social Equality: The Challenge of Today.* Chicago: Henry Regnery, 1971.

Dreikurs, R. and Grey, L. *Logical Consequences: A New Approach to Discipline.* New York: Meredith, 1968.

Dreikurs, R., Grunwald, B. B. and Pepper, F. C. *Maintaining Sanity in the Classroom.* New York: Harper & Row, 1971.

Faust, V. *The Counselor-Consultant in the Elementary School.* Boston: Houghton Mifflin, 1968.

Fromm, E. *The Revolution of Hope: Toward a Humanized Technology.* New York: Bantam, 1968.

Gagne, R. M. *The Conditions of Learning.* New York: Holt, Rinehart & Winston, 1970.

Gelatt, H. B. "Information and Decision Theories Applied to the College Choice and Planning." *Preparing School Counselors in Educational Guidance.* New York: College Entrance Examination Board, 1967, pp. 101–114.

Gibby, R. G. and Gibby, R. G., Jr. "The Effects of Stress Resulting from Academic Failure." *Journal of Clinical Psychology* 23 (1967): 35–57.

Glasser, W. *Schools Without Failure.* New York: Harper & Row, 1969.

Gordon, T. *Parent Effectiveness Training.* New York: Peter H. Wyden, 1970.

Greenberg, H. M. *Teaching with Feeling.* New York: Pegasus, 1969.

Ivey, A. E. and Weinstein, G. "The Counselor as a Specialist in Psychological Education (A Dialogue)." *Personnel and Guidance Journal* 49 (1970): 98–107.

Kohl, H. R. *The Open Classroom: A Practical Guide to a New Way of Teaching.* New York: Vintage, 1969.

Leonard, G. B. *Education and Ecstasy.* New York: Delta, 1968.

Magoon, T. M. "Developing Skills for Educational and Vocational Problems." In *Behavioral Counseling: Cases and Techniques,* edited by J. D. Krumboltz and C. E. Thoresen, pp. 343–396. New York: Holt, Rinehart & Winston, 1969.

Maltz, M. *Psycho-cybernetics.* New York: Pocket Books, 1966.

Maslow, A. H. *Motivation and Personality.* 2nd ed. New York: Harper & Row, 1970.

Matheny, K. Counselors as Environmental Engineers." *Personnel and Guidance Journal* 49 (1971): 439–444.

Michael, D. N. *The Unprepared Society: Planning for a Precarious Future.* New York: Basic Books, 1968.

Moustakas, C. *The Authentic Teacher: Sensitivity and Awareness in the Classroom.* Cambridge, Massachusetts: Howard A. Doyle, 1966.

Neill, A. S. *Summerhill: A Radical Approach to Child Rearing.* New York: Hart, 1960.

Prescott, D. A. *The Child in the Educative Process.* New York: McGraw-Hill, 1957.

Purkey, W. W. "Humanizing and Dehumanizing Students, Teachers, Administrators." Gainesville, Florida: University of Florida, March, 1971. (mimeo.)

Purkey, W. and Harriff, M. "Four Myths about Students and Teaching." *Elementary School Guidance and Counseling* 4 (1970): 287–290.

Randolph, N. and Howe, W. *Self-enhancing Education: A Program to Motivate Learners.* Palo Alto, California: Sanford Press, 1966.

Randolph, N., Howe, W. and Achterman, E. "Self-enhancing Education: Communication Techniques and Processes that Enhance." A training manual researched in the Cupertino Union School District, Cupertino, California, and Menlo Park City School District, Menlo Park, California, 1968. (mimeo.)

Reich, C. A. *The Greening of America: How the Youth Revolution is Trying to Make America Livable.* New York: Random House, 1970.

Roszak, T. *The Making of a Counter Culture.* New York: Anchor Books, 1968.

Spiel, O. *Discipline Without Punishment: An Account of a School in Action.* London: Faber and Faber, 1962.

Satir, V. *Conjoint Family Therapy.* Rev. ed. Palo Alto, California: Science Behavior Books, 1967.

Stotland, E. and Zander, A. "Effects of Public and Private Failure on Self-evaluation." *Journal of Abnormal and Social Psychology* 56 (1958): 223–229.

Thoresen, C. A. "Behavioral Humanism: A Direction for Counseling Research." A paper presented at the American Educational Research Association, New York, 1971.

Toffler, A. *Future Shock.* New York: Random House, 1970.

10

Human Learning and Development Procedures

In the previous section facilitating human potential in the classroom was discussed, and the unique position of the consultant to create a humane environment was presented. The consultant will have increasing opportunities to help teachers to acquire techniques which promote psychological growth in the classroom. In this section a variety of specific techniques, procedures, and approaches to psychological education which will help the consultant to reach these ends are presented and examples of each given.

ENCOURAGEMENT PROCESS

In the day-to-day activities of the classroom, the encouragement process can be a very effective means of reinforcement (Dinkmeyer and Dreikurs 1963). The individual who likes doing school work usually performs better than the person who is not satisfied with his work. Through careful planning and organization, the teacher can use the encouragement process to help pupils to facilitate their own learning process and thereby helping schoolwork to become personally meaningful.

The process of encouragement specifically involves:

1. Valuing the individual *as he is,* not as his reputation indicates nor as you hope he will be—but as he is. Believing in the indi-

vidual as good and worthwhile will facilitate acting toward him in this fashion (Combs et al. 1969, Rosenthal and Jacobson 1968).

2. Showing faith in the individual. This will help the individual to develop a feeling of "can-ness" or a belief in himself.

3. Having faith in the child's ability. This enables the teacher to win the child's confidence while building the individual's self-respect.

4. Giving recognition for *effort* as well as a job well done.

5. Using the group to help the child develop. This makes practical use of the assumption that man is a social being and the need to belong is basic.

6. Integrating the group so that the individual child can discover his place and work from that point.

7. Planning for success, assisting in the development of skills that are sequentially and psychologically paced.

8. Identifying and focusing on strengths and assets rather than mistakes.

9. Using the individual's interests in order to motivate instruction.

(Dinkmeyer and Dreikurs 1963)

Encouragement is a complex process that lets the individual know that the teacher believes in him and will treat him with respect and trust. The individual's value as a person is always apparent. The encouragement process should not be confused with praise. Praise puts the emphasis upon the product, while encouragement stresses the effort or contribution. As Vicki Soltz (1967, pp. 69-71) states in her book *Study Group Leader's Manual:*

Most of us have grown up believing that praise is desperately needed by all children in order to stimulate them into "right" behaviors. If we watch closely when he is receiving praise we may discover some astonishing facts. Some children gloat, some panic, some express "So what," some seem to say, "Well, finally!"

We are suddenly confronted with the fact that we need to see how the child interprets what is going on rather than assume that he regards everything as we do.

Examination of the intention of the praiser shows that he is offering a reward: "If you are good you will have the reward of being high in my esteem." Well fine. What is wrong with this approach? Why not help the child learn to do the right thing by earning a high place in parental (the teacher's) esteem?

If we look at this situation from the child's point of view, we will find the mistake of this approach.

How does praise affect the child's self-image? He may get the impression that his personal worth depends upon how "he measures up" to the demands and values of others. "If I am praised, my personal worth is high. If I am scolded, I am worthless." When this child becomes an adult, his effectiveness, his ability to function, his capacity to cope with life's tasks will depend entirely upon his estimation of how he stands in the estimation of others. He will live constantly on an elevator—up and down.

Praise is apt to center the attention of the child upon himself. "How do I measure up?" rather than "What does the situation need?" This gives rise to a fictive goal of "self-being-praised" instead of the reality-goal of "what-can-I-do-to-help."

Another child may come to see praise as his right—as rightfully due him from life. Therefore, life is unfair if he doesn't receive praise for every effort. "Poor me—no one appreciates me." Or, he may feel he has no obligation to perform if no praise is forthcoming. "What's in it for me? What will I get out of it? If no praise (reward) is forthcoming, why should I bother?"

Praise can be terribly discouraging. If the child's effort fails to bring the expected praise, he may assume either that he isn't good enough or that what he has to offer isn't worth the effort and so give up.

If a child has set exceedingly high standards for himself, praise may sound like mockery or scorn, especially when his efforts fail to measure up to his own standards. In such a child, praise only serves to increase his anger with himself and his resentment at others for not understanding his dilemma.

In all our efforts to encourage children we must be alert to the child's response. The accent must move from "What am I?" (good?) to "How can I help the total situation?" Anything we do which reinforces a child's false image of himself is discouraging. Whatever we do that helps a child see that he is part of a functioning unit, that he can contribute, cooperate, participate within the total situation, is encouragement. We must learn to see that as he is, the child is good enough.

Praise rewards the individual and tends to fasten his attention upon himself. Little satisfaction or self-fulfillment comes from this direction.

Encouragement stimulates the effort and fastens attention upon one's capacity to join humanity and to become aware of interior strength and native capacity to cope.

Praise recognizes the actor, encouragement acknowledges the act.

PRAISE	ENCOURAGEMENT
Aren't you wonderful to be able to do this!	Isn't it nice that you can help? We appreciate your help. Don't the dishes shine? (after wiping) Isn't the carpet pretty now? (after vacuuming) How nice your room looks! Thanks for watching the baby. It was a big help. I like your drawing. The colors are so pretty together. How much neater your room looks now that your toys are put away. How nice that you could figure that out for yourself. Your skill is growing.
I'm so proud of you for getting good grades. (You are high in my esteem.)	I'm so glad you enjoy learning (adding to your own resources.)
I'm proud of you for behaving so nicely in the restaurant.	We all enjoyed being together in the restaurant.
I'm awfully proud of your performance in the recital.	It is good to see that you enjoy playing. We all appreciate the job you did. I have to give you credit for working hard.

In encouragement, as with reinforcement (praise), what is reinforcing to one individual may not be for another child. A good rule of thumb is that encouragement in front of others (e.g., classroom group) usually is effective. Each child and each situation are different, which requires the teacher to constantly use his creative ability in order to facilitate the growth of the individual. Reimer (1967, pp. 72–73) lists ten specific "words of encouragement" which further help to illustrate the encouragement process.

1. "You do a good job of . . ."
Children should be encouraged when they do not expect it, when they are not asking for it. It is possible to point out some useful act or contribution in each child. Even a comment about something small and insignificant to us, may have great importance to a child.

2. "You have improved in . . ."
Growth and improvement is something we should expect from all children. They may not be where we would like them to be, but if there is progress, there is less chance for discouragement. Children will usually continue to try if they can see some improvement.

3. "We like (enjoy) you, but we don't like what you do."
Often a child feels he is not liked after he has made a mistake or mis-behaved. A child should never think *he* is not liked. It is important to distinguish between the child and his behavior, between the act and the actor.

4. "You can help me (us, the others, etc.) by . . . ."
To feel useful and helpful is important to everyone. Children want to be helpful; we have only to give them the opportunity.

5. "Let's try it together."
Children who think they have to do things perfectly are often afraid to attempt something new for fear of making a mistake or failing.

6. "So you do make a mistake; now, what can you learn from your mistake?"
There is nothing that can be done about what has happened, but a person can always do something about the future. Mistakes can teach the child a great deal, and he will learn if he does not feel embarrassed for making a mistake.

7. "You would like us to think you can't do it, but we think you can."
This approach could be used when the child says or conveys the impression that something is too difficult for him and he hesitates to even so much as try it. If he tries and fails, he has at least had the courage to try. Our expectations should be consistent with the child's ability and maturity.

8. "Keep trying. Don't give up."
When a child is trying, but not meeting much success, a comment like this might be helpful.

9. "I'm sure you can straighten this out (solve this problem, etc.), but if you need any help, you know where you can find me."
Adults need to express confidence that children are able and will re-solve their own conflicts, if given a chance.

10. "I can understand how you feel (not sympathy, but empathy) but I'm sure you'll be able to handle it."
Sympathizing with another person seldom helps him, rather it suggests that life has been unfair to him. Understanding the situation and be-lieving in the child's ability to adjust to it is of much greater help to him.

The success or failure of these encouraging remarks will be a direct function of the teacher's attitudes and purposes for using them.

VALUE CLARIFICATION

Values are the guides to the direction of each individual's life. They develop out of experiences, and this development is a personal and a life-long process. Values are not taught; however, they can be learned.

Each individual can learn to develop clear and decisive personal values by using the process of *valuing*. The teacher can contribute to the individual's growth by helping him to find values through:

1. helping each individual to make free choices whenever possible.
2. searching for alternatives in choice-making situations.
3. analyzing the consequences of each alternative.
4. considering what each individual prizes and cherishes.
5. publicly affirming the things that each individual values.
6. doing something or acting on the choices available.
7. identifying and strengthening the positive patterns in each individual's life.

(Simon 1971)

A series of activities are used in the value clarification process. These activities are not designed to inculcate the student with "proper," "good," or "right" values. They are intended to create dissonant-producing issues and situations, to confront the individual with his inconsistent responses, to help him to organize his own values, in his own characteristic fashion, and at his own speed. The following are a few of the techniques used in this process. Raths, Harmin and Simon (1965) and Simon, Howe and Kirschenbaum (1972) offer a detailed look at the theory and more examples of this process in action.

VALUES CONTINUUM

A continuum is used to break down either/or thinking. It takes a problem which usually splits people into two oversimplified camps and opens it up to show a wide range of intellectually-defensible positions.

Take the draft. It is not enough to say someone is a dove or a hawk. There are many complex reasons why one person's values lead to enlistment at the earliest possible date, and why another would rather go to prison than serve in the army.

Set up a preposterous position at either end of the continuum. The hope is that these positions will be so far out that no one will support them. Take the example of this continuum: at one extreme is Eager Egbert. He is so committed to the military that he has been trying to enlist since he was eleven. Now he is fourteen and he is trying for the 90th time to look older so he can go to Vietnam.

At the other extreme is Maiming Malcolm. He borrows his father's shotgun and shoots off five toes so he will never have to be anything but 4F for the rest of his life. Between these extremes is much room for the diversity of opinion which makes for exciting classroom dialogue. Each student is asked to place his name on the line which best describes where he fits and to say something about what that line represents to him.

There will be room for the person who argues for going to Canada to avoid the draft and room for the person who joins ROTC so he can serve as an officer instead of a common foot soldier. As always, the teacher argues that there is no right answer. In the search for values, there must be room for individual choice and the pluralism which makes this society what it is today.

Let's look at the values continuum on racial conflict. This exercise opens up a highly charged topic so it can be discussed with some degree of rationality.

At one extreme we have Super Separatist Sam, whose solution to the race problem is simply to ship every human being back to his original country. He advocates dismembering people whose ancestors came from two different countries. On the other hand, we find Multi-Mixing Mike, who would insist that all babies be distributed not to their original parents but to couples not of the baby's race. In addition, no couples of the same race can marry, and couples of the same race already married must be divorced and marry outside their race.

Between those extremes, students must come face-to-face with where they stand on the issues of integration, Black Power, de facto segregation, and so on (Simon 1971, p. 3).

WEEKLY REACTION SHEETS

The essence of a value-clarification strategy is to get students to examine their lives. A teacher does this in a non-judgemental, non-moralizing way. One simple strategy is to undertake a weekly reaction sheet for a period of six weeks or so. This sheet should include questions like: What was the high point of the week for you? Were you in emphatic disagreement with anyone this week? Did you institute any changes in your life this week? How could this week have been better? What did you procrastinate about this week? Identify three choices you made this week. Did you make any plans for some future event during the week?

At the end of a six-week period, the teacher should return the reaction sheets. Students may volunteer to talk about any or all of the questions. The teacher should try to summarize the patterns revealed. Students can then help each other find alternatives for more satisfying ways of dealing with the issues raised (Simon 1971, p. 2).

Throughout the value clarification process, the teacher is actively involved. He lets the students know that he faces the same value conflicts as they. The teacher states his position and offers it as one alternative among the many posited within the classroom.

Students need to learn more than subject matter; they need to know how to deal with the value conflicts that characterize our times, and they need to discover more effective ways of relating to the world around them. "Those who do not learn these things are likely to suffer from apathy, blind conformity, or irrational rebelliousness; those are the most frequent choices to clear personal values"* (Simon 1971, p. 3).

ENCOUNTER GROUP PRINCIPLES

This approach views the task of education as "to help people bring meaning and understanding into their lives and to determine the nature of their relationship to mankind. This view of education is in contrast to 'training,' which is seen as the development of skill and knowledge in a specific area for a specific purpose" (Roark 1971, p. 1). This approach utilizes encounter–group principles to meet these goals. The following specific techniques will help in implementing the en-counter–group approach:

1. Allowing the students to select their own subject matter and approach for study.
2. Allowing students to evaluate themselves or at least participate in their evaluation.
3. Making clear through both action and words that the student is responsible for what he learns and the teacher is responsible for providing the situation and the resources.
4. Providing extensive opportunities for discussions (large and small groups) where students can see how their ideas compare with others and learn to express theirs. Brilhart's *Effective Group Discussion* and the Stanfords' *Learning Discussion*

---

* If you are interested in learning more about Values Clarification, Sidney Simon and his colleagues conduct two-day weekend workshops, titled "Introduction to Values Clarification," in many parts of the country, e.g., Buffalo, New York City, Detroit, St. Louis, Cleveland, San Francisco, Boston, and Chicago. Longer workshops are offered each summer, including several at the Adirondack Mt. Humanistic Education Center in Upper Jay, New York.

For a brochure on Values Associates and their work, a workshop schedule, and a list of printed materials, write to: Values Associates, Springfield Road, Upper Jay, N.Y. 12987.

Skills Through Games, provide excellent guidelines to leading discussions.

5. Providing opportunities for students to work cooperatively in at least the same proportion as they work competitively.

6. Stressing that the classwork is being done for the present benefit of the students and not as preparation for the future.

7. Using simulation to re-create on a smaller scale the problems and situations in the world in which the students are interested. (Rogers' *Freedom to Learn* is a good source of ideas.)

8. Role playing either in conjunction with other techniques or alone for short periods of time. This is an excellent technique for helping students to put themselves into other situations and see situations from other people's viewpoints.

9. Through "games" providing opportunities for students to learn more about themselves and others as they learn about subject matter. The teacher is urged to enroll in a small group-techniques class to learn how to apply these to the classroom. The following books will serve as an introduction to this area: Schutz, *Joy: Expanding Human Awareness;* Malmud and Machover, *Toward Self-Understanding: Group Techniques in Self-Confrontation;* and Stanford and Stanford, *Learning Discussion Skills Through Games.*

10. Inquiry or discovery approaches to teaching science. These are compatible with the application of encounter-group techniques.

(Roark 1971)

However, the essence of this approach does not center on any technique but rather upon the teacher-pupil relationship. A relationship of open, direct, nondefensive communication at all times will produce the desired results. The outcomes include atmospheric and procedural changes within the classroom and changes within the students. These changes seem to demonstrate an increased interest in learning and subject matter as the "we" feeling among the class develops.

PSYCHOLOGICAL EDUCATION

Stanford (1972) reported empirical validation for the use of affective education activities in the classroom. He discovered: "Giving deliberate attention to social and emotional development in the classroom can have an important positive effect on students" (p. 591). Therefore, he concluded that the consultant can proceed toward the promotion of human potential in the classroom assured that psychological education can work. The following is an example of one of the affective activities that he used with high school students.

1. Each student introduces himself to the group, telling anything about himself that he feels will help others know him better.

2. Students write brief impressions of others and turn them in to the teacher. They then share these first impressions orally.

3. Students take turns being "visiting celebrities." Other members of the group interview them to find out as much as possible about the celebrity.

4. Using only eye contact, each student chooses a partner from across the table and maintains eye contact for 15 seconds. This is repeated frequently, with explanation of the importance of eye contact for good communication.

5. Each student is given a clue to a mystery which the group must work together to solve.

6. In a discussion of a subject-matter question, each student must contribute by responding to a previous contribution.

7. Each student is asked to introduce another to the group, telling them what sort of person he is.

8. Working in pairs, students practice drawing out the speaker by asking questions, displaying empathy, and showing support rather than arguing.

9. Working with the entire group, students practice drawing out the speaker rather than arguing.

10. Students play the "Lost on the Moon" game to learn to arrive at consensus through compromise and careful listening to the arguments of others.

11. Students fill out a questionnaire containing such items as "Whom in this group do you listen to most?" and the results are later discussed by the class.

12. Students play a metaphor game to begin to express their reactions to others in the group. Each student secretly chooses another member of the class and tells the group what music, bird, animal, food, color, and type of weather this person reminds him of. The other students guess the identity of the person chosen.

13. During a subject-matter discussion, each student plays the person on his immediate right.

14. Each student describes how he thinks the group would react to the revelation of his most personal secret. (The secrets are not disclosed.)

15. Students write secrets in camouflaged handwriting on identical slips of paper which are then distributed at random. Other members read the secrets aloud as though they were their own.

16. Each student in turn is asked to answer a question about himself
or his reaction to others in the group. One question is used at the beginning of each period and discussion of the replies follows. Questions
include the following: How does each person here feel toward you?
What would you change about the group's or an individual's behavior
toward you? If you could be anyone else in this group, who would it
be? Who here is happier than you are? What is one thing you would
change about yourself if you could? In what way are you similar to each
person here? Who in this group frightens you? What is the first impression you give other people? Whom in this group are you most comfortable with? Who in this group likes you least? Whom in the group
would you like to know more about? What would you like to know
about him? Who in this group is most nearly like you? What miscon-
ception does this group have about you? How have you attempted to
fool this group?

(Stanford 1972, pp. 588–589)

A more complete description of most of the activities used is available
in an earlier work (Stanford and Stanford 1969).

Another example of psychological education can be found in the
work of Mosher and Sprinthall (1971). They are developing a comprehensive curriculum that aims at "the deliberate development of
positive psychological growth for all children" (p. 72). The program
is an *educational* one and not that of therapy or clinical treatment.
Their work is intended to help both school counselors and psychologists
to move out of the confines of their offices into direct contact with
large numbers of students and the curriculum and instructional life of
the school.

The curriculum is being developed as a series of courses that focus
on the different stages of the "human life cycle," which essentially
means the course of personal and human development from birth to
death. This curriculum in personal and human development includes
a comprehensive set of educational experiences that are designed to
affect personal, ethical, aesthetic, and philosophical development. An
example of one course is that of interpersonal relations and marriage.

What we envisage is that it be taken by a mixed group of adolescents,
young married couples and older married couples. We plan to study
the psychological literature on marriage, family counseling and child
rearing. Case studies of actual marriages and family counseling would
be built into the course as a practicum component.

(Mosher and Sprinthall 1971, p. 14)

Perhaps the most important idea involved in these programs is that
the personal psychological development of each individual should be-

come a primary objective of education. Experiences which foster humane development must be planned, not left to chance.

CONFLUENT EDUCATION

George Brown (1971) states, *"Confluent education* is the term for the integration or flowing together of the *affective* and *cognitive* elements in individual and group learning—sometimes called humanistic or psychological education" (p. 1). The goal of this type of learning is to integrate "what" and "how" the learner feels with what the schools believe he should know. It is felt that if this integration is effective, not only will the individual's desire to know increase, but his future learning will be rich, meaningful, and emotionally healthful. The following is an example of this type of learning using an English unit for tenth graders with the subject matter being Stephen Crane's *The Red Badge of Courage.*

Aaron Hillman, the teacher who developed this exercise, wanted his students not only to gain a greater understanding of the novel, but also to better understand human beings, to see themselves in the lives of others, and to further their skills in critical thinking and in communication (verbal and non-verbal).

In approaching *The Red Badge of Courage* in a humanistic way, Aaron Hillman employed diverse means including daily diaries, readings, discussions, writings, field trips, and affective exercises. Some of the questions explored and exercises used are listed below:

What is your courage?

What is the difference between you and manhood?

A comparison of Civil War and World War II poetry.

Interviewing someone who has known a war.

Debating whether or not war is inevitable.

Collecting a series of pictures that represent courage and weaving them into a story.

Awareness exercises which help the students contact their environment in much the same way the hero contacts his thoughts and actions in the novel "before the battle."

Having the students form groups of six, and then telling each group to get rid of one member followed by a discussion of how it felt to be rejected from a group as the hero in the novel was rejected from time to time.

Listening to war music and writing down freely associated thoughts and feelings that are evoked and then sharing them in small groups.

Having the students (with eyes closed) recall a specific incident in the novel and then concentrate on getting in touch with the environment of that situation—the temperature, the surroundings, etc. The students go through the incidents from beginning to end, and then instead of trying to understand it, they are told to drop it entirely and "with a bounce of the imagination" to jump into another character's place and experience the same incident from the beginning, but this time from inside the other person.

(Lyon 1971, pp. 72–73)

Further pragmatic examples of confluent education can be found in Dr. Brown's *Human Teaching for Human Learning*. This text deals directly with DRICE (Development and Research in Confluent Education), the Ford Foundation project he has been directing.

Perhaps, the following quotation best captures Brown's ideas and feelings:

A unique contribution that confluent education can make to the education of man is that what is now accepted as curriculum at all educational levels can, by introducing affective components, be brought back into contact with the life from whence it came. After all, every curriculum originated in some living reality. It typically lost its vitality as it became an end instead of the means it was originally; a means toward helping the student develop and utilize those characteristics which made him a human being. Thinking about teaching in confluent ways can help restore vital force to education. Man has a mind. Man has feeling. To separate the two is to deny all that man is. To integrate the two is to help man realize what he might be. And none of us knows what that is. It is, however, a most exciting prospect. Let us get on with it.

(Brown 1971, p. 195)

HUMAN DEVELOPMENT TRAINING INSTITUTE

Bessell and Palomares (1967) have developed a procedure whereby the teacher becomes the leader of a modified encounter group called "the magic circle." The teachers are trained in a curriculum which is designed to improve a child's self-confidence, social interaction, and awareness of feelings.

The basic procedure is to have the children sit in a circle and talk with each other and the teacher in a semistructured way. The human development program includes a large number of specific activities and lessons. An example of one of the sessions is described by Borton (1970, pp. 142–143), as follows:

"Today we are going to have a chance to tell how something gives us a good feeling. This little doll makes me have a good feeling because I thought I had broken it, but a friend showed me how to fix it up again. That gives me a good feeling because I have had this doll for a long time, and I didn't want it to be broken. Now would one of you like to tell me something which gives you a good feeling?"

There was a silence in the group. The kids shifted a little uncomfortably, as did we in the audience. Then Joyce put up her hand. We began to crane our necks for a better look. Joyce was a brain-damaged child who had sat huddled into herself on the previous day's session— chewing on a hangnail.

"I can ride my bike."

"You can ride your bike, Joyce! I bet that does give you a good feeling. And you look so pretty when you say you feel good."

Joyce was sitting on her hands now, bouncing up and down, her little blond face aglow. The audience relaxed and glowed with her.

The game went on around the circle, each child getting a chance to express what it was that gave him a good feeling, and being praised by the teacher. The procedure was powerful, since the kids began to discover that some of the things they thought were unique to them were also shared by others—feeling good because a father was coming home from war or because their friend liked them. And the procedure was simple—simple enough so that teachers could handle it effectively.

SELF ENHANCING EDUCATION (S.E.E.)

Randolph and Howe (1966) describe the S.E.E. program in which teachers may help their students to grow in self-esteem through practical and effective practises. It helps the student to improve his scholastic and personal achievement by getting him involved in solving his own problems. S.E.E. achieves this goal through twelve specific processes in which children are guided to become more involved in their own education and development. The twelve processes are:

1. Problem solving
2. Self-management
3. Changing negative reflections to positive images
4. Building bonds of trust
5. Setting limits and expectations

6. Freeing and channeling energy
7. Overcoming unproductive repetitive behavior
8. Changing tattling to reporting
9. Developing physical competencies
10. Making success inevitable
11. Self-evaluation
12. Breaking down curriculum barriers

S.E.E. is particularly beneficial for (1) children whose achievement is less than their potential, and (2) children who employ unproductive repetitive behavior patterns. S.E.E. proposes specific methods that involve the child in solving his *own* problems, exercising his *own* control, and planning his *own* self-direction. The problem-solving process is as follows:

1. *Present the problem* as someone sees it. This person might be a teacher, the guidance worker, a student, principal, parent, or playground supervisor. The problem might be concerned with behavior or with the organization of a study unit.
2. *Gather data.* Talk about it so each person has the opportunity to be a unique and valuable resource of information, feelings, and ideas. The differentiating out of specifics produces significant data as well as increased awareness that each participant may perceive the same incident quite differently.
3. *Clarify.* As participants offer ideas, a direction begins to emerge. The teacher or guidance worker needs to clarify the direction of the data by indicating how he perceived the data and asking for feedback for verification.
4. *Ask for feedback about clarification.* Once clarification is made, it is time to ask for solutions. Since there is seldom one possible solution, it is necessary to consider many alternatives until the favored ones emerge.
5. *Invite solutions.* From the many ideas offered the group determines which are most preferable. Good decisions are made by conducting careful discussion of alternative courses of action and by projecting the possible consequences.
6. *Evaluate.* After action comes evaluation. This gives the opportunity to determine whether the solution and its implementation are satisfactory. Evaluation also brings the group face-to-face with its new position and poses the next problem for consideration.

DEVELOPING UNDERSTANDING IN SELF
AND OTHERS (DUSO)

The DUSO program (Dinkmeyer 1970) is based on a set of planned lessons and experiences for the classroom. The program focuses on the normal problems encountered as the individual develops. The materials are designed to be presented by the teacher in the democratic atmosphere of the classroom. Each child is encouraged to participate and present his feelings, attitudes, and reactions. DUSO is designed to reach children with unique learning styles through assorted media and methods. DUSO D-1 includes recorded stories, music, open-ended stories, problem situations, puppetry lessons, role-playing activities, art, and supplementary activities. The DUSO D-2 program includes these elements and discussion pictures, self-and social-development activities, and career-awareness activities (Dinkmeyer 1973).

> The focus of the material is on enhancing self understanding, aware-
> ness of self and others, and resultant purposeful motivational involve-
> ment in the tasks of life. The experiences are designed to facilitate
> building a positive self concept and feelings of adequacy. The child
> becomes aware of the feeling area of his life and the purposeful, causal
> nature of human behavior (Dinkmeyer 1971, p. 213).

Materials and techniques have been presented which the teacher can apply directly in the classroom. Other procedures are available (e.g., role playing, open-ended group discussions, peer learning) to the teacher and may be used in the establishment of a humane environment.

LARGE-GROUP DISCUSSION

William Glasser has been a leading advocate of large-group classroom meetings. In these meetings, the teacher leads the class in a *nonjudge-mental* discussion about what is important, meaningful, and relevant to them. Glasser (1969) feels there are three types of classroom meetings that should be part of the regular school curriculum:

> the *social-problem-solving* meeting, concerned with the students' social
> behavior in school; the *open-ended* meeting, concerned with intellec-
> tually important subjects; and the *educational-diagnostic* meeting, con-
> cerned with how well the students understand the concepts of the
> curriculum (p. 122).

In his book *Schools Without Failure*, Glasser advocates that such meetings should be held on a daily basis for children of all ages. He provides numerous examples of ways in which he works with classroom groups including separate chapters on "Getting Meetings Started" and "Keeping the Class Meetings Going." The following is a brief description of what happened at one classroom meeting:

> The question was asked, "How many think this is a kind class?" About eight boys thought that it was. Those who did were the boys who were mostly unkind themselves, except for two. The class then gave the opinion that these boys themselves were not kind boys. It was true that especially John (the leader of the dissident group) and Bill (his cohort) had often done cruel things to others. They took great pleasure in ambushing and beating up Mike, making remarks of a very cutting nature to most of the other children, hiding articles belonging to others, stealing money, leaving school early, and blurting out negative opinions in class at will (this last being a problem of John, not Bill). The boys in question were quite shocked that the others held such an opinion of them, and appeared a little shaken. Their own self-images seemed to be a bit different from that of their peers. The class discussed the difference between humor which was funny and that which was cruel. They talked about what it feels like inside when a person laughs at the expense of others, how it hurts. This led to another topic, what feels good in a relationship and what feels bad, a topic which we discussed the next time. Before ending this meeting David wanted to know why the class had not let it be known if he was a kind person. It was explained to him that he had not been one to say he felt it was a kind class. He wanted to know anyway, and was happily shocked to see they felt he was a kind person. He had mixed it up with whether they liked him or not, and beamed when he received this vote of confidence. He said he always felt no one liked him before, and that he was an outsider.

> (Glasser 1969, pp. 150–151)

Glasser feels that the group essentially should be used to attempt to solve the educational problems of individuals or groups. This purpose stems from the premise that the school class is a working problem-solving unit in which each person has individual and group responsibilities. The leader's role is structured along the following inflexible guidelines.

1. All problems relative to the class as a group and to any individual in the class are eligible for discussion.

2. The discussion itself should always be directed toward solving the problem; the solution should never include punishment or fault finding.

3. Meetings should always be conducted with the teacher and students seated in a tight circle (Glasser 1969).

NATURAL AND LOGICAL CONSEQUENCES

It is possible to help children to learn and grow in acceptable ways through the use of natural and logical consequences (Dreikurs and Grey 1968). Through *natural consequences* the individual experiences the consequences of his own behavior. They represent the reality of the social order or the natural course of events without outside interference (which usually occurs in the form of a teacher or parent). For example, the individual who refuses to wear his coat during inclement weather will get cold; the *natural* consequence of not dressing warmly is becoming cold. *Logical consequences,* on the other hand, are arranged or contrived. They are structured around the belief that no individual will willingly do what *he* feels is harmful to him. The individual is then allowed to experience the consequences of his own actions (which have more or less been arranged by the teacher.) If the child writes on the wall, he must clean it up. The child who forgets his gym shoes cannot play the game. Perhaps some may think this is just another name for punishment, but Dreikurs and Grey (1968) feel that there are five fundamental differences between logical consequences and punishment.

1. Logical consequences express the reality of the social order, not of the person; punishment, the power of personal authority.
2. Logical consequences are logically related to the misbehavior; punishment rarely is.
3. Logical consequences imply no element of moral judgment; punishment often does.
4. Logical consequences are concerned only with what will happen now; punishment, with the past.
5. Consequences are invoked with a friendly voice; punishment, with anger—either open or concealed.

In punishment, perhaps, the child who forgets his gym shoes would be asked to stay after school or write a paper on a certain game, while in logical consequences the consequences are tied to the act in a logical fashion. The child is motivated through the reality of life and not the mandate of an authority.

A relationship between the teacher and child that allows for discussion on an equal basis is imperative. A good relationship allows both parties to understand and accept the consequences before they are applied. In a poor relationship, such as when a power conflict exists, the logical consequences turn into punishments.

The consequences need to be applied consistently. The child must be as convinced of the logical consequences as he is of the natural consequences (such as touching a hot stove). The teacher needs to be patient and allow time for the behavior to diminish. A behavior that has been successful for a period of years will not disappear in a couple of days.

There are no patent formulas in using logical consequences. Each child and situation must be viewed as unique. The individual child, his goals, and ways of reaching them must be considered. Having Dennis remain in his desk during the spelling game may work effectively. But to do this in Robert's case may actually be reinforcing and strengthen his behavior.

In conclusion, the consultant should be aware of various human learning and development procedures that he can help the teacher to apply in the classroom. The previous procedures are not inclusive by any means, and the consultant should use his creative power to think of other appropriate procedures and ways of applying them to his unique situation.

REFERENCES

Bessell, H. and Palomares, U. *Methods in Human Development.* San Diego: Human Development Training Institute, 1967.

Borton, T. *Reach, Touch and Teach.* New York: McGraw-Hill, 1970.

Brown, G. I. "Human is as Confluent Does." *Theory Into Practice* 10 (1971): 191–195.

Brown, G. I. *Human Teaching for Human Learning: An Introduction to Confluent Education.* New York: Viking, 1971.

Combs, A. W. et al. *Florida Studies in the Helping Professions.* Gainesville, Florida: University of Florida Press, 1969.

Dinkmeyer, D. *Developing Understanding of Self and Others* (DUSO D-1). Circle Pines, Minnesota: American Guidance Service, 1970.

Dinkmeyer, D. *Developing Understanding of Self and Others* (DUSO D-2). Circle Pines, Minnesota: American Guidance Service, 1973.

Dinkmeyer, D. "Understanding Self and Others: A Relevant, Purposeful Experience." *Canadian Counsellor* 5 (1971): 209–214.

Dinkmeyer, D. and Dreikurs, R. *Encouraging Children to Learn: The Encouragement Process.* Englewood Cliffs, New Jersey: Prentice-Hall, 1963.

Dreikurs, R. and Grey, L. *Logical Consequences: A New Approach to Discipline.* New York: Meredith Press, 1968.

Dreikurs, R., Grunwald, B. B. and Pepper, F. C. *Maintaining Sanity in the Classroom.* New York: Harper & Row, 1971.

Glasser, W. *Schools Without Failure.* New York: Harper & Row, 1969.

Lyon, H. C. *Learning to Feel—Feeling to Learn.* Columbus, Ohio: Charles E. Merrill, 1971.

Mosher, R. L. and Sprinthall, N. A. "Psychological Education: A Means to Promote Personal Development During Adolescence." *The Counseling Psychologist* 2 (1971): 3–84.

Randolph, N. and Howe, W. *Self Enhancing Education: A Program to Motivate Learners.* Palo Alto, California: Sanford Press, 1966.

Raths, L. E., Harmin, M. and Simon, S. B. *Values and Teaching.* Columbus, Ohio: Charles E. Merrill, 1965.

Reimer, C. "Some Words of Encouragement." In *Study Group Leader's Manual,* edited by Vicki Soltz, pp. 71–73. Chicago: Alfred Adler Institute, 1967.

Roark, A. E. "Using Encounter Group Principles in Teaching." University of Colorado, 1971. (mimeo.)

Rosenthal, R. and Jacobson, L. *Pygmalion in the Classroom.* New York: Holt, Rinehart & Winston, 1968.

Rucker, W. R., Arnspiger, V. C. and Brodbeck, A. J. *Human Values in Education.* Dubuque, Iowa: Kendall/Hunt, 1969.

Simon, S. B. "The Search for Values." *Edvance* 1, no. 3 (1971): 1+.

Simon, S. B., Howe, L. W. and Kirschenbaum, H. *Values Clarification: A Handbook of Practical Strategies for Teachers and Students.* New York: Hart, 1972.

Soltz, V. *Study Group Leader's Manual.* Chicago: Alfred Adler Institute, 1967.

Stanford, G. "Psychological Education in the Classroom." *Personnel and Guidance Journal* 50 (1972): 585–592.

Stanford, G. and Stanford, B. D. *Learning Discussion Skills Through Games.* New York: Citation Press, 1969.

11

Parent and Family Consulting

SIGNIFICANCE OF THE FAMILY AND THE CHANGING TIMES

Rationale

With few exceptions, the family and, in particular, the parents exert the most significant influence on the development of an individual. The family is the arena in which love, trust, acceptance, and actualization are cultivated. The child's position in the family constellation and his relationship with siblings also exert a tremendous impact. If this structure is unhealthy, a negative and harmful influence results, characterized by fear and atypical growth.

Family life is perhaps the most important element in the development of personality, for it is in this milieu that the culture and the value, beliefs, and mores of society are transmitted to the individual.

> Parents exert a tremendous influence on the child. They are the earliest and often the only models a child has and it is from them that beliefs, values, attitudes and techniques are chosen. It is the parents' behavior that generally establishes the atmosphere of the home, i.e., whether it is peaceful or warlike; cheerful or depressing; marked by warmth, closeness and mutual involvement; or cold, distant and detached.
>
> (Shulman 1962, p. 34)

For example, it is within the family environment that the original meanings about life are obtained—the meanings of trust, love, adequacy, acceptance, etc. From his place within the family, a child perceives beliefs, customs, and myths and acquires many of his parents' values. The family supplies the situation for dealing with the feelings of superiority and inferiority. It is in the family that the individual formulates his view of self as a social, working, sexual, and spiritual being and develops his fundamental allegiance with people.

The family becomes the first socializing agency as the parents and siblings help the individual to develop an identity and to find a place in the world. Thus, the family should never be underrated in terms of its effect upon the learnings of the individual.

The basic education of the individual in emotional and social areas first takes place within the family. According to Dinkmeyer and Muro (1971), "one of our major societal problems involves the fact that parents almost never have adequate experiences, training and educational background to enable them to function effectively in child training. As a result, many parents who are really largely unequipped play the most significant role in the development of society" (p. 284).

The attitudes, ideas and interrelationships of the parents are frequent sources of problems. The struggle involved with obtaining independence from their own autocratic backgrounds or permissive patterns do not help parents to establish democratic approaches to deal effectively with their children. The acquisition of new techniques in democratic management of children is no longer a matter of choice, but of necessity. Dreikurs (1971) calls this dilemma in social equality the challenge of today. Therefore, a healthy family unit would seem to be the most important ingredient to a healthy society. Margaret Mead relates that every society from aborigine to Maoist China has established some form of family life to raise, socialize, and protect the children—to guarantee institutionally the social, sexual needs of the adult members. A healthy family unit is dependent upon positive human relationships which are based upon the ability to communicate effectively. Recent research, however, indicates that "nine out of ten adults talk to children and youth in ways that are destructive to both the kids and the relationships" (Gordon 1971, p. 1).

"The family dynamics of the home that nourishes productivity are a sharp contrast to the dynamics of the unproductive home. Studies of both types of families have found that the greatest differences lie in four areas: the communication structure, the value system, the presence or absence of a helping attitude on the part of the parents, and the definitive role of the parents, particularly that of the father" (Gilmore 1971, p. 237).

"America's families are in trouble—trouble so deep and pervasive as to threaten the future of our nation," declared a major report to . . . (1970) White House Conference on Children. "Can the family survive?" asks anthropologist Margaret Mead rhetorically. "Students in rebellion, the young people living in communes, unmarried couples living together call into question the stable family unit as our society has known it." The family, says California psychologist Richard Farson, "is now often without function. It is no longer necessarily the basic unit in our society. . . .

(*Time*, December 28, 1970, p. 34)

The crisis in the family unit has far-reaching implications. As Paul Popenoe, founder of the American Institute of Family Relations warns, "No society has ever survived after its family life deteriorated."

The nuclear unit (family) has come under attack as the source of the alienated, bomb-throwing society. Alternative new structures are being advocated. The White House Conference (1970) proposed (1) the establishment of a National Institute of the Family, (2) universal day-care, health, and early learning services in which parents would play a major role, (3) the creation of a Cabinet-level Department of Family and Children, and (4) an independent Office of Child Advocacy. This can result in babies being brought up in day-care centers, the establishment of extended families, new communes—or perhaps as Germaine Greer (1970) proposes, the elimination of connected permanent relationships. Let each man, woman, and child fend for himself. David Cooper (1970) and R. D. Laing (1969) charge that the family unit is the originator of all pathology, personal and political. The family is the source of man's greatest happiness, yet it is also the place of the most savage fights, battles, and rivalries with their corresponding psychological and physical damage.

Some of the forces that appear to be weakening the nuclear family are:

1. Mobility of the population—not only the shifts from rural to metropolitan areas but the impact of modern mass transportation as well.
2. Changing role of women.
3. Glorification of children.
4. Limited usefulness of the family.

According to sociologist Reuben Hill, among others, the family has traditionally performed several functions: reproduction, protection and care of children, economic production of family goods and services, socialization of children, education of children, recreation, and affection giving. But during the past century, he says the economic, educational, recreational and socializing functions have been lost in varying degrees to industry, schools, and government (*Time* 1970, pp. 35–36).

In the areas of reproduction, child care, and affection there has been little change. It is perhaps in these areas that the solidarity necessary for the promulgation of the nuclear family can be found. The role of the family could also become that of facilitator of human development and personal growth, and the family unit could share in many learning experiences. This would tend to add strength to the nuclear family. Is the family out of style? Skolnick and Skolnick (1971) feel,

> Some see changes in sex and family life as frightening evidence that society is falling apart, that we are descending into anarchy and barbarism; others feel that a time of genuine liberation may be. coming. Understandably, students turn to social-science books and causes for enlightenment. They are likely to be disappointed. They will repeatedly encounter affirmations of stability—affirmations that few changes in family and sex life are occurring, and further, that no change is possible in the basic form of the family (p. 2).

It seems to us that the traditional nuclear family will continue, though its form may change. For example, Otto (1971) feels that in the years to come, perhaps 20 percent of the population will explore alternative models of social living. However, all the evidence shows that in order to survive, the family needs help. It cannot function as a healthy institution unless ways are developed to strengthen its concept and spirit. The function of this chapter will be to present procedures and methods for directly working with parents and families.

Organization

Schools have long emphasized the importance of working with the parents and families of the students. Organizations such as the P.T.A. have been created to function in this area. The real issues, however, are not being met in this structure. When communication is established in other than this perfunctory manner, it is usually done in a negative or crisis situation (e.g., behavioral problem, truancy). There is a need to involve parents in a positive program of mental health. Norton (1971) discusses the serious nature of this situation in what he terms "parental apathy." Parents tend to involve themselves only when the purpose for involvement is clear and relevant to them.

There have been theorists, such as Grams (1966), who have advocated the schools helping parents to deal with their children. Several of the major areas needing emphasis are as follows:

1. Teaching the parents ways of providing a solid emotional base for children.
2. Helping parents to convey to children that discovery, curiosity, problem solving, riddles, puzzles, and learning can be associated with happy times.
3. Helping parents to stimulate special abilities and talents in children.
4. Making certain that parents understand readiness as an ongoing concept.
5. Encouraging parents to provide direct experiences which ready the child for learning.
6. Instructing parents in assisting children to think (i.e., being a good listener and a good questioner).
7. Helping parents to assist their children in developing values toward self, others, and learning.

(Grams 1966)

Muro (1970) goes beyond this and feels schools should also "make an effort to instruct parents in the areas of creativity, problem solving, the concept of developmental tasks, the objectives and philosophy of elementary education, special education programs, and the important concepts from child psychology" (p. 236).

Parental involvement must be beyond the typical one-time meeting, such as report card time or P.T.A. meeting. These, like the Sunday sermon, have little carry over. What is needed is a *planned* program of *parent* education. "Where parents have not been sources of nourishment for their children, they must be equipped to do so" (Carkhuff 1971, p. 73).

Perhaps we need to begin to think and conceptualize as Donigan and Giglio (1971). They envisioned and implemented the concept of "family counselor," a professional who works not only with children, teachers, and parents, but who has as part of his assigned role going into homes and working with families. Any program of consulting, counseling, or remediation that proposes to help an unproductive person must contain mechanisms for bringing about changes in his family relationships (Gilmore 1971, p. 259). Traditionally, the school has not provided assistance in helping families to establish policies and principles related to human behavior.

The consultant accepts the challenge of restructuring the school, home, and community. He, perhaps, is best characterized in this role as an architect of change. He is concerned with the whole child and therefore recognizes the importance of working with parents. Previous problems have centered around the resistance of parents to bring their real problems to school. The consultant deals with this by going to the parents! He works in the actual life space of his patrons and helps the family members to develop *solutions* to their problems. The consultant knows that he must go beyond just knowledge "as knowledge defines a problem and does not solve it." The consultant is eager and willing to help formulate ideas, but he is not a judge, umpire, or dispenser of criticism.

A program of parent education which centers on weekly parent group discussions is also an integral component in allowing parents to take an active role. These groups are formed to help parents to understand and work with the affective and cognitive aspects of dealing with their children. Once a program of this nature is begun, it becomes self-supporting (Carlson 1969). Despite common misconceptions, it has been our experience that parents (regardless of socioeconomic status, intellectual level, or ethnic background) *want* and will seek out and support this activity. Perhaps the effectiveness of parent education can be attributed to the many advantages that the participants derive:

> It helps them find a mutual source of support. It enables them to face their actions, their attitudes, their feelings, and to recognize that the problems the parents have are universal. They are not alone in their fears, helplessness and discouragement. The group then provides an opportunity to increase communication skills between parents and between parents and children.
>
> (Dinkmeyer and Muro 1971, p. 285).

Additional benefits might be speculated on the basis of recent research by Duncan (1969). He reported the results of a three-year follow-up study of parents who had attended a *one-hour* conference concerned with their seventh graders entering junior high school. He found during the three-year period, comparing experimental and control groups, that the parents who had attended the one-hour conference made at a statistically significant level more contacts with the school, and the children's attendance was better and grade point averages higher than the control group. There was also a decrease in the dropout rate in counseled families, and there were fewer disciplinary referrals.

Goals and Objectives

According to Van Hoose (1968) the major goals of parent-counselor conferences are:

> (1) to interpret and clarify reasons for certain behaviors, (2) to provide parents with information that will enable them to better under-

stand and help their child, (3) to secure information that will aid the counselor and the school in understanding the child, (4) to identify unsound psychological practices and to help the parent reduce or eliminate such practices, (5) to help the parent understand the child as a learner, and (6) to involve the parent in the school life of the child (p. 131).

Parent group work tends to go beyond this in providing direct assistance to the parents and indirect help to the child. The basic objectives of this activity are:

1. To improve the parent-child relationship. To help the relationship become more positive and mutually satisfying.
2. To assist parents in understanding the meaning and importance of the interactions/dialogues they have with their children.
3. To facilitate the acquisition of effective communication skills. To help parents become aware of their involvement in message sending and receiving.
4. To organize school and home in order to develop consistent efforts in the training of children.
5. To share insights, experiences, and help the parents to develop a deeper understanding of the significant role they play in the development of their offspring. To go beyond this essential level of understanding and explore ways in which they can be of mutual help.
6. To help parents understand the influence the family has on human development, how the specific activities and communication set the pattern for the development of human behavior.
7. To foster the development of social interest which includes helping one's fellow man, creating positive mental health for the community and the establishment of a feeling of togetherness or "we-ness."

The overall purpose lies in establishing a sound communication network and a psychologically positive system for each individual's "primary group."

MODELS OF PARENT AND FAMILY CONSULTING

Gordon's Parent Effectiveness Training (P.E.T.)

The P.E.T. program focuses on improving communication within the family unit and teaching parents how to solve conflicts as they arise. Parents simulate real-life problems through role playing and practise

listening and problem-solving skills. Dr. Thomas Gordon's organization, Effectiveness Training Associates,* has as the motto, "Training Before Trouble—Prevention, not Treatment—Education, not
Therapy."

This approach centers around finding effective ways of changing
the human relationship that has the greatest effect on a child's psychological health—that of the parent-child relationship. P.E.T. is a
planned course that hopes to help parents to change their outlook on
raising children. The program also offers training in the specific skills
and methods needed to bring about a corresponding change in behavior. The twenty-four hours of training involve classroom instruction, which includes lectures, demonstrations, tape recordings,
classroom participation experiences, role playing, buzz sessions, and
general group discussions. The general theory purported is one that
outlines the necessary requirements for establishing and maintaining
a human relationship in which an individual can meet his needs and
reach his potential as well as helping others to do the same. The
ability to resolve conflicts in a "no-lose" fashion as opposed to a "win-
lose method" is also stressed. This is the procedure of joint decision
making that is used by business and labor. Gordon (1970) describes
it as follows:

> Parent and child encounter a conflict-of-needs situation. The parent
> asks the child to participate with him in a joint search for some solution
> acceptable to both. One or both may offer possible solutions. They criti-
> cally evaluate them and eventually make a decision on a final solution
> acceptable to both. No selling of the other is required after the solution
> has been selected, because both have already accepted it. No power is
> required to force compliance, because neither is resisting the decision
> (p. 196).

Gordon's "Credo for Adult-Child Relationships" states, "I respect
your needs, but I also must respect my own. Consequently, let us
strive always to search for solutions to our inevitable conflicts that
will be acceptable to both of us. In this way your needs will be met,
but so will mine—no one will lose, both will win."

An example of the kind of activity utilized is as follows:

> Each parent . . . is asked to demonstrate how he talks with kids in three
> critical but entirely different kinds of interpersonal situations:

---

* Effectiveness Training Associates is located at 110 South Euclid Avenue,
Pasadena, California 91101.

1. When the *child* is troubled, needful, disturbed, bothered, upset, unhappy, frustrated, and so on, because he is having some problem with his own behavior (WHEN THE CHILD OWNS THE PROBLEM);

2. When the *parent* . . . is troubled, needful, disturbed, bothered, frustrated, upset, or unhappy because the behavior of the child is causing the adult a problem (WHEN THE ADULT OWNS THE PROBLEM);

3. When the adult and the child find themselves in a disagreement or in a conflict, involving a clash between the needs of each (WHEN THE RELATIONSHIP OWNS THE PROBLEM).

(Gordon 1971, p. 1)

Another example would be teaching parents to express exactly what they feel rather than sending a command or a judgmental, blaming message.

For example, a teenager arrives home at 1:30 a.m. after agreeing to be home by midnight. Her mother has been quite worried that something might have happened to her and is relieved when she finally arrives. Frequently in such situations mothers say something like, "Well, you cannot be trusted, I see. I'm so angry at you. You are grounded for a month." P.E.T. would encourage the mother to send her real feeling instead: "I have been terribly worried because I was afraid something might have happened to you." The daughter is likely to react less defensively to such a statement (Peterson 1969, p. 369).

Fullmer's Family Group Consultation

In 1963, the American Personnel and Guidance Association presented the Nancy Wimmer Award to Daniel Fullmer for his unique approach to family group consultation. It apparently grew out of the need to have some effective way for working with parents, children, and teachers conjointly. Besides its parent education function, Fullmer and Bernard (1972, pp. 118–119) include the following reasons for consulting with parents:

(1) The counselor needs to interpret change to both parent and child. The difference between parent and child is commonly known as the generation gap.

(2) The increasing urbanization which brings people closer together geographically has resulted in the paradox of separating individuals psychologically. The small group intensive experience in interpersonal intimacy has the potential to overcome this alienating force.

(3) As industry has shifted from individual to group methods of management, we will need to institute such shifts in the parent, family,

teacher, counselor, school concept. Instead of having one individual in charge of many other individuals, we now have groups of individuals who organize and maintain their own social control systems and depend upon self-discipline as the social control force.

The general procedure involves a team of two or more counselors working with several families, including children, discussing specific questions or concerns. All significant persons are encouraged to be present. The method combines the talents of all the people concerned with the child. A team concept involving children, parents, teachers, administrators, and other specialists is utilized to help participants. The focus is on clarifying communcation in the family transactions.

The approach is based on the premise that each individual learns his behavior characteristics inside the family. Therefore, if behavior is to be modified, intervention must center on the interpersonal relationships that occur within the home. The main concern is to share ideas, attitudes, and feelings about "here and now" situations which affect behavior. The process provides an opportunity for the meanings of each person's life events to be examined, verbalized, and clarified for each family member. The consultation procedures employed provide direct intervention in the family communication system. The family is helped when the members begin to understand the meaning that life events have for each other. Fullmer (1972a, p. 271) defines the parameters of interpersonal relationships that group participants develop in the following categories:

Mutual respect	Instead of	Mutual exploitation
"Self" reference	Instead of	"Other" reference
Internal reference	Instead of	External reference
Here-and-now happening	Instead of	There-and-then happening
We share	Instead of	I give-you take (and reverse)
Help-Care game	Instead of	Win-Lose game

Fullmer's style can be more clearly seen in the following case example.*

A family of three was referred to me recently. Here is a selected portion of the sessions.

Father: (enters room) "Are you Dr. _____?"

Counselor: "Yes. Come on in, is your family with you?"

Father: "Yes." (enter mother and seventeen-year-old son)

---

* This material was prepared especially for this manuscript by Dr. Fullmer upon the authors' request.

Son: "How do you do?" (shakes hands)

Father: (shakes hands)

Mother: (looks nervous, pouty)

Chairs are taken in usual fashion with family facing each other and counselor.

Son: "What is this all about? Why are we here?"

Mother: "I don't think it is safe to talk about our troubles in front of him" (son).

Father: (looks helpless in the social stress created by the son and mother)

Counselor: "Are you (family) always this stressed emotionally?"

Mother and son together: "What do you mean?"

Counselor: "You seem so upset that I sense an emotionally tight climate, very distressed. Are you always like . . ."

Son: "Usually."

Mother: "We didn't want to come. Doesn't the idea of telling it all to each other seem to be destructive?"

Counselor: "Oh, how so?"

Mother: "Giving up the secrets—I don't like it."

Son: "What secrets? Now I'm curious. I want to be here."

Father: (still is out of it. He has no role other than to be present physically. Following several exchanges about why the former counselor referred them to family consultation, the session continues.)

Son: "I don't see how our being here will help us. You (counselor) have not told us anything. We talk and you observe— is that all you do?"

Counselor: "What would you like to have me do?"

Mother: "I'm against being here. What do we need to do?"

Counselor: "Why not begin by describing an incident. Tell what happened before, during, and following the incident. Any incident will do."

Son: "Like the one we had this afternoon before coming here?"

Mother: "I don't remember any incident."

Son: "My school work."

Mother: (cuts in) "He is flunking two subjects in the last quarter of his senior year. He won't graduate. He was called in by the principal."

Son: "Only a little time was spent on the school work. Mostly, it was a school politics issue."

Mother: "You are going to fail."

Son: "I can redo the twelfth grade."

The family members continued to expound and challenge each other and myself. The session ran over the one and one half hours by thirty minutes because the family could not decide if they should return. I told them to go home and take with them the task of deciding. I indicated I was disinterested in working with people of such low motivation. "After all, it is difficult work to meet with people like you. It is not difficult to see why you have problems with each other."

The family had a task. They left with directions to phone the center and leave the decision with the secretary. The following day a message was received. They would continue and complete the initial four sessions. (I chose four sessions because it gives enough time to see if family consultation is helpful to the group.)

The family arrived on time for the second session. The first task was to complete the family bond inventory, a projective culture-free test of family relationships (Fullmer 1972b). When each member had completed the task I asked for any reactions each person had during the exercise.

> *Mother:* "I thought it was silly."
>
> *Son:* "The emotional thing kept coming up."
>
> *Father:* "Yes, did you find it that way too?"
>
> *Counselor:* "Anything else?"
>
> *Mother:* "Emotional content? What do you mean?"
>
> *Son:* "Well, you can't place yourself in relation to another person without thinking about whether you're angry or not."
>
> *Counselor:* (to mother) "How do you think everyone else will place the symbols? Do you think your son will place them like you did?"
>
> *Mother:* "Yes."
>
> *Counselor:* "Tell us about it. How do you think he did it?"
>
> *Mother:* "He (the son) would place himself between his father and me."
>
> *Counselor:* "Let's look. Here, take each one and pass them among yourselves. See if you all placed them alike."
>
> *Son:* "Why did you put yours like this, Mom?"
>
> *Mother:* (greatly surprised) "What do you mean? I was just putting the symbols down the way it is."
>
> *Son:* "Sleeping, in a row?"

The mother had tried to defeat the instrument by giving what she thought were bland responses. The directions given included the statement that anyone could rig the responses, but the person doing it would know it if she or he lied. The pattern of placements would not look (or feel) correct. There was no attempt to confront the mother with what she had done. But she did know that everyone knew what she had done.

The second session was a sharp contrast to the initial session. The son remarked about it. He wondered how two sessions could be so completely different. All interaction had been in relation to the instrument. Near the close of the second session I assigned a task. The family was to begin by appointing one member each morning, on a rotation basis, to have the duty of interrupting any escalating interaction by simply asking, "Hey, what's happening now?" The principal participants then were to discuss what had just taken place. If the discussion began to escalate in a similar manner, then the process was to be repeated. Following detailed discussion of the directions, the family went home.

For Session Three the family had tried the task with limited success. However, a marked change in the emotional climate was evident. Strong feelings seemed to have waved toward strong supportive commitments. This phenomenon is not unusual in the second or third session because of a withholding of usual demands on family members by each member. I have called it the "blush of health." The chances that it will last beyond the fourth or fifth sessions is nil. The goal is to interrupt the habitual interaction form with the recalling and recounting of "What is happening?" If a family can get the interruption of their interaction to work, they are ready for step two.

In step two members gain the perception that each of them is a *victim* and has no control over his behavior. This stage requires the family members to identify the sequence of cues which serve as triggers for emotional outbursts. A "head" trip won't help because the person cannot translate reasons into action. But one can learn to manipulate his own input in interactions, and this controls responses from others. Here is the only concrete source of control anyone has in an exchange of messages during an interaction with another person. If an individual family member cannot do the interruption task, he may need additional help in psychotherapy in order to develop a stronger ability to take and maintain a stand.

In the current family, the family bond inventory revealed the existence of powerful normal relationships between family members. (Father-Mother, Father-Son, Mother-Son) We learned from the instrument that the mother is not a reliable informant on family issues. She realized that everybody knew this, but the potentially destructive interaction of confirming it was avoided. During the second and third sessions, the mother gave evidence of conscious effort to be more reliable.

The family was given as much explanation as they wished to have. This write-up is designed to share the intervention technique. No attempt will be made to cover theory. (See Fullmer, D. W., *Counseling: Group Theory and System*, 1971). The family experiences the power of the technique. The counselor must try to avoid "head" trips with the family about their behavior. He must stick with the description of one incident at a time in the sequence of (1) what happened, (2) what happened just before, (3) what happened just after, and (4) what happened during. What response did you make? What happened then? etc. For a group of families—two or more—the interaction discussion takes longer than with one family.

Counselor: "How did it go with your task?"

Mother: "We couldn't do it too well. We made it through most of the weekend."

Father: "I was a mess on Saturday. Whenever I preach on Sunday, Saturday is a lost cause for me with any family activity."

Son: "Just leave you strictly alone—"

Mother: "Immediately following Sunday services, he is a different person. Things improve.

Counselor: "Do you withdraw from the family or stay in close association during such a time?"

Father: "I usually go to the chapel on Saturday evenings. I'm around during the daytime."

Son: "I've been out of school for two days."

Mother: "I'm your mother and I know you are not sick!"

Son: "Can't expect me to go to school with this cough."

Counselor: "Has the school thing remained unchanged?"

Mother: "He has not gone to school so he is around the house all of the time."

Son: "I stay in my room. You two were into an argument last night."

Father: "No we weren't—Oh yes, now I remember."

Mother: "We were in disagreement."

Father: "How can we avoid disagreement?"

Counselor: "You can't. What you need to learn is to manage the interaction to resolve the disagreement so it doesn't become escalated out of your control. This idea is connected to what I told you about the importance of content. Content in interaction is zero. The relationship is all that counts. The relationships in the family are solid."

Long pause.

Mother: "Are we finished for tonight?"

Counselor: "Unless someone has something he wants discussed . . . if not, I'll see you Friday."

Session Three ended a half hour early.

The family arrived for Session Four and set immediately about the task of relating their experiences of the past two days.

> *Mother:* "This thing is not working. I think the whole business has just upset our family."
>
> *Son:* "Things have really improved. I can see how to interrupt the fighting."
>
> *Father:* "We have a long way to go."
>
> *Mother:* "I don't care what you say, things are not good. You haven't helped."
>
> *Counselor:* "Remember that I said in an earlier session you might find the going too rough. You seem to be very distressed today. Perhaps you would prefer to return to your individual therapist who referred you."
>
> *Mother:* "Yes. I do think I should."
>
> *Father:* "I feel the need for more time to try this new behavior."
>
> *Son:* "I think its great! Mother and Dad are always fighting. But I've learned to handle it."

Following Session Four, the parents did return to therapy. Continued follow-up showed the son to be symptom free, but the parents continued to be distressed.

In Family Group Consultation, like other group counseling, everyone improves at his own rate. The gains are more in the area of a realistic evaluation of the functioning status of family members. In the case above, the mother has never seemed to make it with any other person in an interpersonal relationship. Her family members are no exception. The father has spent a quarter century living with the problem. His behavior doesn't change easily. Later, the family may try more sessions together to practice new behavior. This exercise will have to await the mother's development of the ability to level with herself. She has a long history of being an unreliable informant.

Zwetschke and Grenfell (1965) describe the purpose of family consultation as establishing better understanding between individuals in the family, reduction of the cultural encapsulation of members of the family, expression of affection and regard for each other, and greater openness in their behavior with each other. The system was developed on the idea that families seek help because of problems children are experiencing. The family is helped to see that most problems are owned by the entire family and the set of relationships, and not just by the child.

Recently, the importance of the family as a unit of therapeutic focus has been advocated. Ackerman (1958), Bell (1961), Haley (1969), Jackson (1959), Sauber (1971), and other writers have contributed to the literature on understanding the family process.

Satir's Conjoint Family Therapy*

The child's stability or psychological "healthiness" is, in a large part, dependent upon the relationship between the child's parents. The child is trapped between the expectations held for him by the family and his own desire and need for change. Virginia Satir (1968, 1972) operates on the belief that all behavior is learned, and that the members of the family are the most important teachers. She further believes that what is learned can be unlearned, and the quickest and most effective way to work at change is in the family where the learning took place. Previously, the disturbed child was the "symptom bearer" and was treated in isolation. Now we are working with the whole family as the treatment unit and experimenting with using the whole community as a treatment component.

Satir (1968) feels:

A man and a woman are each wholes in themselves. To produce a baby they have to get together. Since babies come into this world as undeveloped adults, the man and woman are essential to bringing the child to adulthood. How a man and woman treat each other and experience each other and themselves becomes the basis for how the growing child will treat and experience them and himself. Over a period of time, this develops into a set of predictable actions and interactions among all of them—their system. The question is, Do these provide experience in growth or distortion? (p. 266)

The therapist becomes involved with the distorted or dysfunctional system. He becomes an active participant and uses his communication to change the system. By communication, Satir means "the process that makes meaning between two people." This process can take five forms: words, voice tone, facial expression, body tones and gesture, and dress including style of hair and make-up. The therapist changes the system in two ways:

Specific therapist communications focus on points of potential change within the system; this kind of therapist activity is common to most therapies. Also, and more distinctive of my approach, is the therapist's use of his own self: the therapist, by his own example, demonstrates a

---

* An audio-tape, "Family Communication and Growth," by Virginia Satir is available from Big Sur Recordings, 117 Mitchell Blvd., San Rafael, California, 94903. This tape describes and demonstrates Satir's technique. A film entitled "Target Five" is available from Psychological Films, 205 W. 20th St., Santa Ana, California, 92706. In this two-part film, Mrs. Satir (with the help of Dr. Everett Shostrom) demonstrates and discusses family communication patterns.

healthier mode of communication. There is no double message in which the therapist prescribes directness and sharing of feelings, but models of self-protection by clinging to his professional inscrutability (Satir 1968, p. 269).

The therapist is a functional communicator who can (1) firmly state his case, (2) yet at the same time clarify and qualify what he says, (3) as well as ask for feedback, and (4) be receptive to feedback when he gets it (Satir 1967).

The following example, typifies Virginia Satir's approach:

Satir:	I've become aware of something. The activity changed here very drastically since we changed the seating. Were you aware of that?
John: (father)	Yes mam. These (Mary and Jane, his daughters) are old enough to understand the cause-and-effect relationship.
Satir:	I don't know what that means.
John:	When they get close to me they know what's going to happen if they're not good. They're handled by rigid discipline. These other two (Jimmy and Elaine) haven't developed this cause-and-effect relationship, and she (Alice) handles them in a different way. I want to say by love, but I love these, too, or I wouldn't be as concerned about them as I am. Nevertheless she doesn't use my disciplinary tactics.
Satir:	You know, John, I have to say something to you. It may surprise you, but I haven't seen one thing, except once you snapped your fingers, about all this disciplining. What I've seen is your making a place for these two girls. I haven't seen anything disciplinary, though. Now are you saying to me that when your arms are around the girls, you are saying to them, "You'd better be good or else?"
John:	No, because I think they understand fully. Elaine, however, doesn't understand that I can be very strict with them and love them at the same time.
Satir:	Are you saying in some way that you don't feel that Alice does that?
John:	Alice is not nearly as strict with them as I am. I think she would agree with that, and yet her control with them is much better than mine.
Jane:	He blows his top.
Satir:	He blows his top! Oh! All right, all right. But I did feel something change. Did you see something change when you changed your positions? Alice, what kind of explanation would you give for that?
Alice: (mother)	I guess these two (Mary and Jane) feel as if they don't have to stay within certain bounds when they're with me as they

Satir: do when they're with him. That's the only explanation that I have. I'm not so good at blowing my top, I guess.

Satir: Do you want to get better?

Alice: I guess so. I mean, I don't know if that would be the solution. I would like to be firmer with them, but I don't want to go into the anger and so forth that is involved with it. We're just so different. I mean, he is a very emotional person and he reacts to every little thing. He just flares up and I don't.

Satir: You know, just let me tell you something that I was feeling. It may or may not be right—that sometimes you ask yourself if you ought to be different from what you are when you don't really really believe it. I don't think you really believe you'd like to blow your top, would you?

Alice: Not blow my top. I would like to be able to be more positive.

Satir: Can you give me an example of what you mean by that?

Alice: I would like to be able to say, "No you are not going to do this," and then make it stick—to be convincing with the children.

(Satir 1971, p. 9)

Behavioral Approach

This procedure generally entails teaching behavioral analysis principles and applications to parents. The behavior modification approaches are simple, direct, and concrete, requiring no complex understandings. The major contribution of the behavior modification approaches has been their systematic methodologies and their resultant ability to demonstrate tangible evidence of human behavior change and its maintenance after short periods of treatment (Carkhuff and Berenson 1967).

In relation to the treatment of children, parents have been trained in the procedures needed to identify and reinforce the child's adjustive behavior (Krasner and Ullmann 1965). Other studies (Hawkins, Peterson, Schweid and Bijou 1966; O'Leary, O'Leary and Becker 1969; Shah 1969; Wahler, Winkel, Peterson and Morrison 1965; Walder, Cohen, Breiter, Daston, Hirsch and Liebowitz 1969) show the efficiency of training parents in behavioral procedures.

Becker (1971), Patterson (1971), and Patterson and Gullion (1968) have developed individually paced learning programs on how to live more enjoyably with parents and children. They believe that children and parents have taught each other to behave in ways that irritate each other and create conflict within the home. The approach is to discover the ways in which parents and children teach each other and then develop new methods of encouraging desirable behavior and eliminating undesirable behavior.

According to Mayer (1972), the two most common objectives of the behavioral consultant are to (1) help the parent to specify the desired terminal behavior for the child or goal selection, and (2) facilitate the parent's acquisition and implementation of the behavioral procedures. After the goal has been chosen, the consultant chooses an appropriate behavioral procedure (e.g., reinforcement, extinction, time-out). For example, the consultant could use "generalization":

> . . . consultants often assume that a procedure the consultee has effectively used with one child (i.e. John) will be generalized to others (i.e. Joe). Yet, this is not always the case. Many times the consultant will find that he must help the consultee generalize a new behavior. He can often do so by *stressing the commonality of elements in both situations*. For example, he can point out to the consultee that Joe's behavior is similar to John's and that the two situations are similar (both in same class, both boys, etc.). He can then suggest that the same procedure (i.e. the use of praise for assignment completion behavior) might work as it did in the other *similar* situation. A similar tack also could be taken to assist the teacher in using the procedure with her entire classroom.

(Mayer 1972, pp. 7–8)

Transactional Analysis: Harris' I'm OK—You're OK

Transactional analysis is a popular approach to mental health that confronts the individual with the fact that he is responsible for the future, regardless of the past. The approach is practical and uses a clear and noncomplex communication system.

The program begins by having the participants (in groups) learn the vocabulary and ideas of Eric Berne's (1964) transactional analysis (T.A.) Among the main constructs are the three active states in each person's make-up: the Parent, the Adult, and the Child (P.A.C.). The Parent is a collection of rules, the don'ts and dos that were learned early in life and are now accepted as governing rules. The Child is perhaps best characterized as feelings or spontaneous emotions. The Adult is the reality-based component of the internal dialogue. The goal of T.A. is "to *cure* the patient by freeing-up his Adult from the trouble-making influences and demands of his Parent and Child. The goal is achieved by teaching each member of the group how to recognize, identify, and describe the Parent, Adult, and Child as each appears in transactions in the group" (Harris 1967, p. 206).

Harris (1967) postulates that there are four life positions underlying people's behavior. These are functions of the "life script" or how life shall be lived.

1. *I'm Not OK—You're OK.* the characteristic position of early childhood.
2. *I'm Not OK—You're Not OK.* the despair or I give up position.
3. *I'm OK—You're Not OK.* the criminal position.
4. *I'm OK—You're OK.* the position of the mature adult who is at peace with himself and others.

Once the language is developed, the central technique, *analyzing a transaction,* is initiated. In the group setting the participant learns about how he responds to others, and practical suggestions for changing his approach to life are provided.

The Adlerian Model*

The Adlerian system feels that most parents mean well but have faulty methods of child training. Therefore, the focus is on providing parents with *specific* principles and not generalities. Adlerian centers (i.e., child guidance centers, family education associations) provide parents with the opportunity to observe practical demonstrations and to get involved in group discussions on how to apply these principles to a specific family. Parents are provided an opportunity to learn more effective ways of relating with their children through observation and identification with the family receiving counseling. Many of the normal problems parents have with children are universal and center around meals, sleep, and dressing. Therefore, in this approach, parents are able to understand their own situation when they observe it in another family. Because of their lack of emotional involvement with children in another family, they can be more objective and understanding of what is occurring.

The elements that are involved in the group counseling process are:

1. The establishment and maintenance of proper relationships, including the counselor as group leader with mutual respect among all members.

---

* A movie of Dr. Rudolf Dreikurs, international leader and spokesman of the Adlerian movement, is available from the American Personnel and Guidance Association, 1607 New Hampshire Ave., N.W., Washington, D.C. 20009. The film is entitled "Individual Psychology: A Demonstration with a Parent, a Teacher, and a Child."

2. An examination of the purpose of each group member's action or behavior.
3. Revelation through group interaction of the individual's mistaken goals or motives. (This comes most easily when group members have common problems.)
4. A reorientation and redirection by the individual through insight on behavior gained in the group and improved interpersonal relationships and group support.

(Sonstegard and Dreikurs 1967).

While the Adlerian approach is based on the assumption that parents and children need to develop new family relationships, the emphasis is to provide education and training—not treatment. The focus is on teaching parents more effective techniques and helping children to become aware of the purposes of their misbehavior (Christensen 1972).

Sessions for parents begin with an introductory meeting where rationale and procedures are explained, questions answered, and a voluntary commitment made. Usually evening meetings of one-and-a-half hours are scheduled. Once a rapport has been established, the interview with selected parents before the group is carefully structured. The parents may be asked to describe the routine of a typical day—behavior of the child and reactions or actions of the parent. The counselor continually includes other parents in the group in this discussion. Then, the counseled parents are asked to leave the room, and the children are brought in to clarify hypotheses made about the children's goals. After the children talk, the playroom director may contribute observations about the children in play situations and the teacher may describe the children's classroom behavior. The parent group is then asked for *action* suggestions, and these are discussed and sorted according to significance. (Sonstegard and Dreikurs 1967).

The characteristic elements of the Adlerian approach, as described by Dreikurs (1949), are as follows:

1. The focus of attention is directed toward the parents, as the parent is generally the problem, not the child. The child responds only in his own way to the experiences to which he is exposed. Especially younger children do not change easily as long as the parent's attitudes and approach to the child does not change.
2. All parents consulting the Center participate simultaneously in a procedure that may be called "group therapy." In these sessions each case is openly discussed in front of the other parents. Many parents gain greater insight into their own situation by listening to the discussion of similar problems which other parents have. In this way an

influence is exerted beyond the scope of individual treatment and the whole community, including teachers, is directed toward a better approach to understanding and handling children.

3. The same therapist works with parent and child. All problems of children are problems of a disturbed parent-child relationship. The therapist is confronted with this disturbed relationship and must approach it from both ends simultaneously. Working with one party alone is almost a handicap. The speed and course of treatment depend upon the receptivity of parent and child alike. It can be evaluated only if the worker is in close contact with both.

4. The problems of the child are frankly discussed with him regardless of his age. If the child understands the words, he can also understand psychological dynamics which they describe. Contrary to widespread belief, young children show an amazing keenness in grasping and accepting psychological explanations. In general, it takes much longer for a parent to understand the psychological dynamics of the problem; the child recognizes them almost immediately.

5. If there are other children in the family, we deal with all of them together, not only with the "problem child." His problems are closely related to the behavior of every other member of the group. One has to understand the whole group and the existing interrelationships, the lines of alliance, competition, and antagonism to really understand the concept and behavior of any one member.

6. The main objective of our work is the change in the relationships between child and parent, and between the siblings. Without such a change it is impossible to alter the child's behavior, his life-style, his approaches to social living, his concepts of himself in relation to others.

Merville Shaw: IRCOPPS Model

A systematic and sustained program of parent contact was advocated by Shaw and the Interprofessional Research Commission on Pupil Personnel Services (IRCOPPS). This model had three basic objectives for pupil personnel services: problem prevention, early identification and treatment, and diagnosis and therapy. Shaw (1969) felt that the role of the specialist should focus on assisting people to change their behavior through understandings that they arrive at by themselves. These were parent counseling groups, different from the traditional groups which focus on providing information about children.

In order to appraise this model, Shaw and others conducted a three-year study involving thirty-eight counselors and fifty-three parent counseling groups. Parents of first-, seventh-, and ninth-grade children were invited to participate in small group discussions focusing upon concerns *they* as parents had about their growing children.

The evaluation conducted at the end of each series concluded that parents who attended more sessions had more positive response to the sessions. Most parents would recommend the group experience to their friends, although there were few who perceived changes in their children's behavior as a result of counseling. More information is supplied by Shaw (1968, 1969), Shaw and Rector (1968), and Shaw and Tuel (1965). A series of films entitled "Counseling with Parents" is available from Psychological Cinema Register at Pennsylvania State University which show this model over the course of the first, third, and fourth interviews.

Other Contributions

The recent work by R. D. Laing (1969), David Cooper (1970) and Jules Henry (1971) has reinforced the need to understand and work with the whole family. They have shown that in some cases certain members of the family become scapegoats or "elected patients" and are not really "ill." The writers not only speak of methodology for dealing with what is, but also expound on alternative forms of living.

Mallars (1968), McGowan (1968), and Heller and Gurney (1968) discussed group counseling with parents of handicapped or underachieving students. Practical suggestions and procedures for this type of program were also discussed.

Bank and Brooks (1971) implemented the "parent principle" in working with the significant adults of inner-city Detroit children. The program involved parents in weekly meetings that centered around planned activities.

Jaslow (1971) reported on parent counseling in the school. She discussed methods such as night counseling, group work with underachievers and their mothers, and pre-school parent training programs.

Sauber (1971), in response to the number of children and families needing help, proposed the use of multiple-family group counseling, in which several families are brought together in weekly discussions.

It is proposed that the public school system provide the services for short-term, multiple-family group counseling which appears to be an effective treatment for family problems of which the student is the "identified client." Since the current philosophy in the school does not give sanction to a long-term therapeutic approach, nor can it afford the financial and time investments of individual family counseling, an appropriate plan of action would be to implement a multiple-family group approach. The concept of multiple-family group counseling (MFGG) is based on the premise that the world of the home and school are inseparable; and with the family being the primary influence, school personnel are often powerless unless communication has been established with the parents. Furthermore, it is postulated that the place to attack the problem is with the people whom it involves and the setting where it occurs (p. 459).

PARENT EDUCATION

Auerbach (1968), Hillman (1968), Kremer (1971), Luckey (1967), Pickarts and Fargo (1971), and Stormer (1967) have presented approaches to parent education. The parent and family education program can be enhanced through the development of parent study groups. The general purpose of these groups is to help parents to understand their children and to develop more effective methods of relating with them. The consultant helps to establish these groups because he realizes that parents often have similar problems which can be discussed in the group setting. The group situation allows parents to realize that they are not alone. The universal nature of certain kinds of parent relationships provides the real setting for experiencing true growth.

Many times the individual consultant has trouble helping a parent to see a new way to relate to his offspring, but the parent group almost always expands his willingness to accept new ideas. Parents begin to reason, "Oh, I see you are doing it," or "If you can do it, then I can certainly do it." The example of other parents who have attempted certain techniques, examined them thoroughly, made changes and modifications, and made them work is much more convincing than a solution postulated by the consultant. The parent study group provides a setting in which parents discuss normal problems of "parenting" in a fashion that evokes mutual help and support.

It is fundamental to understand that parent groups can only be functional insofar as they focus on *practical* problems. As Dinkmeyer and Muro (1971) state:

> The group is never to degenerate into a group discussion, merely talking about certain theoretical points, unless the points can be applied to specific individuals. Principles are never discussed in the abstract, always in the concrete. The leader must make it clear that this is not a theoretical course, but is concerned with helping human beings develop more effective interaction. He always insists that they go back to applying the principles to specific children (p. 289).

If the group continues to function in the abstract, the consultant assumes that they are not ready to deal with their problems and requests that they may feel free to ask him back when they are ready. The consultant is willing to assist the group when they are ready to deal with their problems. However, he does not choose to spend his time in nonproductive tasks.

Therapeutic Forces in Parent Groups

The group provides a unique opportunity for all parents involved to become more aware of their relationship with their children. They are allowed to experience feedback from other parents in regard to the impact that their parent procedures have upon their children. This opportunity for mutual therapeutic effect is constantly available. Concurrently, there is provision for the creation of a strong bond which takes advantage of the universal problems that confront parents. That "all parents have problems" and that solutions are available is experienced. The opportunity for parents to help each other and to mutually develop new approaches to parent-child relationships is provided. Corrective feedback from contemporaries has a tremendous effect upon the participants.

The consultant who conducts parent groups must be careful not to establish the group as if its intention were to provide information and to deal only with cognitive ideas. This is not a lecture, nor is it a discussion, but truly group counseling. This necessitates the use of group mechanisms and dynamic processes that are present in any well-organized therapeutic group.

The consultant realizes the necessity of assuring and encouraging parents (even if only by their good intentions to help the child). The consultant should lead, not push or tell. The parent group is much different from the traditional parent program. It emphasizes the treatment of parents as "whole people" and as equals. They are not lectured at or told how they *should* be, but are dealt with in relation to their own concerns and to where they are at.

Some of the group mechanisms which are particularly pertinent to group work include the following:

1. Group identification or a communal feeling. The idea that they are all concerned about a common problem—relating more effectively with their children.

2. Opportunity to recognize the universal nature of child training problems.

3. Opportunities not only to receive help but to give assistance, help, and love to others.

4. The opportunity to develop cooperation and mutual help, to give encouragement and support.

5. The opportunity to listen which not only provides support, but in many instances provides spectator therapy. Someone else's idea may enable the parents to start a new approach to transactions with their child.

6. One of the basic values involved in the mechanism of feedback —the individual gains from listening to and observing others, but he particularly gains as he becomes able to experience feedback about his own actions, beliefs, and ideas.

(Dinkmeyer 1969)

The mechanisms of group work with parents are the same as with any group. However, groups of parents usually show more enthusiasm (Glass 1971).

Administrative and Organizational Suggestions

Groups of parents can be formed in a number of ways. It is usually a good idea to start with parents whose children are at a given grade or age level. The teacher may initiate the contact or the consultant may present the idea at a community meeting (e.g., P.T.A.). In any instance, the possibility of dynamic sessions for parents is announced at a general meeting which specifies a certain grade level. Notices can then be sent out and some sort of pre-registration collected. It is desirable to keep the group size to a maximum of ten in order to have some type of effective interaction. Therefore, the response will indicate the number of groups that any given consultant can handle.

Once the number of participants has been selected, a time, location, and length of meeting will need to be established. In school settings, it is considered desirable if groups can meet during a school day. The group should preferably meet for one to one-and-a-half hours. The program should allow from six to ten sessions, dependent upon the number of groups it will be necessary to conduct within a given community.

The sessions are always conducted in a setting which permits the parents to face each other comfortably in circular form. The leader becomes a part of the group, a facilitator who helps in the development of understanding.

While the emphasis is upon group discussion and group transaction, it has been found that some printed material often stimulates discussion. Some groups we have lead have used *The ABC's of Guiding the*

Child by Rudolf Dreikurs and Margaret Goldman (1964). This material is used to provide a starting point and to keep transactions from degenerating into complaints or mere sharing of limited ideas and concepts. The ABC's are open to discussion, dialogue, and clarification. They are not learned; they are discussed until they can be internalized to specific situations (e.g., "I see, Sue is biting her nails because I find this revolting and she wants to upset me, to show me who is boss!") The leader uses this material to expand the group thinking, never to distract the group from practical problems, and never to limit dealing with real human transactions (e.g., "Now, perhaps, you can see how 'good' mothers are America's tragedy").

The *ABC's of Guiding the Child* include a number of ideas which can be the basis for discussion. For example:

1. "Children know what's right and wrong."
2. "Acting instead of talking is more effective in conflict situations."
3. "Reward and punishment are outdated."
4. "Don't discourage the child by having too high standards and being overambitious for him."

The leader can begin a group by discussing the implications of such a statement and then throwing it out to the group for comment. These statements are obviously intended to serve as a catalyst for discussion. The leader helps the group members to see the intent of the principle, but directs them to see how this applies to their personal concerns. *Raising A Responsible Child* by Don Dinkmeyer and Gary McKay (1973) also lends itself to parental discussions.

The first sessions are used to clarify the purpose of the group. This is not just verbally stated but actually practiced. It is made certain that parents do not see the group as group therapy. At the same time it is made clear that the group is not a discussion about theoretical children and problems, but *their* children and their concerns. The focus then is on real children and on the transactions which parents have with them. The leader does not pose as a psychological expert or authority. He makes it clear that members are expected to participate in presenting problems, developing suggestions, and assisting each other. It is vital to develop a basic contract about the purpose of the group early in the group's life. Those who participate learn to focus on how they change their behavior rather than on how they change the transactions and interactions with the child.

The consultant recognizes that his long-term goal is to expand the parent education program so that as many parents as possible can be reached. He does this by closely watching people in his group who have potential leadership. Once several groups have developed, he then starts to work with persons who desire to become discussion leaders. These people are acquainted with leadership procedures and group dynamics. At the same time, they are given some opportunity to serve as co-leaders. The co-leaders eventually develop their own groups.

Vicki Soltz (1967) has developed an excellent manual to accompany *Children: The Challenge* by Dreikurs and Soltz (1964) entitled *Study Group Leader's Manual.* It establishes the goals for parent groups and delineates the leader's responsibilities and limitations. Indicating that the leader is not to lecture, counsel, or give advice, the manual makes specific suggestions regarding qualities and skills which must be developed. Specific leadership traits are discussed, such as width of vision, contact with the whole group, sense of humor, use of group pressure, and encouragement. Since the group frequently has individuals who present a specific challenge, a section is devoted to dealing with problem members, such as the challenger, the resister, the chatterbox, the bored one, and the reluctant spouse.

One of the most useful sections for leaders who use *Children: The Challenge* is entitled "Discussion-Promoting Questions and Supplementary Material." This section includes detailed questions on each chapter—actually more than could be used in a single session—and can be used as homework assignment for parents. The manual includes a wealth of material to increase the leader's understanding of this approach.

Principles of Parent Group Leadership

1. The type of parent group leadership that we are suggesting requires awareness of certain basic procedures and skills. The leader must be very cognizant of group process, group dynamics—the therapeutic forces which occur within the group. He works with the group in ways to enhance the development of group interaction and utilizes group mechanisms to foster human potential.

2. He sees the program as a practical program. He is not interested in developing a series of lectures. He intensively avoids generalizations. He stresses specific situations and the application of the general principles to them.

3. He is always interested in the application of theory to practice. Thus, he makes available to parents printed material which supplements the understandings which are developed through their discussion. He always makes certain that parents are able to apply the general principle in a variety of settings. He does not attempt to develop a limited approach.

4. The leader must be careful to recognize that while he provides certain understandings regarding human behavior, he does not take on the role of authority, the expert or the specialist. Thus, in all transactions he is quick to have people look at the meaning of the behavior that is being discussed. He does this in simple form. When one parent finishes describing a situation, he makes certain that the situation has been described specifically. Eventually he sees to it that other members of the group help the parent describe the situation in specific terms. Once it has been discussed, he may ask questions like "What did you think about that? What would you do if you were the parent? How have you handled similar situations?"

5. He stresses the importance of group analysis of the problem, the tentative hypotheses regarding the purpose and nature of the behavior, and an analysis of the solution.

6. He is very concerned with developing commitment. This is not to be just a discussion group. People are to lead the group and come up with solutions and ideas for change.

7. He places emphasis on helping the group develop mutual help and mutual encouragement.

The parent group leader thus combines his knowledge of group procedures and his understanding of human behavior to help parents develop more effective relationships with their children. This is a holistic approach which engages the intellect and feelings of the parents while exacting a commitment to action. The potential good in parents sharing ideas under the guidance of an effective leader should be obvious.

(Dinkmeyer and Muro 1971, pp. 300–301)

THE PARENT "C" GROUP

Examples of the "C" Group Components

The essential elements of the "C" group are collaboration, consultation, clarification, confrontation, concern and caring, confidentiality, and commitment to change. The following are specific examples of what we mean by these factors in parent and family work.

Collaboration

Co.:   "How do you feel when she asks you to repeat something?"

Mo. 1: "I think for a long time we've just been doing it without being aware of it. But now everyone's getting on to her."

Mo. 2: "She might be doing that just to aggravate you? Right?"

Mo. 4: "Is she a slow thinker?"

Mo. 1: "No, not at all."

Mo. 4: "Oh, maybe she's repeating and if you repeat it while she thinks of the answer, then she's got it when you're done."

Mo. 1: "She's got it before I've got it out of my mouth."

Mo. 3: "I think that is the problem of the fast thinkers. They think they know it all. Course, with our son its very much the same."

Collaboration involves working together on mutual concerns. This dialogue shows the mothers and the consultant working together.

Confrontation

Co.: "In regard to report card have you ever made him feel that it was *his* report card and you were not going to get upset. Just ask him what he thinks about it?"

Mo. 2: "I suppose I should try that. Chris is such a passive child . . ."

Mo. 4: "It is easier for someone else to look at someone else's child. But I think your biggest problem is that you are putting the 'round' boy in the 'square' hole. I am speaking as your friend. You are insisting on his conformity to your standards, which you think a student ought to be and hope he ought to go to college and get a job. This is a very artistic boy who will never fit that 'peg.'"

Confrontation produces more realistic and honest feedback. Each individual can better see himself, his purposes, his attitudes, and his beliefs.

Clarification

Mo. 5: "I think the greatest task in the family is teaching responsibility to the children—like taking out the garbage, bed making. I have that problem in my house."

Co.: "I am not clear on what you mean, can you think of a specific example?"

Each group member is helped to *clearly* understand his belief systems, his feelings, and the congruency or incongruency between his behavior, his beliefs, and his feelings.

Consultation

Mo. 3: "A short time ago I had to tell him at least five times, 'Do your homework.' Would you believe that when I went

back to check he had done nothing. He said that he didn't
have a pencil. I was so mad . . ." (pounds on table with
fist).

Co.: "Your telling him several times do his homework did not
succeed. Do you think you could leave him alone and say
nothing? Leave it up to him?"

Consultation is both received and provided by group members and
helps them to become aware of new approaches to children.

Concern and Caring

Mo. 1: "Frank is always fighting with me."

Co.: "Do you think we could help Laura with Frank's negative
behavior?"

Mo. 2: "I know how she feels. It's very discouraging."

The group is concerned and shows that it cares. This concern is also
demonstrated through collaboration, consultation, clarification, and
confrontation.

Commitment to Change

Co.: "Could you ignore her when she does it?"

Mo. 6: "I *think* I *could try* that."

Co.: "What could you *do?*"

Mo. 6: "I know I can do that. I can . . ." (explains her behavioral
commitment)

Members are helped to recognize that only they can change themselves. They learn that *they* must develop a specific commitment which
will involve action that they will take in order to change their approach
to the problem.

Confidentiality

Whatever is discussed in the group stays in the group. The purpose is
to be mutually helpful, not to generate gossip.

Procedures and Steps

The following seven points are guidelines and fundamentals for conducting a parent "C" group.

1. *The size of the group is important.* It is important that the group be kept small; any number between six and ten is desirable. The emphasis is on a size that is small enough to permit active participation by all concerned. The consultant tries to get each parent involved each time in presenting a concern, reporting on progress, or in helping others. This cannot be accomplished in a large group.

2. *The focus is on normal parents and normal developmental problems.* It should be made clear from the beginning that the group is dealing with average parents who have normal developmental problems with their children. The consultant will give the group examples of typical kinds of difficulties that occur. For example, he could state, "We will be concerned with children who don't eat as we wish they would, who neither get up easily nor go to bed willingly, who leave their clothing and toys around the house, and who refuse to come when called or cooperate on simple requests. In other words, we will be talking about our children." This explicitness should help them to recognize that the group will be dealing with the common problems that they all have. This awareness will provide great strength for the group and will enable all to participate productively. Universalization is a basic mechanism for promoting cohesiveness; so, from the start, it is important that parents see how their concerns, feelings, and attitudes are similar.

3. *Integration of the group is fundamental.* The leader should work to help the group to become cohesive as quickly as possible. The leader does this by introducing members to each other. The very first day he should have name tags available so everyone gets acquainted on a first-name basis. In the early introductions each person tells something about himself and the names and ages of his children. Each member could also talk about some good experiences he has had in interaction with his children. This enables the group to develop some fellowship and awareness of their individual situations and to recognize that they all have some assets and strengths to work effectively with children. A good exercise in the beginning is to ask each parent to tell about the good part of his relationship with his child. Each parent must state his strengths in child management and the child's assets. Then each must talk about their concerns and specific problems.

4. At a first setting the leader may *begin by briefly discussing some theoretical principle* that he advocates strongly. This might involve a principle such as encouragement, logical consequences, setting limits, or any other topic which he can illustrate well. The discussion would be brief and serve as an opportunity to acquaint the members with a theoretical point and with the leader's point of view.

After this very brief introductory presentation—never to last over five minutes—the leader gets someone to begin discussing a problem that he has. When the person begins to describe the problem, it is important that the leader focus on having him present the problem in specific terms. This means the person must indicate what the child does, how he responds, and how the child reacts to his response. After he has had an opportunity to survey the group and the kinds of problems that concern them most, the leader then begins to work with problems which are common concerns. This permits the greatest amount of participation, and at the same time, utilizes the mechanism of universalization, which brings cohesiveness.

5. As the group starts to explore specific problems, *members of the group are strongly encouraged to provide each other with ideas.* The consultant is considered an additional resource. In the early sessions he will need to provide tentative hypotheses and tentative solutions. However, the consultant must be aware immediately that if he takes on the role of authority he will not get the kind of group dynamics, group expression, and group cohesiveness that is vital. From the start, the consultant should serve as facilitator and model the behavior he expects of group members. He teaches the group members how to listen, understand feelings, clarify for each other, and begin to offer tentative hypotheses.

6. *Maximum participation of all involved is a group goal.* The consultant attempts to involve each participant during each meeting in discussing some things of primary concern to him and his family. If the group is to serve the purpose of providing help, not merely talk, it is important to provide an opportunity for all to become involved. The consultant tries to schedule the time so that no one becomes dominant and all are invited to raise their concerns.

7. During each session, the consultant has made an opportunity to get maximum involvement. He also tries to *develop some tentative hypotheses and solutions for each parent.* At the end of the session, the group members are asked to summarize what they have learned. This is a very significant part of the group since it permits the members to say what they have really experienced and perceived. It also gives them an opportunity to verbalize and utilize their new information. It is during the session or at this point that the consultant attempts to elicit a public commitment from each member to do something about their situation. It also provides some opportunity to correct faulty impression that parents may have about recommendations that have been developed by the consultant or other members of the group.

An Example of the Parent "C" Group

Five mothers of fifth- and sixth-grade children met with Don Dink-meyer and Jon Carlson (Carlson 1969). After a short introduction about the purpose of parent groups, the mothers introduced themselves and gave the names and ages of their children. The consultants then asked who would like to begin. After a specific incident was related by one of the mothers, the consultant inserted the following statement in an attempt to universalize the problem: "How many of you other mothers have this same or a similar problem?" This tended to increase the active involvement of the group.

From here, the group moved from incident to incident on topics such as waking children in the morning, children not wanting to eat their breakfast, not wanting to brush their teeth, not doing their chores, or not coming to dinner when called. During the summary session the consultant helped each member of the group to develop new approaches to try before the next session. At this time, he also gave each participant a copy of *The ABC's of Guiding the Child* by Dreikurs and Goldman (1964). They were asked to read it and consider some of the ideas that were presented.

The next session began as follows:

Consultant: "What did you get from our meeting last week?" (General discussion and identification of new concepts by the group.)

Mother$_1$: "Well, she is still Sally."

Consultant: "But are you still Mother? Did you do anything different?" (The emphasis in this consultation is on recognition that mothers can only change their behavior and hope that this will change the interaction with their children.)

After a short discussion the mother reported that she had not tried anything different. Another mother asked if she tried some of the things that were suggested to her last week and she replied that she was not sure how to go about it.

Consultant: "What would you like to change? Take one specific thing."

Mother$_1$: "Her attitude in general."

Consultant: "We need something more specific and tangible."

Mother$_1$: "How about when I try to wake her up in the morning. I say 'It is time to get up,' and she says, 'Try and make me.' "

The power contest between mother and daughter was by this time evident to the group. After a short discussion, they recommended that she buy her daughter an alarm clock and let her be responsible for her own awakening. Thus, the mother would be extricating herself from the conflict and leaving her daughter without an opponent. Another mother volunteered.

Mother$_2$: "I already had success using what you said. My daughter tried to get my attention by playing the same song over and over. I used to rush in and tell her to stop it and then the battle would start. This time I shut the door to the kitchen and turned up the radio and went about my housework. She soon stopped and began to play another song."

Consultant: "Very good. In other words, you removed the wind from your daughter's sail. Did anyone else have any other results this past week?" (One mother began to talk about the difficulty she was having with her son swearing and other mothers voiced similar dilemmas.) "What could you do about something like this?"

Mother$_3$: "You could ignore it."

Mother$_5$: "Ignore it; depending on the word. I might tell him this is not very nice."

Consultant: "What about the logical consequences of the situation?"

Mother$_4$: "Well, if they swear, I won't take them someplace they want to go."

Consultant: "Wouldn't that be more of a punishment?"

Mother$_4$: "Yes, I guess it would."

Mother$_1$: "What about if I tell him that if he can't talk properly outside with people, he will have to come inside to his room where there are no people to hear him, until he feels that he can talk to others without swearing." (The entire group felt that this would be a very good way to handle the situation.)

At this time the discussion was shifted to *The ABC's of Guiding the Child*. The group talked about the principles set forth in this pamphlet and discussed similar topics. The members were depending more upon other members of the group for aid and solicited less and less assistance from the consultant. During the third session, the consultant passed out a copy of "Child's Mistaken Goals" (See Chart 1 on page 135). This helped to clarify the previous materials and accelerated the progress of the group.

Consultant: "Did anybody try anything different this past week?"

Mother$_1$: "I've been trying things and I have become so critical of myself. I've been changing and now the entire house is running smoother. I really can understand how 'good mothers are America's tragedy.' "

Mother₂: "Children can do a lot more than we let them do. We do too much for them. As I have realized lately, children are quite capable of taking care of themselves. They really are very capable."

Consultant: "Could it be that you are saying we don't give children enough responsibility?" (All the mothers agreed).

When mothers can realize this fact and begin to do something about it, they have come a long way. With this in mind, the following was presented:

Consultant: "I feel that you are in a position to take this procedure and these concepts and meet with other mothers, some of your neighbors, perhaps, over a cup of coffee, and talk about some of these same things that we have discussed. Concern yourself with normal problems that they might have with their children. It is time for you to help other parents understand the dynamics of their child's behavior while recognizing that their problems are much like the problems of other parents."

Mother₁: "The mothers who need this kind of help won't come to the school for a group of this kind."

Consultant: "Might they come to your house for an informal meeting?"

Mother₂: "Yes, we can work on a different group of people than you work on at school."

Mother₃: "Maybe we can help each other because our children play together and we can encourage them for the changes that they make."

Thus, a core group has been established that will help take the burden of parent education off the consultant's already overloaded work schedule. A group of mothers who has been exposed to new ideas can be leaders in the parent-education program of the community. Under the supervision of the consultant, what started out as five mothers (one group) might well become twenty-five mothers (five groups), and so on.

In conclusion, the consultant becomes directly involved with parents and families. Parent study groups, family counseling, "C" groups, and individual contacts are among the approaches he employs. The necessity of creating a healthy parent and family environment is paramount.

REFERENCES

Ackerman, N. *The Psychodynamics of Family Life*. New York: Basic Books, 1958.

Allen, T. W., ed. "Individual Psychology." *The Counseling Psychologist* 3, no. 1 (1971): 3–29.

Auerbach, A. B. *Parents Learn through Discussion: Principles and Practices of Parent Group Education*. New York: John Wiley, 1968.

Bank, I. M. and Brooks, L. "Elementary Counselors Implement the 'Parent Principle.'" *Elementary School Guidance and Counseling* 5 (1971): 273–280.

Becker, W. C. *Parents Are Teachers: A Child Management Program*. Champaign, Illinois: Research Press, 1971.

Bell, J. *Family Group Therapy, Public Health Monograph No. 64*. Washington, D.C.: Department of Health, Education, and Welfare, 1961.

Berne, E. *Games People Play*. New York: Grove, 1964.

Blocher, D. H., Austin, E. R. and Dugan, W. E. *Guidance Systems: An Introduction to Student Personnel Work*. New York: Ronald Press, 1971.

Carkhuff, R. R. *The Development of Human Resources: Education, Psychology and Social Change*. New York: Holt, Rinehart & Winston, 1971.

Carkhuff, R. R. and Berenson, B. G. *Beyond Counseling and Therapy*. New York: Holt, Rinehart & Winston, 1967.

Carlson, J. "Case Analysis: Parent Group Consultation." *Elementary School Guidance and Counseling* 4 (1969): 136–141.

Christensen, O. C. "Family Education: A Model for Consultation." *Elementary School Guidance and Counseling* 7 (1972): 121–129.

Cooper, D. *The Death of the Family*. New York: Pantheon, 1970.

Dinkmeyer, D. C. "Group Counseling: Theory and Techniques." *School Counselor* 17 (1969): 148–152.

Dinkmeyer, D. C. and Muro, J. J. *Group Counseling: Theory and Practice*. Itasca, Illinois: F. E. Peacock, 1971.

Dinkmeyer, D. C. and McKay, G. *Raising A Responsible Child*. New York: Simon and Schuster, 1973.

Donigan, J. and Giglio, A. "The Comprehensive Family Counselor: An Innovative Approach to School Counseling." *School Counselor* 19 (1971): 97–101.

Dreikurs, R. "Psychotherapy through Child Guidance." *The Nervous Child* 8 (1949): 315.

Dreikurs, R. *Social Equality: The Challenge of Today*. Chicago: Henry Regenry, 1971.

Dreikurs, R., Corsini, R., Lowe R. and Sonstegard, M., eds. *Adlerian Family Counseling: A Manual for Counseling Centers*. Eugene: The University of Oregon Press, 1959.

Dreikurs, R. and Goldman, M. *The ABC's of Guiding the Child*. Skokie, Illinois: North Side Unit of the Family Education Association, 1964.

Dreikurs, R., Grunwald, B. B. and Pepper, F. C. *Maintaining Sanity in the Classroom*. New York: Harper & Row, 1971.

Dreikurs, R. and Soltz, V. *Children: The Challenge*. New York: Meredith, 1964.

Dreikurs, R. and Sonstegard, M. "The Adlerian or Teleoanalytical Group Counseling Approach." In *Basic Approaches to Group Psychotherapy and Group Counseling*, edited by George M. Gazda, pp. 197–232. Springfield, Illinois: C. C. Thomas, 1968.

Duncan, L. W. *Parent-Counselor Conferences Make a Difference*. Saint Petersburg: Junior College, 1969 (EDO31743).

Fullmer, D. W. *Counseling: Group Theory and System*. Scranton, Pennsylvania: Intext, 1971.

Fullmer, D. W. "Family Group Consultation." In *Theories and Methods of Group Counseling in the Schools*, edited by G. M. Gazda, pp. 181–207. Springfield, Illinois: C. C. Thomas, 1969.

Fullmer, D. and Bernard, H. W. *Family Consultation*. Boston: Houghton Mifflin, 1968.

Fullmer, D. W. and Bernard, H. W. *The School Counselor-Consultant*. Boston: Houghton Mifflin, 1972a.

Fullmer, D. W. "Family Group Consultation." *Elementary School Guidance and Counseling* 7 (1972b): 130–136.

Gilmore, J. V. "Parental Counseling and the Productive Personality." In *Guidance for Education in Revolution*, edited by David R. Cook, pp. 231–256. Boston: Allyn & Bacon, 1971.

Glass, S. D. *The Practical Handbook of Group Counseling*. Baltimore: BCS Publishing, 1971.

Gordon, T. *Parent Effectiveness Training*. New York: Peter H. Wyden, 1970.

Gordon, T. "Training Parents and Teachers in New Ways of Talking to Kids." *Edvance* 1 (1971): 1+.

Grams, A. *Facilitating Learning and Development: Toward a Theory for Elementary Guidance*. St. Paul: Minnesota Department of Education, 1966.

Greer, G. *The Female Eunuch.* New York: McGraw-Hill, 1970.

Haley, J. "Whither Family Therapy?" in *The Power Tactics of Jesus Christ and Other Essays*, edited by J. Haley, pp. 99–144. New York: Avon, 1969.

Harris, T. A. *I'm OK—You're OK: A Practical Guide to Transactional Analysis*. New York: Harper & Row, 1967.

Hawkins, R. P., Peterson, R. F., Schweid, E. and Bijou, S. W. "Behavior Therapy in the Home: Amelioration of Problem Parent-Child Relations with the Parent a Therapeutic Role." *Journal of Experimental Child Psychology* 4 (1966): 99–107.

Heller, B. and Gurney, D. "Involving Parents in Group Counseling with Junior High Underachievers." *The School Counselor* 15 (1968): 394–397.

Henry, J. *Pathways to Madness.* New York: Random House, 1971.

Hillman, B. W. "The Parent-Teacher Education Center: A Supplement to Elementary School Counseling." *Elementary School Guidance and Counseling* 3 (1968): 111–117.

Homan, W. E. *Child Sense.* New York: Bantam, 1969.

Jackson, D. D. "Family Interaction, Family Homeostosis, and Some Implications for Conjoint Family Psychotherapy." In *Individual and Familiar Dynamics,* edited by J. H. Masserman. New York: Grune and Shatton, 1959.

Jaslow, C. K. "Parent Counseling." *Caps Capsule* 4 (1971): 6–7.

Krasner, L. and Ullman, L. *Research in Behavior Modification.* New York: Holt, Rinehart & Winston, 1965.

Kremer, B. "A Plan for Parent Education Groups in Elementary Schools." *National Catholic Guidance Conference Journal* 15 (1971): 131–135.

Laing, R. D. *The Politics of the Family and Other Essays.* New York: Pantheon, 1969.

Luckey, E. B. "Parent Education: A Function of the Elementary School." *Elementary School Guidance and Counseling* 1 (1967): 255–262.

Mallars, P. B. "Thinking about Group Counseling for Parents?" *The School Counselor* 15 (1968): 374–376.

Mayer, G. R. "Behavioral Consulting: Using Behavior Modification Procedures in the Consulting Relationship." *Elementary School Guidance and Counseling* 7, no. 2 (1972):114–119.

McIntrie, R. W. "Spare the Rod, Use Behavior Mod." *Psychology Today* 4 (1970): 42–44+.

McGowan, R. J. "Group Counseling with Underachievers and Their Parents." *The School Counselor* 16 (1968): 30–35.

Muro, J. J. *The Counselor's Work in the Elementary School.* Scranton, Pennsylvania: Intext, 1970.

Nikelly, A. G., ed. *Techniques for Behavior Change: Applications of Adlerian Theory.* Springfield, Illinois: C. C. Thomas, 1971.

Norton, F. H. "Parental Apathy: The School Counselor's Albatross." *School Counselor* 19 (1971): 88–91.

O'Leary, K. D., O'Leary, S. and Becker, W. C. "Modification in Deviant Sibling Interaction Pattern in the Home." In *Psychotherapeutic Agents,* edited by B. G. Guerney. New York: Holt, Rinehart & Winston, 1969.

Otto, H. A. "Communes: The Alternative Life Style." *Saturday Review,* April 24, 1971, pp. 16–21.

Patterson, G. R. *Families: Applications of Social Learning to Family Life.* Champaign, Illinois: Research Press, 1971.

Patterson, G. R. and Gullion, M. E. *Living with Children: New Methods for Parents and Teachers.* Champaign, Illinois: Research Press, 1968.

Peterson, B. G. "Parent Effectiveness Training." *School Counselor* 16 (1969): 367–369.

Pickarts, E. and Fargo, J. *Parent Education: Toward Parental Competence.* New York: Appleton-Century-Crofts, 1971.

Roiphe, A. R. "The Family Is Out of Fashion." *The New York Times Magazine,* August 15, 1971, p. 10+.

Sarvis, M. A. and Pennekamp, M. *Collaboration in School Guidance: A Creative Approach to Pupil Personnel Work.* New York: Brunner/Mazel, 1970.

Satir, V. M. "Conjoint Family Therapy: Fragmentation to Synthesis." In *Innovations to Group Psychotherapy,* edited by G. M. Gazda, pp. 256–271. Springfield, Illinois: C. C. Thomas, 1968.

Satir, V. M. "Conjoint Family Therapy." In *Proceedings of a Symposium on Family Counseling and Therapy,* edited by G. M. Gazda, pp. 1–14. Athens: The University of Georgia, College of Education, 1971.

Satir, V. M. *Conjoint Family Therapy.* Rev. ed. Palo Alto, California: Science and Behavior Books, 1967.

Satir, V. M. *Peoplemaking.* Palo Alto, California: Science and Behavior Books, 1972.

Sauber, S. R. "Multiple-Family Group Counseling." *Personnel and Guidance Journal* 49 (1971): 459–465.

Shah, S. A. "Training and Utilizing a Mother As a Therapist for Her Child." In *Psychotherapeutic Agents,* edited by B. G. Guerney. New York: Holt, Rinehart & Winston, 1969.

Shaw, M. C. "The Feasibility of Parent Group Counseling in Elementary Schools." *Elementary School Guidance and Counseling* 4 (1969): 43–53.

Shaw, M. C. *The Function of Theory in Guidance Programs.* Boston: Houghton Mifflin, 1968.

Shaw, M. C. and Rector, W. H. *Group Counseling With Parents: Feasibility, Reactions and Interrelationships.* Monograph 5, Western Regional Center of IRCOPPS. Chico, California: Chico State College, 1968.

Shaw, M. C. and Tuel, J. K. "A Focus for Public School Guidance Programs: A Model and Proposal." *Personnel and Guidance Journal* 45 (1965): 824–830.

Shulman, B. H. "The Family Constellation in Personality Diagnosis." *Journal of Individual Psychology* 18 (1962): 34–47.

Skolnick, A. S. and Skolnick, J. H. *Family in Transition: Rethinking Marriage, Sexuality, Child Rearing, and Family Organization.* Boston: Little, Brown & Co., 1971.

Sloan, N. E. *Family Counseling.* Ann Arbor, Michigan: ERIC (ED 036 674) March, 1970.

Soltz, V. *Study Group Leader's Manual.* Chicago: Alfred Adler Institute, 1967.

Sonstegard, M. "A Rationale for Interviewing Parents." *The School Counselor* (December 1964).

Sonstegard, M. and Dreikurs, R. *The Teleoanalytical Approach to Group Counseling.* Chicago: The Alfred Adler Institute, 1967.

Stormer, G. E. "Milieu-Group Counseling in Elementary School Guidance. *Elementary School Guidance and Counseling* 1 (1967): 240–254.

Time. "The American Family: Future Uncertain." December 28, 1970, pp. 34–39.

Van Hoose, W. H. "The Consultative Role of the Elementary School Counselor." Paper presented at the 1967 APGA Convention, Dallas, Texas.

Van Hoose, W. H. *Counseling in the Elementary Schools.* Itasca, Illinois: F. E. Peacock, 1968.

Wahler, R. G., Winkel, G. H., Peterson, R. F. and Morrison, D. C. "Mothers as Behavior Therapists for Their Own Children." *Behavior Research and Therapy* 3 (1965): 113–124.

Walder, L. O., Cohen, S. O., Breiter, D. E., Daston, P. G., Hirsch, I. S. and Liebowitz, J. M. "Teaching Behavioral Principles to Parents of Disturbed Children." In *Psychotherapeutic Agents,* edited by B. G. Guerney. New York: Holt, Rinehart & Winston, 1969.

White House Conference on Children. Report to the President, Superintendent of Documents, Washington, D.C.: U.S. Government Printing Office, 1970.

Zwetschke, E. T. and Grenfell, J. E. "Family Group Consultation: A Description and a Rationale." *Personnel and Guidance Journal* 43 (1965): 974–980.

Appendix A

Resources for Promoting Humaneness*

BOOKS

Axline, V. *Dibs in Search of Self.* New York: Ballantine, 1966.

Bennett, H. *No More School.* New York: Random House, 1972.

Birmingham, J. *Our Time Is Now: Notes from the High School Underground.* New York: Bantam, 1970.

Borton, T. *Reach, Touch and Teach.* New York: McGraw-Hill, 1970.

Bradford, L. P., ed. *Human Forces in Teaching and Learning.* Washington, D.C.: NTL Institute, 1968.

Bremer, A. and Bremer, J. *Open Education: A Beginning.* New York: Holt, Rinehart & Winston, 1972.

Bremer, J. and Von Moschzisker, M. *The School Without Walls: Philadelphia's Parkway Program.* New York: Holt, Rinehart & Winston, 1971.

Bronfenbrenner, U. *Two Worlds of Childhood: U.S. & U.S.S.R.* New York: Basic Books, 1970.

Brown, G. I. *Human Teaching for Human Learning.* New York: Viking, 1971.

---

* This list is taken in part from Greer, M. and Rubenstein, B. *Will the Real Teacher Stand Up?* Pacific Palisades, California: Goodyear, 1972 and Lyon, H. *Learning to Feel—Feeling to Learn.* Columbus, Ohio: Charles E. Merrill, 1970.

Combs, A. W., ed. *Perceiving, Behaving, Becoming.* Washington: Association for Supervision and Curriculum Development (ASCD), 1962.

Cook, A. and Mack, H. *Schools Are for Children.* New York: Praeger, 1971.

Cottle, T. J. *Time's Children.* New York: Little, Brown, 1971.

Dewey, J. *Democracy and Education.* New York: Free Press, 1966.

Dewey, J. *Experience and Education.* New York: Macmillan, 1938.

Dewey, J. *The School and Society.* Chicago: University of Chicago Press, 1915.

Dennison, G. *Lives of Children.* New York: Vintage, 1968.

Dinkmeyer, D. and Dreikurs, R. *Encouraging Children To Learn: The Encouragement Process.* Englewood Cliffs, New Jersey: Prentice-Hall, 1963.

Dreikurs, R. *Social Equality.* Chicago: Regnery, 1971.

Erikson, E. *Childhood and Society.* New York: Norton, 1950.

Erikson, E. *Identity: Youth and Crisis.* New York: Norton, 1968.

Fabun, D. *Children of Change.* Beverly Hills, California: Glencoe Press, 1969.

Fabun, D. *Dimensions of Change.* Beverly Hills, California: Glencoe Press, 1971.

Fabun, D. *Dynamics of Change.* Englewood Cliffs, New Jersey: Prentice-Hall, 1970.

Fader, D. *The Naked Children.* New York: Vintage, 1968.

Fader, D. and McNeil, E. *Hooked on Books, Program and Proof.* Berkeley, California: Medallion Books, 1968.

Farber, J. *The Student as Nigger.* New York: Pocket Books, 1970.

Featherstone, J. *Schools Where Children Learn.* New York: Liveright, 1971.

Friedenberg, E. *Coming of Age in America.* New York: Vintage, 1965.

Friedenberg, E. *Dignity of Youth and Other Atavisms.* Boston: Beacon, 1965.

Friedenberg, E. *The Vanishing Adolescent.* New York: Dell, 1959.

Fromm, E. *The Revolution of Hope.* New York: Harper & Row, 1968.

Fuchs, E. *Teachers Talk.* New York: Doubleday, 1969.

Fuller, B. *Education Automation.* Carbondale, Illinois: Southern Illinois University Press, 1962.

Gardner, J. *Excellence.* New York: Harper & Row, 1961.

Gardner, J. *Self-renewal.* New York: Harper & Row, 1963.

Gartner, A., Kohler, M. and Russman, F. *Children Teach Children: Learning by Teaching.* New York: Harper & Row, 1971.

Gattegno, C. *What We Owe Children.* New York: Outerbridge & Dienstfrey, 1970.

Gibran, K. *The Prophet.* New York: Knopf, 1923.

Ginott, H. *Between Parent and Teacher.* New York: Macmillan, 1972.

Glasser, W. *Identity Society.* New York: Harper & Row, 1972.

Glasser, W. *Schools Without Failure.* New York: Harper & Row, 1969.

Goodman, M. *Movement Toward a New America.* New York: Knopf, 1970.

Goodman, P. *Growing Up Absurd.* New York: Vintage, 1960.

Green, H. *I Never Promised You a Rose Garden.* New York: Signet, 1964.

Greenberg, H. M. *Teaching with Feeling.* Toronto: Macmillan, 1969.

Greer, M. and Rubenstein, B. *Will the Real Teacher Please Stand Up? A Primer in Humanistic Education.* Pacific Palisades, California: Goodyear, 1972.

Gross, R. and Gross, B., eds. *Radical School Reform.* New York: Simon & Schuster, 1969.

Gunther, B. *Sensory Awakening and Relaxation.* Big Sur, California: Esalen Publications, 1967.

Hamacheck, D. E. *Encounters With Self.* New York: Holt, Rinehart & Winston, 1971.

Hansen, S. and Jensen, J. *The Little Red School Book.* New York: Pocket Books, 1971.

Hart, H. H., ed. *Summerhill: For & Against.* New York: Hart, 1970.

Hendrick, I. G. and Jones, R. L. *Student Dissent in the Schools.* Boston: Houghton Mifflin, 1972.

Hentoff, N. *Our Children Are Dying.* New York: Viking, 1966.

Herndon, J. *How To Survive in Your Native Land.* New York: Simon & Schuster, 1971.

Herndon, J. *The Way It's Spozed To Be.* New York: Simon & Schuster, 1965.

Hentzberg, A. and Stone, E. F. *Schools Are for Children.* New York: Schoken, 1970.

Holt, J. *How Children Fail.* New York: Pitman, 1964.

Holt, J. *How Children Learn.* New York: Pitman, 1967.

Holt, J. *The Underachieving School.* New York: Pitman, 1969.

Holt, J. *What Do I Do Monday?* New York: E. P. Dutton, 1970.

Illich, I. *Celebration of Awareness: A Call for Institutional Revolution.* New York: Doubleday, 1970.

Illich, I. *Deschooling Society.* New York: Harper & Row, 1971.

Jackson, P. W. *Life in Classrooms.* New York: Holt, Rinehart & Winston, 1968.

James, W. *Talks to Teachers.* New York: Holt, Rinehart & Winston, 1964.

Jersild, A. *In Search of Self.* New York: Teachers College, Columbia University Press, 1952.

Jersild, A. *When Teachers Face Themselves.* New York: Teachers College, Columbia University Press, 1955.

Jourard, S. *The Transparent Self.* New York: Van Nostrand, 1964.

Kelley, E. C. *Education and the Nature of Man.* New York: Harper & Row, 1952.

Kelley, E. C. *In Defense of Youth.* Englewood Cliffs, New Jersey: Prentice-Hall, 1962.

Kohl, H. *Thirty-Six Children.* New York: New American Library, 1967.

Kohl, H. *The Open Classroom: A Practical Guide to a New Way of Teaching.* New York: A New York Review Book, Random House, 1967.

Kohl, H. and Cruz, V. *Stuff.* New York: World Publishing, 1970.

Kozol, J. *Death at an Early Age.* New York: Bantam Books, 1961.

Kozol, J. *Free Schools.* Boston: Houghton Mifflin, 1972.

Kunen, J. S. *The Strawberry Statement.* New York: Random House, 1969.

Leonard, G. B. *Education and Ecstasy.* New York: Delacorte Press, 1968.

Lurie, E. *How to Change the Schools: A Parents' Action Handbook on How To Fight the System.* New York: Random House, 1970.

Lyon, H. C. *Learning To Feel—Feeling To Learn.* Columbus, Ohio: Charles E. Merrill, 1971.

Maltz, M. *Psycho-cybernetics and Self-fulfillment.* New York: Grossett & Dunlap, 1970.

Maslow, A. H. *Motivation and Psychology.* 2nd ed. New York: Harper & Row, 1970.

Maslow, A. H. *Toward a Psychology of Being.* New York: Van Nostrand, 1968.

May, R. *Love and Will.* New York: Norton, 1969.

May, R. *Man's Search for Himself.* New York: Signet, 1967.

Moustakas, C. *The Authentic Teacher.* Cambridge, Massachusetts: Doyle, 1966.

Neill, A. S. *Freedom—Not License!* New York: Hart, 1966.

Neill, A. S. *Summerhill: A Radical Approach to Child Rearing.* New York: Hart, 1960.

O'Gorman, N. *The Storefront: A Community of Children on 129th Street and Madison Avenue.* New York: Harper & Row, 1970.

Otto, H., ed. *Explorations in Human Potentialities.* Springfield, Illinois: Charles C. Thomas, 1966.

Otto, H. and Mann, J., eds. *Ways of Growth.* New York: Viking, 1968.

Perls, F. S. *Gestalt Therapy Verbatim.* Lafayette, California: Real People Press, 1969.

Perls, F. S. *In and Out of the Garbage Pail.* Lafayette, California: Real People Press, 1969.

Peter, L. J. and Hull, R. *The Peter Principle: Why Things Always Go Wrong.* New York: Morrow, 1969.

Postman, N. and Weingartner, C. *Teaching as a Subversive Activity.* New York: Delacorte Press, 1967.

Postman, N. and Weingartner, C. *The Soft Revolution.* New York: Delta, 1971.

Prather, H. *Notes to Myself.* Lafayette, California: Real People Press, 1970.

Purkey, W. W. *Self-concept and School Achievement.* Englewood Cliffs, New Jersey: Prentice-Hall, 1970.

Randolph, N. and Howe, W. *Self-enhancing Education.* Palo Alto, California: Sanford Press, 1966.

Reich, C. A. *The Greening of America.* New York: Random House, 1970.

Reimer, E. *School Is Dead.* New York: Doubleday, 1971.

Renfield, R. *If Teachers Were Free.* New York: Delta, 1969.

Repo, S., ed. *This Book Is About Schools.* New York: Random House, 1970.

Rogers, C. R. *Freedom To Learn.* Columbus, Ohio: Charles E. Merrill, 1969.

Rogers, C. R. *On Becoming a Person.* Boston: Houghton Mifflin, 1961.

Rogers, C. and Stevens, B. *Person to Person: The Problem of Being Human.* Walnut Creek, California: Real People Press, 1967.

Rogers, V. R. *Teaching in the British Open School.* New York: Macmillan, 1971.

Roszak, T. *The Making of a Counter Culture.* New York: Anchor Books, 1969.

Sarason, S. *Culture of the School and the Problem of Change.* Boston: Allyn & Bacon, 1971.

Schutz, W. C. *Here Comes Everybody.* New York: Harper & Row, 1971.

Scobey, M. and Graham, G. *To Nurture Humaneness: Commitment for the 70's.* Washington, D.C.: ASCD, 1970.

Siegel, H. and Broedecker, R. *A Survival Kit.* New York: Canfield Press, 1971.

Silberman, C. E. *Crisis in the Classroom.* New York: Random House, 1970.

Skinner, B. F. *Beyond Freedom and Dignity.* New York: Knopf, 1971.

Skinner, B. F. *Walden Two.* New York: Macmillan, 1948.

Skutch, M. and Hamlin, W. G. *How To Start a School.* Boston: Little, Brown, 1971.

Snitzer, H. *Living at Summerhill.* New York: Collier, 1967.

Stein, M. and Miller, L. *Blueprint for Counter Education: Curriculum, Handbook, Wall Decoration, Shooting Script.* New York: Doubleday, 1970.

Stevens, B. *Don't Push the River.* Lafayette, California: Real People Press, 1970.

Sutich, A. J. and Vich, M. A. *Readings in Humanistic Psychology.* New York: Free Press, 1969.

Toffler, A. *Future Shock.* New York: Random House, 1970.

Torrence, E. P. and Myers, R. E. *Creative Learning and Teaching.* New York: Dodd, Mead, 1970.

Turner, J. *Making New Schools: The Liberation of Learning.* New York: David McKay, 1971.

Von Hilsheimer, G. *How To Live With Your Special Child.* Washington, D.C.: Acropolis, 1970.

Walmsley, J. *Neill and Summerhill.* Baltimore, Maryland: Penguin, 1969.

Weber, L. *The English Infant School and Informal Education.* Englewood Cliffs, New Jersey: Prentice-Hall, 1972.

Weinstein, G. and Fantini, M. *Toward Humanistic Education.* New York: Praeger, 1970.

Wigginton, B. E., ed. *The Foxfire Book.* New York: Doubleday, 1972.

PERIODICALS

About Education, 8th Floor, 219 Broad Street, Philadelphia, Pennsylvania 19107.

Anarchy Magazine, Freedom Press, 84A White Chapel, High Street, London, England, UK.

Behavior Today, Human Science Newsletter, Box 2993, Boulder, Colorado 80302.

Berkeley Tribe, P.O. Box 9043, Berkeley, California 94709.

Big Rock Candy Mountain, Portola Institute, Inc., 1115 Merrill Street, Menlo Park, California 94025. A catalog of resources for education.

Change, 59 East 54th Street, New York, New York 10022.

Colloquy, United Church Press, 391 Steel Way, Lancaster, Pennsylvania 17601.

Dialogist, King's College, Wilkes-Barre, Pennsylvania 19702.

Earth, Earth Publishing Corporation, The Agriculture Building, The Embarcadero at Mission, San Francisco, California 94105.

Earth Read Out/SW, Box 1048, Las Vegas, New Mexico 87701.

Eco-Log, Students Organized for Survival and the World, Cornell College, Mt. Hernon, Louisiana 70450.

Expand, Voice of the Children, 200 Gold Street, Brooklyn, New York 11201.

Explorations, P.O. Box 1254, Berkeley, California 94701.

Free People's Exchange Newsletter, Arrakis, R.F.D. 1, Jeffersonville, New York 12748.

Free School Press, Box 22, Santurna Island, B.C. Canada. A mimeographed publication consisting of discussions of philosophical and practical problems related to free schools.

Friends of the Earth, 451 Pacific, San Francisco, California 94133.

Good Times, 2377 Bush Street, San Francisco, California 94115.

Grade Teacher, 23 Leroy Avenue, Darien, Connecticut 06820.

Green Revolution, Rt. 1, Box 129, Freeland, Maryland 21053.

Harvard Educational Review, Longfellow Hall, Appian Way, Cambridge, Massachusetts 02138.

Human Potential, Institute for the Achievement of Human Potential, 1800 Stenton Avenue, Philadelphia, Pennsylvania 19138.

Idea Exchange, Education Associates, Inc., Upward Bound, 171 Massachusetts Avenue, Washington, D.C. 20001.

Inequality in Education, Center for Law and Education, Harvard University, 38 Kirkland Street, Cambridge, Massachusetts 02138.

Insights, New School of Behavioral Studies in Education, University of North Dakota, Grand Forks, North Dakota 58201.

Integrated Education, 343 South Dearborn Street, Chicago, Illinois 60604.

Journal of Humanistic Psychology, 1314 Westwood Boulevard, Los Angeles, California 90024. Published by Association of Humanistic Psychology, 584 Page Street, San Francisco, California 94117.

Kaiser Aluminum News from Don Fabun (ed.) Public Affairs Department, Kaiser Aluminum and Chemical Corporation, Kaiser Center 866, Oakland, California 94704.

Kids Magazine, Box 30, Cambridge, Massachusetts 02139. A magazine written and illustrated by children for each other.

Liberation Teacher, 36 Devonshire Road, Mill Hill, London, NW 7, England, UK.

Los Angeles Free Press, 7813 Beverly Boulevard, Los Angeles, California 90036.

Manas, Box 32112, El Sereno Station, Los Angeles, California 90032.

Media and Methods, 134 North 13th Street, Philadelphia, Pennsylvania 19107.

Mother Earth News, P.O. Box 38, Madison, Ohio 44057.

Motivation Quarterly, Center for Study of Motivation and Human Abilities, College of Education, Ohio State University, Columbus, Ohio 43210.

Motive, Box 871, Nashville, Tennessee 37202.

Natural Life Styles, 53 Main Street, New Paltz, New York 12561.

New Directions in Teaching, a nonjournal committed to the improvement of undergraduate teaching, Department of Education, Bowling Green State University, Bowling Green, Ohio 43402.

New England Free Press, 691 Tremont Street, Boston, Massachusetts 02118.

New Republic, 1244 19th Street, N.W., Washington, D.C. 20036.

New School of Education Journal, 4304 Tolman Hall, University of California, Berkeley, California 94720.

New Schools Exchange Newsletter, New Schools Exchange, 301 East Canon Perdido, Santa Barbara, California 93101. A clearinghouse of news and opinions within the free school movement.

New York Review of Books, 250 West 57th Street, New York, New York 10019.

No More Teachers' Dirty Looks, Bay Area Radical Teachers Organizing Committee, 1445 Stockton Street, San Francisco, California 94133.

Observations from the Treadmill from Mart Yanow, 357 Hidden Road, Norbeth, Pennsylvania 19072. One of the best new publications; education, young people, etc.

Outside the Net, P.O. Box 184, Lansing, Michigan 48901. For those who seek a radical and humane alternative to America's educational system.

Psychology Today, P.O. Box 60407, Terminal Annex, Los Angeles, California 90060.

Radicals in the Professions, Newsletter of Radical Education Project, Box 625, Ann Arbor, Michigan 48107.

Realist, 595 Broadway, New York, New York 10012.

The Red Pencil and *The Red Pencil Bulletin* from Phyllis Ewen, 131 Magazine Street, Cambridge, Massachusetts 02139.

Rolling Stone, 749 Brannon Street, San Francisco, California 94103.

San Francisco Education Switchboard, 1390 Howard Street, San Francisco, California 94103. A resource and information center for alternatives in education. Title of newsletter is *Switched On.*

Saturday Review, 380 Madison Avenue, New York, New York 10017.

Summerhill Bulletin, 339 Lafayette Street, New York, New York 10012 or 1778 South Holt, Los Angeles, California 90075.

Synergy. At the main branch of your public library.

The Teacher Paper, 280 North Pacific, Monmouth, Oregon 97361. Dedicated to reform of public schools.

Teachers and Writers Calloborative Newsletter, Pratt Center for Community Improvement, 244 Vanderbilt Avenue, Brooklyn, New York 11205. Work of kids and teachers.

Theory Into Practice from Jack Frymier, 29 West Woodruff Avenue, Columbus, Ohio 43210.

This Magazine is About Schools, 56 Espland Street East, Suite 401, Toronto 215, Ontario. One of the oldest and best.

Village Voice, 80 University Place, New York, New York 10003.

Wilderness Camping, Box 1186, Scotia, New York 12302.

ORGANIZATIONS

Alternatives Foundation, 1526 Gravenstein Highway, No., Sebastopol, California 97452. Directories of free schools, personal growth, social change.

American Association for Curriculum Development, National Education Association, 1201 16th Street, N.W., Washington D.C. 20036.

American Conservatory Theater, San Francisco, California. William Ball, Director. Reverses "method acting" to make the motion produce the expression.

Association for Humanistic Psychology, 584 Page Street, San Francisco, California 94117. John Levy, Executive Director. Focuses on experience as the primary phenomenon in the study of man; emphasis on choice, creativity, valuation, and self-realization.

Auron Institute, 71 Park Avenue, New York, New York 10016. Harold Streitfeld, Director. Interested in nonverbal activity and body movement.

Center for Educational Reform, 2115 S Street, N.W., Washington, D.C. 20008.

Center for Studies of the Person, 1125 Torrey Pines Road, La Jolla, California 92037. Inaugurated a cooperative program of self-directed change in a whole school system—elementary through college—which brought about innovative and humanizing approaches. Conducts summer training programs for individuals wishing to become group facilitators.

Center for the Study of Development and Social Change, 1430 Massachusetts Avenue, Cambridge, Massachusetts 02138.

Committee for Freedom of Choice in Education, Box 3223, Inglewood, California 92604.

Community Makers, 13 West 98th Street, New York, New York 10025. Uses theater games, etc., to build community involvement and organizational knowledge.

Cooperative Program of Educational Development (COPED), National Training Laboratories, National Education Association, 1201 16th Street, N.W., Washington, D.C. 20036. National cooperative research project on the uses of social sciences in education.

Daytop Lodge, 450 Bayview Avenue, Prince's Bay, Staten Island, New York 10309. Lawrence Sacharow, Director. Renewal center for drug addicts run by former drug addict using confrontation groups.

Development Research Associates, Inc., 1218 Massachusetts Avenue, Cambridge, Massachusetts 02138. Alfred Alschuler, David Kolb, and James McIntyre (President). Runs programs in self-assessment, motive arousal, and "the helping relationship, for Peace Corps, schools, and government agencies.

Education Development Center, EDC Resources Center, 42 Hawthorne Street, Roxbury, Massachusetts 02119.

Education for the Future Project, Stanford Research Institute, Palo Alto, California 94305. Willis Harman, Director.

Education Innovation, Productive Thinking Program, Box 9248, Berkeley, California 94719.

Esalen Institute, Big Sur Hot Springs, Big Sur, California 93920. Mike Murphy, Director. Acts as a broker to bring together all types of psychological educators with groups of people who wish to go through the courses offered.

Fayerweather Street School, P.O. Box 287, Cambridge, Massachusetts 02138. Matt Judson, Headmaster. U.S. counterpart of Leicester Schools in England.

Foundation for Integrative Education, 777 United Nations Plaza, New York, New York 10017. Publishes *Main Currents in Modern Thought.*

Fresh Air Camp, University of Michigan, Ann Arbor, Michigan. Elton McNeil, Director. Here-and-now approach to juvenile delinquency.

Human Development Institute, Inc., Atlanta, Georgia. Produces programmed materials for affective development.

Institute for the Achievement of Human Potential, 1800 Stenton Avenue, Philadelphia, Pennsylvania 19138. Published *Human Potential.* Works with brain-damaged children. Now setting up an experimental school to extend the teaching techniques used with brain-damaged children to normal children.

Institute for Bioenergetic Analysis, 71 Park Avenue, New York, New York 10016. Adele Lewis, Executive Secretary. Interested in body movement and its relation to psychological well-being. Lowen type therapy center.

Integrative Materials Exchange, Center for Integrative Education, 12 Church Street, New Rochelle, New York 10805.

International Foundation for Psychosynthesis, Suite 901, Linde Medical Plaza, 10921 Wilshire Boulevard, Los Angeles, California 90024. Robert Gerard, President. Center for research and dissemination of information on psychosynthesis.

Julian Primary School, 226 Leigham Court Road, Streatham, London, S.W. 16, England. E. A. Osborn, Headmaster. School in London where "discovery technique" is used.

Kairos, Wishing Well Hotel, P.O. Box 350, Rancho Sante Fe, California 92067. Bob Driver, President.

Midwest Center for Human Potential, Oasis, 20 East Harrison Street, Chicago, Illinois 60605.

National Center for Human Potential, 8080 El Paseo Grande, La Jolla, California 92037. Herbert Otto and John Mann, Directors.

National Information Center for Educational Media, University of Southern California, Los Angeles, California 90007. Clearinghouse for films, tapes, etc.

NTL Institute for Applied Behavioral Science, 1201 16th Street, N.W., Washington, D.C. 20036. Vladimir Dupre, Director. Runs training centers and schools for T-groups, basic encounter groups, personal-growth groups, etc. (Publishes *Journal for Applied Behavioral Science*).

Ontario Institute for Studies in Education, 252 Bloor Street W., Toronto 5, Ontario, Canada.

Outward Bound, Inc., Andover, Massachusetts 01810. Joshua Minor, Director. Attempts to build self-confidence and self-reliance through a variety of physical tests of endurance.

Portola Institute, Inc., 1115 Merrill Street, Menlo Park, California 94025. Innovative educational projects. (e.g., *The Last Whole Earth Catalog*. New York: Random House, 1971.)

Psychosynthesis Research Foundation, Room 314, 527 Lexington Avenue, New York, New York 10017. Frank Hilton, Director.

Quest, 3000 Connecticut Avenue, N.W., Suite 237, Washington, D.C. 20008. Bob Caldwell, Director.

Radical Education Project, Box 625, Ann Arbor, Michigan 48107.

School Services Publications, Pinck Leodas Associates, Inc., 2000 Massachusetts Avenue, Cambridge, Massachusetts 02140.

School Works, 33 Union Square W., New York, New York 10003.

Schools for the Future, 821 Broadway, New York, New York 10003.

Seminar House, Bucks County, Upper Black Eddy, Pennsylvania 18972. Grenville Moat, Director. Runs Esalen-like program.

Simulmatics Corporation, 16 East 41st Street, New York, New York 10017. Makes game simulations of life situations, e.g., life-career game, community disaster game, etc.

Social Dynamics, Inc., 335 Newbury Street, Boston, Massachusetts 02115. Paul R. Mico, President; Donald C. Klein, Director. Human relations training and social action programming.

Society of American Value Engineers, Windy Hill, Suite E-9, 1741 Roswell Street, Smyrna, Georgia 30080. Distributes current information, conference reports, bibliographies, etc. on value engineering.

Spanner, Three by Five . . . And Beyond, Box 2602, Stanford, California 94305. Resource pool experimental education.

Summer in the City, 32 East 51st Street, New York, New York 10022. Monseigneur Robert J. Fox, Director. Social action program using mass confrontations.

The Summer Program, Berkeley High School, Berkeley, California. Ann Hornbacker, Jay Manley and Peter Kleinbard. West Coast extension of the Philadelphia Cooperative Schools.

Synanon, 1351 Pacific Coast Highway, Santa Monica, California 90401. Chuck Dederich, Director. Total environmental approach to promoting self-actualization and, in the process, curing drug addicts.

Synectris, a Way of Increasing Creativity, Problem-Solving Ability, Discovery, and Consciousness by using metaphorical thinking. Synectris Education System, 121 Brattle Street, Cambridge, Massachusetts 02138.

Teen Challenge, Program run by the Pentecostal Church in San Francisco and other major cities as a retraining center for drug addicts.

Topanga Human Development Center, 2247 N. Topanga Canyon Boulevard, Topanga, California 90290. Thomas Greening, Chairman.

Western Behavioral Sciences Institute, 1121 Torrey Pines Road, La Jolla, California 92037. Richard Farson, Director.

Wiltwick School, 260 Park Avenue, S., New York, New York 10010. Dr. Hagop Mashikian, Director. Total environment therapy.

FILMS AND TAPES

Inside Out. This film contrasts the complete disaster that urban education has become in places like Bedford-Stuyvesant in New York City and the promise of a "School Without Walls" in Philadelphia. Available from Dr. Jack Robertson, 3 Washington Square Village, New York, New York 10012.

Children As People. This film presents life at Fayerweather Street School in Cambridge, Massachusetts. It presents "the feeling of what children in such a place are like, how they look and talk and relate to the adults in the school." Polynarjsh Films, 331 Newbury Street, Boston, Massachusetts 02115.

Skinner, B. F. Esalen tapes on Affective Education which includes the interviews with Maslow, Skinner, Rogers, etc. Available through Esalen, Big Sur, California 93920.

Borton, Terry (with Oliver Nuse and Jim Morrow), *Prelude* (1966) and *A Lot of Nothing to Do* (1968). Two films about the Philadelphia Cooperative Schools. Audio-Visual Department, Philadelphia Public School Building, Room 327, 21st and Parkway, Philadelphia, Pennsylvania.

The Walsh School. Available from Office of the Superintendent of Public Instruction, State of Illinois, Springfield, Illinois.

OTHER RESOURCES

Vocations for Social Change, Canyon, California 94516. A unique listing of jobs and resources for people interested in working for social change.

The Teacher Drop Out Center, Box 521, Amherst, Massachusetts 01002. Helps alternative schools find teachers and vice versa.

High School Student Information Center, 3210 Grace Street, N.W., Washington, D.C. 20007. Also houses FPS, the High School Underground press service.

Raspberry Greenways Exercises I & II, from Freestone Publishing Company, 440 Bohemian Highway, Freestone, California 95472. "How to start your own school—and make a book." Everything about the practical problems of making a new school.

Start Your Own School, A New School Manual, Center for Educational Reform, 2115 S Street, N.W., Washington, D.C. 20008.

Ant Farm, 247 Gate 5 Road, Sausalito, California 94965. Changing environments.

Catalog for Learning Things, The Workshop for Learning Things, 55 Chapel Street, Newton, Massachusetts 02160.

Catalog of Free Teaching Materials, G. Salisbury, P.O. Box 1075, Ventura, California 93001.

Learning Directory: A Comprehensive Guide to Teaching Materials. Over 200,000 items. Westinghouse Learning Corporation.

New Schools Manual, New Directions Community School, 445 10th Street, Richmond, California 94801.

PERIODICALS DEALING WITH FAMILY AND PARENT WORK

American Journal of Sociology. University of Chicago Press, 5750 Ellis Avenue, Chicago, Illinois. 60637. This is a professional and scholarly coverage of the most advanced thinking and empirical research in the various fields of sociology and social psychology. Most of the articles are a result of field work and research on specific social problems. The signed, evaluative book reviews and the bibliographic listing of current books received (averaging 200–300 titles) provide the means for keeping abreast with the latest and best American and foreign titles available in sociology and psychology. A valuable feature is the yearly listing of Ph.D.s in sociology and newly started Ph.D. dissertations.

Community Mental Health Journal. Behavioral Publications, 2852 Broadway, New York, New York 10025. The only periodical devoted specifically to the burgeoning field of community mental health, it is internationally recognized for its pioneering efforts to coordinate emergent approaches to mental health and social well-being. Forty-seven outstanding consultants, representing all the pertinent disciplines and sub-specialists, select articles to be published from submitted manuscripts on research, theory, and practice in such areas as: consultation, primary prevention, crisis intervention, planned change, suicide prevention, epidemiology, use of nonprofessionals, family therapy, delivery of services, and evaluation research.

Exceptional Parent. P.O. Box 101, Back Bay Annex, Boston, Massachusetts 02117. The *Exceptional Parent* brings professional expertise to parents in a manner and language which they will find of practical use. It also presents the very special wisdom of parents who have developed ingenious solutions to their own special problems in helping their children to develop. Professionals have found this magazine useful as a resource for themselves and as a means of stimulating discussions with parents, both individually and in groups. "The magazine offers advice to help 'exceptional' children live full lives . . . jargon-free articles, which supplement the knowledge of professionals with the special expertise of parents and of the disabled themselves," from Time, June 28, 1971.

Family Coordinator. National Council on Family Relations, 1219 University Avenue, S.E., Minneapolis, Minnesota 55414. This is a professional journal for counselors, psychologists, and teachers working with marriage and family problems. The articles are written by experts and are well documented. While much of the material will be of only professional interest, a few articles touch on problems that concern the layman, e.g., birth control, sex education, divorce, and the sexual behavior of adolescents. A few advanced high school students may find the magazine of value.

Happier Marriage and Planned Parenthood. Parents' Magazine Enterprises, Inc., 52 Vanderbuilt Avenue, New York, New York 10017. The magazine contains articles on all aspects of marriage, such as money problems, in-law relationships, cooking tips, religion, and children. There is also information on planned parenthood. Authors are professionals, the style is basic, the advice is sound. This magazine is more for the adult than the average senior high school student, though it might be of interest to the student who is planning an early marriage. In earlier issues several of the articles were reprinted from Parents' Magazine, and apparently this will continue.

Journal of Marriage and the Family. National Council on Family Relations, 1219 University Avenue, S.E., Minneapolis, Minnesota 55414. This is a medium for the presentation of original theory, research, interpretation, and critical discussion on material related to marriage and the family. It is sponsored by the National Council on Family Relations, which seeks to bring together the leaders in research, teaching, and professional service in this field so as to advance the cultural values secured through family relations. Occasionally, an entire issue is devoted to a single topic, such as the American adolescent in the mid-sixties, the poverty family, and family planning.

Parents' Magazine and Better Homemaking. Parents' Magazine Enterprises, Inc., 52 Vanderbilt Avenue, New York, New York 10017. Parents who raise children by the book will find much of value here. Health, education, personality, and discipline are considered in an intelligent and authoritative fashion. Family and marital relationships are discussed. Finally, there are articles which encourage the parent and the child to take an active role in social matters.

Public Welfare. American Public Welfare Association, 1313 East 60th Street, Chicago, Illinois 60637. This periodical devotes attention to public welfare programs, dependent children, the aged, dependent families, administration, staff training, and general welfare. Articles are written by the staff and directors of welfare programs at federal, state and local levels; deans and professors of schools of social welfare; and civic leaders. The articles are based on the authors' personal, "on-the-job" experiences.

Smith College Studies in Social Work. Smith College School for Social Work, Northampton, Massachusetts 01060. Approximately half of the three to four articles are devoted to reports of investigations based on master's theses and doctoral dissertations submitted to the Smith College School. Presentations are based on the authors' research investigations and practice experiences, but are sufficiently generalized to be applicable to other situations. Papers and reports deal with a range of topics, such as the relevance of ego psychology concepts to social work practice, family relationships, separation problems in children, communication difficulties, identity conflicts, continuity and discontinuity in therapy, and socio-cultural factors related to social work.

Social Casework. Family Service Asssociation of America, 44 East 23rd Street, New York, New York 10010. Written for the social worker, this journal pays particular attention to new approaches and techniques for helping children and adults with problems concerning interpersonal relations and social functioning.

Social Forces: A Scientific Medium of Social Study and Interpretation. University of North Carolina Press, Box 510, Chapel Hill, North Carolina 27514. Brief, scholarly articles report research over the entire range of theoretical and applied sociology. Related subjects include the family, social psychology, regionalism, public opinion, and population. Emphasis is placed on the motivation and reasons behind social action, developments and mobility.

Social Problems. Hyman Rodman, ed. Society for the Study of Social Problems, P.O. Box 190, Kalamazoo, Michigan 49005. Research articles present current data on a full range of social problems. Studies deal with such topics as deviant behavior, comparisons of role behavior, and the differences in activities and occupational pursuits between the sexes.

Social Work. National Association of Social Workers, 2 Park Avenue, New York, New York 10016. "A professional journal committed to improving practice and extending knowledge in the field of social welfare," editors welcome manuscripts which "yield new insights into established practices, evaluate new techniques and research, examine current social problems or bring serious critical analysis to bear on problems of the profession itself." Authors are professional social workers, educators, administrators, and researchers from government and voluntary agencies. They discuss social problems such as poverty, illegitimacy, chronic illness, methods and techniques used in intervention, and the rationale and ideology underlying social work and its specific programs.

Trans-Action. Box A., Rutgers—The State University, New Brunswick, New Jersey 08903. One of the few sociology-oriented periodicals for all general collections, this contains articles on current sociological discoveries and projects.

AUDIO-TAPES

The following audio-tapes are available from the McGraw-Hill Sound Seminars:

The Family as a Social Institution. Howard Becker. Deals with the nature of the social institution, with particular emphasis upon the family. 22 minutes, recorded 1953.

Married Couple Group Therapy. Martin G. Blinder and Martin J. Kircherbaum. Explores the causes of marital conflict and demonstrates techniques suitable for work with couples or groups of couples by which such conflicts may be resolved. 40 minutes, recorded 1968.

Culture and Sexual Intimacy. Harold T. Christensen. Considers the problems associated with pre-marital sexual behavior on three cultural groups. 25 minutes, recorded 1960.

A Mother with Two Sons—First Counseling Session. Rudolf Dreikurs. Shows how a mother is helped to understand the child's goals and need for mutual respect. 98 minutes, recorded 1965.

A Mother with Two Sons—Second Counseling Session. Rudolf Dreikurs. Shows mother reporting on outcome of putting recommended parental changes into practice. 57 minutes, recorded 1965.

Masculinity: The Man's Dilemma. Rudolf Dreikurs. Deals with problems related to the false identification of masculinity as superiority in a democratic society. 55 minutes, recorded 1965.

The Family Power Struggle. Rudolf Dreikurs. Concerns a second counseling session with parents illustrating mutual struggle between children and parents for dominance and power. 44 minutes, recorded 1965.

The Predicament of Motherhood. Rudolf Dreikurs. Discusses the question: Should a mother relate to her child as someone special, or as she would to another fellow human being? 44 minutes, recorded 1965.

Understanding the Difficult Child. Rudolf Dreikurs. Discusses basic principles and practical techniques in child training. 46 minutes, recorded 1965.

A Case of Frigidity Treated with Rational-Emotive Psychotherapy. Albert Ellis. Deals with the application of principles of rational-emotive psychotherapy to a case of impotence. 22 minutes, recorded 1966.

Family Dynamics and Schizophrenia. Jerry Higgins. Examines how family configuration is related to the schizophrenic and the differential development of the child contingent upon the type of family organization. 18 minutes, recorded 1968.

Masculinity and Femininity. Christine Jorgensen. Recorded by Lee Steiner. Relates a discussion with Christine Jorgensen about her book and some of her personal experiences. 21 minutes, recorded 1969.

Woman Power: An Underutilized Resource. Mary Dublin Keyserling. Describes the conspicuous underuse of women in the American labor force. 31 minutes, recorded 1969.

Horror Movies, the Monster Image, and Modern Children. Dell Lebo. Analyzes the ingredients that go into the making of a horror movie, the attraction such movies have for children and adolescents, and possible adverse influences. 21 minutes, recorded 1964.

Children in the One-Parent Home. Howard B. Lyman. Presents suggestions for the single parent, stressing some of the advantages of the one-parent home. 21 minutes, recorded 1970.

Dating as an Adult. Howard B. Lyman. Discusses questions frequently asked by single-again adults, e.g., How do you get dates? Where do you go? How far should you go? 25 minutes, recorded 1970.

How About Sex? Howard B. Lyman. Discusses the importance of sex to single-againers. The author presents his code as a basis for discussion. 24 minutes, recorded 1970.

Preparation for Remarriage. Howard B. Lyman. Discusses the fact that single-again adults are more likely to remarry than are single-still adults of the same age to marry for the first time. 25 minutes, recorded 1970.

Status Unknown. Howard B. Lyman. Discusses the need for a generic term to describe a person who is once again without a spouse, and some of the problems of being single again. 21 minutes, recorded 1970.

The Role of Religion. Howard B. Lyman. Notes the many efforts made by clergymen to help the widowed. It urges clergymen to make greater efforts in accepting the divorced, and suggests positive programs single-againers may employ to better cope with their lives, initiated by churches. 24 minutes, recorded 1970.

New Developments in Sex Research. John W. Money. Recorded by Lee Steiner. Reviews the valid scientific sex experiments and outlines some of the future plans in this area. 23 minutes, recorded 1969.

Some Myths About Child Rearing. Albert Rabin. Deals with child-rearing methods in a kibbutz and draws a comparison with methods of the family situation. 23 minutes, recorded 1968.

Psychology of the Female: A New Look. Leon Salzman. Presents a survey of the advances in the psychological understandings of the female. 36 minutes, recorded 1970.

The Feminine Identity. Esther M. Westervelt. Recorded by Lee Steiner. Discusses the American women's changing identity and satisfaction. 26 minutes, recorded 1969.

Appendix B

Consulting Competencies

Can develop a theoretical base for consultation, which includes rationale and objectives.

Can describe the roles of the consultant and role play these in simulation activities.

Can describe and utilize the therapeutic forces and mechanisms which are essential in establishing a climate for growth.

Can comprehend the consultant's role in the system and develop procedures which enable him to cope with communication, conflict resolution, and social change phenomena.

Can articulate theories of learning and apply them to specific learning problems, life problems.

Understands and can utilize a social-behavioral approach to understanding behavior and can communicate this approach effectively to the consultee.

Understands how to plan organizational change and can implement these procedures in simulation activity. Has the ability to go beyond adjustment to the system and is able to facilitate a planned social system.

Can develop the readiness and the setting for consultation.

Can develop a consultation relationship which enables him to utilize the "C" group process. Can demonstrate "C" group components.

Understands and utilizes the communication processes to avoid the roadblocks to communication while facilitating congruent communication which facilitates growth.

Understands the impact and effectiveness of consultant leads and verbal transactions and can demonstrate the use of consultant leads.

Can conduct a teacher interview which is collaborative while establishing the diagnosis, corrective procedures and a commitment to change.

Can conduct a brief diagnostic child interview to establish the psychological movement and purposive nature of the behavior.

Can develop recommendations which are idiographic and meet the unique needs of the consultee and the client.

Can develop and facilitate productive teacher groups.

Can develop and facilitate productive parent groups.

Can promote human potential and the development of the client's affective, cognitive, and actional elements.

Can demonstrate and use human learning and development procedures in the classroom.

Understands and can apply idiographically logical consequences and other corrective procedures.

Understands family patterns and relationships and is able to make appropriate interventions.

Understands the imperative nature of establishing a humane base for schools and community development. Can identify humane procedures and develop ways to implement them.

Index

AUTHOR INDEX

SUBJECT INDEX